Indie Science Fiction
Cinema Today

ALSO BY CHRIS VANDER KAAY
AND KATHLEEN FERNANDEZ-VANDER KAAY

*Horror Films by Subgenre:
A Viewer's Guide* (McFarland, 2016)

INDIE SCIENCE FICTION CINEMA TODAY

Conversations with 21st Century Filmmakers

Kathleen Fernandez-Vander Kaay
and Chris Vander Kaay

McFarland & Company, Inc., Publishers
Jefferson, North Carolina

LIBRARY OF CONGRESS CATALOGUING-IN-PUBLICATION DATA

Names: Fernandez-Vander Kaay, Kathleen, 1979– author. | Vander Kaay, Chris author.
Title: Indie science fiction cinema today : conversations with 21st century filmmakers / Kathleen Fernandez-Vander Kaay and Chris Vander Kaay.
Description: Jefferson, North Carolina : McFarland & Company, Inc., Publishers, 2018. | Includes bibliographical references and index.
Identifiers: LCCN 2017059866 | ISBN 9781476669335 (softcover : acid free paper) ∞
Subjects: LCSH: Science fiction films—United States—History and criticism. | Motion picture producers and directors—United States—Interviews. | Motion pictures—United States—History—21st century.
Classification: LCC PN1995.9.S26 F35 2018 | DDC 791.43/615—dc23
LC record available at https://lccn.loc.gov/2017059866

BRITISH LIBRARY CATALOGUING DATA ARE AVAILABLE

ISBN (print) 978-1-4766-6933-5
ISBN (ebook) 978-1-4766-3058-8

© 2018 Kathleen Fernandez-Vander Kaay and Chris Vander Kaay. All rights reserved

No part of this book may be reproduced or transmitted in any form or by any means, electronic or mechanical, including photocopying or recording, or by any information storage and retrieval system, without permission in writing from the publisher.

Front cover: Allix Mortis in the 2015 independent film *Magnetic*

Printed in the United States of America

McFarland & Company, Inc., Publishers
Box 611, Jefferson, North Carolina 28640
www.mcfarlandpub.com

Special thanks to all the filmmakers
who generously gave their time and talent
to make this book a reality.
And to Kelly Cline, for turning voices into words.

Dana,
In every distant universe,
in every far-off galaxy,
in every alternate reality,
in every world,
through all time,
you're there.
Thank you.

Table of Contents

Introduction   1

1. EXTRATERRESTRIAL ENCOUNTERS
   Jamie Nash (*Altered*) • Daniel Myrick (*The Objective*)
   • Clay Liford (*Earthling*)   5

2. SURVIVING THE MYSTERIOUS EVENT
   Justin Benson and Aaron Moorhead (*Resolution*)
   • Michael J. Kospiah (*The Suicide Theory*)   17

3. THE SHIFTING SANDS OF TIME
   Merlin Dervisevic (*Cruel & Unusual*) • B.P. Cooper
   (*Time Lapse*) • Kurt Kuenne (*Shuffle*)   28

4. EXPERIENCING A WORLD NOT OUR OWN
   Gerald McMorrow (*Franklyn*) • Darren Paul Fisher
   (*Frequencies*) • Craig Goodwill (*Patch Town*)
   • Juan Solanas (*Upside Down*)   42

5. AN INFINITY OF ALTERNATE DIMENSIONS
   Jeff Waltrowski (*It Came from Yesterday*) • James Ward
   Byrkit (*Coherence*) • Jason Thomas Scott (*Tympanum*)   55

6. THE HISTORY OF ALTERNATE HISTORIES
   Richard Raaphorst (*Frankenstein's Army*) • Timo
   Vuorensola (*Iron Sky*) • Anouk Whissell (*Turbo Kid*)   66

7. NEW INVENTIONS AND TECHNOLOGIES
   Ben Carland (*Shadows on the Wall*) • Timothy Lanzone
   (*Travelling Salesman*) • Brett Ryan Bonowicz
   (*The Perfect 46*)   75

8. JOURNEYS THROUGH AN ENDLESS COSMOS
   Geoff Marslett (*Mars*) • Chance Shirley (*Interplanetary*)
   • Clive Dawson (*The Last Days on Mars*)   88

9. THE ENEMY WITHIN
   Neil Mcenery-West (*Containment*) • Tony Burgess
   (*Pontypool*) 100

10. DEALING WITH ARTIFICIAL INTELLIGENCE
    Shane Acker (*9*) • Christopher Ford (*Robot & Frank*)
    • James Felix McKenney (*Automatons*) 109

11. THE FALL, AND WHAT COMES AFTER
    Paul S. Myers (*5 Shells*) • Conor Horgan (*One Hundred
    Mornings*) • Harry Ralston (*The Last Man*) • Jim Mickle
    (*Stake Land*) 119

12. THERE CAN BE ONLY ONE
    Paul Hough (*The Human Race*) • Ben Carland (*Sol*)
    • Stuart Hazeldine (*Exam*) • Mario Miscione (*Circle*) 132

13. DYSTOPIAN FUTURES
    Brandon Drake (*Visioneers*) • Josh Feldman (*Senn*)
    • Justin Trefgarne (*Narcopolis*) 146

14. ALONGSIDE THE SECRET SOCIETY
    Jeff Pointer (*Ink*) • Tom Woodruff, Jr. (*Fire City:
    End of Days*) • Jennifer Liao (*End of Days, Inc.*) 158

15. UNNATURAL SELECTION
    Alec Gillis (*Harbinger Down*) • Oklahoma Ward
    (*Crawl or Die*) 167

16. CONFRONTING GLOBAL DISASTERS
    Todd Berger (*It's a Disaster*) • Sophia Cacciola (*Magnetic*) 176

17. THE RISE OF SUPERPOWERS
    Andrew Droz Palermo (*One & Two*) • Kyle Roberts
    (*The Posthuman Project*) • Jordan Galland (*Alter Egos*)
    • Justin Dix (*Crawlspace*) 185

18. SCIENCE FICTION AND FAKE DOCUMENTARIES
    Karl Mueller (*Mr. Jones*) • Philip Gelatt (*Europa Report*) 198

19. THE FANTASTICAL WORLDS OF MUSICALS
    Cory McAbee (*The American Astronaut*) • Paul Bunnell
    (*The Ghastly Love of Johnny X*) • Rod Bingaman (*Ripped!*) ... 206

20. THE ROMANCE OF SCIENCE FICTION
    Justin Benson and Aaron Moorhead (*Spring*)
    • Brian Ackley (*Alienated*) • Tom Large (*Beyond*) 216

21. THE FUTURE OF OUR CINEMATIC FUTURES 227

Further Reading 241

Index 243

Introduction

Cinema is an escape.

While there are many joys to be found in watching a film, and many things that can be learned, the positive experience gained in watching a movie can be boiled down to a single primary purpose: escape. You can learn things about other people or societies in a documentary or a biopic, and you can explore the vast reaches of outer space in an IMAX film about the cosmos, but even in those cases, the element of escaping the standard experience of everyday human life is the motivation for watching.

Humanity loves to watch films. Of all the various media of artistic expression, it is one of the most popular because of the visceral nature of film. A book requires a certain amount of effort from the reader in order to fully come to life; a film, however, happens to you. Cinema is an escape, and it is an experience.

So why is it that so many of the genres of film are confined to such mundane circumstances? Of the 20 or so mainstream genres (the number changes depending on who is defining the individual genres), most are confined to the standard rules of everyday life. Sure, believability can be stretched with an outlandish action sequence or the behavior of a character in a comedy, but for the most part, films operate according to the rules of the known universe.

Not all of them, though. There are a few special genres whose primary appeal is their determination to break free of the constraints of the real world. That is where science fiction comes in. In science fiction films, there are endless possibilities, good and bad, a vast and varied universe to explore.

The popularity of the genre, from the early adaptations of stories like *Frankenstein* and *The Wizard of Oz* to the modern DC and Marvel superhero uber-franchises, has always been tied to the fears and hopes of society throughout the decades. Unlike the fears of the moment on display in horror films, science fiction and fantasy also explore the curiosities and hopes of humanity, the light that goes along with the dark.

Science fiction stands in as an allegorical representation of everything man wonders about: the future, society, ourselves, machines, new discoveries, outer space, the changing definition of life consciousness, cutting edge scientific breakthroughs, and the mysterious and very human circumstances of life and death. They speak to us as much now as they did when Georges Méliès made *A Trip to the Moon* in 1902.

However, in 2000, 98 years after Méliès sent his explorers into space, humanity had new curiosities, new questions created by new discoveries and problems. It would be hard to argue that the events of September 11, 2001, were not instrumental in the shift towards darker visions of the future with domineering dystopias and devastating apocalyptic events. The advent of the smartphone changed the nature of communication and the ease with which live recordings can be made; this has also influenced the style and themes of the genres. Technology and culture have been changing faster than ever before, and the genres that explore those changes the most have been moving apace.

Our preoccupations as a society always filter out through our entertainment. Not until we look back at the work in retrospect do we notice them. The purpose of this book is to look back through the years of 2000 to 2016 and observe and discuss the new preoccupations of a post-millennial society.

The focus of this book, however, is not on the big-budget, popular films that all mainstream moviegoers would know from extensive advertising, online reviews and availability in theaters and on DVD. Another change that has come about since 2000 is the advent of new technologies that allow for the ease of creation and distribution of smaller films.

We can certainly learn something from a popular film; however, the primary purpose of a big-budget studio film is to make money, possibly enough money to turn a single film into a series of films. As such, those films tend to steer clear of the controversial subjects, the sticky philosophies, the probing questions. Larger films want larger audiences, so the instinct of film studios is to be broadly appealing while avoiding pushing any buttons.

The new venues for smaller films, from online streaming to video-on-demand, have created a market for the smaller, more daring films, in a way that independent films have never enjoyed, even back to the beginning of the independent filmmaking movement. These films will be the primary focus of this book. We will occasionally use the more popular films of the era primarily as introductory material to illuminate the major subsections of the genre.

For the purposes of strict definition, the films included in this book are considered independent films if they have not been funded or released by the major American studios often referred to as the Big Six: Warner Bros., 20th Century–Fox, Paramount, Sony (formerly Columbia Tri-Star), Universal and Walt Disney. Regardless of the budget, notoriety or stars, a film released outside of the American studio system is an independent film.

Some of these smaller films may not have the slick gloss of a Hollywood blockbuster, the recognizable faces of superstars or the elaborate sets and special effects on display during the summer in a typical Cineplex. What they do have is ingenuity, passion and a restless spirit of exploration. They dig into the thoughts, hopes and psyches of a culture at the dawn of a new era for humanity.

Science fiction as a filmic genre has close neighbors in horror and fantasy, genres that also trade in fantastical scenarios and unlikely worlds. Because they live so close to each other in the neighborhood of film genres, they can often overlap. Some of the films in this book could additionally be placed in the genres of fantasy or horror, but they are included here because we feel they are primarily or significantly science fiction films, for a number of reasons: They focus on technology and/or science, they avoid magical explanations, or they adhere to worlds that are primarily realistic aside from their central outlandish conceits.

While the films in this book fall broadly into one major genre, science fiction, there is a trend of certain subject matters, themes and sub-categories being the focus of numerous films of the era. This is true of every era since the inception of film. However, those subject matters, themes and sub-categories change based on the events of the time in which the films are made, and that is the purpose of this book: to discuss the categories which science fiction films have frequently fallen into during the first two decades of the new millennium.

Many of these categories have existed in some form for many years, often for as long as the genre itself; however, new changes in society and politics, as well as the big shift in technology and communication, have given modern filmmakers new perspectives on these old ideas.

Each chapter of this book will begin with a brief discussion of where the subgenre or movement has gone from the inception of science fiction film through to the end of the twentieth century. Then, an observation of the changes it has undergone since the new millennium, both in the mainstream and from an independent perspective. The discussion of individual films of the era begins after that, complete with interviews with some of the filmmakers who were kind enough to share their thoughts about their related films and the subgenre in general. And finally, we recommend a few other titles from the subgenre that might be of interest for devoted fans and explorers.

1

Extraterrestrial Encounters

Functionally, the experience of the alien in a science fiction story is most clearly allegorical to the experience of the foreigner in a new land. Dealing with strange customs and languages, the foreign visitor has no one to commiserate with about the constant struggle to fit in. Of course, not all science fiction films are from the perspective of the alien itself, and as such, films often display the reactions and feelings of the people with whom the aliens or foreigners are interacting. It is this aspect of the subgenre of Extraterrestrial Life science fiction that is most clearly reflected in film, and therefore the changes in those sentiments can be seen clearest.

In one of the earliest science fiction films to feature an extraterrestrial character, 1924's *Aelita, Queen of Mars*, the influence of the alien is a meddling and destructive force. The irony in this early example is that its alien is a human man from Russia named Los. He has fallen in love with Aelita, who watches him from Mars through a telescope. When he finally ventures to Mars in a rocketship, he finds that Aelita's Martian society is built on a dual class system of aristocracy and slavery. When Los' friend stirs up revolution and the workers fight for their rights, Aelita takes charge of the army and tries to subdue the workers. This horrifies Los, who kills Aelita to save the workers. Los and his friend, representatives of the (admittedly propagandistic) culture of the Soviet Union in the 1920s, shattered the status quo on Mars, and societal upheaval led to murder.

Sometimes, the invading alien force wasn't an individual or group from another place, it was an ideology. Two 1951 films observed the issues of the day from opposing perspectives. In *The Thing from Another World*, an Air Force crew ventures to the North Pole and aids in unearthing an alien spacecraft frozen in the ice. An alien, freed from the ice, begins to reproduce quickly, using the blood of the dogs and humans at a polar station to create pods. The crewmen are able to stop its spread, but just barely. As a reporter begins to tell the harrowing story over the radio, he ends his message with the warning: "Every one of you listening to my voice, tell the world, tell this to everybody wherever they are. Watch the skies. Everywhere. Keep looking. Keep watching the skies." This allegory for the spread of communism in America is portrayed as an invading threat, ready at any moment to insinuate itself into all avenues of life.

Nineteen fifty-one's opposing viewpoint of alien visitation is *The Day the Earth Stood Still*. A benevolent alien named Klaatu arrives in Washington, D.C., to broker discussions with humans in attempts to calm their paranoia and escalating fears and suspicions. After being shot in the initial meeting, Klaatu escapes from the hospital and walks among humans. He learns that his fears of growing violence and destruction are well-founded, with the development of atomic weapons and other forms of mass destruction growing. This film ends with a different caution than that of *The Thing from Another World*, a message that makes clear that the danger doesn't come from others but from the violence of the culture itself: Klaatu tells a crowd,

> It is no concern of ours how you run your own planet, but if you threaten to extend your violence, this Earth of yours will be reduced to a burned-out cinder. Your choice is simple: join us and live in peace, or pursue your present course and face obliteration. We shall be waiting for your answer.

The fear that Klaatu speaks of, the fear of "the other" in society, is far more dangerous than the targets of the fear itself.

This back-and-forth battle, the struggle to accept vs. the desire to scapegoat, defines the Extraterrestrial Life subgenre for much of its existence. In the 1950s, at the height of the Cold War, films like *The War of the Worlds* and *Invasion of the Body Snatchers* drew clear lines between humans and aliens as heroes and villains; there was no room for nuance in the battle between cultures and ideologies. However, in the 1970s, when organizational mistrust was at an all-time high following the Watergate scandal, films like *The Man Who Fell to Earth* and *Close Encounters of the Third Kind* framed the government and the military as obstructionist at best and villainous at worst; the aliens themselves were as much victims of the system as Earth citizens.

The increasingly corporate make-up of the film industry in the 1980s and '90s meant that personal stories and narrative nuance were even more rare. Nineteen eighty-two saw the spiritual allegory of the Jesus-like *E.T. the Extra-Terrestrial*, a being of pure good stalked and kidnapped by the evil military, and likewise saw the slow and inevitable takeover of the shape-shifting monster from John Carpenter's *The Thing*. Seemingly gone were the emotional complexities of the conflicted aliens of the 1970s.

The alien villains of the 1990s took on an almost cartoonish quality in films like *Independence Day*, appearing only fleetingly in smoke and fog, here only to decimate our planet and destroy our iconic landmarks in spectacular fashion. As the new millennium approached, however, the dominant perspective of aliens in film was that of hapless or naïve victims. In *Men in Black* (1997), the aliens were wandering weirdos and rejects from across the galaxy, attempting with varying degrees of success to integrate into Earth's shining society. In *Galaxy Quest* (1999), a race of technologically advanced aliens seeks out the help of former sci-fi television stars because they're unaware of the existence of acting or even the concept of lying. The aliens were the innocents, and it was we, the citizens of Earth, who were taking advantage of them…

Beyond the Millennium

The events of September 11, 2001, changed everything. A new perspective on the threat of global terrorism loomed large, and the whole world mourned the deaths of people on three airplanes. Conscious or otherwise, the perception of the visitor from another planet in films of the era was altered as a result.

Steven Spielberg, responsible for the childhood innocence of *E.T.* 20 years earlier, remade *The War of the Worlds* in 2005, embracing the us vs. them mentality that reflected the fear and divisiveness of the world in the new millennium. The initially hopeful *Men in Black* franchise couldn't exist in this new world, and in 2012, the third entry in the series traveled back in time to the late 1960s. Occasional films like *District 9* and *Avatar* snuck through the filter, but even then, it was only because of the clout of popular iconoclastic directors and producers like James Cameron and Peter Jackson.

It took a full 20 years, from 1996 to 2016, for creator Roland Emmerich to make *Independence Day: Resurgence*, the sequel to the wildly popular original. The sequel earned just under $400 million at the box office, less than half the take of the original, and it's not hard to see why. After the United States experienced an attack on some of its most iconic real-life landmarks and lost human lives in the process, audiences were reticent to embrace a series which had gleefully plastered the destruction of the Empire State Building and the White House on its action movie posters.

The Independent Perspective

Independent filmmakers found new ways to embrace the Extraterrestrial Life concept of the stranger in a strange land, and some even found a way to address the aftermath of 9/11 in oblique but emotionally affecting ways.

Gareth Edwards, who eventually directed the American reboot of *Godzilla*, began his feature film career with the indie sci-fi drama *Monsters*. Existing in a world where an alien invasion has already taken place and a large section of North America is an uninhabitable infected zone, *Monsters* tells the story of human beings learning to live in a vastly different world in the aftermath of a massive and unexpected tragedy. The aliens, considered dangerous in the opening of the film, are eventually revealed to be merely creatures trying to stay alive themselves, to mate and to procreate. The message is masked but clear: Those different than us who we consider enemies may be as much the victims of the tragedy as the rest of us.

Indie films also discussed the individual human toll of violence through the allegory of alien abduction and attack. *Alien Abduction* (2014) showed a family trying to survive and remain together in the midst of an attempted abduction, while in *Almost Human*, director Joe Begos explored the devastation of losing a loved one and the struggle of having them return considerably changed. In the Featured Films section, these independent filmmakers explore Extraterrestrial Life themes as varied as shattered masculinity, the war on terror, and the fluid nature of gender and sexuality.

Featured Films

Altered (2006)
Director: Eduardo Sánchez
Writers: Jamie Nash, Eduardo Sánchez
Starring Adam Kaufman, Catherine Mangan, Brad William Henke

Wyatt shares a dark past with his friends: Fifteen years earlier, five of them were abducted by aliens, and only four of them survived the experience. Wyatt has struggled to regain a normal life, including a relationship with his girlfriend Hope, while the other survivors still take hunting trips out into the woods where they were taken, obsessed about the night that changed their lives. When Wyatt receives a phone call from his friends,

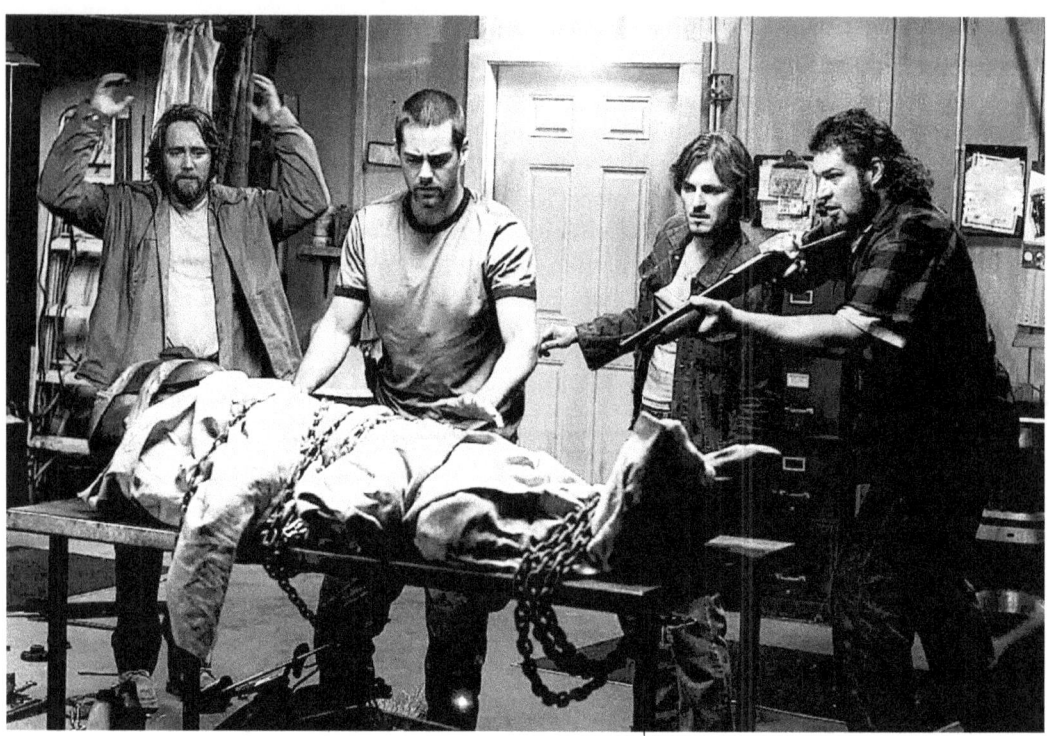

Alien abductees Michael C. Williams, Adam Kaufman, Paul McCarthy-Boyington and Brad William Henke turn the tables by kidnapping their abductor in *Altered* **(2006).**

he meets them in a cabin in the woods to discover that on their last hunting trip, they came back with something. Wyatt's friends have captured an alien.

A dark and thrilling inversion of the typical alien abduction film, *Altered* is a contained nightmare of a science fiction film that operates equally in the arena of horror. As disturbing as the physical disintegration of certain characters in the story is, the psychological de-evolution of the lead characters is just as unnerving. The narrative allows us to watch men who are so unable to process their trauma that they continue to revisit it. The film was a precursor to the social discussion of toxic masculinity that was first seen in 2001's *Fight Club* before being addressed more overtly in mainstream films like *Moonlight* and *Goat*.

~

Two thousand six was a good year for Jamie Nash, who co-scripted *Altered* and wrote and directed the dark fantasy comedy *Two Front Teeth*. The collaboration between Nash and director Eduardo Sánchez on *Altered* was successful, leading the two to work together on several other films: *Seventh Moon*, *Lovely Molly*, *VHS 2* and *Exists*. Though the shooting script for *Altered* was a sci-fi/horror written by Nash and Sánchez, the film was originally written by Nash as a much different kind of story.

Jamie Nash: *Altered is an interesting script. It was in some ways kind of my career-breaking script.... I met Eduardo Sánchez through that script. I wrote it on spec, I wrote it by myself. It was very different when I originally wrote it. It was more a horror-comedy. It had the same basic beats and set-up. It was almost played in an* Evil Dead II *sort of way, for* laughs. So it was very different after I met Ed, he really responded to that version, the horror-comedy, but his experience in Hollywood and horror was that horror-comedy was generally a tough sell. He and I kind of embarked then on some development that turned it into "quirkier funny" and less "ha-ha funny." He was heavily involved in the rewrite in that way. He gave notes and guided the tone of it. Then he also added a lot to an overall mythology to it. I think my original script was probably a little more contained. He was really interested in a bigger picture, a small snapshot of a big world.

There are very interesting subversions of the expectations of an alien film. I'm curious if they were present in the original draft or if they came about because of the script changes. The first one that interests me is the idea of alien abduction being seen in the context of molestation or sexual abuse. The element of the four lead characters who never really coped with their abduction the way that sometimes people don't cope with sexual abuse. I'm curious, was that present in the comedic version or was that something that came about because of taking it more seriously?

That whole backstory of them being abducted was there. It was definitely there. It was certainly a dark comedy, no doubt, kinda edgy independent comedy. I notice a lot of my scripts have that kind of dark secret. That thing in the past, long in the past, that you just buried deep inside you and can you get past that thing or will it come back to haunt you? I noticed a lot of my screenplays have that same central theme. There is even one right now that we're working on that has that same central theme, but it's a possession movie. It's like the same thing and it kind of treats possession like molestation in a woman's past. The person who suffered that must deal with the ramifications years later. I think it's one of those themes that has reoccurred a few times in the stuff I have done.

One of the things you touched on is the idea of alien abduction scenarios, because normally an alien abduction story is about people being abducted by aliens, and you did the exact reversal. This story is about four men who abduct an alien. Was that the kernel of the idea for you? Is that where the concept was born?

There are two origin stories, and I think they both kind of collided. On one hand I was watching Taken, *the alien abduction TV series produced by Steven Spielberg. I was at the Austin film festival, and the only reason I went to see it was because Tobe Hooper was there to introduce it. He directed the first episode. I was watching the episode, and I remembered that I had this other idea for a few weeks that was going through my head. It was, if E.T. had come to my friends back in the 1980s or 1970s, my friends were kind of degenerates, and they would have beaten E.T. to death or put him in a cage or done something horrible to poor E.T. So I had that dark thought going through my head while I was at the Austin Film Festival and I saw* Taken. *I hadn't really seen an alien abduction film since* Fire in the Sky *and* Communion. *So, given all those things, I think of one of the reasons we haven't seen another alien abduction movie is because you really can't top* Fire in the Sky's *alien abduction scene. So, you almost have to give it a new spin or you have to give it a new twist. You have to come at it from a different angle.*

Many films in this book are in some way reacting or commenting on films from the '70s and '80s, the formative years for the filmmakers now making movies. That's interesting, because the filmmakers in the '80s were doing the same thing with films that they grew up with in the '50s and '60s. In many ways, *E.T.* is the reaction from the compassionate kids who felt bad for aliens in the '50s movies.

Right, right. Ed and I are a few years apart, and generally the same movies are our favorites. You'd almost be able to predict what my favorites are: Star Wars, Jaws, Close Encounters of the Third Kind, E.T., Poltergeist. *These are my favorite movies. I do go outside of that, like I have* RoboCop *in there and some weirder ones. I'm a huge* Evil Dead II *fan. But for the most part, it's Spielberg-y and the 1980s.*

It's interesting that you guys have four lead characters who are males. There's an interesting observation to be made there because, for years before that, male sexual molestation was not something that was discussed a lot. It was into the '90s with *Prince of Tides* and movies like *Sleepers* before anybody was even comfortable having that conversation. I think because of the perspectives that people had about masculinity, it just wasn't a thing you talked about in movies. I think it's interesting that your film talked about it, but often in a way that movies do, where they will slightly veil a conversation so that it's a little bit easier to talk about it honestly.

I can definitely see that. I think probably I'd have to look back on when the Catholic Church scandal was and things like that. We were probably coming off that when Altered *was written. I think it had been in the zeitgeist; I don't know that I was directly thinking about that, but it occurred to me in a very literal way that, that's what the metaphor that story was. While I was writing, it was certainly a little of what I was trying to channel into, no doubt.*

If you look at the nature of the masculinity and especially as it is in features and on television, it has changed. When I was a little kid, movies were full of the John Wayne, "I'll knock your block off" kinds of characters, and with Altered … *most of the characters I've written since then aren't really like that. The* Altered *characters are almost old-fashioned masculinity, western style. As if they are the last of their era in a way. The notion of them being almost like western characters, I think that was always there as well. I mean, the guy's name is Wyatt; they have that certain era of masculinity. I think that's an interesting observation. Again, nothing that I was conscious of, but looking back at it many years later, I can definitely see that.*

The Objective (2008)
Director: Daniel Myrick
Writers: Daniel Myrick, Mark A. Patton, Wesley Clark
Starring Jonas Ball, Jon Huertas, Michael C. Williams

In the months following 9/11, a Special Forces team is assigned to accompany a CIA agent into a remote area of Afghanistan to find a valuable Afghan cleric. The team finds themselves isolated, uncomfortable with their reception, and questioning the truth of their assignment. After their technology breaks down, their supplies dwindle, and members of their team start vanishing, they push the CIA operative to tell them the truth, and they discover why they're really there: to search for a mysterious group of invisible creatures in the desert that can only be seen with infrared cameras.

Though the enemy in *The Objective* is a mysterious alien race, the film deals allegorically with the unfathomability of war with an ideology rather than a country or an army. Brilliantly remixing fears of terrorism, genuine questions of belief and freedom, and the struggle to achieve political wins with incomplete information, the film is a treatise on the problems plaguing the War on Terror.

Director Daniel Myrick was one of the creators of *The Blair Witch Project*; the lost, confused protagonists, the obsessed central character who won't stop using a camera, and the mysterious and ambiguous creature that eludes capture by the pursuers and the viewer are all familiar elements from his first film. Myrick, however, finds a way to make them fresh, surprising, and grittily realistic in a brand-new way. He made two other films after *The Blair Witch Project*; *The Objective* is a halfway point between the mystery of *Solstice* and the religious exploration of *Believers*. The motivation for the film, however, came from a much more basic fascination.

Daniel Myrick: *I've always been fascinated with UFOs. Not only from the prospect of potential intelligent life in the universe, but also under [the] premise of the social and cultural ramifications they have on society and people in particular. I wanted to do something that's sort of sci-fi and thriller and a quasi–UFO encounter, coupled with sort of this political commentary on the war in Afghanistan, sort of our misadventures over there and a bit of an allegory of getting into something we really don't understand. I thought those two topics that were sort of close to me at the time would be an interesting premise. I also thought it would be cool to do something in the desert, kind of a military-esque film was an interesting challenge I wanted to take on. I did a little research and the producers I was working with helped, but tapping into the kind of folklore in the Middle East, Southeast Asia, and places like that. Of course, it's just like it is over here. There's a lot of ancient history regarding otherworldly spirits. The Vimana sort of came up and that fell very much into the wheelhouse of western folklore with regards to ancient astronauts, so I thought it was a cool premise and a little bit of a different take on a military sci-fi thriller.*

This film wouldn't exist, or at least not exist in a format that it does, without the events of 9/11. It's a film that is drawn directly from that circumstance, isn't it?

Absolutely. It represents this clash of cultures and our sort of inherent and amplified paranoia post–9/11. [It] gave us a blank check to go do that, and there's a lot of motivations that, were they not born solely out of 9/11, certainly were reinvigorated and used as a pretext for some of the adventures we got into overseas. Certainly The Objective *casts into a lot of that, but I was cautious to not turn it into a political movie. I didn't want to hit anybody over the head with some big political statement and it was a bit more subversive than that. If you could read between the lines of what was going on, you could see it there, but it's housed within a good old-fashioned sci-fi thriller and UFO movie.*

If we use the Bush administration as sort of the allegorical blanket for this film, then the idea of these soldiers being led into a place under false pretenses because they're looking for aliens rather than a cleric, the idea of being hopelessly unprepared for the task at hand, brilliantly takes actual events that are entirely unrelated and just uses those as signposts to create a really solid narrative.

Yeah, that was the whole intent, and the trick is to have this military movie taking place in the world that was already rife with political chaos and terrorists around every corner. At the same time, I wanted to portray a human element that gets left out whenever we read headlines regarding these kinds of big, world-changing events. I wanted to portray the soldiers themselves as real guys, not your typical Hollywood gung-ho military jarheads and the people of Afghanistan as real textured individuals. There are consequences to these actions and there's a human cost and it's complicated. Our geopolitical machinations aren't easily distilled into your newsfeeds, so that's a lot there that is going on that I'm trying to portray but not get too heavy-handed with it.

This movie does a great job showing the battle of ideologies and divisions many of the characters have. Just because they're with one group doesn't necessarily mean they're part of that group or that they're not manipulating that group. It's an interesting way to show how difficult a task like this is when you don't even know if the person next to you can be trusted, let alone anyone else.

Exactly. I was careful to not portray the Vimana itself as aggressive. It's arguably acting in self-defense, whenever its space is infringed upon by the soldiers. It's because we don't understand it; we try to force it into our realm of understanding. I think that's where our CIA guy represents an internal conflict in America. We have a whole other institution within our own country that can be at cross-purposes with the military we are all supposed to be supporting. That was an interesting component as well.

The Vimana take on a religious or mystical element in this story. It dates back to the '70s, the *Chariots of the Gods* concept about aliens throughout history being mistaken for encounters with divine creatures. You found ways to take all the elements that would normally be part of an alien encounter, abduction scenario, or attack, and flipped them just slightly so that they take on a metaphysical and religious aspect.

The ending scene is as much of a religious experience for our CIA operative as it is an alien abduction. I wanted to portray it where those distinctions were blended together because one could make that argument. What if some of the religions in the world throughout history could have been from visitors from another planet? Is religion itself inspired by somewhere else or somebody else? There are a lot of arguments to be made that it's all coming from the same place. The Vimana is a sort of representation of one person's God, another person's UFO. It could be all the above. I didn't want to fall into any one category. I wanted to play into that ambiguity and point a finger at us all looking at the same thing here and calling it a different name.

At the end of the film, the CIA operative's experience makes me wonder, "Is this what Mohammad experienced? Is this what Jesus went through when he went into the desert?" It's brilliant, because you draw that conclusion, and even people who are irreligious could say, "It's not what I believe, but in this context, maybe it's not crazy."

Absolutely. If you're a Christian and you were around during the time when the claims were made that Jesus rose from the dead, or you're Mohammed in the cave and you're talking to the Angel Gabriel or ancient astronauts. It all could be the same thing, right? That was the message I wanted to get across: one part abduction, one part religious experience, a spiritual awakening, and then a good old fashioned 1970s ESP-telekinesis event. You see him levitating at the end. It's all coming from the same source that we simply don't understand, and we're trying to put a label on it, form a religion out of it, or build a conspiracy theory around it.

It reminds me of that Arthur C. Clarke quote about how "any sufficiently advanced technology is indistinguishable from magic."

Exactly. There is no way we could understand what it is, what it's made of, what its intentions are, how long it's been here, or if it's just visiting. There are so many things out of our scope of understanding, yet we're compelled to try to dissect it and break it down, co-opt it for our own use. We learn the hard way that it's not as simple as it might seem.

I'm curious as to what your motivation was for bringing the visual element of the FLIR (Forward Looking Infrared) camera into the film.

One of the original themes in my head when I started formulating the premise was inspired by all the postings online from soldiers in battle in Iraq and Afghanistan with night vision goggles. There's countless hours of fire fights and engagements with this greenish, spooky green night vision war footage; it's creepy. I just got to thinking, how scary would it be that some monster is revealed in the distance that you can only see through this technology? That was the kernel of creativity behind wanting to do this kind of different visual, that reveals the monster, if you will, that is a bit out of the ordinary. This camera was experimental at the time, so we had to get clearance from the State Department to bring it over to Morocco where we shot. It was a great way for our CIA guy to have one more layer of technical complexity to what he's doing as well as have a visual exposition of the artifacts that were important and the reveal at the end where you can see the actual Vimana on screen via this camera.

Why do we, as both viewers and filmmakers, continue to gravitate back towards the idea of aliens in our science fiction stories? What's so fascinating to us?

There are a few reasons. I believe human nature is always looking for explanations, and we're uncomfortable with the notion of being completely by ourselves. We're the only intelligent thing sitting on this little boondock in the middle of the nowhere, so I think there's a certain level of comfort knowing that we are not the only ones in the black and vacuous space. There's a natural innate fascination that all humans share and it's cross-cultural, which I think plays very well for filmmaking when you've got an idea that can pretty much play anywhere in the world. I think that's the reason why horror does so well, as opposed to comedy or topical drama. There's a certain amount of insecurity we have with aliens that makes them scary. There's a lot of creative license behind what an alien premise can be. Certainly, they're extremely visually compelling for film. It's why we're fascinated with Bigfoot and the Loch Ness Monster. I think it's just a fascinating subject to explore.

Earthling (2010)
Writer-Director: Clay Liford
Starring Rebecca Spence, Peter Greene, William Katt

A strange event takes place in the vacuum of space. As a result, a small group of people begin to go through strange physical changes. More disturbingly, buried memories surface. They are not human at all, but aliens living on Earth in disguise. Struggling to negotiate their past lives with a newly discovered truth, they have to decide if they want to try and go back to the existence they knew before the change, or to embrace their real origins and try to find a way back home.

Quiet and beautiful and fully deserving of the descriptive "human," *Earthling* is a film whose science fiction allegory is broad enough to encompass the concerns of numerous marginalized groups. Exploring sexuality, immigration and the difficulty of living an authentic life in a judgmental society, it's a sci-fi parable and story of unrequited love. Its literary and cinematic influences are as varied as Virginia Woolf and Andrei Tarkovsky.

∽

A film as ambitious as *Earthling* needed an equally ambitious creator, and Clay Liford brought the experience and passion necessary to achieve it. Aside from writing and directing the feature films *Slash*, *Wuss*, *Earthling* and *A Four Course Meal*, he has also been a producer, editor, cinematographer and actor, and even worked in visual effects.

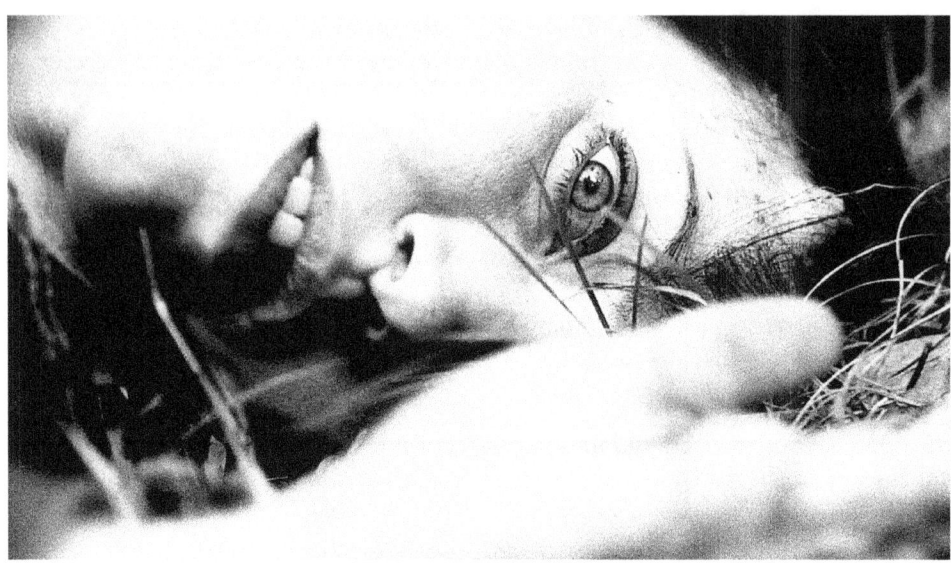

Judith (Rebecca Spence) collapses at a shocking revelation in *Earthling* (2010).

His love for science fiction runs deep, but it was his desire to see recognizable human emotion within those science fiction narratives that inspired him to make *Earthling*.

Clay Liford: *It was always the idea of wanting to do science fiction where it wasn't about robots or rockets or ray guns, it was about people. But it was still hard sci-fi at the same time. The gestation of the alien entity was a fun mental exercise. The concept of "How could an alien being traverse the cosmos?" The idea of being these freeze-dried seeds that were required to be inside of a host organism to unpack itself, that was the key idea.*

One central theme of the movie is that the aliens assimilating into society so well that human beings can't tell the difference between the aliens and themselves. The first thing I thought of was the immigrant allegory, of total immersion into the society you're joining. But there's also this idea of the aliens learning of their true nature and having to decide how to handle the realization, which feels like it's more an allegory of a gay person coming out for the first time. Were these both elements you recognized allegorically when you were writing it?

I think that's a good way of saying it. It wasn't in those exact terms, but they were both in my head at the time. I was a big fan of Orlando, *the Virginia Woolf story, this cross-time, cross-gender romance where the story existed before and after their current incarnations. That was a major jumping-off point, the idea of whether you can accept your identity when you realize what it is. One of the core relationships in the movie is a character who fully remembers what she was before and the emotions she had in her previous life, who is in love with someone who has no interest in that. It's about two people being presented with information that may be too much to handle and making two different choices. Some of that has to do with the sexuality of the characters, and is metaphorically tied to sex- and gender-based fluidity, but also the idea of immigration. It was slightly less about immigration, but it was definitely there.*

I also thought of *Orlando* while watching it. It's not just that the aliens' consciousness was changing, it's that they were also going through physical changes. With the alien elements like the skin alterations and the bumps, the actual changing of their body to reflect their true nature, it even extends to the idea of actual gender identity. There's a connection that can be made to the trans community as well. Was that intentional?

It was definitely something I thought about directly. It's using sci-fi to tell stories that are political, but being able to look at the emotion behind it while hiding the politics. That's what Star Trek *did best. There was an episode of* Star Trek: The Next Generation *where Commander Riker fell in love with an alien who identified as female but whose society wasn't supposed to have females or males. And when her people found out, they basically neutered her gender traits. You can talk about stuff like that, this idea of the political nature of what it means to be trans. In that episode, it was tied to this concept of the "un-gaying" of people, the right-wing desire to fix people in gay camps.*

Science fiction is a great place to create an allegory where it's not just a one-for-one replacement. The thing can mean more than just one thing. In the case of your film, we've already talked about three kinds of people who are marginalized and could be fit into this story framework. Horror and science fiction are the only genres which are broad enough to do that.

Yeah, you have more tools in your toolkit. The concept of playing with genre is that you have more tools to tell human stories. It's not an excuse to talk about rockets or whatever, it's about having a broader expanse of my playing field to explore ideas.

While there are obvious science fiction elements in this film, there are also complex lyrical and artistic qualities that reminded me of two science fiction films that have deeper themes in mind as well: Andrei Tarkovsky's films *Solaris* and *Stalker*. Were they influences for you on this film?

Tarkovsky is a huge influence. I made my first feature in Russia because I was obsessed with Tarkovsky. The film before Earthling, A Four Course Meal, *had a Russian fairy tale segment, and we actually had a cast member from* Stalker *in that. He was a minor character in* Stalker, *but we had him in the movie, and it was amazing. Tarkovsky has a certain pacing and quietude, even though his films are about grandiose things. In Solaris, the drive to the airport is almost a ten-minute sequence where he's driving for the last time to the airport, essentially saying goodbye to the Earth. The last part of the movie is more plot-centric, but the first act and into the second act of* Earthling *tends to feel more Tarkovsky-influenced, and that was intentional.*

Aside from directing, you've done a lot of cinematography. Is that part of what appeals to you about Tarkovsky? Because a cinematographer doesn't have an enormous amount of control over the dialogue or actors, so a cinematographer's job is to tell the story the best he can with just images. The first half of your film is told with pure image, or just image and sound, without a lot of dialogue interaction. I'm curious if the cinematography experience was influential on that.

I think it was more unconscious there, but I can definitely see that. I always try to use imagery when I can. My biggest problem with Earthling, *and why it's one of the few movies I've made that is difficult for me to watch, is that we shot the movie out of order and inexpensively. We shot the climax of the film first, and when the effects didn't work, we had to lean on dialogue to make up for it. That hurts me so much about the movie, even though most people give it a pass. The third act of* Earthling *is a bit of a factor of its limitations, and one of the casualties is the lyricism that we built up to that point that was replaced by expository dialogue. That was my only regret, was that I couldn't maintain that. It's always better storytelling in general to tell story with images.*

Is there any connective tissue between having made *Earthling* and interacted with science fiction fans that may have led to you writing *Slash*, your follow-up film about young people who write erotic sci-fi fan fiction?

I've always been a genre fan, so that was always there, but as my work became more character-based, there was some part of me that expected not to work in genre material because it's hard to be taken seriously. But Slash *is the weird joining of my previous two features. After* Earthling, *I made a high school comedy called* Wuss, *which has no genre elements to it.* Earthling *and* Wuss *were actually shot at the same high school. Then, I wanted to take the dark comedy of* Wuss *and combine it with the spiritual exploration and humanity of* Earthling.

Earthling is probably the most human film I'd made up to that point. I was looking for something about people being outsiders because of their interests as much as their sexuality, and that's how Slash *came about. Metaphorically, it hit all the ideas of how to build a community of people with your interests, and then what is still taboo even there.*

Geek culture has been mainstreamed now due to shows like *The X-Files* and the advent of the Internet, and a new subculture has grown to replace that subculture. Now that sci-fi is mainstream, bigger studios are making sci-fi films. Except for smaller films and indie films, we're robbed of the interesting observations that were made in older studio films like *2001: A Space Odyssey* and *Silent Running*.

I love Silent Running, *which oddly enough was released overseas as 2002. My buddy who made* Kumiko the Treasure Hunter, *David Zellner, had an Italian poster for 2002 in his house. I was reading it, and it said "Featuring the music of Joan Baez," and sure enough, it was* Silent Running. *But to the point about the interesting observations, you're right. Movies have to play across the world now. You can't have specific cultural elements because it has to play in China or Africa.* Warcraft *was a bomb in America, but it was a gigantic hit in China. Movies with nuanced conversations or with cultural specifics don't translate everywhere. Movies are regressing because they have to find a baseline of education that will appeal to that lowest level, the grade school level where things will translate easily.*

Your film falls into the subgenre of alien stories, which have been around nearly since the inception of science fiction film. Why do you think we continue to revisit the alien subgenre again and again over the history of film?

I think it's the idea of a life form that you don't instantly relate to, but has thoughts and feelings. They can see and comment on our culture because of that. It has an intelligent and emotional response to its surroundings, but because of its alien nature, it can reinterpret and give us a clean view on our own society. People always joke about how, if aliens landed and all they saw of our culture was The Golden Girls, *what would they think of us? You wonder about that; think about the cultures that we've lost even within our own human history. How much do we really know about the Roman Empire or the Macedonians?*

More Films of Interest

Terminus (2015), *Alien Trespass* (2009), *The Box* (2009), *Ejecta* (2014), *Extraterrestre* (2011), *Extraterrestrial* (2014), *Hangar 10* (2014), *The Quiet Hour* (2014), *The Substitute* (2007), *The Wild Blue Yonder* (2005), *The Signal* (2014), *The Visit: An Alien Encounter* (2015)

2
Surviving the Mysterious Event

The subgenre of the Mysterious Event is predicated less on the event itself and more on the reaction of the people who have survived the event and how they cope with the results. Several genres have an equivalent to the Mysterious Event; in horror films, it comes as the nameless, faceless monster or the motiveless masked killer. It takes the shape of the unexplained curse in the fantasy film.

In all these instances, the event acts as an introduction to a world much like our own, but with a drastic event or circumstance that redefines the way people live. The event or the aftermath often reflects the anxiety of the age, and that is never truer than in science fiction.

The Cold War threat that permeated America in the 1950s left people with daily fears of an attack or explosion, and with it came the constant concern of losing loved ones or ending up alone. Multiple episodes of *The Twilight Zone* tapped into that fear, as well as features like Roger Corman's *The Last Woman on Earth*; in this 1960 film, a pair of newlyweds and their lawyer are on vacation in Puerto Rico when the air becomes unbreathable and everyone dies but them. Isolated and struggling to survive, the three soon battle each other. The Cold War lasted through to the 1980s, and the fear bubbled up in numerous films, from 1974's *Where Have All the People Gone* to 1984's *Night of the Comet* to 1985's *The Quiet Earth*.

Humans weren't the only threat. In the 1960s and 1970s, as scientists discovered the devastating effects of pollution on the planet and sounded the alarm on the possible drastic environmental change, films began to reflect that fear. In Alfred Hitchcock's classic *The Birds*, flocks of previously docile birds start attacking people, seemingly without reason or explanation. A character in the film observes: "I have never known birds of different species to flock together. The very concept is unimaginable. Why, if that happened, we wouldn't stand a chance! How could we possibly hope to fight them?"

The smallest creatures in the ecosystem were the first ones affected by our mistakes, so they were the first to retaliate. Smaller even than Hitchcock's birds were the insects of Saul Bass' *Phase IV*. Ants quickly evolve due to an unexplained cosmic event, and Dr. Lesko and company find themselves in an escalating struggle with them as they try to study their changing dynamics. As the ants begin the process of changing humanity to suit their own needs, Lesko realizes that the ants are now in charge, and the world belongs to them, expressed in the ominous final voice-over: "We knew then, that we were being changed ... and made part of their world. We didn't know for what purpose ... but we knew we would be told."

As the Cold War threat ebbed, new technologies created new fears. Computer systems and automated machines were replacing human jobs, and the irrational fears of them taking over were fed through the filter of the Mysterious Event. Strange solar events gave life to a series of homicidal trucks, ATMs and other electronics in the Stephen King-directed *Maximum Overdrive* (1986). The trend expanded with another King-written story, turned into 1995's *The Mangler*, and continued through to the edge of the new millennium. *Virus* (1999) brought self-building machines to life via an alien signal that works its way through the Mir space station and onto a Russian research ship.

After the Millennium

As the complexity of new technologies and their almost magical abilities grew exponentially in the new millennium, humanity's appetite for the Mysterious Event grew comparably. However, the desire for mystery grew more complex as a result. When average people on the street could pull phones from their pockets and play interactive video games in real time with people halfway across the globe, it took more than a simple mystery to sate their desire. Luckily for humanity, television stepped in to fill that void.

With television seasons that lasted between 12 and 22 episodes, the time spent on mysteries could expand, and with it could come more complicated, convoluted and elaborate narratives. From the six seasons of the increasingly intricate desert island thriller *Lost* to the universe-altering *Fringe* to the short-lived high-concept series *FlashForward*, *Day Break* and *Awake*, television allowed viewers to relish the extension of the mythos that was relegated to two hours or less in the world of feature films.

The Independent Perspective

Independent films have the luxury of touching on personal and controversial subjects that would be a harder sell in a mainstream film meant to appeal to broader audiences. In the new millennium, discussions of equality found their way into the Mysterious Event subgenre.

In 2004, director Sergio Arau used a mysterious event in California to discuss immigration and race relations with *A Day Without a Mexican*. A strange fog surrounds the state and causes the disappearance of every Mexican, which throws the economy into turmoil and brings normal daily progress to a grinding halt. The more divisive the conversation about immigration gets, the more prescient the film becomes.

The evolution of the feminist movement was discussed in a similar manner in 2001's *The New Women*. A strange rainstorm in the small town of Lacuna puts the entire community to sleep. After a few days, only the women wake up while the men remain comatose. Men die off and food supplies dwindle. The women discover that the rest of the world has experienced the same rainstorm. For better or worse, the world is a fully female society.

The Mysterious Event in many indie films boils down to the inciting event that puts characters on journeys to face traumas, a cinematic form of therapy. In *Another Earth*, student Rhoda tries to use the shocking discovery of a duplicate Earth to make amends for tragic mistakes of her past; in *The One I Love*, troubled couple Ethan and Sophie make a mysterious discovery in a guest cottage which changes the nature of their relationship forever; and in *Ultrasonic*, a stressed-out musician's ordeal with mysterious sounds only he can hear makes him reconsider the conspiratorial ravings of his mentally disturbed brother-in-law. Changes in the world around them cause these protagonists to look further inward. In the Featured Films section, these filmmakers invent compelling Mysterious Events to explore the power of media to transcend all barriers, the almost supernatural power of retribution and justice, and the complicated dynamics of romance in isolation.

Featured Films

Resolution (2012)
Director: Justin Benson, Aaron Moorhead
Writer: Justin Benson
Starring Peter Cilella, Vinny Curran, Emily Montague

After receiving a video showing his former best friend Chris, drug-addled and isolated in an unfinished house in the middle of the woods, Michael goes to try and convince him to seek recovery. After a tense greeting, Michael overpowers Chris and handcuffs him to a pipe, intending to keep him there and get him clean. As their confrontations become more heated and the encounters with others become stranger, they start to find photos and recordings of themselves left on the premises, somehow captured without their awareness. Some of the images show the two of them dying, and all the images seem to start coming true.

Michael (Peter Cilella) and Chris (Vinny Curran) realize that someone is watching them in *Resolution* (2012).

On the surface, *Resolution* appears to be a contained two-person horror film that effectively utilizes its single location and cast; however, just beneath the surface, the film enjoys tearing at the edges of expectation and subverting the clichés of both the science fiction and horror genres. The plot makes the villain Media itself and, in so doing, forces the audience to be an unwilling participant in the suffering of the characters. Sophisticated, challenging, and worthy of its cult reputation, *Resolution* stands alongside *Mr. Jones* as a film which helped reinvigorate the found footage concept.

~

Resolution was the first feature film project from directors Justin Benson and Aaron Moorhead, who met at a commercial production company. They went on to work together on the equally groundbreaking *Spring*, and their most recent film is the cult thriller *The Endless*.

Though *Resolution*'s narrative seems complicated in passages, the directors found the heart of the film in a single, seemingly simple element.

Justin Benson: *It all started with the idea of finding out at the end of the movie that everything you've been watching is the POV of a real ancient entity that communicates via thoughtography, then everything was reverse engineered from there. A lot of what was reverse engineered was guided by the theme of control, and more specifically as it relates to addiction and unique experiences I had with my mom's substance abuse problems. That said, though this theme of control did guide the story, it was something that was realized in retrospect, not like "Hey, the theme is control, let's do this," but rather on a less intellectualized level, more instinct. We've made movies since where we more consciously let the theme guide the story, and it works out about the same. I guess the lesson there is that sometimes the writing tools still work even if you don't know you're using them.*

Aaron Moorhead: *I wish I could take credit, but Justin came up with this thing the whole way through. In development, the biggest thing we worked out was the red herring aspect of the film. We have all these strange (what I now know is sometimes referred to as "Lynchian") characters popping in and out of the story at will. In the finished film, it leaves viewers disoriented so we can swoop in and blast that crazy ending on them, but it wasn't working how we wanted in earlier drafts. We tried a draft where we cut most of them and elevated one of them (the girl in the window) to appear in several scenes and even the climax, but it felt silly. So the idea was hatched to "red herring" the hell out of it. If Chekov's gun is on the wall in the first act and must go off in the third, we'll put a dozen guns on the wall and in the end someone who you didn't notice was in the room all along will stab you with a knife.*

Smaller projects with single locations and only a handful of characters have always been a part of horror films, but in recent years, the films have been growing in concept to be far more ambitious in their narrative scope than the trappings of the production would lead you to believe. What was your interest in framing such a complex narrative into a relatively simple physical production?

Moorhead: *The biggest compliment I remember getting on* Resolution *was when someone called it a "mind-fuck." From a production standpoint, messing with someone's perception of reality can be pretty low-cost and comes down to how much time you spend crafting your story. No feature film is easy, but the kind of low-budget production you describe is simpler than others. What's hard is making it effective, making it a movie that keeps you up at night thinking, that sits with you for days. Massive scope doesn't do that, but ideas do. Ideas don't* cost anything. We hope that all of our films have a massive narrative and thematic scope but feel personal. The worst failure for us as filmmakers is if at some point our reach exceeds our grasp and we make a film that ends up feeling "try-hard."

Benson: *I think complex narrative is the only thing we really know how to do and our stories just end up that way whether we like it or not. But the small cast and one primary location was guided by the economics of indie film. Something Aaron and I learned real quick as DIY filmmakers is write for what you can accomplish with the resources you have so your movie doesn't look like a YouTube fan film. There's obviously nothing wrong with fan films, where the charm often lies in scope beyond the means. But we set out to make original content, which is nearly impossible to get financing for in the first place. And for it to work artistically, it often needs to have a high degree of realism. So you just don't put stuff in the script that can't be done well with the money in your checking account. Thus, the thrills often come from ideas and getting to know real, interesting people, rather than a big shoot-out between giant robots or destroying a city with superpowers.*

The film is about many things, but one of them is about how relationships are damaged by addiction. Did you choose this central theme because you felt it was simply a good entry into the larger narrative, or did you feel like there were thematic connections to their plight and how it folded into the greater story?

Benson: *It was more of an instinct thing that again, in retrospect, works really well thematically with the science fiction component. But the addiction stuff was more about having a lot of experiences with it that I had never seen honestly expressed in a movie, and there was something fun about that stuff being as fresh as the antagonist and other sci-fi and horror elements.*

Moorhead: *I'm lucky enough to not know many addicts (at least not admitted ones), so this didn't have any personal connections per se, but it does seem to dovetail just right with the sci-fi aspect of the story. Here's an unseen thing trying to control them and make it do its bidding for its own unknown gain, and one of those guys is forcing his best friend into an unasked-for sobriety so that "he can have something to save and feel good about himself."*

You cleverly place several people in the path of the main characters, each positing a possible (albeit unusual) explanation for the strange circumstances they're experiencing. Is this part of the meta-experience of the film, placing the characters and the viewer in the same circumstance?

Benson: *I didn't know what meta meant when we were making the film, so can't say it's intentional. The only way I know how to honestly describe that one is that it very coincidentally turned out that my own relationship with genre films that inspired those red herrings turned out to be very similar to the audience's relationships with those same films. Which is actually quite odd, because the genre films that inspired those red herrings are relatively obscure.*

Moorhead: *I think it's hard when you make something that can be considered a meta film at what you draw the line at between being meta and not. Because at a certain point, it's still a movie. That is, if someone lampooned bad movies but the movie itself was unwatchably crappy, it's a cheap out for the filmmaker to just say, "No but that was meta" unless they're some kind of visual artist and have no aspirations of actually making films in the industry. So, short answer, no, those characters weren't meant to be proxies for the audience members, although there's definitely a lot of things that bleed over on themselves once you start seeing the movie entirely in a meta context, and that was intentional.*

The lead characters receive recorded media of themselves throughout the film, from places and angles and times which should be impossible to have captured. Aside from the ultimate revelation of the film, is this act a commentary in some way on media itself, the progression of it, the purpose of it, the manipulation of it?

Moorhead: When you look at footage of game shows from the 1950s or crowds of people watching horse races from the 1920s, you're looking at a bunch of people that are very likely all dead. I don't have much of a belief in the supernatural, or ghosts specifically, but the closest thing I can think of to ghosts is old media. It's the image and creation of someone long gone. You could also think of it as the closest we have to a time machine. And that unfamiliarity, no matter how banal it was when it was used at the time it was captured, gets under my skin.

Benson: Not really a commentary, but I love the idea of an ancient entity who operates via media and who has also evolved its communication as humankind developed new technology. Basically, what started using cave paintings is now using a hard drive—that's really fun and creepy.

The end of the film: While you don't have to go into a clear and unambiguous explanation of the final moments, do you feel there is a definitive explanation for the events in the film, or are you more interested in having the viewers bring their theories to bear on what can seem like an open ending?

Benson: There is one very detailed explanation that is answered in the film if you watch very closely, but also there's an undercurrent of something bigger that was just discussions mostly between us and our sound mixer Yahel. It's been fun watching all the interpretations, though. The craziest thing is when you read a review that nails the actual explanation so hard, it's like they were in the room with us when discussing even the more subtle aspects of it.

Moorhead: We never set out to make a movie with a deliberately perplexing end, because we can trace every event back to its origin in the film. The only issue is, with all mystery stories, most things only make sense in retrospect. It relates well to what you asked in the beginning about our narratives being inherently a bit complex. I think a good mystery is one that keeps you thinking after the credits roll, but one that isn't purely open to interpretation. That said, I much prefer to leave it to the viewer if they ask me point-blank, because there's a lot less joy in knowing what's inside the mystery box.

This film is an excellent entry into the sci-fi subgenre of the Mysterious Event. What do you think it is that draws us over and over again as both filmmakers and viewers to stories about unexplained events?

Moorhead: Most of the natural world has been nearly inexplicable to humans until the modern era. We lived in a universe of miracles. Now, we're getting closer and closer to feeling like there aren't all that many frontiers left. But there will always be frontiers in storytelling, especially in the sci-fi genre, and that's exciting through the end of the world.

Benson: Could be as simple as "cool as science is, we all still love magic, too."

The Suicide Theory (2014)

Director: Dru Brown
Writer: Michael J. Kospiah
Starring Steve Mouzakis, Leon Cain, Joss McWilliam

Several years after the tragedy that killed his wife, Steven is now a contract killer. In the midst of hunting down a mark, he meets Percival in the strangest way possible: by crashing onto his cab while attempting to commit suicide from atop a building. Percival pursues Steven after discovering he's a contract killer, begging Steven to kill him. It seems that Percival is unable to end his life, no matter how many times and how violently he has tried. Steven tests the theory, leaving Percival injured but not dead, and Steven senses this challenge might be worth exploring in more depth.

The Suicide Theory takes what could be simply a mainstream high concept idea and utilizes it in dark and inventive ways. The film uses the interaction of individuals in this narrative to comment from a more global perspective about the effects of off-handed violence on the lives of unexpected people. Also exploring multiple aspects of mental illness, the film's ending is both a fantastic *Twilight Zone*–esque shock and a well-deserved and thoughtful conclusion.

∽

Director Dru Brown was no stranger to film, having helmed the thriller *Sleeper* in 2012. But writer Michael J. Kospiah thundered onto the screen for the first time in 2014 with *The Suicide Theory*. The year was a good one for Kospiah, who wrote the similarly gritty short film script *The Dead Guy in the Trunk*. The central concept of *The Suicide Theory* is so outlandish that one might expect the plot was entirely an invention; however, Kospiah used some very real elements of his recent past to give the film its dark heart.

Percival (Leon Cain) and Steven (Steve Mouzakis) discover their lives are oddly intertwined in *The Suicide Theory* **(2014).**

Michael J. Kospiah: I was going through a rough time in my life during my mid-20s. It was one of those things where I was like, "Fuck everybody." It was me against the world. I guess I was a late bloomer in terms of maturity because I was experiencing the type of angst and depression usually associated with teenagers. Now, I got a girl pregnant—a girl I was madly in love with—and I sort of crumbled under the pressure. And it cost me, not only the relationship, but the baby. She decided an abortion was the best thing for the both of us. And, despite being somewhat against my moral beliefs, I went along with it. But I felt solely responsible for this. But I didn't want to feel like the bad guy through all of this. So, I lashed out and acted immaturely, pretty much burning as many bridges as possible. But it didn't make me feel any better. It was very self-destructive and it took a toll on me. Deep down, I felt like a monster. Not only did I lose the girl I was deeply, deeply in love with, but I lost a child. And I really, really thought about suicide. A lot. There wasn't a day when I wouldn't think about it. I'd spend many sleepless nights ruminating about my existence. But, at a time when I felt like a failure in every way possible—as a human being, professionally as an aspiring writer, etc.—I thought that I'd probably fail at suicide. In my mind, I'd probably end up surviving no matter how drastic my suicide attempts would become. And I'd probably either end up a vegetable, confined to a wheelchair or something else really fucked-up. Like my dick wouldn't work any more or I'd have to get a limb amputated or something shitty like that.

As horrible as that sounded, and as depressed as I was, I couldn't help but kind of laugh at the irony of that scenario if it were to play out. It sounded like a really fucked-up episode of The Twilight Zone. And it inspired me. And actually helped me deal with the depression in somewhat of a healthy way. Though, as I was writing the script, I was actually stuck in this deep, dark, depressing, shitty hole. But as I got closer to finishing, I felt myself getting closer to escaping this hole. And as I got closer, I started lightening up a little bit. And I started injecting a little humor into the script rather than making this a horror film (which was the original intention). Though the humor was pitch black, it was humor nonetheless. But I based a lot of the story on myself whilst exaggerating everything greatly— I felt like a monster so I made the Steven character a guy who killed people, the scariest kind of monster. I lost a baby and the girl I was in love with. So, I injected that into the story, but in a more tragic kind of way to draw more sympathy towards this despicable character who just so happened to be my story's hero. The Percival character was the antithesis to the Steven character, opposite in every way imaginable. Even his sexuality. But he was still based on me. The good side of me. The sensitive side. Now, I'm not gay, but I had a lot of gay friends who were genuinely great people and I wanted to use that likability that they had in order to create a likable character. And, because he's likable and friendly, the "suicide dilemma" that he has in the story, this "curse," felt more intriguing than if I gave Steven this "curse" instead. Plus, it added to the contrast between the characters—Percival wants to kill himself, Steven wants to kill others. Percival is an artist in the film. He creates. Steven destroys.

I got the idea for the oft-repeated line, "You're lucky to be alive," when I'd bitch and moan about the situation and people would tell me that. And nothing pissed me off more than to hear "You should just feel lucky to be alive." It felt like an out to me, just so they didn't have to hear me complain any more.

And then came one of the central themes: Fate. During that rough time in my life, I didn't feel like I had control. I questioned my destiny and asked myself whether all this bullshit was meant to be. When I'd asked for advice or words of encouragement, a lot of the *time, the answers would be "It just wasn't meant to be." And, I'd be like, "What the fuck is that supposed to mean?" But it got me thinking, at a vulnerable time in my life when I was looking for answers and constantly reflecting. I thought that maybe all of this was happening because of Karma and for all the things I did wrong at earlier times in my life. And I started concentrating on little things, looking for signs out of desperation. Maybe the universe was trying to tell me something, stuff like that.*

While there are several genre elements in this film, one of the main themes is the idea of loss and the strange and dangerous ways that humans deal with loss. Why were you drawn to that idea as subject matter?

Well, obviously, it was something very personal to me. And I saw how I self-destructive I became after losing something I loved. I was dangerous. To myself. And to others, though not in a violent kind of way but in a way that did hurt people, emotionally. And it wasn't until after the damage was done that I realized this. Also, as a screenwriter, I thought it would be something that people could relate to in some way. At least that's what I was hoping for. Sure, artistically, I thought it was a theme that people could relate to. But personally, this was sort of a way to indirectly find some kind of empathy for myself. If an audience could sympathize with a despicable character like Steven, in a way, they'd be empathizing with me.

This film is as much a crime drama as a high-concept sci-fi-fantasy. Was part of the decision to make the story about a hit man and a series of crimes in order to ground the fantastical elements in a strong reality?

Yeah, in a way. The Twilight Zone *was a big inspiration. To me, it's the greatest TV show ever created and Rod Serling is God. But, if you watch a lot of those old* Twilight Zone *episodes, much of it is grounded in reality. So, when these weird things happen, it does feel surreal. In Serling's intros, you'd hear him say, "He was a normal man" or "It was just another normal day," or something like that. Something that relates to the audience. Something based in reality. But then something strange happens, something otherworldly, something unexplained. Bending reality. Skewing it.*

Also, I was always intrigued by true crime and the psychology behind serial killers and hit men and what was going on upstairs in their heads. And it was always frightening to me how "normal" aspects of their lives were. These monsters actually had human emotions. I remember watching that HBO special about the Polish hit man from Jersey, Richard Kuklinsky. He was so cold and frightening in his interview. And he killed a lot of people, whether he was getting paid for it or not. But this guy had a family. He had kids that he cared about. I just found it very, very interesting that someone like that can feel something one moment, then not feel anything the next moment.

Anyway, to directly answer your question, yes, it was a way to ground the fantastical elements in a strong reality. Because the fantastic becomes even more surreal in contrast to that reality.

The ultimate reveal of the film, and the connections the characters actually have, makes it feel as if the central conceit of the film about Percival's immortality is actually a cosmic justice scale that bent the rules of the universe to right a wrong. I was reminded of *Groundhog Day*, a film that used a similarly mysterious event to teach someone a lesson. Was that film influential on this one? Were there films you consider influential on the story and style of *The Suicide Theory*?

There were a lot of influences on The Suicide Theory. *And, yes,* Groundhog Day *was one of them. That montage in* Groundhog Day *when Bill Murray tries killing himself over and over again…. It felt like the most honest and beautiful part of that movie which, overall, is kind of whimsical in tone. That sequence really stood out. You could see the pain in Bill Murray's eyes. His urge to end it all was palpable.*

Alfred Hitchcock was a big influence, I'd say the biggest influence (that and The Twilight Zone*). You'll see a little bit of* Strangers on a Train *and* Psycho *with certain elements. Not sure if they're Easter eggs or not, but the main characters meet on a train in one of the first scenes. And Steven wears his dead wife's clothes (though for reasons different from Norman Bates). I was also going through a little bit of M. Night Shyamalan phase—I was a huge fan in particular of* Unbreakable *and the duality of that film's characters, how opposite they were.* Taxi Driver *influences a lot of what I write, the lonely anti-hero who may or may not be losing his mind. You could probably also throw in* Midnight Cowboy, Fight Club, American Psycho *and* Collateral *as minor influences.*

You juxtaposed a lot of dark elements (mental illness, homophobia, the death of loved ones) against the idea of the Suicide Theory itself, which Percival explained as his inability to die unless he feels genuine happiness at the moment of death. Is part of the theme of this film about the need to embrace the inherent darkness in life in order to be able to deal with and survive life? What do you feel is the ultimate meaning of the Suicide Theory (as posed in the movie)?

That's a huge part of the theme. You have to take the good with the bad. Because bad things will happen to you. There will be darkness. That's life. But I feel the ultimate theme of The Suicide Theory *is this: What we do in our lives doesn't just affect us. It affects others. Others we might not even meet or know. There's a chain reaction to everything we do, whether on a small or grand scale. Someone will be affected by the choices we make. And somehow, those decisions will come back to you in some way. Maybe not directly, but in some way. The universe is both large and small at the same time. That nerdy kid with the braces you used to make fun of in school may shoot up an office building one day—and you may be working in that office building. Or have a loved one who works in that office building. On the other hand, that same nerdy kid could become an advocate for anti-bullying and write books about it. Books you may one day read because your own child is being bullied in school—like the kid you used to pick on. You never know. I'm sure we all experience our share of strange coincidences. But maybe coincidences aren't just coincidences. Maybe they're signs. Maybe it's karma. Who knows? To sum it all up, and I know this will sound generic and clichéd—but what goes around comes around. In some form, whether we notice it or not.*

The idea of the Mysterious Event, the thing we can't explain but which has an enormous effect on our lives, is a growing subgenre in the sci-fi world. Why do you think filmmakers are drawn to tell stories about them, and why do you think audiences enjoy seeing them so much?

I think audiences are drawn to fear. When people go to see a movie, they want get some kind of feeling or emotion out of it, right? You go to a comedy, you want to laugh. You go to a horror movie, you want to be scared. And horror films (or sci-fi with horror elements) are the most marketable—because everyone is afraid of something. It's a natural human emotion. And, a lot of the times, that fear comes from not knowing "why" or "how." And when we don't know the whys and hows, we create theories. And some of those theories frighten us.

We try to use logic to explain the whys and hows as a way to comfort ourselves. But logic doesn't always explain that. Logic only provides us with the most logical answer—an answer that isn't definite. If our civilization depended solely on logic, we'd all still think the Earth was flat. Even the most logical thinkers have doubts about certain things. Like ghosts, for instance. I don't believe in that shit. If I hear strange noises in the house, I'll tell myself that it's the pipes or something. Because it probably is. But it's not definite. I don't believe in the paranormal (so I say). But would I ever spend a night in an abandoned prison where they used to perform executions? Fuck no. Would I ever spend a night in a cemetery? Fuck. No. Not happening. Because what if I'm wrong? What if my logical presumptions are proven wrong and everything I believe in or don't believe in is proven wrong? That's some scary shit. Ghosts and aliens and poltergeists ... it's highly unlikely that stuff like this exists. It's not probable. But they haven't completely proven to be impossible. And that's what we're afraid of. That the worst-case scenario could be very real. It's the "could be" part that drives a lot of that fear.

As for the horror and sci-fi world, I don't see that as a subgenre. In fact, I believe that Mysterious Event, the thing we can't explain that affects our lives—it's been the driving force of these films since films were films.

More Films of Interest

The Corridor (2010), *After* (2012), *Nothing* (2003), *The Wall* (2012), *Vanishing on 7th Street* (2012), *It's All About Love* (2003), *The Frame* (2014), *Enter Nowhere* (2011), *Donovan's Echo* (2011)

3

The Shifting Sands of Time

Time travel is one of the most common themes in the science fiction film genre. And much like films about robots, time travel films began pragmatically, focusing on purpose-driven stories and the novelty of the invention itself.

Generally considered one of the first time travel stories ever written, Charles Dickens' beloved *A Christmas Carol* is one of the most-filmed adaptations of a story in history. Beginning with the earliest known surviving version, 1901's *Scrooge, or Marley's Ghost*, the story has been told again and again, even with Mickey Mouse and The Muppets. In each version, the element of time travel has the same utilitarian purpose: to walk Ebenezer Scrooge through his past, present and future in an attempt to help him see the error of his ways and change his destiny. The mission is successful: Scrooge cries in the final moments of his interaction with the Ghost of Christmas Future, "Spirit! Hear me! I'm not the man I was!"

In director George Pal's movie *The Time Machine* (1960), based on the classic 1895 novel by H.G. Wells, the focus of the story isn't on correcting any particular issue in the timeline, but rather to watch with reverence and awe as the chains of linear time are broken. The Time Traveler goes forward and backward through time at the turn of a handle.

Previous time travel stories showed a person moving from one time to another, but never focused on the process of the travel itself; here, director Pal uses cutting-edge effects to show the changes and ravages of time blasting past the inventor in real time. Buildings crumble and fall, societies shift. Plot and character take a backseat to the sheer excitement of innovation and discovery. No matter who the scientist meets and what he discovers, what the audience takes away from the film is the miracle of the invention itself. After the Time Traveler's final journey into the future, the friend he left behind muses on his possible destination and destiny: "One cannot choose but wonder. You see, he has all the time in the world."

The longer the concept of time travel existed in movies, the more complicated the narratives became. Later journeys would be far less controlled and goal-oriented. In 1972's *Slaughterhouse-Five*, main character Billy Pilgrim has become unstuck in time and is careening back and forth between his past in World War II, his present in upstate New York and his future as a captive on an alien planet; no greater goal or purpose guides his travels, and he is whisked along through time like a leaf on the wind. Moving through time was wilder and more chaotic; time travel became the solution to nothing more than cleaning up the messes it was creating itself. In *Time After Time*, H.G. Wells ventures into 1979 after Jack the Ripper steals his time machine to escape the law. The Supreme Being chases a boy and a group of *Time Bandits* throughout history to retrieve his time map and stop them from stealing everyone's treasure. The ability to travel through and alter time didn't make things more orderly, it made them less so.

Audiences and filmmakers became so accustomed to the presence of time travel in films that it became a tool for solving the most mundane problems. Stale marital relationships were reinvigorated in *Back to the Future* and *Peggy Sue Got Married*, while a time-traveling phone booth helped two failing high schoolers pass their History final in *Bill & Ted's Excellent Adventure*. Though occasional darker and more serious entries like *12 Monkeys* and *Freejack* appeared in the 1990s, they were matched with light comedies like *Groundhog Day* and *Austin Powers: International Man of Mystery*. The idea which was groundbreaking in the early days of cinema had been reduced to a mere plot device relegated to a supporting role in the background of big-budget comedies and action films.

After the Millennium

The first few years of the millennium saw studios doubling down on big-budget remakes of previous time travel stories, with another version of *The Time Machine* in 2002 and a new *A Christmas Carol* in 2009; even the classic *Planet of the Apes* franchise was revisited in 2001, adding a time travel element that did nothing to re-ignite the series. Even the bigger hits in the subgenre (*Hot Tub Time Machine* and *Edge of Tomorrow*) were homages or amped-up reinterpretations of films like *Back to the Future* and *Groundhog Day*.

Romance became the new vogue for time travel, incorporating what would have been standard comedies and dramas with the genre element in the hopes of breathing new life into both. With films like *The Time Traveler's Wife* (2009), *The Lake House* (2006) and *In Time* (2011), the results were mixed.

Popular franchises used time travel as plot devices to fix continuity or expand outside the original framework of the established series. Hermione's time-turner came in handy during the events of *Harry Potter and the Prisoner of Azkaban*; Will Smith went back to 1969 for a brand-new old adventure in *Men in Black III*. In *X-Men: Days of Future Past*, an aging Professor X convinces Wolverine to send his consciousness back to the 1970s to change the dire fate of the future.

In big-budget Hollywood, time travel was no longer the star of its own films; it was no more than a bit player in someone else's story.

The Independent Perspective

Independent filmmakers were less beholden to corporate masters when making their films, which meant they could take them to task more easily. *Synchronicity* (2015) tells of a group of men struggling to invent time travel under the thumb of the corporate investor who wants their idea; without him, they cannot find the funding to continue their work. The film is a sharp commentary on the invasion of private businesses and corporations on scientific research (and a sly swipe at modern Hollywood too).

The most refreshing element that the time travel movies of the new millennial indies brought about was the reinterpretation of what time travel looks like in film. *Primer* and *+1* both played with the idea of clones and doppelgangers through the time travel conceit of multiple versions of one person at a single point in time. Australian filmmaker Rolf de Heer's *Dr. Plonk* uses the technological style of its time, 1907, to make a modern-day silent film. *Donnie Darko* weaves a tale of violence and romance, of apocalyptic end times and disillusioned youth, where time travel might be the thing that destroys the world or saves it. *Timecrimes* and *Triangle* turn *Groundhog Day*'s repeating timeline motif into something resembling the punishment of Hell, a loop of action and violence acting as reminder and retribution for past transgressions.

In the Featured Films section, these filmmakers use the Time Travel subgenre to examine the judicial and prison system, existentialism, addiction and free will.

Featured Films

Cruel & Unusual (2014)
Writer-Director: Merlin Dervisevic
Starring David Richmond-Peck, Michael Eklund, Richard Harmon

Edgar is having a strange day. When he gets seriously ill, he asks his wife Maylon to call an ambulance. During an argument with her, he accidentally kills her, then dies moments later. He wakes to find himself in an unusual facility with other "patients" who

Julien (Michael Eklund) reveals a disturbing truth about fellow patient-prisoner Doris (Michelle Harrison) in *Cruel & Unusual* (2014).

are also there for having killed people. Edgar believes he shouldn't be there, since his wife's death was an accident. The facility still requires him to go back and relive the death over and over; Edgar continues to struggle against his punishment, eventually devising a way of possibly escaping the afterlife prison and altering his fate.

The classic framework of the wrongly accused man thriller is given a clever science fiction makeover with *Cruel & Unusual*. Like the amendment from which it takes its name, the film explores what the proper punishment is for violent criminals. It also examines questions of mental illness, fate vs. free will, and the need for perspective and compassion in judicial verdicts.

∼

Cruel & Unusual was director Merlin Dervisevic's first feature film. From his work in the art department on the series *Supernatural* and set-decorating on *The Andromeda Strain* to his directing on short films and TV projects like *The Unprofessionals* and *Our Hero*, Dervisevic already had over two decades' worth of filmmaking experience. *Cruel & Unusual*'s themes touch on existentialism and bureaucracy, but Dervisevic found his inspiration in a less likely place.

Merlin Dervisevic: *The idea came about as I was watching TV one day, and one of the lead characters of this TV show found himself in Hell. His version of Hell was a fiery pit, and he was chained up to it and there were whips and all kinds of other physical torture that he had to endure. As I was watching it, I was thinking, "Is that what Hell would really be, or would it be something more than that?" I think that eventually you would get used to that. I've always thought the hell you create for yourself is worse than anything anyone else can do to you. It leads me to think about people who are guilty of crimes of passion, especially against their loved ones, and how they feel about it once they have time to reflect on it. The hell that they go through in their own mind must be much worse than anything we can dole out to them.*

Around the same time, there was a case here in Western Canada about a guy who killed his own kids; his reasoning for it was to get back at his ex-wife. At the time, they were talking about the different kinds of sentencing they were considering for him. It just seemed so futile and senseless. Provided he wasn't a psychopath, wouldn't whatever was going through his own mind, dealing with what he had done, be a million times worse than any way we could have punished him?

Given the title of the film, *Cruel & Unusual*, which is a reference to the eighth amendment of the Constitution, is it safe to say that this film is an allegorical conversation about the idea of justice and the prison system?

I never thought about it through political terms like that. I've always been more interested with the human nature side of storytelling. For me, it wasn't a statement so much on the prison system, but more about punishment being given to us vs. us punishing ourselves, essentially. It's like saying a person's conscience and remorse are much more powerful than anything else that another person can do to them.

The film extrapolates the idea of purgatory; you made a physical representation of the concept of constantly having to relive the most horrible moment of your life. One of the great things about science fiction is the ability to turn the figurative or the abstract into the literal to discuss it in a more direct way.

I agree with that, and that's what storytelling allows us to do, whether it's filmmaking or writing fiction. It allows us to bring to life these "what if?" scenarios. I've always been a fan of films that take us one step outside of reality, just a slightly surrealistic world, so we can go further than just imagining, but actually seeing and experiencing what life could be like in these other instances.

The film re-envisions the crime procedural because we have a detective character of sorts who's looking at a crime, investigating it and discovering it a piece at a time. The brilliant twist in your film is that the person who's the detective is one of the people involved in the crime and is piecing it together as he realizes what level he is involved in it himself.

That's an interesting way to look at it. I've always been a fan of films where the story unravels and we learn at the same time as our protagonist what is happening. We're learning with him, we don't know anything more than he does, and he discovers it at the same time. It makes for an engaging experience as an audience member. In a movie like this, it's important that you're paying attention and you're picking up on the clues just as Edgar does so that you can unravel the story as well. When the audience is engaged, they're asked to make connections, and not just connections, but to make opinions about characters as well. Some people think that Edgar is someone that they want to root for and other people really dislike him. Same thing with Maylon. It's interesting when people have different interpretations of a film and its characters, rather than the filmmaker saying, "This is the good guy, you should like him," or, "This is the antagonist, you shouldn't like him or her." For my films, I'd like for the audience member to come to their own conclusion as well.

It brings me to another important theme in this movie, and I think it's that perspective changes perception. Earlier in the movie, it seemed apparent that Edgar is completely innocent of this and he is in the wrong place just as he cries to anybody who will listen. As our perspective changes through the film, every time he goes back into his life, we see that it's all not as we thought.

Even though this is obviously rooted in science fiction, one of the other genres I thought of was film noir because most of the characters in the noir films are not a clear-cut good or bad. They're all varying degrees of gray, and depending on where you are mentally as an audience member, you may be in sympathy with any of the characters because they all exist on a spectrum.

Yeah, and isn't that more interesting? I truly believe so. When we look at a character, we can see some of the things that character does that we believe are with a good heart, and maybe some things aren't. Humans are like that: everybody has a dark side and everybody has a good side. I don't think anybody is purely evil or purely good. I always appreciate seeing true human qualities in film characters. I try to display that in my work as well.

The troubles that Edgar had were circumstantial, and he had problems in his life, but he wouldn't be what we would traditionally consider mentally ill. However, the woman who killed herself does represent that element. I thought that was an interesting commentary on the difference between regular criminal behavior and crimes that stem from mental illness.

Yeah, the laws are in black and white like the laws that we live by in real life. This version of Hell in the film is very much a bureaucracy and there are certain rules that are followed regardless of the circumstances. In her case, her committing suicide is considered a crime against family members, especially in her case where her children found her body and we can assume it scarred them for life. That's the reason for putting "suies" [suicides] in this version of Hell. As you said, there are other circumstances behind it, where she's not well and she's depressed. I've got a whole backstory about her, why she came to this point where she felt she had no other choice but to hang herself.

Bureaucracy is also evident in how Edgar ends up in Hell. He died by being poisoned by his wife, but he strangled her and she died moments before him, so technically when he dies, he's a murderer, so that's why he's there and she's not. There's a bit of irony and comic relief when they're explaining that to him. But it's true, the bureaucracy in this version of Hell mirrors what we live through as well.

It reminded me of the judicial system and the prison system, how we have all these frustrating technicalities and circumstances. It reminds me of how, if you've gone to prison and you're there wrongly, you must admit guilt for a crime you didn't even commit in order to gain parole. It's an amazingly byzantine series of technicalities.

It's true, and in this film, we think that admitting to it will help you graduate out of this place or be excused of your crime in some way. In fact, William doesn't want to leave because he realizes the only comfort he has is from feeling the pain of guilt over killing his parents, but there is no escape from this place. A lot of people have asked me that question: Where do they go after; once they've accepted their crime and their punishment, where do they go? The answer is hidden in there, but it was expressed by William; the better place he describes is just the acceptance of the punishment and the guilt and the pain. The best he can hope for is feeling horribly about what he did. It's not a very bright future for any of them, and I find that interesting.

We're introduced to the woman who committed suicide earlier in the story, and she's looked upon as the lowest of the people in the group there. You do a brilliant reversal when Edgar's actually willing to take his own life to spare someone else the same suffering, so he wears that derision proudly. The perception changes because of the perspective.

I like the way it works out in the end because, although Edgar is now the pariah in Hell and he will never escape that place and it's an eternity of torture for him, what he does have is the knowledge that he helped Doris escape and he relieved his wife Maylon of this cycle as well. So even though he's there for eternity, he has a sense of satisfaction that nobody else will have and so it's a dark, bittersweet ending.

You know how hard I had to fight to get that ending in the movie? I almost had to walk away from the film because the financers said, "We can't end the film with Edgar in Hell, he has to escape, he has to come back to life, once he's realized the error in his ways, we need to give him a second chance. We want him to come back to life. It's going to be too depressing if he's in Hell in the end." I said, "No, you don't understand. He is victorious in the end." The film almost didn't happen, but eventually they let me make the ending the way I wanted, and I'm so glad that I did. If he came back to life in the end, it would have had the same effect of him waking up from a bad dream, or the end of A Christmas Carol. *It's not very satisfying.*

I'm curious about the antiquated technology in the film. Was there some sense of commentary in using that? Was there some deeper reason you went with that, or was it just an aesthetic decision?

It was definitely aesthetic. I like the idea of going back to the basics of filmmaking. I didn't want this movie to be saturated with CGI, because I am getting tired of that. I'd rather see a film made the way that we used to make them, where it's relying on the directors' decisions and the tools of cinema to convey the story, not just these sets made on a computer. So, this Hell that I've imagined seemed institutional to me, and that's what I wanted to use as a backdrop for where he is. I wanted to move away from the fiery pit, and the idea that reliving the worst moments of their lives repeatedly and talking about them in group therapy seemed to lend itself to a cold, timeless institution. That was the main influence for the production design of the set. As far as the tube televisions, I wanted to make sure that we didn't confuse the gatekeepers in this Hell with the inmates, so I wanted to separate them and I was thinking of how I could do that. Do I put them in costumes? Do they wear masks? What is it that makes them not human? The idea of the tube television came up. It puts enough of a separation between the actual inmates and the counselors to realize that they're not human and that they weren't inmates before. They are just something else and the fact that they can communicate through the television tells us that. As a fan of the movie Brazil, *it had that same vibe, where there was some stuff that seemed futuristic, but then they had old typewriters around.*

Even though there have been hundreds of films about time travel, we continue to revisit the theme so frequently.

I think it's interesting to fathom what could be possible, if we had the technology to do that. But I also think, as human beings who make mistakes in our lives, who hasn't thought, "If I only could just go back a day or a week or several years and change that one thing in my life"? I think everybody on the planet has those thoughts weekly, if not daily.

The other thing that's interesting about it is the domino effect of changing something in the past. I think people have always been fascinated by that. If you change one little thing, how does that affect everything else on the planet?

Time Lapse (2014)
Director: Bradley King
Writers: Bradley King, B.P. Cooper
Starring Danielle Panabaker, Matt O'Leary, George Finn

Finn lives with his girlfriend Callie and best friend Jasper. After a neighbor in a nearby apartment passes away, they go into the apartment and find a strange camera machine the middle of the room, pointed out the window and across the yard to their front window. They find pictures the machine took of them, and realize that the images are not from the past; the camera can take pictures 24 hours into the future. Profit-minded Jasper devises a way for them to make money off the revelation, but complications arise that put the trio in debt and possibly at risk of their lives.

Time Lapse uses the classic get-rich-quick framework of many time travel movies to touch on the aimless youth of post-millennial America to excellent effect. Unproduced artists, get-rich-quick slackers, and endlessly complicated relationship dynamics are the elements that swirl around the central concept, and they all feed into the driving theme of lost twentysomethings still trying to find their moral center. The ending is as destructive and uncertain as the characters' lives, and feels wholly appropriate and simultaneously devastating.

∽

Finn (Matt O'Leary) discovers a strange secret in a deceased neighbor's house in *Time Lapse* (2014).

Time Lapse was B.P. Cooper's first feature film as screenwriter, but his experience in independent filmmaking is extensive. After a few short films, he worked as producer on *Special*, *Flourish* and *Cement Suitcase* before teaming with director Bradley King to devise the concept for *Time Lapse*. As is often the case, Cooper recounted how a single minor moment from another film created the thought process that led to the story.

B.P. Cooper: *We knew we wanted to make a sci-fi-based movie, but it had to fit conceptually within the confines of a very limited budget. The origin stemmed from me mentioning to (co-writer-director) Bradley King about the camera they put into a time machine in the movie* Time Line *[2003]. In that movie, its intent is to take pictures of where and when in time a person was sent by snapping a photo of the night sky and determining position and time based on constellations. I always enjoyed that clever story trick (regardless of however scientifically inaccurate it may be) and said to Bradley it would also be cool if a camera itself could be a time machine of sorts by taking pictures of the past, that I hadn't ever seen a movie that used such a contraption.*

That was on a Saturday. The following Monday, he storms into our writing office and says, "What if the camera can take pictures of the future but only a limited time frame, say 24 hours? This way, we never have to show any slick future stuff we couldn't afford. And what if it's a giant immovable invention so we stay anchored in a single location the entire time?" And with these rules, we were off to the races formulating the story of the three roommates in the apartment complex.

Once we worked our way through the rules of the world and how the camera works, we quickly realized the "time-shifting" aspect was going to drive our narrative along nicely. We were also beholden to it, however, and knew that we couldn't necessarily deviate from the established rules. This made it very enjoyable to write when the ideas were flowing and a few times felt like an impenetrable wall when a story branch idea would get stuck. The puzzle pieces all have to fit in the end. Not an easy thing to do with a time travel–ish, causal loop movie since paradoxes will always exist in one way or another.

A lot of the plot and information is delivered through still images, both through the photographs taken and the paintings the artist creates. Is there a commentary here about the ambiguity of the still image, given that they are used to distract or mislead the characters throughout the story?

Having the characters try to determine, or assume, what is actually happening in any of "tomorrow's photos" was certainly a fun aspect to create. It's fair to say that their perceptions of what the pictures represent are usually correct but it's within the getting there that's the interesting part. Our attempt was to indeed throw curve balls at the characters and audience alike and try to keep things interesting and constantly moving forward. There is a deliberately slower pace to the movie overall, so a lot of time was spent making sure moments leading up to a big photograph reveal or picture pose had some punch to them to help with pacing.

The paintings go a lot deeper in a way as they are always foretelling something in the background. Sometimes it's small and other times it's dark and ominous. Oftentimes the characters, other than Finn, aren't paying attending to the painting but instead to their presence or lack of it within the picture. But the idea was to always be foretelling and signaling things to the audience through them. So even if many clues are missed on first viewing, it's an enjoyable discovery upon a second viewing.

The concept of time travel, time-manipulation pops up frequently in science fiction films. Why do you feel like viewers and filmmakers seem so drawn to the idea over and over?

There is near-infinite wish fulfillment potential story-wise in witnessing or changing the past and visiting the unknown future. Certainly, there is a lot of derivative material on the subject at this point but I am confident that time travel, time manipulation still has a vast well to draw from in storytelling. I do think it's the wish fulfillment aspect that people are so drawn to. We romanticize the past with nostalgia and certain life simplicities, and romanticize the future with inventive technological advancements. Doing this makes it easy to think "what if?" and daydreams of living in or at least seeing another era beyond our present is nearly impossible for any human to not do at least a few times in their lives. Because of this, I think we gravitate to stories that send us beyond our present reality.

The film has a similar sensibility to Shane Carruth's *Primer*, not just because of the time manipulation story but also because of the economy of characters and locations coupled with the complexity of the narrative. Was this film an influence on you, and were there other films or stories that also served as influences?

Bradley and I are both big Primer *fans. We certainly used that movie's proof of concept success in the marketplace (being lo-fi sci-fi, no special effects, complex storytelling, etc.) as motivation that it can be done. Additionally, that movie helped us a lot with how certain technical information is explained to the viewer.* Primer *is super- smart, almost too smart! We knew we wanted to be slightly hard to follow to engage a thinking audience but not to the degree of difficulty many might have found* Primer *to be.*

Other movies that served as inspiration to craft the story were: Timeline, *merely for the initial camera going into an actual time machine idea they portrayed that we morphed into a camera that sees the future.* Shallow Grave, *for the three roommates committing a crime and trying to cover it up, plus the "bad guys disrupting their lives" aspect.* Time Crimes, *we really dug the causal loops in this and how the time travel information was presented from one character to another.* Rear Window, *for the one location apartment looking into another voyeuristic aspect, plus excellent thriller elements. And to a lesser extent, but also serving purpose to help craft storytelling aspects in our film,* Blood Simple *and* A Simple Plan. *These final two might seem far off considering they are bigger-budget movies, but one of Bradley's favorite movies is the original* Total Recall, *and he always finds a way to review it when we are looking for inspiration to break a storyline or a character arc. I do essentially the exact same thing with* Back to the Future!

Shuffle (2011)
Writer-Director: Kurt Kuenne
Starring T.J. Thyne, Paula Rhodes, Chris Stone

Lovell Milo is losing a lot of sleep, trying to stay up for days at a time. The reason he is avoiding falling asleep is because every time he does, he wakes up at a random point in his life; one moment, he is a child, and the next, he is an old man. As he struggles to understand his dilemma, others tell him his experiences must be designed to help him save someone. When he discovers that, later in his life, he marries a woman named Grace whom he first met as a child, he thinks she must be the one he needs to save. But time and fate seem to have a different plan for him.

It's rare that a high concept science fiction-fantasy film taps into such a universal truth that it has the potential to connect emotionally with anyone who watches it. *Groundhog Day* had that power, and *Shuffle* also reaches that status. The film uses the premise of the uncontrolled shifts through time to emulate the tragedy of an unguided and unconsidered life. Reflecting the struggle to give meaning to a seemingly arbitrary existence, the movie creates a small, honest relationship to portray humanity's journey as a whole.

~

Lovell Milo (T.J. Thyne) wakes as an old man in the time travel tale *Shuffle* (2011).

Director Kurt Kuenne had already worked with star T.J. Thyne in the short film *Validation* (2007) before they reteamed for *Shuffle*. Kuenne is a multi-talented filmmaker, having directed documentaries (the nostalgic *Drive-In Movie Memories* and the heartbreaking *Dear Zachary: A Letter to a Son About His Father*), worked as cinematographer and producer, and even composed scores for several films.

As effective and inventive as *Shuffle* was, Kuenne explained how it almost never became a film at all.

Kurt Kuenne: *The idea for* Shuffle *came out of a conversation I had with a development executive who had been a big fan of my script* Mason Mule, *which won the Academy's Nicholl Fellowships in Screenwriting in 2002, and he invited me in to discuss ideas for future projects that we might be able to do together. Because* Mason Mule *made clear my fondness for playing with structure, we started discussing ideas where that could be exploited to great effect, and one of the ideas that came up in that conversation was: "What if a guy lived his life out of order?" I didn't even know what the sentence meant at the time, but it contained a kernel that excited me, so I went home, brainstormed a story, wrote up an outline and brought it back to him. It turned out that he had more of a Jim Carrey–style broad comedy in mind for that idea, whereas I'd come back with something that approximated a big episode of* The Twilight Zone *crossed with* A Christmas Carol. *He said his company would never make that particular take on the idea, but he thought it was a cool approach, encouraged me to write it on my own and said, "Just make sure I'm one of the first people to get it when it goes out to producers."*

So I developed the story for a while, then finally sat down to write a first draft. When I was about two-thirds of the way through my first draft, my managers called with bad news: Chris Columbus had just sold a script to Warner Bros. called Will Sebastian—*and the logline was that it was about "a guy who experiences his life out of order," which was literally the same logline I was using for* Shuffle. *They told me to forget about* Shuffle *and get started on something else, as we no longer had any shot after a similar idea had just made a high-profile sale. But the story was fully present in my head and it would have killed me not to get it down on paper, so I quickly wrote the last third of the script in about two days, then put it away.*

Later that year, my friend Dan Austin asked if he could read that "out-of-order thing" I'd been working on, so I let him read it with the caveat that it was a first draft and needed a rewrite, but would probably never get one because the project was essentially dead. A couple of months later, he called me up and said, "Dude, I read Shuffle—*and I was expecting not to like it because you sounded so down on it after what happened ... but this is really good. I cried. Take another look at it. Maybe you could do this as a low-budget indie someday." So I re-read it, fell in love with the story all over again, rewrote it just because I wanted to in my spare time ... but there was still nothing my managers could do with it at the time because of the other sale, so I put it on the shelf again. Years later, I made a short film called* Validation *starring my friend T.J. Thyne, one of the stars of the hit TV show* Bones, *and it became a huge hit at film festivals and on the web. T.J. floated the idea of the two of us doing an indie feature together on his summer hiatus from* Bones *that year, and asked if I had any scripts that could be right for him. I sent him* Shuffle. *He read it, loved it and said, "Let's do it. I think I can find the money." So he raised a couple of hundred grand and we shot it that summer at his house, some other friend's houses and an abandoned hospital using a lot of the same folks with whom we'd made* Validation. *It was very much a family affair.*

This film concept is a clever way of doing a time travel story without confining yourself to the standard structure of the time travel device and the intentional decision to travel, a concept that was explored by Kurt Vonnegut in *Slaughterhouse-Five*, and has been revisited a few times in the new millennium in films like *The Butterfly Effect*. What interested you about redefining time travel in this way?

I had never read Slaughterhouse-Five *at the time we made* Shuffle, *though so many people brought it up to me during production that I finally read it shortly after locking and mixing the movie. I don't really think of* Shuffle *as a time travel movie, actually—and without giving away the ending for those who haven't seen it yet, those who've seen it know that it really isn't a time travel movie at all, it's more of an "experience" and the film's closest narrative cousin is probably* A Christmas Carol. *What interested me about the idea was the ability of this conceit to give us a unique storytelling experience structurally, where we could get pieces of information out of order, creating a mystery in the audience's mind where they would wonder (along with the character, who knows as much as they do) what happened during the intervening time gap that we missed and how we got to where we were. I also had gone through some personal tragedy right before writing the script (anyone who's seen my documentary* Dear Zachary *will know the events to which I'm referring) and the idea of what you do with grief was very much on my mind; you can let it destroy you or you can let it empower you to make the most of the time you have. And I wondered how those who'd died would feel if they looked down and saw grief destroying their loved ones, and if they could speak to us, what would they say? So for me, that's really what the film is about: not letting grief destroy you after a tragedy. And the out-of-order conceit was a fresh, fun way to tell that story.*

The idea of Lovell bouncing through moments in his life, desperately searching for an answer to why it's happening, is in some ways an allegory for life itself, isn't it? Was that an intentional parallel?

No, that wasn't an intentional parallel; it actually created a huge writing problem for me that he was bouncing around inside his own life, because the character of Lovell can't actually do anything to change his circumstances for most of the film (though he doesn't know that at the time). All he can really do is observe like a detective and put the puzzle together. But since movies are all about characters taking action, it became a challenge to find the forward thrust for the character to keep the movie moving along, so I finally decided that this really was a detective movie and he was an observer inside of his own life, watching what unfolded and taking notes to solve the mystery using the few breadcrumbs that his "guides" give him along the way as a framework for understanding his experience.

Though the film has science fiction elements, it is in many ways a hybrid film that is as much drama and romance as it is science fiction. Was the choice to use the sci-fi element simply a way of finding a new perspective on the classic romantic and dramatic narratives?

One of my favorite things about the way Shuffle *unfolds is that it sort of throws away the character of Grace during the opening passages when Lovell is just trying to get his bearings and figure out what is going on. And slowly, we realize that the film is really about her: This girl who's been in the background for so many scenes is actually the centerpiece of the film ... and the audience has the opportunity to realize, "Oh, wow, this is a love story; I didn't see that coming." Movies are so "on the nose" these days that it's a rare occurrence when a movie has an opportunity to unfold and reveal itself to be something deeper than you thought it was going to be. That was what my friend Dan told me he reacted to when he first read the script all those years ago. From what I'd told him about it, he thought it was just going to be this interesting experiment in messing with story structure, but when it revealed itself to be a love story, that was when it grabbed him emotionally. As I mentioned earlier, what I was really doing in this story was exploring the idea of what you do with grief after you lose someone, how you move past it, and my deep hope that those who have passed are still nearby watching over us. And the out-of-order conceit gave me a new way to approach that subject that I didn't feel like I'd seen before.*

How difficult was it to shoot a film in which not only the shooting schedule is out of order, but the actual narrative itself is as well? Does it make tracking character development more difficult? And how does involving child actors (one of whom is supposed to be playing a grown man mentally) complicate that further?

This is an 82-minute movie that has 195 scene numbers in the script, and the costume designer told me she'd never seen a script with so many wardrobe changes—so there was a lot to keep track of. But since movies shoot out of order anyway, keeping track of the emotional through line wasn't a real difficulty for me because I had internalized the film's structure so completely by the time we shot it that I just knew where we were at all times. It may have been more challenging for the actors, you'd have to ask them. But one thing that made production a true challenge due to all of the age jumps was the old age makeup. We were extremely fortunate to have Barney Burman, who won the Academy Award for Best Makeup for Star Trek *shortly after the* Shuffle *shoot, do all of our old-age makeup, and his work was mind-blowing. He's a true genius; I still can't believe he did our little movie for the money we had. But it was absolutely essential that you believe the age shifts or the film wouldn't work, so we needed someone of his caliber—and I love that people rarely bring up the aging when talking about the movie because his work feels so effortless, it just feels like the characters are getting older or younger. That makeup took a long time to apply, so it created some scheduling headaches with our limited time, but Barney pulled it off with flying colors.*

The child actors were tremendous, we were just so lucky to find Dylan Sprayberry and Elle Labadie. Dylan has gone on to play the young Clark Kent in Man of Steel *and he's currently on the MTV show* Teen Wolf. *Elle was just so effortlessly natural and unaffected, and Dylan was so precocious that at ten years old, he totally understood that he was playing a grown man's perspective inside of his child's body and how to communicate that. He blew me away.*

At what point in the process did you make the decision to have the main character address the audience, and what was your thinking in making that an aspect of the storytelling?

Lovell is essentially a detective gathering information about his own life as he pops in and out of each day, but he has no one he can talk to about it once the psychiatrist in the opening sequence has to leave the story. Detectives on TV crime shows can always discuss their cases with one another, but here I had a guy who was essentially stuck inside of his own head, so all of his puzzle-building was going to be happening internally. It became clear pretty quickly during the writing process that the only way to follow what conclusions he was drawing was to go inside of his head. While I suppose that could have been done in voice-over, it just seemed way more fun, stylish and energized to have him address the camera when "talking to himself." When he looks into the lens, starts talking and floating on the dolly through the wedding reception at about 12 minutes into the movie, it just kind of kicks the movie in the ass in a great way for me, announcing that we're now moving into a different chapter of the story in a very active way. I did, however, limit the "talking to the camera" thing to three instances, as I didn't want it to become a constant presence in the movie—and three felt like the right dramatic number.

Time travel is a subgenre that has been frequently revisited over the years. What draws filmmakers and viewers back to it over and over?

I think there's something inherently compelling about wanting to go back and visit the past, about the concept of being able to undo your mistakes, about the concept of two people who didn't temporally co-exist in real life having the opportunity to meet, and about the concept of seeing what lies ahead for all of us by jumping into the future. Taking pictures is time travel; that's what people are doing on Facebook, they're "stopping time" just like Lovell does so that they can go back and revisit that moment again and again in their heads and share it with others. So we do it all the time, we're just doing it mentally and not physically. That's one thing I love about filmmaking itself is that it allows you to stop time and hold on to the past. When making my documentary Dear Zachary, *which is about the murder of my best friend, that was a huge time travel experience for me, because I was spending every day working with old footage of my friend—and while he was dead physically, he was very much alive in my editing software, so I had, in a sense, the opportunity to go back and spend time with him every day I worked on that film. I love going to see old movies on film on the big screen because it's the closest thing we have to time travel back to a period before I was born. If you see a 70mm print of* Vertigo, *you feel like you're there in San Francisco in the late 1950s. I think we long for what we can't have.*

More Films of Interest

11 Minutes Ago (2007), *Found in Time* (2012), *Blood Punch* (2014), *I'll Follow You Down* (2013), *Paradox* (2016), *Repeaters* (2010), *Sound of My Voice* (2011), *The Butterfly Effect* (2004)

4

Experiencing a World Not Our Own

Though the opening text crawl sounds like it would be more appropriate for a fantasy film, *Star Wars* began with one of the most iconic phrases of all time: "A long time ago in a galaxy far, far away…"

Those ten words are the perfect encapsulation of the Strange Land subgenre of science fiction film. The story takes place in a world previously unseen that resembles our known world in almost no way. Characters may be humanoid, with emotions and interactions like humanity, but that is often where the similarities end. But unlike the classic "fish out of water" stories where aliens arrive amongst humans or vice versa, there is no fish out of their water here. Everyone belongs where they are, and it is we, the members of the audience, who are out of our element. This is the elemental draw of the subgenre: to experience a world that is not ours.

This science fiction subgenre is one of the latest to bloom for multiple reasons. Firstly, the idea of the "world unlike anything we've seen before" is equally a concept of fantasy films and novels, and many films that fall into the Strange Land subgenre belong to the fantasy genre as well as science fiction. And secondly, the formative years of film had limited abilities when it came to costuming, sets, special effects and makeup, all elements that aid in the seamless building of a truly Strange Land.

Even the most iconic worlds of early science fiction were not genuine worlds unto themselves. Fritz Lang's *Metropolis* (1927), with its fantastic architecture and flying machines, still began as our society before devolving into the dystopian society we see in the film. In Sir Arthur Conan Doyle's *The Lost World* (1925), the "world" of dinosaurs is nothing more than a Venezuelan plateau untouched by modern man. It took the advancement of the technical aspects of filmmaking to bring those Strange Lands to life.

But even as the technology advanced, filmmakers were wary about a fantastical world that had no connections to our own. Large budget or small, from *Planet of the Apes* to *Barbarella* to *Death Race 2000*, all used some common human experience as the jumping-off point for their narrative. It wasn't until a visionary young filmmaker named George Lucas decided to cut ties with Earth in 1977 that a fully formed Strange Land came into true existence. The audience was immediate and enormous, and the path was clear for future science fiction filmmakers: Sci-fi narratives needed recognizable human emotion, but little else from the real world, to capture the attention of viewers.

Though *Star Wars* would seem a far-flung adventure of aliens, robots and mystical powers, Lucas always noted the influences of feudal Japan and the conflict in Vietnam on the character design and story. This was the back-and-forth volley of Strange Land stories; sometimes filmmakers created new worlds that reflected aspects that we would like to see and have never had the chance to experience, and other times, filmmakers created new worlds that reflected aspects of the world that they don't like and wish they could change.

Films like *The Ice Pirates* and *Dune* could work simultaneously as escapist worlds where deserts, sandworms, Templars and robots act out elaborate pulp fantasies as well as subtle commentaries on the real-life fear of dwindling resources on a finite planet. Even the darkly comical and ultra-stylized sci-fi fairy tale world of *The City of Lost Children* (1995) comments on reliance of technology, child labor and the questionable ethics of scientific experimentation. Clever and subversive filmmakers found ways to use imaginary worlds to speak about very real problems.

After the Millennium

The heyday of the Strange Land film in Hollywood was the 1980s, after the studio system had collapsed and new, young filmmakers were testing the boundaries of what their new corporate owners would allow. Later into the 1990s and the new millennium, companies found their comfortable rhythms and rarely ventured outside a known intellectual property or easily explainable "high concept" story.

Dune was remade in 2000 for the Syfy network, stripped of much of the fantastical otherness that made David Lynch's original a cult phenomenon. The worlds of *Sky Captain and the World of Tomorrow* (2004) and *The Golden Compass* (2007) were nothing more than elaborately designed alternate versions of our own world, pretend pasts or alternate presents. Even high-concept comedies like Ricky Gervais' *The Invention of Lying* (2009), which posits a world in which humanity never learned how to be dishonest, was still otherwise exactly like our everyday world.

As the technology of CGI made the possibility of creating fantastic and unseen worlds more achievable, the desire for films to make more and more money kept science fiction at an arm's length from those Strange Lands. It would take the inexhaustible passions and singular visions of filmmakers working outside the film industry, without the primary objective of immense profit, to bring those Strange Lands to reality.

The Independent Perspective

An independent film budget doesn't always allow for the kind of world-building that Hollywood films have, but some enterprising indie directors found ways to create mostly new worlds or Strange Lands with only tangential connections to our reality that exist primarily as cost-saving measures that allowed the films to be produced in the first place.

Director Ari Folman's follow-up to his animated documentary *Waltz with Bashir* was the live-action-animation hybrid *The Congress* (2013), in which actress Robin Wright sells her digital likeness to a movie studio only to eventually merge with it in a strange animated world in which humanity has been altered by its conversion to digital material.

Though the story began in the apparent real world, the animated world she ends up in and the eventual bizarre real world she returns to are powerful images that touch on the real-world ramifications of computer-based fantasy life.

The world of injured stuntman Roy Walker's hospital in 1920s Los Angeles is grittily realistic, but the Strange Land he creates in stories for a fellow patient is something exquisite and exotic, sprung fully developed in the film *The Fall* from the mind of director Tarsem Singh. Singh's vision brought to life the alien landscape of a serial killer's mind earlier in his career, with 2000's *The Cell*, and he is one of the few Strange Land filmmakers who has worked with equal success within the studio system and without.

In the Featured Films section, four bold and visionary filmmakers use Strange Lands to discuss the human toll of modern war, the damages of consumer society, colonialism and corporatism, and the hierarchical constructs that keep humanity divided.

Featured Films

Franklyn (2008)
Writer-Director: Gerald McMorrow
Starring Eva Green, Ryan Phillippe, Sam Riley

In the otherworldly Meanwhile City, Jonathan Preest stalks the streets as a masked vigilante, hunting his nemesis, The Individual. Preest is the lone atheist in a strange society in which belief is a requirement for citizenship. In a parallel narrative in our world, a troubled young woman crosses life paths with a naïve man looking for true love and a

Who is the face underneath the blank mask of the vigilante Preest in *Franklyn* (2008).

minister searching the homeless community for his missing son. Events continue to draw them near to each other, bringing the two worlds crashing into each other.

The shadow of the Iraq War aftermath hovers like a specter over the events of *Franklyn*, an assured and mature science fiction drama. The film's four main storylines each touch on troubles facing modern society, from relationship troubles and mental illness to homelessness and the deep religious divisions in humanity. Even the design of Meanwhile City and the costuming hold symbolic meaning, including the featureless mask that represents Preest's shattered sense of identity.

∼

After studying film in New York, Gerald McMorrow premiered his skills as writer and director with the short film *Thespian X* (2002), about a man trying to get a job in a bleak dystopian future. It's a thematic progenitor of McMorrow's first feature film, Franklyn. The narrative of *Franklyn* is impressively complicated; McMorrow originally intended that this complex narrative be much smaller.

Gerald McMorrow: *It started out as a short film idea–I had a concept about an apartment building in front of a restaurant and what happens in the restaurant and the building over the course of one night. In the restaurant, there is an elderly man dining on his own. In the first floor flat opposite is a young woman about to take her own life and in the top floor flat is an armed assassin about to take the life of the elderly man in the restaurant. The assassin can't get a bead on the elderly man due to the angle and height of the window and realizes he must take the shot from the floor below—so he interrupts the young woman from committing suicide and charms his way into her flat. From then on, she becomes the hero, going from trying to take her own life to trying to save it as well as the life of the elderly man.*

This idea started me thinking, reverse-engineering the story if you like—I wanted to know who the elderly man was to the assassin. I immediately felt it would be interesting if the man was the assassin's father. If so, then why would the young man be trying to kill his own father? What if he didn't think it was his father? Maybe he saw his father as somebody or something else? That's where the idea of Jonathan Preest's and David's parallel skew on reality came from. Preest saw David's father as the embodiment of evil and the cause of the girl's death in Meanwhile City while he was simply the cause of David's sister's death in reality. Everything spread from there and in a sense the film was written from the end to the beginning.

You tackle a lot of issues that were on the minds of society at the time (and many of which are still relevant) like the Iraq War, homelessness and the struggle to deal with mental illness. Did you choose the fantastical aspect of this story to marry with these issues because it helps to make difficult conversations more palatable to viewers?

It was definitely a time to question the motivations and aftermath of the Iraq war, there was a lot of soul-searching at the time as well as many documented cases of PTSD in the British armed forces. I was also interested in the different aspects of mental illness in the story. David's was a complete break, he is a schizophrenic traumatized by the death of his sister and his time in Iraq. Milo was innocently deluded and in a romantic madness that consumed him after his failed relationship, and Emilia was on a path of self-destruction that she chose to mask by camouflaging her masochistic urges with her creativity, her performance pieces. I guess what was more interesting to me was to take those ideas on even further. There are many moments in the story, especially at the denouement, that imply that there may be some truth lying behind the individual delusions. I always liked the idea that once David had died in this world, he carried on as Jonathan Preest in the other.

The film's structure, with the broken narrative slowly revealing itself to be interconnected in unexpected ways, is a storytelling concept that has become more utilized in recent years. Do you feel that in some ways this storytelling style more accurately reflects the way we experience life (with fragmented understanding), or was it just an attempt to adjust storytelling styles to an increasingly sophisticated viewing audience (in order to retain and maximize surprise and drama)?

I think it's a bit of both. I've always been a fan of parallel storylines and there is something to be said for this structure reflecting real life. There are constantly changing threads of fate in our lives, other people's stories endlessly running parallel with our own, some tying in, some veering off. But I guess this is the nature of storytelling and drama, how these happenings intersect, how different people affect each other. I also think that audiences are becoming more sophisticated (despite what we see from the studios!). I think people are crying out to be challenged, to be manipulated, to be surprised and tested.

In the film, the lead character Jonathan exists in a parallel reality from many of the other characters. What do you think it is about the idea of alternate realities, other worlds or secret societies that continue to draw us in as filmmakers and viewers?

I've always liked the idea of alternate realities, especially where it comes down to perspective. Who's to say that the world that someone who is deemed insane is experiencing is any less valid than our own? In storytelling terms, the parallel world opens up infinite possibilities and that is of course desirable to writers and filmmakers. All fiction is based on a sense of "what if?," and essentially, we are only restricted by our imaginations. It has also been a useful tool recently for rebooting classic story arcs. Star Trek, for instance, has been sent on a brand-new journey due to J.J. Abrams' deft use of an alternative Star Trek *"timeline."*

Franklyn is clearly touching on issues regarding religion: the main character being an atheist named Preest, the world of Meanwhile City being a largely religious society, and one of the other characters being a church warden. Did you have any specific goals thematically in the inclusion of these elements as part of the larger narrative?

I tend to look at many of the problems in the world today as dogma-based. Meanwhile City is somewhere where we see the ultimate melting pot of religion, all as ridiculous as each other, but the more powerful [The Ministry] rising to the top and being in ultimate control. Meanwhile City is run on faith, and I took this to its ultimate level where you simply had to believe in something (anything, in fact) to have a permit to live and exist in the city. Religion is a manmade thing and so it is ultimately flawed. Jonathan Preest is the only atheist in Meanwhile City and this makes him the only rational person in an insane metropolis. All of this, of course, is simply a reflection of Preest-David's deeper problems where his vendetta against the theists is a result of his rejection of the same in the real world, namely his father. David's father tried to explain away his sister's death by saying it was God's will, his work as warden shows his commitment to the church. Sadly, it seems that his father has lost everything because of his blinkered faith—his daughter, his wife and then of course, finally, his son.

Frequencies (2013)
Writer-Director: Darren Paul Fisher
Starring Daniel Fraser, Eleanor Wyld, Owen Pugh

In an alternate world, luck is a measurable phenomenon, tracked through a person's individual frequency. The higher the frequency, the better the luck, and this measurement is what determines your opportunities in life. Schoolboy Zak is in love with Marie, but his status as low frequency bars him from being able to pursue her. But after experimentation with his friend Theo throughout their teenage years, he discovers that frequencies can be altered, and he renews his pursuit of Marie. While fighting to be with Marie, Zak also discovers that a mysterious government organization is after him because of his discovery, but not for the reason he thinks.

Alternately titled *OXV: The Manual*, *Frequencies* is a high-concept science fiction film that tackles some of humanity's biggest questions: fate vs. free will and true love. That the film also finds room for a smart commentary on hierarchical social systems is equally impressive. Playing on the alternate dimension element of a single divergent element in an otherwise similar world, the concept allows the viewer to understand real political and social complexities like the manipulation of the public without facing the same scrutiny as non-fiction or drama.

∼

Writer-director Darren Paul Fisher began his career as a filmmaker with the back-to-back teen comedies *Inbetweeners* (2001) and *Popcorn* (2007). After a brief break from filmmaking in which he began teaching at Bond University, he created 2013's *Frequencies*. The film's narrative, which deals with some heavy subjects, came from a simple initial interest.

Darren Paul Fisher: *I've always been obsessed with luck. We all know those people, those with what is often described as a natural sense of "timing," who always land on their feet. This is not simply a matter of perception or the mentality of those involved (such as projecting positivity) but more, seemingly, a purely mathematical thing. Someone who regularly wins at raffles (as an ex-girlfriend of mine once did) does not win by an optimistic interpretation of events, nor by being emotionally open to the world. The concept of the "lucky person" is currently inexplicable in the real world and I wanted to explore this through fiction, find some way of explaining, if in a playful way, how luck might work scientifically. All the ideas and science are based in fact, but hijacked to a more or lesser degree for the story. It was important for our acceptance of this alternate universe that the science felt intuitively right and had a simple internal logic to it. The idea of frequency is real. All physical objects resonate on some level, but linking it to luck is pure invention.*

I originally had an idea for what would eventually become Frequencies *in the late '90s but a film that explores theories of knowledge, destiny and free will was not one that was a natural choice for most commercially-minded producers. Then Charlie Kaufman happened, and people became a little more prepared to accept that a film that deals with some very abstract intellectual concepts could be a commercial prospect. We're not talking commercial in the make-huge-money sense, but in the sense of connecting with any audience at all.*

The central theme of the film, about how people have different frequencies which determine their lives to a large degree ... there are several allegorical possibilities that the idea could represent (genetics, class hierarchy, etc.). Was there one specific allegory you felt strongly about while writing it, or did many of them make themselves known to you as you wrote and directed the film?

This is a discussion that came up a lot during the Q&As on the festival run of the film, and everyone had their own take on it. Obviously, as I was writing the script, there were clear allegorical opportunities that I made sure I kept open—class and race perhaps the two most overt. But other interpretations, such as genetic elitism or the idea of science being in tension with the arts, are equally valid. What was interesting for me was that as much as the layering of the themes were important, all were secondary in the writing. The priority was always having fun with the thought experiment of "What if luck could be measured?" and exploring the effect this would have on free will. For me, ultimately, it's a story about knowledge.

Though it is sometimes more expensive to make, science fiction films that create entirely new worlds are often the most immersive experiences in film. Why do you think we are drawn to stories that take place in worlds so vastly different from our own. And how do you as a filmmaker ensure that the world isn't so alien that we can't connect to and relate to the events taking place there?

All narrative film is fantasy to some degree. The power of the "what if?" is incredibly seductive. Even when it's not sci-fi, film is essentially a time-travel (and location) device, as most "worlds" we visit through film—even in the here and now—are different from our own. Sci-fi is just at the more extreme end of the spectrum and is actually more freeing. If you do it right, and by right, I mean create a fully realized alternate world or future with characters that we can understand and root for, I believe it really taps into, for lack of a better phrase, the essence of cinema. It's what the form is particularly good at, and unlike the written form it really lets the viewer experience the world in a visceral sense. There is a lot of fun to be had. And fun is very important. I feel like we are sharing the joy of unrestrained imaginings in that pure childlike sense.

I think the key with any world-building is to keep it relatable on a fundamental everyday level. What put me off a lot of pure fantasy novels and pushed me into sci-fi as a young reader was the density of information you were often forced to navigate within the first few pages. I remember one time I opened a book to read the first few lines only to read something like: "J'n'grthi was a Raga, and was destined to be the Abnerath of the Nnraljr. He had a pet Yuyul who was always sjdii." There was literally no entry point. I couldn't even pronounce the names in my head and there was no way to visualize the story. Obviously, film visualizes for you, and I love stories to have density and texture but the viewer must always have an entry point at all times. It may not always be advisable but it is possible to delay understanding, but only so far. If it becomes too much to physically track, or not enough information is given—or if they get the sense you're simply trying to show how clever you are in a mocking sense—you will lose the audience forever.

There are always three strategies when bringing an audience into a new world. Either get it all up front in the setup, stagger the exposition slowly throughout the story or completely and willfully ignore the fact it's a new world and let differences come naturally through the drama. We went for option number three. It's a riskier strategy, as there's a strong chance you'll end up on the wrong side of too subtle, but if you get it right, it's much more convincing. It also saves you inventing spurious devices or characters to explain things that inevitably slow down the pace of the story and allows the film to retain a sense of mystery and depth.

You should be able to understand everything from context but not everything is explained. In fact, in the transmedia universe we now live in, it's actually a benefit that we leave some things open. If there is enough interest, the mosaic storytelling can very easily expand beyond the limits of the film itself. There are a lot of stories to explore in this world across all different platforms.

The other way you draw an audience into your world is to have recognizable and relatable characters and quandaries. You can plot all you want, but the audience is ultimately watching people. At its heart, Frequencies, for all the puzzle structure, cold hard science, and thematic analysis, is really a very simple romance following a boy-meets-girl dynamic. We billed it as the world's first scientific-philosophical romance, although by the time the film hit iTunes, it had become a sci-fi romantic mystery, which is also pretty fair.

What was the inspiration for having your lead characters named, at least partly, after famous scientists like Isaac Newton and Marie Curie? Since the film is partially about changing your destiny, are you comparing the hopeful romantic dreamers of this film to the scientists whose ideas changed the real world?

It was really just about texture. As part of the world-building, I wanted to imply that this world valued scientists and philosophers over athletes and actors—the mental over the physical. In my initial outline for the film, there was a prologue about how the world came about but I decided there were things I'd rather leave implicit and this was one of them. Instead of naming your child Tyson or Jennifer, you'd name them Albert-Einstein or Marie-Curie. The idea is that the values these scientists and inventors hold are the key values of the society. In the same way young children idolize and want to become actors and athletes, most in this world idolize and want to become scientist-philosopher-dreamers!

This film touches on some heavy concepts, in particular the eternal discussion of fate vs. choice. Do you feel that one of the advantages of making a science fiction film is that you can have more complex and important conversations about human existence by framing the conversations around entertaining fantastical circumstances?

I think if you keep the action interesting on a moment-to-moment level, you can discuss pretty much anything thematically in any genre. Ultimately, most films are thematically about how to be a better person, however that is conceived and expressed. Sci-fi can do that, but also is very well-suited for you to make films not just about how to be a **better** *human but what it means to be* **human,** *which is quite different and particularly complex.*

In the film, the solution to changing your frequency, using sound waves and certain words, feels like it might be an allegory on how an individual's life (frequency) can be controlled in some way by external circumstances, sometimes by people other than yourself. Is this in some way a commentary about social systems, hierarchies, governments, etc., and how their behaviors and rules can exert influence on an individual's life?

Yes, it's a bit of a meditation on social control but ultimately brings us back to the idea of free will. Is it an illusion, either because we are being controlled by specific external forces for external gain (government, police, other people), or just how the universe works? And does it matter? It's this last question I find particularly intriguing. The idea of being controlled is a scary concept but we are all controlled to some degree. Yet is this always bad? I wanted the audience to really think about these questions and have time to consider the answers beyond the usual immediate instinctive response.

Patch Town (2014)
Director: Craig Goodwill
Writer: Christopher Bond, Jessie Gabe, Craig Goodwill, Trevor Martin

Jon began life as a tiny toy doll. He lived with his adoptive "mother" for many years until, like many toys, he was forgotten and left behind. His life took a dark turn, and he discovered that rejected toys go to work in a factory that births babies from heads of cabbage and turns them into new toys for children to enjoy and then discard. Jon eventually marries, and the two of them decide to take one of the newborn cabbage children as their own. An evil child hunter is soon on their trail, so Jon must summon all his courage to help his family escape their miserable lives and possibly reunite with his long-lost adoptive mother.

An ambitious and wildly imaginative world peppered with commentaries about consumerism and even a few musical numbers(!), *Patch Town* is a true hybrid film in every sense of the word. Playing on elements of several well-known science fiction and fantasy subgenres, from the dystopian society of *1984* to the man-child fantasy-adventure of *City of Lost Children*, the movie borrows images and concepts from its inspirations, but the sensibility of the film is in a class all its own. Equal parts light-hearted fantasy and Tim Burton–esque dark comedy, Jon's tale works as a brilliant metaphor for marginalized workers whose lives and products are used and disposed of with abandon.

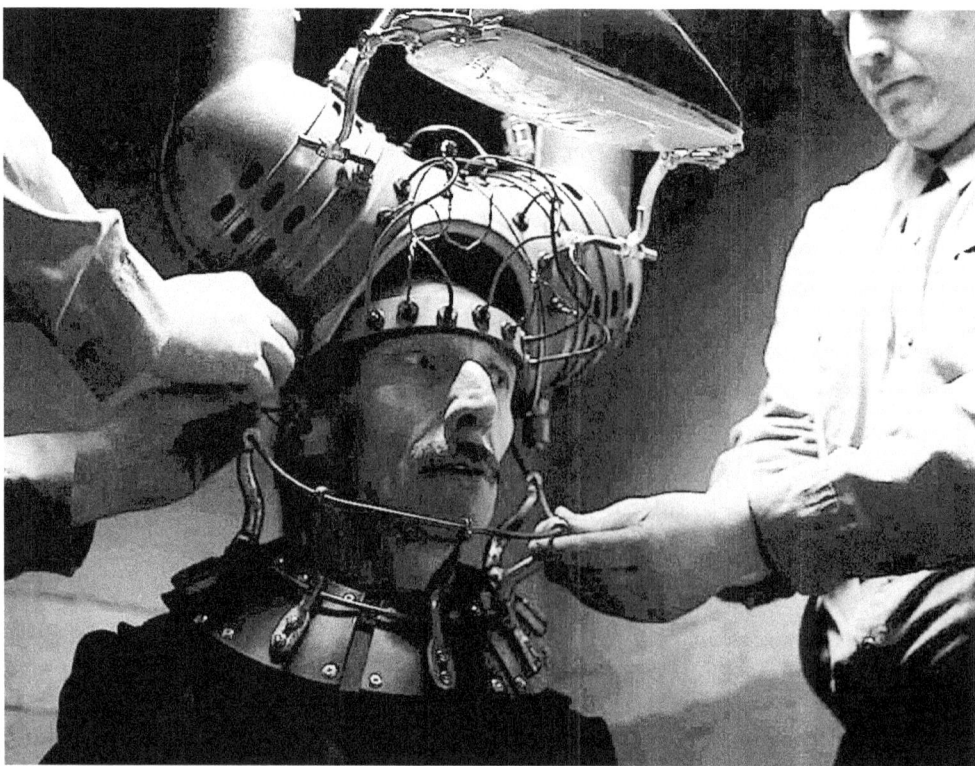

Yuri (Julian Richings) is punished for not finding his target in *Patch Town* (2014).

The journey to the creation of *Patch Town* began when Craig Goodwill, a television documentary producer, decided to bring his unique vision to the screen as a short film in 2011. Three years later, the dedicated filmmaker was finally able to secure the funding for a feature version, which opened up new narrative possibilities for his very personal story.

Craig Goodwill: *I was working with a Russian script supervisor on set and we were waiting for the next set-up and we started speaking about where babies come from. I said in North America we believed the stork delivered us, and she said in Russia and Eastern Europe, you are born in the cabbage patch. That night, she sent me a picture of a fetus inside a cabbage, and my imagination started running. It was first produced as a short that premiered at TIFF and then made into a feature film.*

Because of the presence of the "cabbage patch"–style characters who were rejected by their original owners, do you feel this film is an examination of consumption culture (cultures driven by the acquisition and quick disposal of material goods)?

Yes. That was the point. There is a tendency to label the film as a family film, and though I do see that, the intent was to comment on consumerism and our culture of disposal of those things we once loved. It's about what happens to that transference of love and the responsibilities of people who physically sign adoption papers for these dolls.

This film touches, perhaps indirectly, on the idea of forced and child labor with its story element about what happens to rejected toys. This is a serious problem which has grown more concerning as globalized business has grown in recent years. Was this element intentional on your part?

Yes, very much so. I was inspired by old Disney films in a way; within their films, there was always embedded a much deeper and darker message. This commentary was further to highlight not only the consumerism attached to these items but the same production process of the same toys (children) working the line to ultimately dispose of themselves. Would leaving you feeling rather worthless, wouldn't it?

This film falls into the subgenre of the "dark fairy tale" film which has grown in popularity in recent years, beginning with Jean-Pierre Jeunet's *City of Lost Children* and many of the films of Tim Burton and Terry Gilliam. Were these films influences, and were there others? What is it about the dark fairy tale aesthetic that appeals to you as a filmmaker? What do you think makes it appealing to viewers in general?

Yes, Terry Gilliam was my childhood idol. I loved his films, along with Monty Python, and City of Lost Children *was certainly in there as well. I was also attracted to the wacky ideas of John Carpenter and movies like* Big Trouble in Little China, *which adds an air of levity to the film.*

As for the appeal, I am not sure if dark is an adequate word. I think humans and their stories are deeper and have much more meaning overall and it is important to show that layer. If it is labeled dark, then that is fine, but I would venture to say that we all must have a "dark" side and therefore I feel audiences are attracted to the authenticity of that idea.

Upside Down (2012)

Writer-Director: Juan Solanas
Starring Jim Sturgess, Kirsten Dunst, Timothy Spall

Two planets are joined in their orbits, pressed right up against each other but having their own separate gravities. One world is rich and successful, the other is ravaged by overpopulation and poverty. Poor Adam meets wealthy Eden when they are children, and when they get older, they begin a clandestine relationship. After she is injured in an accident and authorities separate them, Adam schemes to get up to her world in order to reconnect. He brings an invention of his to a corporation that straddles both worlds, and uses the towering office building to sneak in and meet her. Struggling to conquer bureaucracy, Eden's injury-related amnesia, and the literal world itself keeping them apart, Adam discovers the element most important to changing their fates.

A visionary film that discusses colonialism, class systems and the enduring hope of love to bring divided factions together, *Upside Down* is a marvel of ingenuity in plotting and execution. Using primarily practical effects to bring a mind-bending story to life, the film's world-building and action sequences are all in service to the central romantic narrative. Nominated for multiple awards, including a Saturn Award for Best Independent Film, *Upside Down* is an achievement of imagery, theme and passion.

∼

Juan Solanas' rise to recognition as a unique voice in cinema was a quick ascent. From his first short film *The Man Without a Head* (2003), it was only two years before he made the multi-award-nominated international drama *Northeast*. He directed a documentary, *Jack Waltzer: On the Craft of Acting*, and followed it up the next year in 2012's *Upside Down*. The entire narrative, with its dual worlds and elaborate details, came from a single simple image.

Juan Solanas: *The idea came one morning when I woke up. I saw an image of a guy and a girl, and one is upside down and the other is not. I understood there was a great story in that, and that it would be a love story. The same day, I started to think how we could shoot a movie like that. Because of course, you cannot put an actor upside down for a whole film. I didn't want to shoot a heavy special effects movie, with a green screen all the time and shooting a guy talking to another guy in gravity and then shooting the other guy a week later. I love to work with actors, and acting is reacting, so how can you react with someone who's not there? I tried to find a way to shoot my scenes in real time like a normal movie, have the two actors talk to each other, one being in one gravity and one being in the other gravity, on the same set. How could we do that? How could we shoot and direct? More than that, I like to make the actors improvise a little bit around the lines to bring life into the scene.*

If I couldn't find the way to do that, I didn't want to make the movie because it would be like I often say, "the dinosaur syndrome." You see an actor looking at a dinosaur on-screen and you feel he's not looking at a dinosaur.

So, on this first round of making the script, I theorized a kind of technology to achieve my idea of shooting, and a couple of years later when we start to produce the movie, we went to see a few companies around the world with my idea of the technology. Finally, we found our company who said, "Oh yeah, nobody has done that, but we think it's doable. Very challenging but doable." That's the package of the idea and how to do it and how it came together.

This story is essentially similar to *Romeo and Juliet* or *West Side Story*, where two people from different worlds come together; in this case, they're from literally different worlds.

One of my favorite parts of those stories is that you usually have some sort of commentary, whether it's social or political, about the two different worlds. You have Up Top and you have Down Below, and one of them is a rich society and one of them is poor and is being taken advantage of. It had a sense of colonialism. Were these themes influenced by real-life events?

Yeah, of course. For me, it was a metaphor, especially when you come from this kind of country. When I was young, we got exiled from Argentina because of the military strike. For me, Upside Down *is my metaphorical way of speaking about my story. I have lived 37 years of my life as an Argentinian guy living literally upside down. France and Argentina, that's what this is all about. I'm very happy that you saw that.*

The lead character, Adam, is able to reach Eden and for their relationship to continue because of his ingenuity and his invention. He looked at the world in just a different enough way so that he could get the attention and get where he needed to be. In America, you might hear about a filmmaker from Detroit who didn't have any money or any resources, but it was the passion and the vision that helped to complete a project that created a career. In some ways, that's a metaphor for what you did, too, as a filmmaker in using your vision and your passion for filmmaking to break out of where you were and to bring your message to a larger audience.

Yeah, absolutely, you need to use a lot of creativity because you don't have other things. I mean my childhood was very, very happy for me, but I used to play with cocoa, little nuts, and a piece of wood. When we got rain in the street where I lived, it would get overrun by water. My street became a river, and for me it was incredible. They were great moments. Again, creativity and your brain, at the end of the day it's everything that you need.

There's an interesting commentary on corporatism in this film as well. While it was good that he could find a place to take his invention and his ingenuity, this corporation is looking for someone with a good idea they can profit from, that they can absorb without benefitting the individuals who created the idea. That's a story with a long history, since corporations first came into existence.

Absolutely. One of my favorite characters is Boruchowitz, the guy who helps Adam in the company.

Boruchowitz and Albert, Adam's mentor, are flip sides of the same coin. Their roles could have easily been reversed. It's interesting that you have two figures who Adam looks up to in both worlds, who serve the same purpose.

Absolutely, 100 percent. These two characters were the ones that I really love. When I was writing, every time Boruchowitz or Albert came into the story, it was a great pleasure. Because I understand them very well.

Throughout the film, we see elements like conversations between people from Up Top or snippets of newscasts where we hear information about crimes, and it's always blamed on people from the Down Below. Down Below is this world where people have no money, they're desperate, and they are sometimes stealing things from Up Top because they can use them for energy. People are desperate, and they are doing things to survive, and it ends up feeding into this false impression that people from Down Below must be worse people because they are committing crimes. It creates a fake narrative that allows people from Up Top to feel better about the fact that they are oppressing people.

Yes, absolutely. And the other great thing about the ingenuity of Adam is that he is the opposite of cynical. I don't want it to sound silly, but you need to be a little naïve, you need to believe that not everything is shit, not every human wants to use another human for a purpose. That is why, to me, Adam tries to achieve great things, to believe and try and then achieve.

You created an entire other universe where we recognize humans, but all the other rules have changed drastically, down to the idea of the dueling gravities and the interaction of the world. What do you think it is that draws audiences to worlds that they don't recognize, as opposed to the worlds they already know?

Sometimes you watch a film and it feels like you've watched it two hundred times. You know every ten minutes or every 20 minutes what's going to happen. You know when one's going to die. I get bored, it's like a machine.

We talked about some heavy elements in this conversation: ideas of class systems, colonialism, corporations, things like that. I wonder if people are more comfortable in a made-up world where you're not talking about things directly. If you go out tomorrow and make a movie about a kid from Mumbai who fell in love with a girl from New York City and it was the exact same story except it wasn't allegorical, it was just a real-world story, I wonder if it would find the same audience.

The idea of Upside Down, *the morning I saw this image, I understood that this idea was a metaphor for the north and south, first world and third world, whatever you want to call it. The power of the idea was so strong, it would allow me to speak about other things, but not be too direct about it. You can pass that idea to an audience that didn't go to the movies to see that, so it's a second story that came for free.*

More Films of Interest

Beyond the Black Rainbow (2010), *Yesterday Was a Lie* (2008), *Dark Portals: The Chronicles of Vidocq* (2001), *Timer* (2009)

5

An Infinity of Alternate Dimensions

The phenomenon of the alternate dimension is relatively new in the world of film. It was long confined to the worlds of science fiction novels and short stories, comic books and role-playing games; film producers considered the concept not quite mainstream enough for general moviegoers.

Television was more permissive, particularly with adventurous science fiction series like *Star Trek*, which virtually created the popular portrayal of the alternate universe with its episode "Mirror Mirror." It focused on dark doppelganger versions of the well-known series leads, and it blew open the possibilities of where to go with alternate dimensions.

It was the comic book, sci-fi novel and video game arena, however, that finally made Hollywood comfortable with traveling outside our own dimension. The year 1980 brought *The Lathe of Heaven,* based on the novel by Ursula K. LeGuin, in which the dreams of a psychiatrist's patient are slowly reshaping the reality around him. The sense of pulp adventure that brought about *Raiders of the Lost Ark* was refitted with a satirical sense of humor and an old sci-fi bent with 1984's *The Adventure of Buckaroo Banzai Across the Eighth Dimension*; the film was humorous and chaotic, and would become a blueprint for later sci-fi comedy epics like *Guardians of the Galaxy*.

The idea of alternate dimensions soon became the go-to explanation for film companies looking to explain away high-concept franchises being brought to the screen from other mediums. *Howard the Duck* used alternate dimensions to explain away the strangeness of talking human-like ducks, and *Masters of the Universe* did the same thing to give He-Man and his friends a few normal human companions. Even *Super Mario Brothers* borrowed the concept.

The alternate dimension films reached a fever pitch in the 1990s with films like *Crossworlds*, *The Lake* and *Run Lola Run*. The idea of alternate realities quickly became a comfortable arena for film, expanding into less exotic concepts; *Sliding Doors* took the concept of alternate realities as a centerpiece of a drama about the possible divergences in a woman's romantic life.

After the Millennium

The remake cycle continued in this subgenre as well, with another version of *The Lathe of Heaven* in 2002. Even *Star Trek* revisited the idea of alternate realities when it leapt to the big-screen for a rebooted franchise that was an offshoot of the original timeline of the many TV series.

The post-millennial movie arena was no longer timid about embracing alternate realities. *Final Destination* co-directors Glen Morgan and James Wong put martial arts superstar Jet Li in *The One*, a high-concept action-adventure that literally had Li battling multiple versions of himself in hand-to-hand combat. *The Mist* allowed writer-director Frank Darabont to create a treatise on military overreach and religious apocalyptic authoritarianism through the guise of an inter-dimensional portal that brings evil into our world.

The subgenre even allowed for an exploration of the War on Terror and government surveillance post–9/11 in 2011's *Source Code*. The film follows an Afghanistan veteran traveling into an alternate past to try and solve a train bombing.

The Independent Perspective

Indie film has always been more daring in its embrace of new and unusual storytelling elements, and the idea of alternate dimensions is no exception. From the dissolution of the family unit in *Coraline* and *The Hole* to an exploration of the cast-off aspects of society and culture in *Re-Cycle*, independent film pulled no punches in the new millennium.

Phantasm director Don Coscarelli created another dream delusion of a film in *John Dies at the End*, about a drug that causes the user to experience shifts in time and space. And even in more traditional plots, like Sam Esmail's *Comet*, the idea of a romance that is meant to be is given cosmic import. In the Featured Films, these filmmakers use new technologies to hearken back to the early days of filmic storytelling, chronicle the struggle of a family in turmoil, and explore the seductive opportunities of easy social advancement.

Featured Films

It Came from Yesterday (2011)
Writer-Director: Jeff Waltrowski
Starring Jeff Waltrowski, Nathan Hollobaugh, Nayli Russo

Heroic scientist Professor Jack is an adventurer in a retro-futuristic version of the 1940s. Along with the Electric Club (the name his sidekicks Buddy and Penny Precious go by), Professor Jack is on the trail of a strange mystery. Bug-like creatures have been sighted, and no one knows where they came from. Professor Jack discovers that they are inter-dimensional beings who traveled to our dimension to enslave the human race, and only he stands in the way of their success.

The love of movie serials from the 1940s colors every frame of *It Came from Yesterday*, a loving homage to a subset of earnest but lo-fi science fiction films whose lofty story ambitions were greater than the budgets and effects they contained. The lead character is a pastiche of great adventure serial heroes, the same films and set-ups that brought Indiana Jones and Allan Quatermain to the big screen in the 1980s. The jokes

A faux-vintage lobby poster featuring Professor Jack in *It Came from Yesterday* (2011).

in the film are laughs of recognition that are never at the expense of the characters or the story.

∼

Nearly a full decade before Jeff Waltrowski directed *It Came from Yesterday*, he was already dabbling in similar interests. In 2002, he wrote, produced, and directed another adventure, *Project: Valkyrie*, also starring in the role of Professor Jack Cranston, a prototype of the *It Came from Yesterday* lead he later played. He worked as cinematographer in documentary (*Spicy Sister Slumber Party*) and narrative film (*Splatter Movie: The Director's Cut*), and even acted in *A Feast of Flesh* and *Demon Divas and the Lanes of Damnation*. Waltrowski talked about the film's long gestation period, from inception to reality.

Jeff Waltrowski: *The character of Professor Jack has been with me for a long time. While I was a film student at Point Park University in Pittsburgh in the late '90s, I shot a 16mm short that was meant to be one chapter of a '40s serial. It was totally played straight but had tons of laughs if you were a fan of the genre (similar to* It Came from Yesterday's *tone). The character had always stuck with me as I had grown up on '50s sci-fi,* Star Trek *and '40s serials. He even appeared very briefly in my first feature, a micro-budget horror-comedy called* Project: Valkyrie, *shot when I was 23.*

Before It Came from Yesterday *came to be, I was developing an entirely unrelated sci-fi film, when the script became too big for the budget that I had. Rather than scrap the project or rewrite, my fellow producer and I decided to switch gears. We needed to come up with something fast. Luckily, Professor Jack was sitting in the back of my brain with nothing to do. It was always my dream to do a feature film like this. I wrote the first draft in a week. The story just poured out from me from being bottled up for so many years.*

We now live in a world where we're paying homage to original films from the past *and* the material that was created as an homage to that original material. Would you say this film is more influenced by the original serials from the 1920s, '30s and '40s like *Buck Rogers* and *Flash Gordon*, or from the resurgence of films based on the serials in the 1970s and 1980s like *Raiders of the Lost Ark*, *Allan Quatermain* and *Star Wars*?

I am a massive fan of Indiana Jones, Star Wars *and* The Rocketeer. *As I was growing up, I had all the modern stuff fed to me right alongside George Pal and Buster Crabbe. I knew that one influenced the other, but my love was equal for both.*

When it comes to It Came from Yesterday, *however, my main intent was to capture the feeling of the vintage material. Probably the main influence on my entire artistic career (for some reason) has been* Radar Men from the Moon, *the Commando Cody serial. I can't explain it, it's just something that has always resonated with me. I think you can easily see the shades of that in* It Came from Yesterday *as far as the dynamics between the heroes. One thing that I wanted to communicate to the audience was my love of the golden age of sci-fi, the hokey mumbo jumbo science, the cheesy performances, the crazy monster suits. When you watch* It Came from Yesterday, *you're not watching a strict recreation of the films of that period, but rather a recreation through my eyes and how I see that genre. Of course, being a child of the '80s, it was really difficult to not have some influence of the modern era. The spirits of* Buckaroo Banzai *and* Indiana Jones *are scattered throughout.*

The idea of "retro-future," visiting the imagined future that we looked towards in our collective past, has become a phenomenon, with films like yours, *Sky Captain and the World of Tomorrow* and many others. What do you think is the draw in revisiting futures that never came about?

A dieselpunk retro-future vibe is all over It Came from Yesterday. *The futuristic jet plane, robots and other goofy tech featured in the film, besides letting the designers have a field day, was really meant to evoke a sense of optimism. I think that's why the retro-future aesthetic remains popular. It shows us that people of the past had an eye on the future that was hopeful, that technology would make life easier and not be a burden, and that their children would live in a safer, more advanced world. Most visions of the future today are dystopian and don't offer much hope for our future generations. I think that's where we are as a society, unfortunately. For me, it was great to delve into a world where the future looked bright.*

Many of the original films and serials you're emulating in this film were filled with paranoia and fears about nuclear weapons, communism and many other things including rock'n'roll and wayward youth. Is there something about the fear mentality of that era that makes it relatable to an audience decades removed from it now?

The fear and paranoia that you'd see cleverly disguised in the films of that era is just as relatable now, if not more so. Right now, that same fear is in our society just wearing a different mask. Terrorism is the new communism. Mass shootings, police violence, everything you see people posting their "thoughts and prayers" about on Facebook have put our country in a state of fear that I don't think has been seen since the Cold War era. I'm surprised that we haven't seen more horror films and sci-fi films tackle these fears. As far as the films of the '50s that spoke to that fear, I think that's why they remain great. The topics are timeless and universal. It Came from Yesterday *taps into those topics of the time briefly when we are not going for the goofball cheese, but I think that helps ground it in that period.*

Though the film is an homage to films of the past, in many ways this film could never have existed without many of the modern technologies and techniques like CGI and greenscreen that allowed for such a unique and specific film to be made on a reasonable budget. This is kind of a film of two distinct eras, isn't it?

Definitely. Even though it is in a style reminiscent of the past, you can't overlook the road we took to get there. We would never have been able to tell this story if we didn't make it the way we did. One thing that was very important to me was recreating the Technicolor look of the time. Having today's digital technology was key to that. Also, building models, finding props and sets, and building that time period on a stage or on location would have been impossible on our budget. Building it digitally not only let us create our world without limitations, but we could give it that hyper-real quality that the movie has. Not only did it give us a unique look, but it also helped convey the tone as well.

When you have that real but unreal look to the film, it helps get the idea across that we aren't taking ourselves too seriously and that it's okay to have fun. In the end, it was the modern technology that was available to us that really nailed the vintage feel. One hand washes the other, I guess.

One of the film's central themes is about creatures from another dimension threatening the existence of humanity. Alternate dimensions are a long and proud tradition of the science fiction genre; what do you think it is about the subgenre of alternate dimensions that continues to be so appealing to viewers as well as filmmakers?

For my money, alternate dimensions will always be fascinating, since the first time I saw Jerome Bixby's excellent Star Trek *episode "Mirror Mirror." It's the idea of presenting us a "what if?" scenario. Somewhere, there's a world where things worked out differently. You went left instead of right. Your life turned out differently. Granted,* It Came from Yesterday's *alternate dimension shows us a world very different from our own, but I think it still speaks to that same sense of wonder. Here's a dimension where humans may not even exist, where creatures share the same mind. The alternate dimension concept is something I hope never goes away.*

Coherence (2013)
Writer-Director: James Ward Byrkit
Starring Emily Baldoni, Maury Sterling, Nicholas Brendon

Emily and her boyfriend Kevin have been invited to a dinner party at a friend's house. Some of the people attending, including Kevin's ex-girlfriend, could make it an uncomfortable experience. Most of the interpersonal drama is set aside, however, when conversation about a comet-sighting turns into a night-long ordeal as the aftermath of the comet knocks out power in the neighborhood. Venturing out of the house to find help, the friends discover that the neighborhood has vanished, and the only light they see in the distance looks exactly like the light from the house they just left.

Coherence is a dizzying puzzle box of a movie whose central conceit is as narratively complex as its locations and cast are limited. Finding a brilliant allegory for the angst of an educated but aimless generation, the film shows a version of Robert Frost's "road not taken" to be as much the terrifying, shadow-filled mystery as it is the hopeful silver-lined cloud we've become accustomed to in stories of this nature. The film is designed to be watched repeatedly; every viewing adds a new narrative wrinkle or character detail.

~

After several successful collaborations with director Gore Verbinski, from illustrations on *Mousehunt* to storyboarding and consulting on the *Pirates of the Caribbean* films to writing the story for the animated *Rango*, James Ward Byrkit directed several short films and a short prequel to the first *Pirates* film. Having worked on enormous sets with gigantic budgets, Byrkit went in a bold direction for his feature directorial debut.

James Ward Byrkit: *The initial motivator for* Coherence *was certainly the micro-budget aspect, using the limitations to inspire creative choices. But the more we started forming a plan, the more we began to crave pushing past the obvious constraints. For example, almost any other film like this would make a conceit out of never leaving the interior of the house, and using the walls as a hard boundary to where the camera can go. But we quickly decided that complexity was going to be our friend, and that made me want to get more and more audacious with the scope of the puzzle.*

Em (Emily Baldoni) wakes to wonder if the whole strange night was a dream in *Coherence* (2013).

Eventually, what I found most exhilarating was the concept of doing one of the most challenging, ridiculously complicated mind-benders of a story with the least amount of support in terms of crew and budget. It felt like scaling a mountain, not just without oxygen, but without shoes, food or any support. Normally, that's a terrible idea. But we were very aware of being in a unique situation, with an amazingly adaptable cast and a way of shooting without a script that made the complexity work for us.

The way you constructed the narrative, by having guidelines and plot points rather than a traditional shooting script, is something that has recently become more popular, starting with *The Blair Witch Project* and developing through the mumblecore film movement. Why was this process more interesting to you than scripting it out? Also, do you feel like this style of filmmaking is more prolific in recent years because the technology of filmmaking has made it easier to do this way?

Definitely the technology has influenced that process. No longer are you spending tens or hundreds of thousands of dollars just to assemble the equipment and process the film. So experiments are much more doable.

For Coherence, *I had always wanted to try doing away with the script ever since I was a kid and saw an episode of E.R. that had been shot in the style of a "real" documentary. I was amazed at how the style of filmmaking suddenly exposed the artifice of what was normally considered a well-crafted show. Suddenly, the acting seemed false. The writing revealed how utterly unnatural it was, all because the documentary style didn't match the tone of the performances. They changed the camera without dealing with the other creative elements.*

This was fascinating to me, and it was clear that the solution would have been to give the actors much more autonomy in crafting overall scenes, and not having every single word scripted for them. So I couldn't wait to try my theory. Normally a movie as complicated as Coherence *demands that every twist be immaculately scripted, every plot point wordsmithed to make a perfect Swiss watch of a story. In doing the exact opposite of that, we found ourselves in completely new territory, and realized that something that ambitious had never been attempted without a script before. I wouldn't recommend it, but somehow it worked for us.*

What is it that you think continues to draw audiences (both viewers and readers) back to stories about alternate dimensions or alternate realities?

There will always be something fundamentally fascinating about versions of reality, branches that life could have taken. We are beings that have a hard time processing life, and the flow of time, and the idea that major consequences result from tiny causes. So stories that allow us to rub up against the inherent weirdness of the fragility of the one random reality we happen to be in will always be relevant.

Humans are obsessed with thinking about changing one little thing in our past, to fix a mistake or see how a different choice would have affected things. "Variations on a theme" is one of the most automatically entertaining concepts, whether it's looking at celebrity hairstyles or listening to classical music. Alternate realities will continue to be used to process different aspects of life as long as we have imagination.

I get the impression when I watch the movie that there is an allegorical element to the multiple dimensions that points towards some sense of post-millennial angst about identity and people's places in the world. Was this intentional on your part in the creation of the story and the events?

That really is the whole idea, although I think that specific kind of identity angst was first crystalized by Rod Serling. Some of the most effective Twilight Zone *episodes were set in the more mundane realities, with someone starting to get glimpses of existential terror by feeling they didn't actually belong in whatever reality matrix they were sensing. These stories worked so well because for many people, we feel like reality is actually much stranger than anyone admits.*

Coherence *takes this a little further just by the function of the characters making a complete mess of their situation, to the point of the story feeling incoherent and unsalvageable. But the underlying metaphor is the same: that we are fundamentally in conflict with ourselves by creating our own worst enemies from inner fears.*

There's also an element of nihilism (or perhaps realism) in the sense that for all the elaborate machinations the characters go through to get back to normal (or even to find a slightly improved circumstance), there's ultimately no escaping the reality of yourself. Is this movie in some ways a cautionary tale to the millennial dream of the easy road to a good life?

That is certainly an intended commentary, although it probably applies to all generations. This is a night where Em is trying to figure out the grand lesson, what she's supposed to learn from her own pattern of indecision that led to suffering. We all have a fantasy of getting to change one thing, or redo a choice from the past and Em gets the unique opportunity of literally "choosing" the outcome of her life by inserting herself into the reality she desires most. But the cost is high, and she shows that even a good person, who would never consider hurting someone else, is willing to inflict harm on "themselves" to get what they want. She ultimately learns too late that she can't just force her way into a reality she didn't earn.

Was the information cited in the film (about other comets and their effects on Earth) based in reality, and did you do a lot of research into quantum physics phenomena in order to create this elaborate narrative?

We had great fun in combining fact and fantasy in those stories. Clearly, there are serious scientific debates to be had about the multiverse, and quantum phenomena leads to some brain-bending places. But we used a lot of misdirects, false facts and misinterpretations to get the characters to the utterly lost state they needed to arrive at. They had to assume that the night was a "Schrödinger's Cat Box" so that they would be convinced there was potential danger in the other house. They used a combination of movie tropes (the evil double), halfway science and just pure anxiety to work themselves up to a state of paranoia.

Ultimately, the film is not about science fact, but the emotional truths of people being in conflict with themselves and being their own worst enemies.

Tympanum (2012)

Director: Jason Thomas Scott
Writers: Shannon Corder, Jason Thomas Scott
Starring David Tenenbaum, Bobbie Prewitt, Nicol Zanzarella

Maron and Lilith, a young suburban couple, move into a new home with their daughter September. They are struggling to keep afloat because of financial issues; the home Maron can afford is small, and September makes the living room her new bedroom. Something strange is happening in the house, though. Inside a small closet, Maron discovers

Maron (David Tenenbaum) puts his daughter (Bobbie Prewitt) and wife Lilith (Nicol Zanzarella) at risk in their new home in *Tympanum* (2012).

a dimensional portal to some kind of underwater world. Sensing the financial opportunities possible from such a discovery, Maron decides to keep the portal a secret. While Maron is saving money to buy equipment to explore the place himself, the family discovers that the portal goes both ways, and something has been visiting them…

Balancing science fiction exploration with the moving everyday experiences of a struggling American family, *Tympanum* is a film that wears its love of the 1980s aesthetic on its sleeve. The complex family dynamics are always on equal par with the intriguing sci-fi premise, and the closet's dimensional wormhole acts as an intelligent allegory for the buried and unacknowledged problems plaguing a seemingly perfect family.

～

With clear nods to *Poltergeist* and *E.T. the Extra-Terrestrial*, director Jason Thomas Scott channels the best aspects of Steven Spielberg's Amblin-era work. Utilizing nearly a decade of production experience on television series like *Pit Boss* and *The Amazing Race*, Scott drew inspiration for his first feature film from a more personal place.

This is a unique take on the alternate dimension story seen through the perspective of a single family dealing with the fallout of a strange discovery in their home. How did this idea first come about?

Jason Thomas Scott: *My day job is producing documentary television series, but like many, I came out to Hollywood wanting to direct movies. As a fan of science fiction and genre pictures, I've always favored stories about regular people dealing with extraordinary things.… I think it grounds, and makes personal and relatable, what would otherwise seem silly.*

In 2010, I moved into a loft apartment in Studio City, and it had this crazy, Harry Potter-style closet under the stairs, and I joked it was large enough to hide another world in there. And so it hit me: What if it did?

The advice I'd heard for lower-budget fare was to try to limit your story to a maximum of three locations, so our apartment became one of them, not only for the odd closet space, but to also take advantage of a location I figured would be "free," and for its ease of use. Turns out it's a huge imposition to shoot a film in the privacy of your own personal living space!

This film has a distinct Spielberg sensibility, particularly *Poltergeist* with its family dynamics and otherworldly circumstances. Was this film an influence? Were there others? Why was it of interest to you to revisit this style of film, which has become popular in recent years with *Monster House, Super 8* and the Netflix series *Stranger Things*?

I've wanted to make pictures since I was two years old, after seeing Willy Wonka and the Chocolate Factory. *My parents brought me to Disney World, telling me they were taking me to Wonka's factory, and when I didn't see Gene Wilder or a river of chocolate, I was horribly disappointed. Between spoonfuls of oatmeal fed to me by Pinocchio and the White Rabbit at our Disney hotel, they explained that Wonka's factory didn't actually exist, and I felt this was a true injustice; the world deserved such a place! So I told them, "Then I will make it myself!" I wanted to put that sense of awe into the real world, and filmmaking allows for that.*

The films of Steven Spielberg have been a huge inspiration to me, again because they seemed grounded in a reality that I could identify with, but they also contained pure, unadulterated awe! Even though their plots are built of B-movie subject matter, the fact they portrayed regular suburban families dealing with these things made them seem all the more real. Close Encounters of the Third Kind, E.T. the Extra-Terrestrial *and yes,* Poltergeist *were all huge influences on* Tympanum.

I actually tried to shoot and cut the film to feel like a Spielberg movie from the 1980s. I shot on DSLRs not only to reduce cost, but for the grainier look. We could never afford a period piece, but I wanted it to look and move like those films. I got a lot of flak for it, actually, in that it moves at a slower pace; it's boring, it's too simple, it doesn't feel modern. But then Stranger Things *came out and I was like, "Oh my God, I was right, there are people out there who do feel like I do!" I'm bummed that people haven't discovered my film to the same extent, because it shares so many of the same elements. I fear people will think I stole from* Stranger Things, *right down to specific shots, characters, themes, costumes and ideas! But in reality, it was all things Spielbergian I was emulating, as were the Duffer Brothers, so there can't help but be similarities. They were able to pull it off far better than I could.... Their budget just for the Eggos probably exceeded that for my whole film!*

I was honored to actually finally meet Spielberg in person at the Producers Guild screening of his film Bridge of Spies, *where I was able to thank him personally for what his works have meant to me over my lifetime. He was truly kind; he put his arm around me and snapped a selfie with me that he took himself using my cell phone. It was an amazing moment for me personally; it felt like the culmination of so many things, especially because I belong to the same guild and met him not as a fan at a convention or something, but as another producer in the industry.*

The struggle of the family to stay together in the aftermath of this startling discovery in their home can be seen in some ways as an allegory of family issues in the wake of a tragedy like the death of a family member or divorce. Was this an intentional corollary?

Most definitely. Tympanum *was truly a personal journey for me. It exposes a lot of what was going on in my own head at the time.... I'm embarrassed to look at the tape of* it now, but at the Q&A for the first screening of the film, I explained to the audience that the movie is literally a metaphor for divorce; not only the one I personally suffered, which served as the catalyst for me pursuing my dreams in Hollywood, but also the divorces between my parents, and between my mother and stepfather.

In the film, Maron is a horrible father. Dave Tenenbaum did an admirable job portraying him, but his character's name is a play on the word "Moron." Maron chooses the water, just as Roy Neary [in Close Encounters of the Third Kind] chooses going aboard Sky Harbor. The child character of September is a direct reference to 9/11, which was the catalyst for my own first marriage. (It's amazing what thinking the world might be ending does to one's personal planning!) That is why in the film, Lilith references "the surprise of September" as the catalyst for her own marriage to Maron.

Again, I wanted to put normal, non-heroic people into a story where they had to confront something so unusual, they wouldn't know how to deal with it; drop them into a no-win scenario without the proper tools to cope, and watch them crawl their way out. In my opinion, the fact that their bond as a family is so tested helps make the inherent silliness of an Einstein-Rosen bridge in their home closet more digestible and interesting!

Why do you feel that audiences and filmmakers continue to come back to the idea of the alternate world-alternate dimension story throughout the years?

I think the best stories science fiction has to offer are the ones where real world problems are explored using the slightly foreign backdrop of science fiction as a chaser…. It just goes down easier. Just like Quentin Tarantino switching to black-and-white footage in Kill Bill, Volume 1 *to make his hyper-violence watchable, science fiction allows storytellers to tackle subjects that might otherwise be too complicated or taboo to discuss.*

Other than The Twilight Zone *or the 1960s* Star Trek, *one of my absolute favorite television series is the 2003 reboot of* Battlestar Galactica. *A 9/11 parable using robots and spaceships? Genius. We're watching what's left of humanity struggle with base questions of morality. You couldn't get away with their conversations on rape, torture, dirty politics or collateral damage as easily with a sitcom set in a bus station.*

I personally happen to believe in a concept known as Many Worlds Interpretation: There's an alternate universe where Gore had the votes in Florida, there's one where JFK lived, there's one where I've already won an Oscar, or even one where I've fallen off a cliff. Every action we take builds a whole new series of events, a new chain, a new branch of the tree, but the world I'm in now is the one I observed and am observing. So why not tell a story that illustrates that point?

People make choices in life and have to live with them, and our entire existence is a direct result of those personal choices. You don't actually have to go to work today, no one's forcing you; it's a choice. There are consequences, sure, and some restrictions based on circumstance, but what you do and what happens to you are really entirely up to you.

I think it's that self-awareness, and self-doubt about our choices, that drives us to ask, "What if?" And "What if?" is the start of any good story.

Other Films of Interest

The Nines (2007), *III: The Ritual* (2015)

6

The History of Alternate Histories

The subgenre of the alternate history film is unusual for science fiction, a genre so accustomed to always looking forward. Science fiction film is most frequently interested in what is new, what is coming, what might be around the corner, while the alternate history subgenre is predicated almost entirely on looking back.

What could possibly make us want to go back, to re-evaluate so intensely that it could create an entire subgenre? One of the single most defining events of the 20th century: World War II. The nightmare of the Nazi rise, as well as the efforts to stop their spread, became a uniting and defining element of global society for the last half of the 20th century. Jewish people, gypsies, gay people and many other minorities bore the brunt of their cruelty, and soldiers who arrived to liberate the concentration camps were forever scarred by the things they saw there.

Film is often a reflection of the feelings of the time, and World War II was no different. In the years after the war, films portraying the horror and heroism were plentiful. However, after two decades of films about the war, the message began to lose its power. That's where science fiction came in.

In 1965, directors Kevin Brownlow and Andrew Mollow made the film *It Happened Here*, which chronicled the fake rise of Hitler after the invasion of Great Britain. The film was starkly realistic, similar to another false history film of the same year, Peter Watkins' *The War Game*—a film terrifying not because it was so outlandish and fantastical, but because it was frighteningly possible.

The Boys from Brazil (1978) merged the alternate history narrative with a modern-day thriller about an escaped Nazi doctor cloning children from Hitler's DNA. The film played on the fears of a world that may have forgotten Hitler's atrocities, one that might not be prepared if it were to happen again.

The re-evaluation of World War II extended into the American wing as well, with 1980's *The Final Countdown* chronicling the accidental time travel of a modern aircraft carrier back to the day before the Pearl Harbor bombing. The film deals in the sticky ethical arena of time travel as well as alternate history, weighing the effects of preventing that single tragedy against the possibility of the U.S. never becoming involved in World War II.

The subgenre grew in popularity, from Gregory Peck and Laurence Olivier in *The Boys from Brazil* and Kirk Douglas and Martin Sheen in *The Final Countdown*, to Rutger Hauer and Miranda Richardson in *Fatherland* (1994).

World War II ended in 1945, but we continued fighting it in film for another 50-plus years.

After the Millennium

The new millennium saw more Hitler rehashes. The Nazis recruited Russian madman Rasputin to help conjure *Hellboy* from another dimension in 2004, and Quentin Tarantino used the flammability of film itself to destroy the Third Reich and let Eli Roth machine-gun Hitler to death in 2009's *Inglourious Basterds*. It was posited that Hitler actually worked with a crazed villain with a skull for a face in *Captain America: The First Avenger*.

Enterprising filmmakers found interesting alternate histories in various time periods. In 2000, writer-director Robert Dyke showed what the world might have looked like if John F. Kennedy hadn't been assassinated in *Timequest*. Before reinvigorating the DC Comics universe, Zack Snyder brought Alan Moore's dark *Watchmen* to screen, showing a different past Nixon administration and a super-powered Cold War with the Soviet Union. Gonzalo López-Gallego revealed a secret untold trip to the moon in *Apollo 18*, and another of Alan Moore's graphic novels brought classic literary figures to nineteenth-century life in *The League of Extraordinary Gentlemen*.

Comic books were dominant in their rewriting of history, with *X-Men: First Class* and *X-Men: Days of Future Past* taking on the decades of the '60s and '70s with the addition of mutant heroes and villains. The undead crept into political history with *Abraham Lincoln: Vampire Hunter*, and even animation company Pixar got into the game with *The Good Dinosaur*, imagining a world in which dinosaurs and humans co-exist because the meteor which killed dinosaurs barely missed hitting the Earth.

The Independent Perspective

The indie film arena saw an opportunity to use alternate histories to observe our own under a microscope, and it didn't always show a pretty picture. The films, by virtue of the concept itself, allowed for challenges to expectations and norms.

The Man from Earth supposed a world where Jesus was actually an immortal man with no ties to any God. In 2004, there was the one-two punch of *CSA: The Confederate States of America* and *The Old Negro Space Program*, mockumentaries that shined an unflattering spotlight on America's whitewashing of history and its still-unbalanced social systems. Andrew Currie's *Fido* put a zombie spin on the perfect sitcom family of the 1950s, and *Osombie* cheekily referenced the War on Terror by bringing a famous murdered terrorist back to undead life.

Featured Films

Frankenstein's Army (2013)
Director: Richard Raaphorst
Writers: Richard Raaphorst, Miguel Tejada-Flores, Chris W. Mitchell
Starring Robert Gwilym, Luke Newberry, Karel Roden

A group of Russian soldiers is on a reconnaissance mission during World War II when they get a distress call. The group, followed by propaganda filmmaker Dmitri, head

Russian soldiers deal with Propellerhead, a monstrosity created to help build up *Frankenstein's Army* **(2013).**

to the coordinates of the call, where they find a robotic zombie guarding an abandoned church. After venturing into catacombs under the church, they discover the call was a ruse to get the soldiers on a mission to kill the crazed Nazis who created the zombie abominations. The trail leads straight to a descendant of Victor Frankenstein, picking up where his ancestor left off.

    A unique perspective on both the World War II horror film and the found footage concept, *Frankenstein's Army* is a boldly original and weird vision. It deftly balances the gritty wartime imagery with the outlandish central premise, and the result is a fun, dark ride.

∼

Richard Raaphorst's first feature film as director was *Frankenstein's Army*, but his career in film is extensive and varied. A director of several short films, including *Zombi 1*, *Popo* and *The Rocketeer*, Raaphorst's experience was mostly in the art department, working on *Faust*, *Beyond Re-Animator* and *Black Book*. He described the humorous conversation that led to the creation of *Frankenstein's Army*.

Richard Raaphorst: *I was joking about it with my friend and producer Bart Oosterhoorn. We were talking about movies we really want to see, and the idea of a post-apocalyptic Nazi zombie film was what we wanted. At the time, nothing like that was being made.*

There are many movies that tell the story of secret alternate histories, and many of them have to do with Hitler and the Third Reich. Why do you think that is one of the pieces of history that people want to revisit so much?

Because the Third Reich represents pure evil. It is something we can all relate to because it looks so shiny and polished. Hugo Boss designed the costumes of the Nazis to be elegant and classy. The combination of that with the fascism makes it very disturbing and evil. We are programmed to think evil has to be ugly, but the Nazis transformed it into a slick appearance.

Why did you decide to choose the fake documentary style to tell this story?

I thought it was more original. I'm very much intrigued by documentary filmmakers, and I always wanted to make a fake doc. In Frankenstein's Army, *the subject of the documentary is violence as heroic deeds. Of course, the deeper layer is to get information. But in my movie, the person filming becomes the victim of his own subject. He becomes the target.*

Were there other films that influenced this film? I think of one film about a military cameraman during Vietnam, called *84 Charlie MoPic*, and I wonder if you were influenced by this film.

I was not aware of that film until we were writing. But it was a very interesting flick. I'm actually very much influenced by the European comic book artist Don Lawrence.

Are there parts of this film that came about as a result of the film you were trying to make before this, *Worst Case Scenario*, not being made?

Yes, everything. When I realized Worst Case Scenario *was never going to get off the ground, I switched all the ingredients 180 degrees. Americans became Russians. The future became the past. Slick motion tracks became hand-held, etc.*

The Russian Front is one of the less-seen settings in films about World War II. Is there a reason you chose to set this story here?

Yes, I'm fascinated by Russian history because of the Cold War situation. It always triggered my imagination and fear of nuclear holocaust. At the moment, that fear is coming back to me. [Authors' note: This interview took place in late 2016.]

The practical effects were fantastic and believable. Did you use them because they were less expensive, or because they worked better for the kind of film that you were trying to make?

I think practical works better, if you work with physical stuff. There is some CGI in it, but I hope no one will notice. I think there is 90 percent practical, and I hope to do the same thing in my next movie.

Iron Sky (2012)

Director: Timo Vuorensola
Writers: Jarmo Puskala, Michael Kalesniko, Timo Vuorensola
Starring Udo Kier, Julia Dietze, Peta Sergeant

Two American astronauts are sent to the moon in 2018 as a publicity stunt to support the re-election bid of the U.S. president. Upon arrival, the astronauts discover the Fourth Reich, a secret group of Nazis living on the dark side of the moon after their escape from Earth in 1945. The astronauts are captured; a Nazi discover that his one astronaut's iPhone could power an invasion better than their dated technology. After an exploratory visit to Earth, the moon Nazis declare all-out war, using zeppelins, flying saucers and weaponized asteroids to conquer the world.

A tongue-in-cheek response to the sharp rise in conspiracy theory obsession in a post–9/11 world, *Iron Sky* is as impressively created as it is strangely hilarious. Touching on controversial issues like race, global politics and the white nationalist rebranding of Nazi belief into a pseudo-religious following, the film uses its satiric punch to hit home some deeply disturbing truths about the survival of hate groups.

~

Director Timo Vuorensola was well-trained to be the man heading up the difficult and ambitious undertaking of *Iron Sky*. In 2005, he directed *Star Wreck: In the Pirkinning*, which satirized *Star Trek*, *Babylon* 5 and other sci-fi TV series. It showed Vuorensola's versatility and skill. Beyond his directing, writing and acting experience, Vuorensola is also one of the founders of the dark industrial band Älymystö.

Sanders (Ben Siemer), Vivian Wagner (Peta Sergeant), Renate Richter (Julia Dietze), Klaus Adler (Götz Otto) and the President of the United States (Stephanie Paul) wage war in *Iron Sky* (2012) (photograph by Mika Orasmaa, copyright Blind Spot Pictures).

Even with his varied experience, Vuorensola himself was unsure of the viability of the *Iron Sky* concept when he first heard it.

Timo Vuorensola: *It was originally an idea by Jarmo Puskala, our community manager. One day in a sauna after a long shooting day, he told us about it: Nazis on the moon. We thought it was a fine idea, but too crazy to be made into a film. Luckily, we eventually decided to go for it.*

Recent years have brought about a lot of films where a secret history of the world has been revealed, one that only certain people know about. Why do you think that the idea of secret histories or alternate histories are such a popular idea for science fiction films?

They offer an interesting mix of facts and fiction which we people like to tangle in our heads and make part of the story we consider the world around us has. Conspiracy theories, secret histories and such offer an interesting explanation and a set of interesting possibilities for the world, which in many cases actually is really quite boring. Sci-fi has always had its way of elevating realism and what better than a thing that's tied to realism, even though loosely.

Many of the alternate history stories often involve Hitler, Nazis and the Third Reich in some way: your film, *Frankenstein's Army*, *Man in the High Castle*, etc. Why do you think that the Nazis are still such a popular subject matter?

So much of Nazi achievements, especially in the field of warfare, technology and so forth, were lost at the end of the war, mainly because both Americans and Russians stole everything they got their hands on, and kept them hidden after that. The need for secrecy is always the breeding ground for imagination. Also, we are still suffering from the Nazi trauma, as humans, and are looking for explanations for it, however crazy they might seem.

This film also touches on some sensitive current topics, from race relations to the divisiveness of American politics. Do you find it easier to talk about controversial subjects by creating a film with a dark satirical comedy perspective, one that allows you to discuss serious things in a humorous way?

For me, science fiction has always been that: a tool to discuss our current world, a projection of our current world issues into a setting that allows us to look at them from outside the box, and re-project them back into our own world. Hopefully, we end up learning something from it.

Because of the clash of different eras, this film taps into the idea of advanced versions of classical technology, more popularly known as Steampunk (with flying saucers and zeppelins traveling side by side). Was this story idea chosen so you could use Steampunk style, or was it just a bonus of the concept that you ended up with a great visual concept to work with?

It was something that was born after the story idea was there. It's more actually Dieselpunk than Steampunk world, which is very precise time in history—World War II— so it came naturally to illustrate the film.

This is a film that in some ways could not have existed before the new millennium. Because of the digital technology used to record it, the visual effects and the ability to crowd-source funding to bring the film to life.

Absolutely. Starting with affordable visual effects, the film's visual look couldn't have been done in the '90s with the same quality without at least ten times bigger budget. Tech and programs have become so much cheaper since the turn of the millennium. And yes, without the Internet there wouldn't be this film in the first place. So yes, it's definitely a child of the new millennium.

Turbo Kid (2015)
Writer-Directors: François Simard, Anouk Whissell, Yoann-Karl Whissell
Starring Munro Chambers, Laurence Leboeuf, Michael Ironside

The imagined post-apocalyptic future of 1997 is a miserable wasteland. A young man known only as "The Kid" scavenges the landscape, searching for supplies, objects to sell and, most importantly, any memorabilia from his favorite comic book superhero, Turbo Rider. When he meets sweet but crazy Apple, he develops feelings for her. When Apple is kidnapped by Zeus, ruler of the wasteland, the Kid finds the remains of Turbo Rider's body. He takes on the armor and weaponry of his hero and heads out to battle Zeus and save the girl of his dreams.

Marrying the absurdly silly 1980s children's films *BMX Bandits* and *The Dirt Bike Kid* with dark post-apocalypse films like *Mad Max*, *Turbo Kid* is a fantastic primer for the subgenre and a nostalgic look at a dark future that was conceived of in a more innocent past. The sophistication of the film, along with the surprisingly graphic violence, makes it an interesting commentary on the changing perspectives on children's films and action filmmaking in general. Fantastic locations and set design hint at a much larger world than the story we see on-screen, and a sequel is already on its way.

∼

The Kid (Munro Chambers) and Apple (Laurence Leboeuf) find friendship and possibly more in *Turbo Kid* (2015).

Co-writer-co-director Anouk Whissell already had a deep love for the aesthetic of the 1980s before she brought *Turbo Kid* to the screen. Writing and directing several short films such as *Demonitron: The Sixth Dimension* and *Ninja Eliminator 4: The French Connection*, Whissell eventually brought the concept of *Turbo Kid* to life in the short film *T Is for Turbo*. She continued the narrative into the feature, then followed up with another short film in the series, *No Tomorrow: A Turbo Kid Tale*. The various permutations of the story show, as Whissell notes, the flexible nature of its inception.

Anouk Whissell: *It really started from a concept: "Mad Max on BMX" (which could also be read as* Mad Max *meets* BMX Bandits*), and also from our love of Italian post-apocalyptic films and the movies that rocked our childhood.*

Watching *Turbo Kid*, aside from the obvious inspirations of *Mad Max* and *BMX Bandits*, I also thought of films like *Six-String Samurai*. Were there other films that were inspirations?

Mad Max *and* BMX Bandits *were definitely inspirations, but also all the Italian* Mad Max *rip-offs, such as* The Last Barbarians *(everybody needs to see this!) and more films from our childhood, such as* The Goonies, The Neverending Story, The Dog That Stopped the War *and so on.*

There's an interesting thread in this film about the main character's fandom of a comic book character from before the fall. Is this in some way a commentary on the new millennium's growing and expanding fan arena? Comics and sci-fi have become mainstream in a way it wasn't previously; is that reflected here in the film intentionally?

The three of us are comic book geeks, and though you're right about the movement becoming mainstream, it has always been popular around us. The commentary was mostly pointing at the use of comic books, superheroes and even animated series that were created and/or used as army propaganda. In the particular case of Turbo Rider, *which we imagined for the movie, this superhero was created for a recruitment campaign directly aimed at the youth. And because the Kid lost his parents, his only true way of learning was through these comic books he found. Of course, we kept the message subtle, and it's only part of the universe backstory.*

This film has the framework of a classic '80s, '90s kids' film, but the subject matter is considerably darker than the material of the day. Was that intended to reflect the more complex kids' films of the '80s, like *Explorers* and *Night of the Creeps*? Films which were intended for younger audiences but dealt with more mature themes than children's films do now?

Definitely. We always say that Turbo Kid *is a kids' movie that's not for kids. The three of us grew up in the '80s, and we remember that movies of this era, even when they were targeted at kids, often treated and showed more mature content, as opposed to now. And that was great; it was definitely the best time for movies. Also, we remember seeing classic horror and sci-fi films way too young! It left some marks (good ones we'd say—ha ha) and so we wanted to play with this contrast of the friendship story, full of heart and the darkness and violence of the universe they evolve in.*

Were there specific social or political elements of our current world that played into the story, setting or characters you decided to create for *Turbo Kid*? How did the events of the new millennium play into the creation of this film?

We think it's almost impossible not to be inspired or influenced in some way, from the current political or environmental issues. So yes, we do have a critique of the corporate power, and climate change. Which were also major concerns in the '80s and '90s and were often depicted in their vision of a dystopian future. It's frightening to witness that it's becoming reality.

This film travels back into a nostalgic past, but then extrapolates that nostalgic past into a dark false future we never saw. What do you think is the general appeal of the alternate history sci-fi film?

We decided to set our future in the '90s, following the codes and aesthetics of the sci-fi post-apocalyptic cinematography established in the '80s. It really is to be consistent with our desire to stay true to our concept. It's always strange, in a good way, to watch back a cult movie and to see that their visions of the '90s were a dystopian future where people are dressed in sports gear and studs.

Other Films of Interest

Radio Free Albemuth (2010), *2009: Lost Memories* (2002)

7

New Inventions and Technologies

Science fiction is excellent at imparting a sense of wonder. Much of what draws us to science fiction is the idea of a peek behind the curtain, as if we're auto enthusiasts waiting outside the car show for a glimpse at what is coming next year.

Science fiction is the building block that takes our imagination from concerns about today to possibilities for tomorrow. If we allow for our science fiction to be tinged with just a little bit of horror, we can peek all the way back to the early 1930s, when James Whale introduced us to pioneering scientists with amazing new technologies in *Frankenstein* and *The Invisible Man*. Distanced from the films of their supernatural friends Dracula, the Mummy and the Wolf Man, these two films were about driven inventors shattering the boundaries of previous human expectation.

In the early studio years of Hollywood, science fiction-tinged films about new inventions and technologies held that sense of wide-eyed wonder. The 1950s showed us stain-proof clothing in *The Man in the White Suit* and a fantastical underwater vessel in *20,000 Leagues Under the Sea*. In the '60s, we learned a bit about the inner workings of the human body by miniaturizing and traveling inside it in *Fantastic Voyage*.

It was in the 1970s that a healthy mistrust of the government and technology found a voice in the work of Michael Crichton. The original *Westworld* film (before it was remade into an HBO TV series) and the lesser-known *The Terminal Man* expressed humanity's fear of rapidly advancing technology. The popularity of Crichton's technology-gone-wrong ethos continued into the 1980s with *Looker* (a commentary on plastic surgery and deceptive advertising tricks) and *Runaway* (about a near-future world in which we entrust most of our lives to robots).

The 1980s also began to tackle the fear of technology encroaching on our minds and bodies, seen best in David Cronenberg's *Videodrome* and Douglas Trumbull's *Brainstorm*. In some cases, like 1982's *TRON*, technology was no longer happy being subservient; it wanted to run things.

The early 1990s was a mix of terrifying views of a near future, as in Kathryn Bigelow's *Strange Days*, and adventurous romps from the past, like Joe Johnston's *The Rocketeer*. But in the late 1990s, we began to feel the angst of the coming millennium, with apocalyptic visions of a secret mathematical code that will bring about Armageddon in *Pi* and an elaborate machine in which seven people must work together to survive in *Cube*.

After the Millennium

Y2K came and went; no satellites fell from the sky, no computers blew up from confusion about the rollover from one century to the next. Society took a deep breath, and filmmakers were allowed to go back to having just a little bit of fun with new technologies.

It is no coincidence that the real technologies of computer generated imagery in film came along as part of the package. Ideas that were barely imaginable could now be put on the screen with something approaching photorealism. Now, audiences could fully believe that a rich man could construct a robotic suit and become a hero in 2008's *Iron Man*. The fantastical realms of dreaming were within the reach of some technologically savvy criminals in 2010's *Inception*. Even the hazardous dissolving landscapes of a slowly fading memory became achievable in 2004's sci-fi romance *Eternal Sunshine of the Spotless Mind*.

The Independent Perspective

Independent filmmakers wasted no time using the New Inventions and Technologies subgenre to discuss real-life concerns society was already facing. The increasing globalization of the world due to technology illuminated already existing cultural imbalances, and films like Alex Rivera's *Sleep Dealer* and Jennifer Phang's *Advantageous* showed the effects of that system.

The ethical ramifications of technology on human morality have always been a topic of concern for scientists and professors, but some indie films brought that conversation to film. *The Phoenix Project* and *Listening* explored what scientists will do to successfully complete a breakthrough, while *Life Tracker* and *Jackrabbit* dug deeper into the troubling questions of genetic manipulation and technological dependency for which mainstream audiences only scratched the surface.

They broke the laws of nature in David Gelb's *The Lazarus Effect* and imagined a virtual world that lives in tandem with our own with Benjamin Dickinson's *Creative Control*. The Featured Films in this section touch on the hubris of inventors who reach beyond their grasp and bring back something horrifying, mathematicians who have to deal with the ethical aftermath of an explosive discovery, and the questionable nature of a seemingly positive matchmaking company.

Featured Films

Shadows on the Wall (2015)
Writer-Director: Ben Carland
Starring Chris M. Kauffmann, Tim Fox, Nicole Lee Durant

College student Palmer is working on a new project with roommate and cousin Chase. Palmer's tutor in mathematics is Alice; the three of them become close, and Palmer confides in them about his penchant for inventing weird machines. His most recent, it seems, has some potential, and he needs their help. They end up constructing a device

7. New Inventions and Technologies 77

Chase (Tim Fox), Palmer (Chris Kauffmann) and Alice (Nicole Lee Durant) prepare to test their new invention in Shadows on the Wall **(2015).**

that can see into distances beyond the known galaxy. It works well, but unfortunately for them and perhaps the rest of the world, something else might be looking back.

A simple concept and a small cast give *Shadows on the Wall* the look of an unambitious film designed to be a stepping stone in a filmmaker's career. But it is anything but unambitious. Finding a way to shrink an enormous thematic concept into a chamber piece with only a few speaking roles, the film operates on numerous levels. A taut thriller, it also comments on the danger of unchecked scientific exploration with no oversight.

∼

Ben Carland's directing work in *Shadows on the Wall* exuded a confidence despite the film's limited budget, and that came from previous experience working in the arena. With a career bookended by the fantastic science fiction short films *The Forgotten Future* and *Possession*, Carland's feature-film career began with the high-concept film *Sol*. Carland described the process by which all of his ideas come to fruition.

Ben Carland: *Most of the stories to my scripts come about from me asking a question myself, and the story is an exploration of an answer to that. For the story of* Shadows, *it came about because I was interested in what would happen if someone wholly unprepared to make contact—or even trying to make contact—succeeded in it. In most instances of sci-fi, it's great scientists or explorers or combat veterans or something that always make contact. There are several exceptions to that norm but more often than not, it's people that are prepared or are seeking something huge to happen, who make alien contact. I wanted to see what would happen if we took someone who was not any kind of role model or great figure—someone who could barely even handle everyday life—and thrust him to the center of this great situation and see what happens. On top of that, I love stories about things that are going on right under our noses. Alien contact always jumps out to me as one of the greatest "what if?" scenarios, and I thought it would be fun to make that come together in an unassuming, rundown warehouse that most people wouldn't even bother to notice. It's* *no starship, it's no high-powered government lab, it's just a small, forgotten warehouse where this great event is taking place without anyone even being aware of it.*

In some ways, this film is a throwback to the mad scientist tales of the 1950s. Was that intentional, and were there films of that era that influenced the writing and shooting of this one?

I love old sci-fi. There was no particular film that really influenced Shadows, *but I've always been drawn to the idea of someone just messing around in their "laboratory" and before they know it, some great discovery or terrifying experiment comes about that either changes the world or ruins the mad scientist's life (or both). Small-scale stories with larger-than-life consequences. I think that's just a blank canvas for fun, especially when you're working on a small indie budget.*

There is an element of "science caution" in this film, the idea that inventing for the sake of inventing can have terrible outcomes. Is this an allegorical reference to anything that might be going on in the scientific community in recent years, from artificial intelligence to cloning?

I wouldn't say that it's meant as commentary to any specific topic in modern science. There are a lot of awesome things going on in the scientific community and I'm excited to see where they go. But I think with Shadows, *it's fun as a storyteller to explore the notion that you can never really know where a road will lead until it's too late to undo it. Plus, I think it makes it more frightening if a character that opens Pandora's Box wasn't even trying to. It's one thing if a character is seeking out danger or adventure and finds it, but I think it's more unnerving if someone who had only the smallest, most innocent intentions unleashes something big because that could potentially happen to anyone.*

This movie is part of a recent trend in science fiction, with very contained stories about a small handful of people changing the world in a huge way. From *Primer* to *The Phoenix Project*, these films have been exploring the world-changing events, but also the intimate human interactions. What do you think is so appealing to audiences about these kinds of stories?

I think that answer is twofold. I think we're seeing these kinds of films because filmmakers are wanting to tell "big" or world-changing event stories through the means that are within their grasps. These are often very, very small films we're seeing, and that constraint is making people be very inventive in how they depict these huge, larger-than-life events. The best way to do that effectively on a small budget is through the eyes of a very small group that we get to know very well or care a lot about. Then with the "big" plot, we only need to see the tip of the iceberg because it's really being told through how it impacts that small group of characters we've come to know. I think audiences are enjoying these types of films because (A) a lot of the time they're done in ways that are inventive and fun to watch unfold, and (B) they're just not getting that substance from most of the large films you see in theaters these days. When I think of the blockbusters that I've seen in the last year or two, I can barely remember anything about them. When I think of the indies that have climbed to the top, I can remember every little nuance of them. I often liken modern blockbusters to eating cake for dinner. Two hours of delicious sugar. What kid wouldn't want that? But you don't really get much out of it and you're hungry again before you know it. These little sci-fi films can be more inventive and tell more personal human stories than large blockbusters because a lot of the time, the personal elements of modern blockbusters get lost in the noise of the rest of the film.

There is a lot of "lingo" in this film, spoken by characters educated in the fields of electronics and mathematics, and that gives it an authentic feel. Did you have to do much research to execute these sequences, and how much of the science you discuss in the film is based on actual scientific knowledge or theories?

Thank you, I'm glad it feels authentic! I tried to be as accurate as I could with the writing of the film. The space and cosmos elements were largely of my own research because I'm a huge space nerd and love following that type of stuff. With the math and electronic elements, luckily one of my very good friends is an electronic engineer. So I made my first stab at those while writing, then sent the script to him to review. We sat down and fact-checked it and made any adjustments as needed. I can still hear myself back in high school asking "When will I ever need to use this?!" during math class. I'm sure this isn't what they had in mind but still goes to show that you never really know...

Aside from the obvious science fiction elements, this film falls into another subgenre, that of the new technology subgenre. These films generally revolve around the impact of a new invention or technology, as well as the effect it has on the inventors. This subgenre has been growing rapidly in recent years. Why do you think that this kind of film has started to attract viewers and filmmakers so much?

This answer plays back to your earlier question about cautionary tales. It's a tremendously exciting time to watch everything that's going on in modern science. With so many new discoveries and possibilities being unlocked, I think it encourages filmmakers to come up with their own "what if?" stories. We try to imagine the far-reaching consequences of what a new discovery or invention may lead to in the real world. That can be both daunting and scary in certain cases, so it's fun to explore similar ideas under larger-than-life (and thankfully more fictional) circumstances in film.

Travelling Salesman (2012)
Director: Timothy Lanzone
Writers: Andy Lanzone, Timothy Lanzone
Starring Danny Barclay, Eric Bloom, David John Cole

Four mathematicians are sitting in a conference room, getting ready to meet with a representative of the U.S. Department of Defense. The four were asked by the government to try and crack a complex mathematical stumper known as the Travelling Salesman problem. The team members believe they have solved it. However, when the government offers them a huge sum of money for part of the algorithm they created, one of the scientists balks at the staggering ramifications the solution could have on the world when in the possession of a single world government.

A smart thriller that finds its suspense in intelligent conversations and ethical quandaries rather than explosions and artificial plot devices, *Travelling Salesman* is a rare science fiction film that dives deeply into mathematical theory and doesn't slow down or dumb down in the assumption that the audience can't keep up. Themes of governmental influence on scientific research and the weaponization of knowledge was prescient when it was released, and in the wake of massive social shifts due to hacking of governments and individuals, the movie is all the more realistic and terrifying now.

Unnamed scientists and mathematicians (Tyler Seiple, Eric Bloom, Matt Lagan, Danny Barclay, Marc Raymond) discuss the ramifications of their discovery in *Travelling Salesman* **(2012).**

Timothy Lanzone began his career with the comedy-drama *Road to Pecumsecah*, about a young filmmaker seeking his big break. He did a lot of commercials and short form work for NBC, but found himself drawn back to the world of feature filmmaking.

Timothy Lanzone: *When I graduated from film school, I putzed around and made some short films. Some became longer form pieces, but neither unlocked the golden door to making multimillion dollar films. I knew I needed to do an intermediate film to get into festivals and have a larger showpiece picture to build my career. That was kind of the genesis; the question became how to start doing that.*

I knew I wanted it to be contained. I needed it small to get the budget that we wanted. It couldn't be a large picture because I was working full-time as a producer for NBC; I couldn't take months off to go shoot something big. I didn't necessarily want to go down that route of trying to figure out how to finance a half a million dollars, so we just kept this very, very small and tried to execute this over 10 or 15 days.

I effectively put myself in a box from a conceptual standpoint. I couldn't have special effects, I couldn't have multiple locations, we couldn't be traveling. It had to be very self-contained. I remember at film school, one of the big tenets is that the hardest thing to shoot is a dinner table conversation for a variety of reasons: the geography of the table, the eye lines, getting that emotional zeal out of the characters, and all just sitting flatly in this weird self-contained table. I always thought this was interesting and [a] challenge. One of the great one-on-one moments in cinema is the Pacino-De Niro scene in Heat *which is 20 minutes of two people just looking at each other across the table, but it's just riveting. That is the ultimate rare example of these two great actors at this apex moment of their careers just going one on one, but literally nothing else happening other than them looking at each other and just talking.*

12 Angry Men *is one of my favorite movies. I started thinking how to tell this very dramatic story but contain it. I wanted to challenge myself to keep it around a table like* 12 Angry Men. *But how do I tell a dramatic narrative given that context? The films I had done before were a little more whimsical, a little more playful, so I just gravitated toward more dramatic at the time, with a more science fiction bent. I thought, "Let's tell the story of five or six guys around this table that have discovered something amazing"; what could that be? When we figured out how we could do this, we figured out a budget number. That's when I sat down and started to write the script. Most films at this level—the kind of the concept of containing this world in effectively one room—started literally out of necessity budget and ability to execute a film, so hopefully I can make more.*

Why did you decide to take on such complicated and possibly hard-to-understand computer science concepts like P vs. NP and the Travelling Salesman problem?

When I initially wrote the script, it was more mystical. It was about factoring the prime number. It was this idea of "What if these guys unlocked this mystical thing while factoring the prime number [that] could lead to the keys of the world." It was a little less fact-based, even though it was all grounded in the mathematical principles of factoring the prime. We had a few more characters in the room that add a little more.

I sent the script to my brother, who's a computer science electrical engineer. He works at Google now, and he just graduated from Michigan's computer science program for his Masters. He'd just been studying all sorts of crazy tenets and principles, and P vs. NP was a relatively new concept at the time even though the idea of it stems 50 years in the past. He said, "Tim, this is exactly what you're trying to get across. This plot of these scientists, these mathematicians who work together to solve this problem which leads to a lot of power could be more fact-based and less mystical." That's where P vs. NP came in. We went back and retooled the script. Interestingly, we only changed 20 percent of it to fit the P vs. NP narrative. I don't know if it was luck or coincidence, but the idea of factoring the prime and what it allowed them to do really played nicely with the P vs. NP story. The Travelling Salesman problem is a subset of P vs. NP, and there's a lot of problems in that subset. We looked at all the names and there's tons of them. Travelling Salesman was one of the most popular, and one of the most notable. We found that strange but perfectly connected name to call the picture; it just seemed to fit right for us.

One aspect of sci-fi writing that is rarely covered is the complexity of research in the field of the narrative's subject. How much of the subject matter of the film did you already know about, and how much did you have to research?

I'd never heard of P vs. NP until my brother told me about it. In terms of initial research on the prime number and factoring, it was a lot. Once I got the narrative arc in my head, I made the story outline, and then I went in and bolstered that narrative arc with as much fact and research that I could do online whether it was reading around Wikipedia or trade papers, or talking to my brother and other people in this world.

We walked a tightrope with Travelling Salesman. *You don't want to be so into the math and data that a regular person wouldn't understand the narrative or the dramatic story arc. They'd be totally baffled and bored. You have to get a baseline understanding, but then distill it and make it interesting to a broader base of people, a larger audience. You want to have a good knowledge base as a writer, but you also don't want to get too geeked out and esoteric and confusing to your audience.*

Once I developed these five characters, I was inside their heads and how they behaved and reacted, which I think was important to understand them. As I was writing their dialogue, it did take me in different directions, and I'd have to research that to make sure things made sense and it was clear. Often that would be very unexpected. A lot of it was a big journey in the script development progress with all this information that I had to distill and make clear to access a large audience.

Much of the running time of the film is devoted to discussion of the ethical consequences of the discovery. Though the breakthrough in the film hasn't been made in real life, this is a genuine concern with any scientific discovery, isn't it? Particularly with today's advanced technologies?

I grew up fascinated with the Manhattan Project. The idea that some of the smartest people in the world put their brains together and did something almost unfathomably crazy in the creation of the nuclear bomb always struck me as interesting. Oppenheimer is often quoted as saying the "Now I am become Death, the destroyer of worlds" line, which resonated with me as well. They did that for years, and at the end, they realize, "Oh crap, we have this thing. Now what?" We created this thing, this horrible device we all live in constant fear of, and it really shaped an era of American history. It seemed to be more an ethical question of "just because you can do something, should you?" That heads into things like the genome, and stem cells and cloning, and all sorts of other avenues.

Sometimes I wonder if that's the only way something great can be done, if you put your head down and blinders on. You focus on this end goal with almost this intense obsession and you worry about the results once you execute it, and that's what these guys did. Then the larger ethical question comes as to who owns those ethical judgments. Is it the people in the scientific community who did this, the ones who know about the power and the ramifications and the nuance of this discovery? Or is it people who have a broader base of people that they consult, whether it's politicians or philosophers or influencers? Who should be the one to determine how this should be used, what it should be used for, or what the ethical realities of it are?

If you create something super-powerful and suddenly it's taken out of your hands, you go, "Whoa! I didn't want it to be used for this." That becomes an interesting debate. I think anything that is super-powerful, like anything on a scale of this magnitude, it's never going to be controlled by the people who invented it. It's always going to be taken out of their hands on some level by people who are going to use it, hopefully for good. That's one of the main dramatic elements of this movie is these guys learning they did this and now they're going to lose it. Do the people who are using it know exactly what it can do and is that okay? That notion stemmed from my historical interest in this crazy idea of the Manhattan Project and these intensely dedicated, obsessive scientists and physicists coming together to do something extraordinary that changed mankind.

This film is part of a recent movement of sci-fi films in which a single group of people in a small office or room make world-changing discoveries or breakthroughs. I'm thinking of *Primer, Listening, The Phoenix Project* and your film. What do you think the appeal is about the low-budget, high-concept sci-fi drama, and what drew you to it?

Primer *is definitely an influence on the film. I think a lot of the influence was just the scale. Obviously, we didn't pull too much from the plot or anything. When you have a small budget and you want to tell a science fiction story or a big idea story, you've got to be creative and you can't have huge armies of people at NASA headquarters developing things.*

I think what it all boils down to is the human brain is like this limitless potential that you can sell in a script. Geniuses do exist. We've seen them, we've read about them. They're romanticized. They are Einstein, they are Henry Ford. They are people we all recognize, they are people we know and we know what they've done. People will believe the idea that the human brain can create these unimaginable realities, so you can just put these really smart people to work, and what they create can have these massive consequences.

A lot of it, frankly, is what I was saying earlier about budget and price. It's out of necessity. When you can't do something huge, but we have this semi-perfect machine in our heads that can come up with these great ideas, why don't we base a science fiction film around that? "What if they came up with this idea, and what are the realities of it?"

Primer is similar; they came up with this idea and they faced ethical consequences. It then becomes whether we do it well and the idea is interesting enough. Part of *Primer's* magic was the garage invention idea, which we've all heard of from Hewlett Packard and Apple and a lot of these places. These groups of smart people get together in literally the humblest of places like a garage or, in our case, a conference room, and they create something big. It's a cheap but still very powerful story idea.

There's enough people out there who like to watch movies and to think and to be challenged. There certainly is a market for that. You're not going to get rich off that market, but there is a market for people like that. I have a lot of friends who are very interested in cinema, and they search on Amazon and IndieFlix and places like that to find unique films or science fiction-based films that are going to push them a little bit. There's a sense of every science fiction film being some level of escapism. It's a slightly different reality we are bringing you into. Any time you can do that for at least a certain segment of the people, they appreciate it and seek it out.

This film also falls nicely into another great indie sci-fi tradition of recent years: the mathematical puzzle film. Movies like *Fermat's Room* and *Cube* explore the solving of complex mathematical equations as a central aspect of their narrative. Do you feel that this has been lacking in film until recently? That films don't want audiences to think or be challenged, and films like yours are a hard sell to audiences seeking only a fun diversion.

We just haven't had the digital technology to produce almost any type of niche film. It's a relatively recent reality, and the distributor of our film was a niche distributor. They did a lot of LGBT films, most of them from Sundance and larger film festivals, but they would find a niche like weird rom-coms that weren't mainstream, things that weren't at the top of the Sundance slates, horror films. Ours fit in with that, a crazy small math film about a crazy big idea, but we have the ability now to tell these stories that just didn't exist 20 years ago.

With the Internet, we also have the audience accessibility. I mean, we found all our ideas on the Internet. Ten, 20 years ago, pre-social media days, we would never have found this audience. This film would have never made a cent. So, I think financiers and distributors are learning there are a lot of niche audiences.

Regarding the film being challenging, I don't know of a film that doesn't want the audience to be challenged. We knew making Travelling Salesman that we were never going to get the casual 16-year-old popcorn popper going to the AMC Cinema on a Friday night. We thought we had the ability like Pi and Primer, *the ones that went on to wider theatrical releases. I'd rather be known as someone who writes films that challenge people, that are smart, that talk about a big idea and bring you along for an unexpected ride.*

This film lives right on the border of real science, barely stepping over into the realm of fiction. Is that what interests you about science fiction? Its proximity to (and possibility of becoming) real life?

My favorite part about science fiction is the limitlessness of it. The idea that you can create your own rules. As the creator, you bring your own construct, then you tell your story within it. In a film like Inception, *Christopher Nolan created a set of rules in a world and then the question becomes, "Can you tell a good story with good characters in the world you created?"*

I don't want to sit down to an intense family drama. That doesn't help me escape from anywhere. It doesn't take my imagination to new heights. The other scripts I've written have often been science fiction-based. I just like that idea of being able to build a world. If you just tweak one thing: What if these people could see a murder before it happens? You just tweak one small thing and everything else is the same. It's all you need to create this fascinating world and fascinating story. Children of Men *is a good example, a simple but fundamental change to our day-to-day experience and what that means to humanity at large.*

The Perfect 46 (2014)
Writer-Director: Brett Ryan Bonowicz
Starring Whit Hertfod, Don McManus, James Kyson

CEO Jesse Darden founded a genetic screening company called The Perfect 46. The premise was simple: A couple considering having children can send their genetic samples to Darden's company, and they will use a proprietary technology to tell the couple what the likelihood is that their children will have any genetic defects. As groups boycott the company and accuse it of eugenics, Darden's world starts to crumble around him when his marriage falls apart and the algorithm upon which the technology is based turns out to have troubling bugs in it.

A complex story that presupposes a concern that may be just around the real-life corner, *The Perfect 46* is as interesting and challenging as it is sobering in its implications. It works in multiple thematic narratives, exploring both the social ramifications of the technology on the future of child-rearing and the personal, political and financial decisions that cause corporate figures to make the decisions they do.

∼

Steve (Don McManus) and Leslie (Robyn Cohen) try to talk sense into CEO Jesse Darden (Whit Hertford) in *The Perfect 46* (2014).

Brett Ryan Bonowicz had a long journey to the creation of *The Perfect 46*. With a career that started primarily in documentaries like *Signs and Voices* and *Pressing the Public Opinion*, he moved into feature filmmaking with the dramas, *The Comedian at The Friday* and *Waterhole Cove*. After that, he was drawn to the idea of producing films that touched on real scientific principles and concerns. His first was *The Perfect 46*, and he followed it up with a doc called *Closer Than We Think*. Bonowicz talked about how his motivation for the film was in part the desire to create a compelling dialectic.

Brett Ryan Bonowicz: *I wanted to make a chamber drama, something where two people were debating an issue that had no right or wrong answer. That intrigued me a lot. I think I had just seen Steve McQueen's film* Hunger *[2008]. So I had two characters talking and they needed to be debating about something. The character of Jesse was established at that time as more of a stereotypical "mad scientist" but I didn't know what he had done. I was working with a collaborator at the time and we had talked about having him doing experiments with plants. This was later dropped as the human genetics angle came to me.*

I had an interest in genetics, and a few years prior to the writing, I had done the 23andme.com genome test. That got me thinking about the future of that industry and the idea of The Perfect 46 *came from that thinking. I knew I wanted the film to lean science fiction, and I knew I'd be working on a limited budget, so car chases and spaceships were out of my reach. But looking at genetics, a lot of what I wanted to explore revolved around ideas and not traditional action set pieces.*

I'd met Whit Hertford a few years prior for a different project. That didn't end up working out, but in my meeting with him, I saw this side of him where I just started realizing the character I was writing was him, or my impression of him. So we started meeting every month or so as I was writing and we'd talk about the character and eat sushi, and it was a good way for me to bounce ideas as they were coming to me.

The writing of the film would continue until I'd reach a science stumbling block. I'd read a book or two and then get back at it, and that's how a lot of the film was shaped. It was more organic than it probably appears in the finished product.

This film is part of a very recent trend in film with the examination of the bioethical ramifications of the rapid advancements in technology. Was part of your hope in making this film to open up the discussion of what technology can be used for, why it is used and how it affects us?

My largest ambition with The Perfect 46 *was to create a dialogue with the audience. The goal was to create a film with no right, no wrong, just the biggest gray area imaginable.*

I've had a large variety of reactions to the film and I love hearing people's perspectives on it. Everyone can grab onto a line or a character and use those things as their throughline.

While watching this film, I was reminded of the goal of many pharmaceutical and medical companies, which is to get customers to use their product, regardless of the ultimate helpfulness of the product. Were aspects of the real-world for-profit medical industry on your mind when creating the company in the film?

I was thinking a lot about rock star tech CEOs while I was writing. Looking at how personality can be tied to company and how dangerous that can be when things go wrong. I think at the time I was proposing the idea of "What if the iPhone 4 Antennagate had been people?" You can't solve that with a free bumper case and that kept me asking more and more ethical questions during the writing phase of the film.

I think that we continue to see how Silicon Valley thinking bleeds into all aspects of the real world. Driverless cars are an example that comes to mind immediately. There's a huge ethical debate over how the AI will decide who dies in an accident, the driver or a group of pedestrians.

During production, we decided to make Jesse's car driverless and if you look in the film he's in the backseat, and no driver is ever shown. I think it added to our "subtle future" production design and also exists as a comment on the ethical debates that exist in almost every aspect of technological innovation.

This is a film whose reviews come from just as many scientific magazines as entertainment ones. Was it your intent to try and bridge the gap between those two communities, to create a film that educates and cautions equally with entertaining?

We needed something that would set the film apart from other science fiction. We knew that with the emphasis on science in our film, we weren't going to be able to market ourselves in a general way towards other science fiction films.

Our first screening was at the Consumer Genetics Conference in Boston. We got our first press from that screening and I think it gave us an opportunity to… Not exactly bridge the gap, but to give us an opportunity to find the very particular audience for the film. That screening allowed us to move forward with the science front and center in the marketing of the film, and we didn't have to rely on any bait-and-switch type marketing with a monster baby movie or something that doesn't properly represent the film.

Why did you choose to have portions of the film in documentary style? Was this a budgetary consideration, or did you do it to lend even more realism and credence to the conversation being had in the film?

A lot of the thoughts on using the documentary style stemmed from not wanting to give the chamber drama actors an unnecessary amount of exposition.

The film spun out from having one story with the chamber drama, to having two stories with the documentary. At a certain point in the writing, I toyed with the idea of a third timeline where we could see more of Jesse's personal interactions with people around him and eventually that worked its way into the film as well.

The way that I wrote this film is not something I would ever recommend to anyone. I would end up writing a scene, and if there were scientific elements to the scene I might stop writing for a few days as I read up on what was required to complete it.

As a filmmaker, I always feel like transitions are the most important things. So I would always look for the connective tissue, what was a good break in the dialogue or the perfect visual to connect one piece to the next.

I would often describe the film as a tapestry. As a viewer, one should feel they're looking at one large story, made of smaller pieces of fabric, and if I was able to weave them correctly, it would create a sense of world-building that simply wouldn't exist without the doc story and the non-linear timeline. I always feel it's more interesting to see A to G and then skip back to C. As a viewer, you get to fill in those blanks and have a richer experience.

Many sci-fi films used to tell stories about fantastical futures generations down the line, and imagine what the future might bring. Do you feel your film is part of the ushering-in of a new sci-fi era in which the conversations are less fantastical and more pragmatic, and the events are closer and closer to the reality of now?

I think audiences want something relatable. I think the feelings and discussions that come from something like The Perfect 46 *resonate specifically because they're pertinent to people's lives. These are real questions we're beginning to look at scientifically in our society and that to me is infinitely more interesting than seeing something that I find unrelatable or something that I know is unrealistic. I can connect to that directly and there doesn't necessarily have to be a metaphor as a conduit or be a parable to find a connection with the story and the audience. I think pragmatism can still have interesting world-building and I think we're seeing that in a lot of the new science fiction.*

Other Films of Interest

Zero Theorem (2013), *Cypher* (2002), *Extracted* (2012), *The Cell* (2000), *LFO* (2013), *Listen* (2013), *Love & Teleportation* (2013), *Memory Lane* (2012), *The Infinite Man* (2014)

8

Journeys Through an Endless Cosmos

The subgenre of science fiction films involving space travel is an interesting one because the subgenre began before we had the ability to do it. As mentioned in the opening, *A Trip to the Moon* came out in 1902, and while it was far from accurate scientifically, it showed humanity's interest in exploring the floating rock orbiting closest to us. However, unlike most science fiction films which posit a world or technology which we have little to no hope of seeing become reality, we achieved this.

It is no coincidence that a number of films about space exploration came out in rapid succession beginning in the mid–1950s: In August 1955, the United States and the Soviet Union both expressed their intention of putting a satellite into orbit. Two months earlier, *This Island Earth* was released theatrically. *Forbidden Planet* followed in 1956.

Hollywood even took a stance on who might make it to the moon first. In 1964, the aptly titled *First Men in the Moon* followed a modern space crew who arrived on the moon only to discover that a Victorian era man completed the journey over six decades earlier.

The closer to reaching the moon we got, the more realistic film portrayals became. The realism on display in 1967's *Countdown* was an early window into director Robert Altman's naturalistic style, and Stanley Kubrick changed the face of filmmaking forever with the quiet beauty and scientific accuracy of *2001: A Space Odyssey*.

Then, the day came when traveling to the moon was no longer fantasy. On July 16, 1969, Neil Armstrong set foot on the surface of the moon. Science fiction aficionados no longer had to wait and wonder; the future was here.

Of course, the accomplishment spawned fictions of its own. Months after the successful landing, November 1969 saw the release of *Marooned*, a tale of three astronauts stranded and suffocating slowly.

Feelings about space travel shifted quickly, and outer space went from being uninhabitable and inhospitable emptiness to mankind's hope for survival. In *Silent Running*, humanity has destroyed the Earth and orbiting satellites are filled with the last living plants. In *Dark Star*, human space travel and superiority is advanced to the degree that crews of Earthmen travel the cosmos destroying unstable planets in a bid to keep themselves safe.

The magic of space travel remained in the youth-aimed films of the late 1970s and

1980s. Disney released *The Black Hole*, their first PG-rated film, about a spaceship facing the titular trouble. In 1984 came Universal's *The Last Starfighter*, in which an intergalactic rebellion pinned all its hopes in a poor teenager from a trailer park who was very good at video games; filmmakers were bald-faced in their attempts to court both the spacefaring fandom and the new video game aficionados.

Though there were still visionary films that made space travel frightening and wondrous, such as Robert Zemeckis' *Contact* and Paul W.S. Anderson's surprisingly effective *Event Horizon*, much of the science fiction of the 1990s had become used to space travel and saw it as rote. In 1996's *Space Truckers*, the technology is so commonplace that workaday blue collar heroes populate the film. After only 30 years of actual space travel, filmmaking had become a little bit bored with it.

After the Millennium

A renewed interest in space travel and its realistic portrayal in film boomed in the new millennium, an irony considering the actual frequency of space travel was in steep decline. The cancelled TV series *Firefly* was resurrected on the big screen as 2005's *Serenity*, and the 1972 Russian classic *Solaris* was remade by Steven Soderbergh in 2002.

Danny Boyle's *Sunshine* (2007) was an offspring of the contained space horror of the original *Alien* (1979), while the realism of *Countdown* and *2001: A Space Odyssey* returned in the form of *Gravity* from Alfonso Cuaron and *The Martian* from director Ridley Scott. Scott began his journey to space with the original *Alien* and returned to space and the franchise with *Prometheus* and *Alien: Covenant*.

The Independent Perspective

The frequency of space travel films in the independent arena is limited given the difficulty of capturing that landscape realistically on modest budgets; even the studio releases of previous decades with plentiful budgets look laughably cheap and shoddy now.

One perspective taken by director Jack Plotnick was to incorporate the dated iconography of the subgenre's past into its aesthetic make-up; 2014's *Space Station 76* poked fun at the fashion, effects and outdated social behaviors of the 1970s.

Director Nicolas Alcala broke the mold with his 2013 release *The Cosmonaut*, one of the first films successfully crowdfunded on that level. It was eventually released for free under a Creative Commons license.

Two slightly higher-budget productions made smart decisions that secured them production funding: *Infini* director Shane Abbess cast Luke Hemsworth (brother of *Thor*'s Chris Hemsworth and *The Hunger Games*' Liam Hemsworth) in a lead role, and *Dante 01* was brought to the screen by Marc Caro, visionary filmmaker and co-creator of *Delicatessen* and *City of Lost Children*.

The Featured Films in this section show outer space as just another workplace, a vast and unexplored canvas for dreamers and romantics to get lost in, and an untamed expanse teeming with dangers we can't understand and from which we can't escape.

Featured Films

Mars (2010)
Writer-Director: Geoff Marslett
Starring Mark Duplass, Cynthia Watros, Liza Weil

After proof of life on Mars is found, two crews are sent on a race to Mars. One is a robotic expedition, the other a crew of humans with the same mission. The crew includes celebrity pilot Charlie, doctor Casey and questionable leader Hank. Their journey is constantly monitored by Mission Control and TV journalists. On the long trip to Mars, the crew members bicker, struggle and even find love.

A bold undertaking to accomplish on an independent budget, *Mars* is a computer-rotoscoped film made from live-action performances that is half *Moon* and half *Safety Not Guaranteed*. Many members of the impressive cast of young actors were either already indie darlings or went on to renown after this film. While it is different from *Waking Life*, another challenging mind-bender that utilizes similar technology, the films have a restless curiosity and positive core in common.

~

While *Mars* is an animated movie, and director Geoff Marslett has worked in animation elsewhere (*Everything Changes* and *Milton Is a Shitbag*), Marslett's interests are as vast as his skills. Aside from directing his other feature film, the improvised drama *Loves Her Gun*, he also wrote the scripts for several films including *The Day Before the Wedding* and *Bubblecraft*. Marslett describes the origin of the film as a convergence of two distinct but surprisingly similar elements.

Geoff Marslett: *This feature really came from two initial ideas. The first was a general theme I had been toying with for a couple years. I wanted to explore the parallels between exploration and love—basically the idea that when you look across the room and see someone to whom you are attracted, they are an ideal. They are something in your head and they are something in reality, but the minute you approach them and talk to them, your perceived version of them is different* and *you change them (and they change you) by the act of meeting—so they aren't what you approached any more, and you aren't the same as before you started your journey across the room. Exploration is the same game. When you strike out toward a new frontier—you arrive at a new place that immediately changes you, and you immediately change it—so you can never explore the place you thought you were going. You can only explore the new place you created. That idea of exploration as romance was the core of the film.*

To build that core out, I went back to a short film I wrote but never made several years earlier. It was just about the Beagle 2 *[a real Mars lander lost by the European Space Agency]. I theorized it never opened its solar panels and essentially starved into hibernation on Mars after a landing mishap (a theory that was just recently mostly confirmed, I believe). My short was a robot romance in which a new lander thumbs its metal nose at Mission Control and goes to save its own kind instead, changing landing sites and rescuing the* Beagle 2.

I took that short, expanding the minor Marsnaut characters, and added a whole cast of Earthlings and wrote the script for Mars *while I was teaching a summer in Portugal. I gave the astronauts, the scientists, the robots and even the planets their own romantic entanglements.*

I'm interested in the film's animation process, which involves rotoscope animating over live-action scenes. Why did you decide to use this process?

First, budget. When I went about thinking through an exploration film, realistically I could go out west or to Europe or to an island and shoot actors in the real world on a small budget, but if I wanted to really go to the new frontier [space], an actual full live-action film would be more than my micro-budget would allow. Animation would let me go anywhere I wanted. Second, I wanted that feeling of romance or exploration being just out of reach, like something approachable on a top shelf that you could see, but never wrap your fingers around. The almost realistic rotoscoping allowed me to make the whole world feel "almost real"—approachable, but still other. I wanted that graphic novel separation from reality aesthetic, and the animation style let me do that. Plus, it let me make the hairstyles their own narrative convention!

What do you feel animation adds to this story, and what did you feel that the live action performances added to the animation process?

The live action actors allowed the characters to still be very nuanced and subtle. Expressions still shaped the scenes in a way that is very difficult to do in straight animation. I wanted that. I wanted that separation from reality, but I didn't want to lose the emotional weight and attachment. So, this hybrid style of live action-processing-hand drawing let me diverge far from photorealism without losing realistic performance—or, at least I hope it did!

This film uses space travel as a backdrop for relationships and workplace drama. Is there some commentary here regarding how accustomed we have become to both real-life space travel *and* the portrayal of it in films?

For sure. I even made a few jokes about "they," and conditioning us for the widespread acceptance of aliens. Whether real or not by design, my generation grew up on Star Wars *and* E.T. *and* Close Encounters. *The existence of aliens, the day-to-day of space travel. It's honestly what we expect now—not an event that shatters the foundations of our beliefs if it occurs. So I definitely wanted space travel to feel like a regular job.*

In this film, even the space travelers are so unimpressed by it that it's business as usual.

And I do think that is where we are headed.

The combination of the science fiction setting, the minimal cast and the focus on comedy and character reminds me of the 1974 film *Dark Star*, written by Dan O'Bannon and directed by John Carpenter. Was that film an influence on this one? Were there other influences on this film and its subject matter and style?

We have gotten that comparison a lot, and it definitely factored in there. A few films more so, but Dark Star *is there. Oddly,* Dark Star *was more of an influence as comedic style than sci-fi for me ... but it's pretty great to sometimes get compared to it.*

As far as direct influences, I think David Byrne's True Stories *and Hal Hartley's* Trust *and James Kochalka's graphic novels had more of a stylistic influence on the storytelling than anything else. And visually there was a healthy dose of Bob Sabiston's work in there. And* 2001, *of course.*

I love comics and I love movies. I even enjoy a lot of movies based on comics, but almost all of them do not feel like comics (maybe with the exception of Ghost World*). They feel like comics adapted into movies, but the storytelling is straight movie and no comic. Comics make dialogue confront you directly and usually wrap it up in three or four panels.*

Lines define the action. Characters say things bluntly and do not rely on pauses and pregnant expressions. They say things that hit each other like clubs ... and that style can be pretty cool. I wanted the performances to be "like a comic book." I wanted people to say what they meant and let the dialogue do battle. I wanted scenes to play like those three-panel moments. Early Hal Hartley did that kind of dialogue wrestling, David Byrne did it. I tried to do it. Some people are going to like it, some won't, but I hope watching the film felt like reading a comic.

Would you say that the ease and relatively inexpensive nature of modern technology allowed you to take a handful of actors and a few sets and turn it into a film about intergalactic space travel? One that doesn't look like *Plan 9 From Outer Space*?

MARSLETT: *Yes. And if I made it today, it would have been ten times easier than it was when I did it. One terabyte was like 1500 bucks when we made this, and now it's 50 bucks. Trying to get a camera to send uncompressed 1920 × 1080 to the editor to process with the program I wrote for the film was tough in 2007. Now it would be laughably easy and we would use 4K. Entertainment and technology go hand in hand. Five years before we shot* Mars, *my process would have been impossible on a sub-$100K budget. Five years after we made* Mars, *it would have been pretty easy. When we made* Mars, *it was really hard but possible. So we found a sweet spot of doing it as soon as you could and still have aesthetically pleasing results. Still, it put gray in my beard. The five of us that mainly animated this film worked all night, every night for a year. I still dread the sunrise now.*

Space travel has been a solid subgenre in science fiction since its inception. Though stories have been told about it for 100 years, we as viewers and filmmakers continue to go back for more. Why do you think that is?

I think it's the same reason we like westerns or any other adventure film. Even regular stuff is cooler when it's happening somewhere else. Space is the ultimate "other." It is by its very nature different than anything any human has ever known, so it is exciting. It is a blank slate, it is scary, it is fun. Plus, it is so big that even when we go there in real life, we only scratch the surface—there is always more a little further on. So I think it will always be a prime setting for films and books and songs.

I wanted to explore exploration as love. For me it was the obvious choice, and probably my movie is a textbook case of why people choose space as a setting so often. The fact that Mars *is a romance is an outlier in space movies, but my reasons for choosing space are still pretty similar to the myriad of more action-based space sci-fi flicks.*

Interplanetary (2008)
Writer-Director: Chance Shirley
Starring Cary Borders, Alison Britt, David Brown

This film concerns nine of the employees of Interplanetary Corporation, a conglomerate that conducts much of its business on Mars. Their job is not particularly exciting, and they spend most of their time bickering, until their jobs and their safety are suddenly threatened. A group of marauders has attacked them, and if that weren't enough, a reptilian alien creature of some kind has started attacking them as well.

According to *Interplanetary*, you can travel across the solar system, but you'll never escape mind-numbing jobs and annoying co-workers. The film's mix of horror, science fiction and comedy blend into a fun satire of office politics and alien film clichés. The

Corporate employee Steve (Michael Shelton) isn't prepared for a Martian war in *Interplanetary* (2008).

low-budget film has an infectious charm and the locations and costumes add a level of DIY cleverness not seen in larger films.

∼

Chance Shirley wrote and directed *Interplanetary*. As a director, he sandwiched *Interplanetary* between two zombie films, *Hide and Creep* and *For a Few Zombies More*. He is also an accomplished cinematographer; his work can be seen in the short films *Golden Age*, *Nine Minutes* and *Lullaby Procedure*. Most of his films are horror or science fiction; he is a longtime aficionado of both genres.

Chance Shirley: *I've been a science fiction fan for just about as long as I can remember. And I was kicking around ideas for "my Mars movie" before I knew anything about filmmaking.*

The germ of the idea was an unfinished novel called Rocket Science. *Its plot posited that a Microsoft-like corporation mounted the first manned mission to Mars. After landing on the Red Planet, the corporate astronauts encountered a secret race of Martians and hijinks ensued. I was working on this idea in the late 1990s. It seems a little less far-fetched now that guys like Elon Musk are building rockets.*

After I made my first feature Hide and Creep, *a zombie flick I co-directed with Chuck Hartsell, I started trying to come up with an idea for a follow-up movie and returned to the idea of a corporate-shenanigans-on-Mars story. This time around, I threw some monsters into the mix. And a few months later, I ended up with the screenplay for* Interplanetary.

You've created a complicated hybrid here: not only science fiction and horror, but also comedy. How hard was it to keep the balance between genres, both in the scripting and the actual shooting of the film?

Tone is always tricky. And it's subjective. Like so many creative endeavors, there isn't necessarily a right or wrong way to do things. You just do the thing and hope others are entertained by your work.

The "elevator pitch" for Interplanetary *is "it's* Office Space *meets* Alien.*" And that idea was pretty much my guide to tone when it came to writing and filming.*

Horror comedies and sci-fi comedies don't seem to be as common as straightforward horror movies and sci-fi movies. Especially in studio pictures. Maybe it's because the hybrid movies don't generally make much money—that seems to be the perception, at least. I guess that leaves the hybrid field more open for us indie guys.

The hard work of balancing the genres changes depending on whether you're writing or actually shooting. During the screenplay phase, the hard work is coming up with the basic plot and making the dialogue funny where it needs to be. During the shooting, the hard work is selling the sci-fi and horror elements—making the sets and costumes believable and shooting the horror stuff in a scary or gory or suspenseful way.

I still struggle with the horror and suspense. I mean, just about everything about making movies is difficult, but I'm mostly comfortable with filming a funny conversation. But shooting a good horror scene is so tough. I'm not sure if I've ever totally pulled it off. So, though all of my movies are in some sense horror-comedies, they tend to lean more toward comedy.

The film's humor comes quite a bit from the juxtaposition between the violence of the attacks and the mundane nature of the job (the big boss, possible downsizing, etc.). It's obvious there's commentary here about what it's like working in an office, but is there also commentary on the fact that we've become so used to space travel in sci-fi that even the characters themselves have grown accustomed to the activity and see it as just another job?

Yes. Exactly. When I was a kid, I was fascinated by computers. I mean, think about HAL in 2001: A Space Odyssey *or the talking computer in* Star Trek. *The idea that you could ask a computer a question and get an answer was pretty mind-blowing in the mid–1970s. Now the phone I carry around in my pocket can basically do that. The amazing has become mundane.*

I figured that in a future where space travel is relatively cheap and simple, working on another planet might become mundane. Especially when one is working in the confines of a corporate bureaucracy that is all too familiar to us earthbound folks.

In many ways, yours is a throwback film in terms of technique, from the film stock to the practical effects, etc. Was this a response to the "slickness" of modern, CG-driven science fiction and horror, producing films that may look polished but rob the viewer of a sense of connection and emotion?

I'm not sure the "old school" approach was reactionary. It was really more of a byproduct of the tiny budget and my personal tastes. I'm 45 now and came of age as a film watcher when I saw Star Wars *in the theater. That one movie still informs much of my idea of what a movie should look like. I love all of the spaceships and hand-built sets and crazy cantina aliens.*

I didn't realize it at the time, but the original Star Trek *series was an even bigger aesthetic influence on* Interplanetary. *I grew up on* Star Trek *reruns, and the aesthetic of* that show was a little more in line with our budget than the look of Star Wars. Or Alien, another beautifully realized 1970s sci-fi movie.

As much as I love film, the decision to shoot Interplanetary on 16mm was really a market consideration. When we started making the movie in early 2007, the DVD home video market was still relatively healthy, and distributors had a strong preference for shot-on-film movies over flicks shot on video. Unfortunately, we bit off more than we could chew, and the movie took almost four years to complete. And by that time, most of the Blockbusters and Hollywood Video stores were out of business. And distributors had gotten past their aversion to video.

If I ever make a big-budget movie, I will totally shoot it on film. But for shoots with a low (or no) budget, film just doesn't make any sense these days. I'm currently finishing up on my third feature, For a Few Zombies More, again co-directed with Chuck Hartsell, and we shot it on a slightly modified Canon 7D DSLR camera.

Why do you think, of all the subgenres of science fiction, that filmmakers and audiences alike gravitate back to space travel films so frequently?

I think we like space travel movies because they appeal to our curious nature. For whatever reason, people are driven to find out what is around the next corner. Galileo couldn't travel to the stars, but he created a telescope so he could at least see them in a little more detail. People climb mountains and scuba dive to explore places on Earth that aren't easily accessible. It only makes sense that, if the technology were available, people would travel to the stars. Since the technology isn't available for us yet, we like to watch movies about people traveling to the stars.

The Last Days on Mars (2013)

Director: Ruairi Robinson
Writer: Clive Dawson
Starring Liev Schreiber, Elias Koteas, Romola Garai

Twenty-five years into our future, the Tantalus Base outpost on Mars is manned by eight workers who have less than a day left in their six-month mission. When a worker finds what he believes might be evidence of life on the planet, he heads out on a final journey with another crewmember to find definite proof. When he is swallowed up by a sinkhole, other members of the crew go down to find him only to be taken over by the very bacteria they sought. With crewmembers quickly succumbing to the bacteria which turns them into mindless drones, the remaining uninfected crew have to try and protect themselves until the transport vehicle arrives to take them home.

A tense and claustrophobic variation on *The Thing from Another World* (which also owes its origins to a pulp sci-fi story, "Who Goes There?"), *Last Days on Mars* began life as the story "The Animators," written by Sydney J. Bounds. Balancing equal parts reanimated corpse horror à la *Night of the Living Dead* and isolated space travel thrillers like *Sunshine*, it's an interesting hybrid that touches on two big fears of the new millennium: uncontrollable pathogens and the devastating isolation bred by technology.

~

Screenwriter Clive Dawson began his career in British television as an animator on *The Wind in the Willows* and *Funnybones*. He transitioned into writing, eventually working on the long-running London crime series *The Bill*.

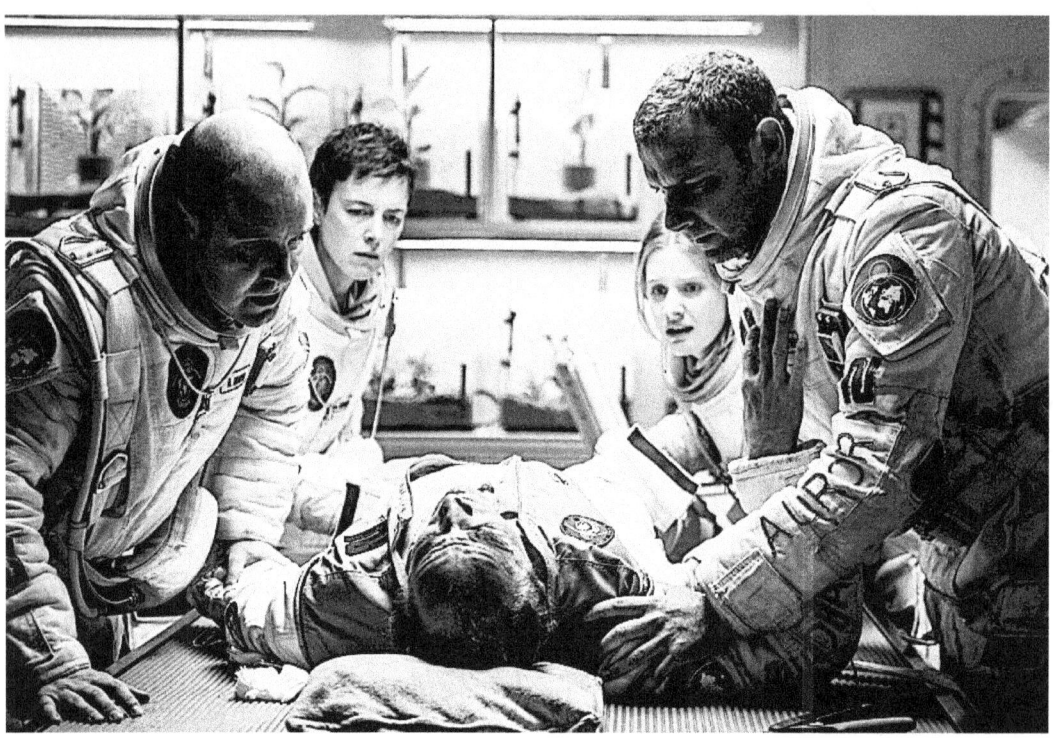

Astronauts Marko (Goran Kostic), Kim (Olivia Williams), Rebecca (Romola Garai) and Vincent (Live Schreiber) help Charles (Elias Koteas) when he is attacked in *The Last Days on Mars* (2013).

I know that the film is based on the short story "The Animators." Was a lot of alteration needed, given that nearly 40 years has transpired since the story was first published?

Clive Dawson: *The adaptation of the story into the early drafts of the script was remarkably straightforward, though it became more of a chore later in the process, due to a number of changes that were imposed on the story. The original short story is a terrific read, despite its age. In fact, it's one of the most memorable short sci-fi stories I've ever read, due to its tight prose and the creepy atmosphere it generates. I'd always wanted to do something with it and, in 2008, I finally tracked down the rights and optioned the story.*

I wrote a two-page pitch document, and it was this that secured interest from the production company, Qwerty Films. I then followed up with a detailed, seven-page story outline, and on the basis of this, Qwerty commissioned the screenplay.

Basically, the original short story consists of three key set pieces: the accidental cave-in on Mars that 'kills" astronaut Pugh; the horrific and deadly return of the reanimated Pugh to the inflatable habitat in which the rest of the astronauts live; and the final chase, in which the sole remaining human, Brunel, is relentlessly pursued across the desolate Martian plains by his colleagues, who are all now dead and reanimated. I built the structure of the screenplay around these three sequences but, yes, there was a considerable amount of material that needed adding, to ensure it would sustain as a 90-minute screen story.

The short story has dated somewhat (for example, all the characters are men, so one of the changes I made was to make some of them female), but it remains reasonably sound from a scientific point of view. Nevertheless, I did a large amount of research into the current science relating to Mars, and the various mission architectures that NASA and others had devised for a real-life Mars shot. Many of the "changes" I made to the narrative were actually additions, building upon what was there already, rather than alterations. The characters in the short story are sketched only briefly, so for the screenplay each needed to be fully defined and given individual character arcs. I also added several new set piece action and "horror" sequences, including an extended, climactic Act III sequence set aboard a relief ship sent from Earth. Unfortunately, this end sequence, and several others, were either dropped completely or changed during pre-production because of budget constraints.

Writing the initial adaptation was great fun. The producer, Michael Kuhn, kindly gave me the space to take it in the directions I wanted it to go. I was determined to capture the essence of Syd's short story in the screenplay, and I was extremely happy with these first iterations of the script.

How prominent was the "zombie" element in the original story? Was it accentuated to take advantage of the post-millennial uptick in interest for living dead stories?

That's a very interesting question, because the "zombies" in the film went through several incarnations.

The zombie element is extremely prominent in the original short story, though the actual word itself is, I believe, used only once in the prose. Syd Bounds' reanimated astronauts are without question "undead," but they are actually far more interesting than the mindless creatures that typify most movie zombies. The dead astronauts of the story are reanimated by an intelligent Martian virus that invades the dead host and takes control of the body and the brain. These undead creatures are not mindless, shuffling things; instead, they are directed by a coldly reasoning intelligence, moving purposefully, operating the equipment and airlocks when necessary; working in unison to track, trap and kill those that still remain alive and human. In this sense, Syd's zombies have more in common with the pod people of *Invasion of the Body Snatchers* than with traditional movie zombies, and this was the approach I embraced in the early versions of the screenplay.

I expanded upon Syd's concept, reasoning that the invading bacteria (I changed it from a virus, because of the research I'd done into possible fossil bacteria that had supposedly been found in Martian meteorites) would need a certain amount of time to gain full control of the body and mind of the dead host. As a result, the reanimated bodies would be slow and inefficient when first reanimated, but would gradually display more speed and dexterity as the bacteria took complete control. I also implied that the undead astronauts shared a telepathic "hive mind" to explain their coordinated efforts, putting to joint use the knowledge accrued by the host bodies during life. They shared a clear, logical, common goal: to reach Earth so as to continue their unique method of procreation. To punctuate this horrific scenario, I developed a backstory which hinted that early evolutionary animal life on ancient Mars had been rendered extinct on a planetary scale by the same process.

As the script went through development, many of these concepts were dropped, one by one. The evolutionary backstory was the first to go, then the "hive mind" idea. Then, progressively, the intelligence and dexterity of the reanimated astronauts was downplayed. As a result, the "undead" in the finished film share many of the traits of the infected people in *28 Days Later*. I'd originally tried to do something a little different in the way the zombies were presented, and I have regrets that the numerous rewrites of the script diluted that approach. It's fair to say that the director's vision of the zombies was not the same as mine, and many heated discussions took place over the manner in which they should be portrayed.

At one stage in the process, the idea was even raised that the astronauts should not be dead at all, but merely infected and "taken over." I still believe that Syd's original conception of the zombies would have been a far more interesting approach.

This film falls into a popular subgenre of science fiction, that of the space exploration film. Why do you feel we as viewers and filmmakers continue to be drawn back to the idea of space travel and exploration, no matter how many times these kinds of stories have been told?

I suppose the vast unknown of outer space has always had a fascination for us, particularly as it resonates with the bigger questions of who we are, whether we are alone in the universe, and our significance as a species in the vast order of creation. Interestingly, the more we learn about our neighboring planets and the wider universe, the more our fascination seems to increase. Instead of answering questions, newfound scientific discoveries seem only to increase our curiosity and raise even more questions. It's such a fascinating genre, with so many inherent possibilities, that it will no doubt continue to inspire stories almost indefinitely.

This story has the sensibility of a classic alien rampage story, but with changes and additions to bring the narrative into the new millennium. Can you speak to some of those changes from the classic alien structure (the alien being microscopic rather than a rampaging beast, the nihilistic ending where the hero doesn't make it, the focus on hard science)?

To be honest, I didn't consciously set out to update the genre for a new millennium, but naturally I was instinctively aware that something new should be added to the pot each time it is "re-cooked," if that makes sense. The main thing I wanted to do was update the concept of the zombie and present them in a slightly different way, but ultimately that approach didn't make it onto the screen.

The microscopic nature of the "alien" is part and parcel of Syd Bounds' original story, and that's one of the things that makes it so interesting. However, the research I undertook into the hard science of Mars and its environment unearthed a host of interesting and related topics. For example, back in 1996, a NASA scientist claimed to have found fossilized bacteria in a meteorite that originated on Mars. This claim was subsequently proved to be unfounded, but the subject fitted in perfectly with Syd's story, so I engineered Act I of the screenplay around the idea that one of the astronauts finds the first conclusive evidence of fossilized Martian bacteria, and while he's investigating this he is killed in a cave-in.

Much of the tension in the screenplay is generated by the unique dangers and restrictions that the protagonists labor under—such as the need for an oxygen supply, the use of airlocks, the claustrophobic confines of the habitats, the limitations of the batteries in the Rovers and the fuel supply in the Mars lander, etc.—all of which grew out of the exhaustive science research. I wanted the story to be grounded in scientific reality as much as possible, so that the audience would better relate to the protagonists and the jeopardy they face. If the backdrop to the story is unrealistic, it undermines the suspension of disbelief required for the "horror" element to work effectively.

I was drawn to the story because of two key dramatic elements: firstly, the relentless nature of the threat, as one zombie becomes two, then three, then four, and so on, while the living humans are simultaneously and inevitably reduced in number until only one remains, alone; and secondly, the fact that, on Mars, there is simply no place for the humans to go to escape. I particularly liked the idea that, no matter where the survivors ran across the barren landscape, or how far they drove in the Mars rovers, all the zombies had to do was follow the footprints and tire tracks in the Martian dust and, sooner or later, they would catch their prey. I'm not sure that came across in the finished film, due to the changes that were made along the way, but it was one aspect of the situation that fascinated me more than most.

The "nihilistic" final scene was devised very early in the process, and remained intact right through to the final shooting script, with only minor tweaks. No other ending was ever seriously considered, to my knowledge, simply because it seemed so powerful and appropriate. A happy ending would have been too easy and too contrived, but equally, it didn't seem appropriate to kill off every last one of the characters. An open-ended, unresolved, "will he make it, or won't he?" ending simply felt right. You say in your question that the hero "doesn't make it," but actually I've always felt that he at least had a glimmer of a chance of surviving, no matter how unlikely that might be.

When Bounds wrote the story about the rampaging virus, he would have had no knowledge of the events of the last 15 years; however, when you were writing this story in 2008, you had a backdrop of diseases like SARS and Avian Flu, and even frightening events like white powder Anthrax being mailed to people. Did this environment of disease and outbreak paranoia influence you while writing it?

It influenced me to some extent, since I've been interested in pandemics and diseases ever since reading The Hot Zone in the 1990s. I'm also a fan of movies such as Outbreak, and I've done story research into diseases and biological warfare at different times in my career. Much of that accumulated research naturally went into the scientific backdrop to the story, and informed the paranoia of characters threatened by a virulent pathogen. It's fair to say, though, that my focus was less on the scientific reality of infections here on Earth, and more on creating a speculative life cycle for the Martian "zombie" bacteria. Nevertheless, even wild sci-fi concepts need a certain level of logic underpinning them if they're to be believable, so an existing interest in the topic was certainly of help.

For Last Days on Mars, the presumed ability of the zombie bacteria to jump-start a reanimation process in a dead body was only the starting point, as far as I was concerned. More interesting was its ability to use the accumulated knowledge and skills stored in the dead brain of the host, as implied in Syd's original story. Another aspect of the idea that I found particularly fascinating related to the question of whether the soul exists. If so, what would be its place in a dead, reanimated body controlled by an alien bacteria and, secondly, would the brain of the dead host body still possess some level of consciousness and self-awareness when reanimated? Many of these ideas didn't make it to the screen, but that's where my main interest lay while I was writing the early drafts of the script.

Other Films of Interest

Pandorum (2009), Red Planet (2000), Ghosts of Mars (2001), Humanity's End (2009), Stranded (2013)

9

The Enemy Within

The most interesting aspect of sci-fi's Diseases and Pathogens subgenre is that it was born from real life. Before there were science fiction films about diseases, there were already diseases. In fact, throughout most of history, diseases and pathogens were an expected element of life. From the bubonic plague to cholera to malaria, humanity has been ravaged numerous times by the spread of deadly diseases. What led to the creation of science fiction films about diseases was the weaponizing of disease.

The idea of intentionally infecting people with a disease is not a new one; the Native American population in the U.S. was intentionally infected with smallpox-infested blankets, and a similar circumstance has long been rumored about the spread of smallpox among the aboriginal population in New South Wales, Australia. However, what changed the intentional spread of disease into science fiction was the idea that the diseases themselves could be altered and manipulated.

One of the classic science fiction horror films, 1964's *The Last Man on Earth*, tells the story of a single normal human man living in a world overrun by vampires due to a strange plague. It is not coincidence that much of the new biological warfare pioneered during World War II took place less than 20 years earlier, and the public was just finding out about much of it.

In the understandably paranoid decade of the 1970s, when the peace movement was shattered by violence and government crackdowns, films turned towards the government as the villain. A team of scientists is assembled by the government to quarantine and research a virus in a small town in the Michael Crichton thriller *The Andromeda Strain*. In *The Crazies*, military men are sent to cover up the accidental release of a virus called Trixie. *The Last Man on Earth* was remade with a more cynical edge as *The Omega Man*, and body horror auteur David Cronenberg used the idea of behavior- and body-altering disorders for the double impact of *Shivers* and *Rabid*.

Though many of the titles in the subgenre would deal directly with the fear of the disease itself, other films took on other concerns while disguising themselves as straightforward breakout thrillers. Both 1985's *Warning Sign* and *The Stuff* deal with a spreading public danger due to problems within the American food production industry, a real-life worry turned into fodder for science fiction.

Using real concerns to fuel science fiction storytelling is common in this subgenre. An uneducated public panicking about the spread of AIDS in the 1980s led to several films that commented obliquely about the reaction: *The Stand*, *Outbreak* and *Twelve Monkeys*. The appearance of monkeys in the latter two are of note given the simian origins of HIV.

After the Millennium

There is perhaps no sci-fi subgenre more affected by the events and aftermath of 9/11 than that of Diseases and Pathogens. While the events of the day itself were not used in any specific film, many films alluded to it. *28 Days Later* included a sequence where a comatose man wakes to find a frighteningly empty London, the streets devoid of people; this image is familiar to citizens in the days after the World Trade Center Towers fell.

American society lived in a state of near-constant panic, with health and attack scares and the everpresent color-coded Threat Advisory system that almost never dropped down into the "safe" green. Even college students on vacation in the wilderness, as in *Cabin Fever*, and news reporters out on a seemingly innocuous assignment, in *REC* and *Quarantine*, were not safe from a terrifying biological outbreak. New fears led to remakes of old movies: *The Last Man on Earth* was revisited a second time as *I Am Legend*, *The Andromeda Strain* got a television mini-series, and *The Crazies* got a bigger budgeted theatrical treatment.

While some of it was played for dumb fun, like the highly popular video game adaptation series *Resident Evil*, more often than not the films reflected a deep angst in the human psyche. *Blindness* and *Carriers* reminded us that it wasn't simply the disease that put us in danger, but also humanity's violent and divisive reaction to it. As we lived through news reports of anthrax scares and dirty bombs, films like *Contagion* and *The Bay* showed us, up close, the process of the spread, discovery and attempt to contain a disease.

The Independent Perspective

Oftentimes, independent films will replace the large-scale set pieces of blockbuster films with clever concepts and unique perspectives.

In the post-millennial whirlwind of constantly improving technologies, films like *The Signal* and *Antisocial* posited the idea that diseases could now be spread by electronics. *The Last Days* created a virus that made everyone agoraphobic, tapping into a uniquely modern circumstance of humanity becoming disconnected from its environment.

The indies also had a love for what came before; *Doomsday* was a throwback to the classic *Mad Max* films with the added layer of a worldwide plague, and *Cabin Fever* may have set a record for fastest and strangest reboot of a series (only 14 years between the original and the remake, with two sequels in between).

The two films in the Featured Films section discuss the perception of a disease through multiple lenses: the media, the victims and the cross-section of society forced together due to medical necessity and circumstance.

Featured Films

Containment (2015)
Director: Neil Mcenery-West
Writers: David Lemon, Neil Mcenery-West, Antony Woodruffe

Mark, an artist, lives in a council flat in Southampton. One morning when he wakes up, he finds that he has been sealed inside his apartment. The water and power are off, and the phone doesn't work. After hearing a strange transmission through the speaker system for everyone to remain calm, a neighbor smashes through the wall and Mark realizes they're all imprisoned inside their own homes. Outside the windows, they see people in hazmat suits patrolling the grounds.

Containment is a perfect title for this film about tenants imprisoned in the home they previously thought was safe. The film taps very effectively into the universal fear of a quickly spreading disease and the isolating methodology needed to combat it. The tenants themselves don't know each other well; the film is an interesting commentary on how society grows further apart the closer together they exist.

∼

Neil Mcenery-West began his filmmaking career with the short film *Undertow* in 2009. It was well-received, garnering awards for Best Director and Best Actor at the New York Independent Film Festival. Six years later, Mcenery-West directed *Containment*, which won numerous awards for its excellent ensemble cast. The psychological impact of tragedy on large groups of people was something that was of interest to Mcenery-West, and he discussed other films and stories with that element that were influential to him.

Neil Mcenery-West: *I've always been a fan of stories that explores human nature. Particularly in circumstances where our societal structures are taken away. There are great*

Residents of a quarantined building flee their heavily protected captors in *Containment* (2015) (photograph by Chris Carr and Lenka Rayn).

stories like Lord of the Flies, Concrete Island *and* High Rise *that have done that brilliantly.*

For Containment, *the basic premise was actually adapted from a story I wrote in the '90s about a group of people trapped inside their homes as a result of an environmental disaster. Then it became a story about a huge social experiment. And when David Lemon came on board in 2009, the script went through several more iterations. But the basic set-up remained the same. A group of residents wake up to find they've been locked inside their homes, all communication to the outside world cut off, and gradually they start to turn on one another out of fear.*

This circumstance (the fear of quarantine and separation from loved ones and the world at large) was once a paranoid fear that actually became a reasonable concern in the new millennium, after multiple attacks, diseases like SARS and Avian Flu, people being mailed anthrax powder, etc. Did any real-life circumstances influence this story?

Yes, but interestingly not the more recent high-profile events. Mary Kings Close in Edinburgh was a big influence on the story. The Close can be found under buildings that still exist in the city. There are several urban myths surrounding them. One in particular tells the story of a plague outbreak so bad that the council sealed the building up during the night, with everyone inside. And the residents were left to starve. Once they'd died, a pair of butchers were paid to go in and remove the bodies.

It's a fascinating story. And although I didn't consciously take that idea, the aspect of being sealed inside your home was almost certainly inspired by that story, as I already knew of it from my time living in Edinburgh.

The principal drive was to tell a story about human nature. What's really interesting is that the more progressed we become as a society, the more we try to deny our primitive instincts. This need to disown them and believe we have risen above it all is fascinating. Even though it's probably healthier to acknowledge their continued (albeit repressed) co-existence with our progress. People are cruel on a daily basis, just in a much more socially acceptable way than beating someone's head in with a club. For much of society, we've got to the point where a large portion of us don't really encounter the sorts of hardships and ethical dilemmas our ancestors would have been forced to confront all the time. And I'm often amazed at the amount of projection we employ to make ourselves feel better by making "other" people the "bad" ones. Or our refusal to acknowledge that we might, as individuals, be capable of making pretty dark choices. I wanted to tell a story about a group of ordinary people that the audience would identify with. And have the audience coming out of the film reflecting on what they might do in a similar situation. And whether their choices might be morally right or wrong. That's the real horror of the story. The plausibility of the choices made.

In some ways, the location of the film is itself a commentary on the activities; the likelihood of people in much more affluent living spaces being treated this way is quite low. Was this an intentional commentary on your part?

It's an interesting question. The answer is yes, but I'm not sure whether that class distinction on how you'd be treated is as clear as you might think. Taken from the point of view of the hazmat teams, if the outbreak was in a five-star hotel, then we'd probably have had them quarantined in a similar way. In fact, High Rise *is a great example of how class is both important, and yet strangely irrelevant when faced with extreme circumstances. In that story, the rich have more control over the building and see the lower classes as animals, but ultimately the people become indistinguishable as they turn towards savagery.*

Our film isn't about class in the way that High Rise *is, but our intention was to have a range of people and classes to reflect the mixture of people that live in council flats these days. They are fascinating microcosms of society. In one flat, you might have an elderly working class resident who has lived there all his life. But his neighbors might be a young middle-class couple working in the city and just starting off on the property ladder. It can vary, and I liked that quality, as it lent itself to a story that examines the universal aspects of human nature. This could happen anywhere, to anyone.*

There's also an inherent irony in tower blocks. They are designed to cram hundreds of people together into a confined space, and yet people often live in them for years without ever knowing who their neighbors are.

Was it intentional to keep the details of the disease to a minimum because the point of the film is less about the specifics of the disease and more about the reactions of humanity to the perception of the danger?

Absolutely. The disease is fairly irrelevant. It's the initial driver of the plot, but it's not what the story is about. Inevitably the film was marketed as a viral outbreak film, which makes commercial sense as it's a subgenre with a built-in audience. Also, the hazmat suits are strong iconic images for a poster. But I'm not surprised that some people have had trouble with the fact that the film doesn't deliver on the details of the virus. That's simply not the story we were telling. It's absolutely about the complex nature of morality and human nature. Where is the line drawn between self-preservation and social concern? It's also the reason the story ends on what might feel like an abrupt note. It's not about the bigger picture. It's the story of this group of people and how they react. Once they are either dead or have escaped, the story is finished. To end the film by shifting the attention onto the wider world, and how everyone else has been affected, would have been a disjointed closure to the film, as we've barely hinted at that throughout the story. Interestingly, that was discussed, as there was concern from audience test screening reactions that we didn't elaborate enough on the source or impact of the virus. But I'm glad that in the end we kept it focused on just this group right through to the last moment. It's a stronger resolution.

For me, the scene that sums up the film is when Mark talks on the intercom to the other residents, and our group choose not to let the other residents in, particularly when faced with a desperate plea from one of the residents that his wife is sick and needs urgent medical attention. What a hideous choice to be forced to make. Leaving them outside is almost certainly a death sentence. But the risk of them infecting the group, or lynching the hazmat they've captured, is a logical and compelling reason to deny them access. These kinds of existential-moral choices having to be weighed up is where the horror of the story lies. Not in zombies or gore. In ordinary people making terrifying choices.

Why do you think that audiences and filmmakers are drawn so frequently to stories about outbreaks and pathogens, something that in real life is terrifying and which we try to avoid? What makes it such a touchstone for the science fiction film world?

I think partly it's because of what you mention in the question. The plausibility of it. We know it's possible and that outbreaks do occur, but it's also so alien to us. Just as a thought experiment, it's interesting to play out these types of scenarios to see what might happen and how we might react.

I imagine it's not dissimilar from the thrill of watching a gangster film or a post-apocalyptic movie. We've all daydreamed about what it might be like and what we might do. But we don't actually want to experience it for real life. This is much the same.

This type of fictional scenario also has dramatic benefits. It's immediately gripping, and places characters in a life-or-death situation. It can be played out on any scale, from a small contained outbreak all the way up to complete global collapse. But ultimately, it comes down to the choices characters are forced to make in extreme circumstances. That's what makes these types of stories really compelling. What if? What would you do?

Pontypool (2008)

Director: Bruce McDonald
Writer: Tony Burgess
Starring Stephen McHattie, Lisa Houle, Georgina Reilly

Grant Mazzy was once a popular drive time shock radio host, but the downward trajectory of his career now has him working in the tiny Ontario town of Pontypool reporting local news, like updates on a neighbor's missing cat. While butting heads with his producer Sydney, Grant starts receiving news of riots, attacks and strange behavior breaking out all over the town and nearby cities. With increasing weirdness and frequency, the radio station crew discovers that a strange disease is spreading, causing people to mimic one another and attack seemingly at random. Worst of all, they discover how the disease is transmitted, and its spread might be partially their fault.

An audacious and darkly absurd refitting of the zombie-outbreak film, *Pontypool* is an assured vision from a distinct and idiosyncratic filmmaker. The decision to keep the action almost entirely confined to a radio station could have been a tension killer, but the script and direction create a palpable sense of separation and isolation for the leads. An ironic observation of the breakdown of language, the film allows for multiple allegorical interpretations of what might have caused the demise of meaningful communication: Did humanity destroy words, or did the words themselves revolt out of self-preservation?

~

The idea was born not as a screenplay, but as the second book in a trilogy by Tony Burgess which began with *The Hellmouths of Bewdley* and concluded with *Caesarea*. Burgess'

Small-town deejay Grant Mazzy (Stephen McHattie) has an unexpected day at work in *Pontypool* **(2008).**

career varied widely, from stage performer in *Oklahoma!* to punk musician to telephone psychic, before he found success as a novelist. In a rare circumstance for first-time novelists, Burgess wrote his own screenplay of the book *Pontypool Changes Everything* for director Bruce McDonald.

Pontypool began life as a book. Can you talk about the inspiration for the story, as well as how the story had to change in the conversion from book to film?

Tony Burgess: *For the book, the idea came from a few places; however, to be honest, it sort of just popped into my head, and in retrospect I mostly guess where it came from—oddly enough not Burroughs—his language as a virus from outer space is very different, I think. I know this, though, that I wanted to make concrete a sensation I have had on and off my whole life: that if the ability to use language deteriorates, then my personality ceases to exist, or at least, is not recognizable as a personality to others. I have felt that at times, almost physically, and it is terrifying, and, even as it resolves itself, leaves the distinct impression that it will return as our inevitable condition. So the idea of a language virus that pulls a person apart came, primarily, from my mind, not as an idea but as a difficult and ultimately devastating obstacle to being here. The literary roots range from Jarry's* Pataphysics *to Marlowe's* Faust *and peculiar art of occulted rhetoricians and memory machines in the early modern period and on. Basically, I was looking to design a swap of physics for metaphysics and have that pull everything apart. The language virus appealed because I could use it in a freewheeling way—yes as a threat in a conventional monster way, but also as a mechanism for pulling areas of the book apart, the narrator, the present tense, etc.*

There were a number of scripts prior to the adaptation that was filmed. Many different approaches and narratives—with more or less some relationship to the book. The Pontypool *script that we did film was originally commissioned as a radio play by the CBC. It all fell together naturally after that—I always loved the breaking news on the small black-and-white TV in the background of* Night of the Living Dead ... *it gives the insane zombie plot a plausibility because media can't help but verify what is. This worked well, I think, because the* Pontypool *virus is even less believable. But what if someone had to, was obliged to, as a service to those experiencing this wild and unknowable event, give context with the little that is known? Any mad tangent might explain things. It allowed me to have things said* sous rature—*that is, some things are almost said—partially taken back but still heard. Tricky to do in film and not everybody buys it. It's fancy cheating, really. Ha ha.*

Was the choice to have the story take place primarily in a local radio station in part because it is a commentary on the way that most people get their news in the modern age, i.e., from possibly unreliable sources whose news is filled with as much opinion as hard fact?

Well, I would say no to the idea that there was commentary in the decision to use that setting. However, it was something we discussed often, and I was probably very frustrating about it. I wanted the commentary-editorial level of the film to be a bit crumbly ... for instance, the French vs. English element. It is a given, regardless of whether or not I want to convey something, that it will feel like it's making use of an editorial thread. (You see I'm terrible at fortifying metaphors. Thread? Level? Element? Conveyance? What is it? Pick one, dammit!)

I have since adapted the script as a stage play, and it has been produced a number of times. I tell the director to replace all of the geographical details to fit specifically with their location. I also ask that they use whatever is the most prevalent second language. In Texas, for instance, it might be Mexican Spanish, and in England it could be Welsh. That stands in for the French Canadian. And with Mendez, who is speaking in Armenian [in the film], I ask that they get an actor whose second language is English. In the U.K., they had a Swedish-speaking doctor. But importantly, no dialogue should be changed to make these changes meaningful. They are arbitrary. The sensation of meaning and commentary will still be strong and empty.

Outbreak-disease films have been around for a long time, but the numbers of films about them have risen steadily in the new millennium. What do you think it is about the idea of an illness reshaping or destroying society that is of such interest to filmmakers and audiences that we revisit them constantly, either in films about diseases or in post-apocalyptic stories about worlds ravaged by a past disease?

Well, there's lots of reasons for the current fear. We're sort of due ... and the monster has been taking peeks at us from under the bed. SARS, Ebola, scarier influenza strains, super bacteria, and you can feel terror in our fear. Disease and medieval zealotry and direct challenges to our survival are supposed to be relegated to fairly distant past times and places. We don't want be dragged kicking and screaming back to smallpox and polio and childhood fevers that can wipe out a generation. But it now appears that these things are so persistent and so adaptive that they somehow have a guarantee of return ... and our homes and even ourselves ... will always grant privilege to these things, in spite of or because of our occasional calm. We are conflating them now; the viral terror, viral nationalism, pandemics, etc., leave us wondering, like you might with disease, "How did I get this? When did it start? Where is it now?" And because there is no answer, you close your eyes and picture this monster, its face, its name. I'd like to make Outbreak 4 *where you can actually hear the virus growl.*

We are, after all, none of us, going to survive. You see this odd, childish reaction to celebratory death on social media—a panic that somehow it has come for our best this year, and if it can, what's to stop it from getting us all?

In the closing act of the film, the lead character attempts to save people in a unique way: He attempts to use gibberish as a weapon (or perhaps as a shield). Was this part of an overall message in the film about the inherent difficulty of people to communicate meaningfully with one another?

Well, in a way ... except that I far prefer gibberish to meaningful communication. That's partly a cynical preference (we don't know how to be meaningful) and partly joy (we can mean nothing in exhilarating ways). It's one of the reasons I love art that fails catastrophically. I detest consensus, even the impulse to seek it. Grant Mazzy's gibberish falls away because there is no audience for it.

Do you have a specific intention that you hoped the audience would take away in the final moments of the film with the two lead characters? Or do you prefer that viewers define for themselves what that final scene says about the events and the outcome? There are multiple theories floating around online, and everyone seems certain their interpretation is the right one.

[Laughs] I most certainly am thrilled that there are different interpretations, reactions to that scene. Contradictory, angry, dismissive, blissful reactions. No reaction, even. I would

be breaking a promise with myself if I ever said it's this or that. It **is** this or that, however; that is, its meaning is singular ... and by that, I mean both unique to it and only in one very specific way.

Other Films of Interest

Phase 7 (2010), *Cemetery of Splendor* (2015), *The Hive* (2015), *Pandemic* (2016)

10

Dealing with Artificial Intelligence

When robots and other artificial intelligence first started populating film screens, it seemed that they served one major purpose: to emulate humans. In 1927's science fiction classic *Metropolis*, inventor Rotwang creates a robot which he is ordered to shape into the likeness of rebel leader Maria. The trend continued all the way through *Westworld* and *Futureworld* (both from author Michael Crichton) and *The Stepford Wives* (from author Ira Levin).

The late 1970s and early 1980s took it a step further, showing that robots weren't just emulating people because of their programming; they wanted to have their own human-approximate lives. *Star Wars* introduced us to two scrappy robot heroes with defined individual personalities; *Android* (1982) showed us that robots can have the same romantic feelings (and jealousies) as their human counterparts. *Blade Runner* was the capper, proposing that robots wanted to be free, to blend in, and possibly to even forget that they are machines at all.

Robots in the 1980s and 1990s no longer wanted to just be human; they wanted to dominate humanity. *TRON*'s Master Control Program digitized and kidnapped its creator to rule over him and make him participate in his own video games. In *Screamers*, self-replicating killing machines disguise themselves as humans in order to hunt them as prey more efficiently.

In the late 1990s, mere steps away from a feared millennium in which we believe machines would malfunction or stop working outright, our collective fear of the machines coalesced in a series of panicked films. *The Matrix* warned us that our world was already controlled by machines that didn't want us to wake up and change anything; *Virus* warned us that, when sentient machines need new parts, human beings will do the trick. In their own quiet, humorous ways, even *Mystery Science Theater 3000: The Movie* and *Bicentennial Man* remind us that robots can do our jobs and live our lives, and so humanity is no longer needed.

After the Millennium

When the dust settled after the turn of the millennium and the world remained as it was, unsullied by a mass strike by unwilling machines, humanity recognized that humans and machines could co-exist peacefully. *A.I.* (2001) showed us that robots were not the aggressors, and in fact they were often the victims. We warmed to robots as companions in underdog battles, as in *Chappie* and *Big Hero 6*. We teamed with them to save the world in *Transformers* and *I, Robot*. We even fell in love with them (or watched them fall in love with each other) in *S1m0ne*, *WALL-E* and *Her*.

Though films like *Eagle Eye* and the remake of *The Stepford Wives* tried to remind viewers what could still be terrifying about machines, society had by then grown too comfortable with social media and wireless devices to ever go back to a world without constant machine interaction. Like Hugh Jackman's boxing manager in *Real Steel*, society was using machines to fight its battles and score its victories. Machines and humanity were inseparable.

The Independent Perspective

Indie films are known for their intense and close-up examinations of human interaction, a trait that often replaces the expensive set pieces and effects that smaller films can't afford. Because of that previous training in character observation, it was no surprise that indie films decided to turn that trained eye on the machines, telling their intimate personal stories.

The Machine and *Ex Machina* wade into the waters of self-awareness and consciousness, questioning whether machines could be as unique and individual as humans, and whether we could ever truly know if it had even happened. *Automata* tells the story of a future world in which a new kind of programmed slavery exists with robots who are unable to repair or augment each other. The anthology film *Robot Stories* tells four touching stories that are bold and futuristic.

The featured films in this section deal with the reliance on machines in old age and illness, the use of unthinking mechanisms of war, and the disturbing possibility of a planet in which the only remaining humanity is what has been programmed into a small group of manufactured machine people.

Featured Films

9 (2009)
Director: Shane Acker
Writers: Pamela Pettler, Shane Acker
Starring Elijah Wood, Jennifer Connelly, Crispin Glover

An animated rag doll named 9 awakes in a workshop in a post-apocalyptic world with no knowledge of what or where he is. As he travels the ravaged landscape, he runs into other rag doll creatures, all of whom are confused about their existence. While fleeing mechanical beasts that are trying to destroy them, they discover that they're the only living things left on Earth after humanity has gone extinct, and they were created for a purpose greater than any of them could have imagined.

Dark and somber but ultimately hopeful, *9* is an interesting juxtaposition of beautiful animation and ugly and devastated locales. The film cleverly discusses humanity's issues with peace and global communication by actually removing them from the story almost

9 and 5 discover a talisman in the post-apocalypse world of *9* (2009).

entirely, making the plight of the rag dolls the central focus. While the film is grim in its assessment of humanity's future, there is hope in its showcase of technology being embraced as a way to save the world as opposed to only being able to destroy it.

∼

Director Shane Acker's career began as many animation directors' careers do, in the field of visual effects. After working on the short films *The Hangnail* and *Major Damage*, he was hired as an animator at Weta Digital to work on *The Lord of the Rings: Return of the King*. The short film version of *9* was nominated for an Academy Award for Best Animated Short Film. That got the attention of well-known filmmakers Tim Burton and Timur Bekmambetov, who helped him turn the film into a feature. Acker described several other filmmakers who were influential in the creation of his film.

Shane Acker: *I was inspired by the work of the Launstein Brothers, specifically their animated film* Balance, *as well as the work of the Brothers Quay and Moebius. I loved the worlds they created and their focus on non-verbal, visual storytelling.*

Because of the fact that the creator of the Stitchpunks imbued part of his soul into them, do you feel in some way that this film, with its struggle between characters and its ideological divisions, represents the individual human struggle within each of us that leads to the struggles we have with others?

Well put, that was definitely a theme we were exploring. I feel that we each contain many different identities within ourselves, some of which manifest when we are in different social situations, or we are pushed to certain extremes, or the need arises for us to adapt in order to function in society. But if you were to extract those identities and distill them down into a purer form, I'm not sure they would all get along or function in an idealized way. So this film explored that. The loose concept is that each of the dolls has a strength, a concentrated facet of the soul that was divided, and each of these strengths combined help the group to survive. But at the onset of the movie, they are missing the last doll, 9, who is the true leader. 9's strength is that he can unite them and lead them to the truth. But at the beginning, they are fracturing under the politician 1, the false leader. It isn't until 9 comes and pushes them in the right direction, that they can actually come together again.

You found a clever way to subvert the standard battle of man vs. machine that often comes about in stories about artificial intelligence. By making the "human" element also a machine, what different dynamic were you hoping to bring to the story here that you hadn't seen in a science fiction story before?

This is a post-human tale, one that takes place after we humans are gone, which I think is an interesting genre. This film embraces cyborg theory, which suggests the next evolutionary step for us is to merge with our machines. So it questions what happens to our humanity when we take that next step. In this film, the cyborgs are the heroes, but we identify with them because they contain humanity within—which is exhibited in their creative energy, their moral code and their spirituality.

It's also a cautionary tale, because our technology has the ability to disconnect, dehumanize and destroy us as well, so it's all about finding that balance.

You combined two sci-fi subgenres here, the artificial intelligence film and the post-apocalypse film. Which of them came first in the creative process, and how did one inform the other?

I was fascinated by Oppenheimer as a historical character. He was a genius, but he was blinded by his own ambition. He chose not to consider the full ramifications of his work and was swept up in the scientific pursuit of splitting an atom. The result of which was of course a technological marvel, but also the most destructive force ever created by mankind at the time. In the end, when it was used, he was crushed and filled with regret. The remainder of his life he spent pursuing peace and trying to undo the thing he created.

So in 9, the scientist who creates the Fabrication Machine is a surrogate for Oppenheimer. After he sees the destructive nature of his creation, he tries to undo his transgression by making machines with a human consciousness. The big irony is that humans are fallible creatures and can become morally corrupt, so there is no guarantee that these creatures will find a better way. So the struggle of the human condition continues in a post-human and post-apocalyptic world. The whole concept with the number 9 is that it is close to perfection (10) but not quite, it's still imperfect, as are we all.

Is part of the message of this film that technology isn't inherently good or bad? It's subtler than that, it's more about what you choose to use technology for that makes it good or bad. It's an interesting irony that a movie which discusses the merits of technology could not exist without heavy reliance on amazing new storytelling technologies.

Yes, exactly. That and the drive humanity has to make technology, even if we don't fathom all the ramifications of what we create. If we dream it, we make it. But some dreams actually turn into nightmares.

True, there is lots of CG animation and effects, but we actually relied heavily on tried-and-true techniques like matte painting. Sure it's digital matte painting, but it's still a technique that's been around since the beginning of film and one that relies heavily on classically trained painters. For me, it's all about telling the story in the most effective way and not so much about the whiz bang of the latest technology. But I get your point, I love irony and contradiction.

The artificial intelligence story is a frequently visited sci-fi subgenre, with numerous fantastic concepts that explore the idea. Why do you feel that filmmakers and audiences alike are drawn back time and again to the artificial intelligence story?

Well I think these types of stories have always been a part of human storytelling. In some sense, you can see the core of them in the ancient stories of the Golem and the Homunculus, as well as in Mary Shelley's Frankenstein. *The concept that we create something that is stronger or more powerful than we are—and then that something exhibits a free will and turns on us or betrays us. These creations are a facsimile of us, or an evolutionary step beyond us that has no conscience or soul, and we can't control them. That's a pretty frightening concept. Not to get too Freudian here, but maybe it represents our deep-rooted fears that our own children will grow to become monsters. I mean in some way, maybe it relates to the Creation story. God made us in His image and we royally screwed up—we're His technology gone awry.*

The design of the film is stunning, with visual references to various elements like Steampunk, H.G. Wells' *War of the Worlds* and the work of Tim Burton. Are there specific films or filmmakers you would cite as influences on this project?

City of Lost Children, Akira, Balance, Street of Crocodiles, Delicatessen, Brazil, Time Bandits, The Nightmare Before Christmas, 12 Monkeys and Metropolis *are a few of the big ones, but the list goes on....*

Robot & Frank (2012)

Director: Jake Schreier
Writer: Christopher Ford
Starring Frank Langella, Susan Sarandon, Peter Sarsgaard

In the very near future, an aging career thief named Frank is struggling with mental deterioration. He lives alone, and simple daily tasks are getting more challenging. His son, recognizing the need for change, buys him a robot to keep him company, remind him about his medications and make sure he is active. Frank dislikes the robot at first, but when he discovers that he can talk the robot into helping him with his shady activities, they form an unlikely criminal duo.

Robot & Frank is equal parts sweet and heartbreaking. The seemingly light-hearted caper film is actually a sobering rumination on aging, mental illness and the positive impact new technologies can have on humanity. It film also touches on the struggle between old and new media. But the heart of the story is a relationship between man and machine that is, in its own way, as powerful and touching as the romance in Spike Jonze's *Her*.

~

Christopher Ford's ascent to the mainstream with his script for *Spider-Man: Homecoming* came in an unusual way. After writing some online material and several TV movies, he wrote a buzzy short film called *Clown* that circulated online and was eventually picked up by producer Eli Roth, who wanted to turn it into a feature. As that was being made, Ford released *Robot & Frank*, a film with an impressive cast that heralded a career jump.

His next two films, *Clown* and *Cop Car*, were made with director Jon Watts, and those films got the two of them the writing and directing gigs on *Spider-Man*.

Christopher Ford: *The idea for* Robot & Frank *came out of a story I heard on NPR about how they were trying to build robots in Japan specifically to take care of their growing elderly population. I thought it was a really interesting use of robots that I hadn't heard of before and I started thinking of how a grumpy old man would interact with a perfect little robot buddy. The other aspects in the film, like Frank being a cat burglar, came into it much later.*

There are elements of this story (Frank's illness, the waning popularity of print media) about obsolescence. Did you choose technology as a central story point because technology so often creates the impression that older people, machines and ideas are obsolete?

I didn't start with the idea of obsolescence. In fact, it wasn't until several drafts in that my filmmaking friend Ben Dickinson pointed out that I was dramatizing the robot's memory being erased at the same time as Frank's memories being destroyed by disease. After that, I really focused on this idea and found ways to use it as a theme throughout. It helped inform the kind of house Frank would have, and his attitude toward technology, and lead me to the idea of taking all the books out of the library. You have to remember that the movie didn't come out that long ago, but even so, technology has already changed. When I was writing it, I tried to coin a term for a technology that we now have in the form of iPads and tablets. It was still science fiction at that point. So the idea of all of the books being removed from a library in favor of ebooks wasn't an obvious one.

This film has a more hopeful outlook on the relationship between humans and machines than many movies do. Why were you interested in telling that side of the human-machine story? Is it closer to your feelings about the real-world relationship we have with technology?

Robot & Frank *is definitely more optimistic about robots than, say,* The Terminator. *But that isn't to say I intended everything to be perfectly rosy. Characters bring up the idea that people are out of work, that there's some kind of movement happening about the encroachment of robots. I wanted the "character" of the robot to be very neutral and interested only in following its programming. My real-life views on robots are that they will only continue the problems we currently face. If robots do something bad, it is because human beings wanted it. Likewise, if robots are going to be a force of good, we have to actually adapt our society to their presence and be the source of that good. In the end, behind the robots are always human beings.*

The idea of combining a sci-fi film with a heist film is interesting. Both of those genres have expected dynamics and plot elements; how did you navigate which elements to keep from which genre in order to most effectively tell your story?

I found that I gained a lot from using the genre elements of a heist film to give the movie structure. You hatch a plan, carry it out and try to survive the consequences. I don't really see sci-fi as a specific film genre in the same way. It's often a setting or an aesthetic, but the topic of science fiction—or speculative fiction—is too broad to be as specific in film as a western or a gangster movie, etc. I believe a science fiction movie can be of a genre. We just most often see it set as high-concept action-adventure because it used to be so expensive to include sci-fi elements that you had to have broad appeal. I am seeing a more recent trend in low-budget movies to explore the genre possibilities of science fiction due to the increased ability to shoot cheaply and include professional-level effects cheaply.

Is the copy of Don Quixote that Frank steals intended to be symbolically representative of Frank's seemingly crazy journey?

Yes, the Don Quixote *was a little joke because Frank is such a Don Quixote figure. Originally the book was a copy of* Treasure Island, *just because I loved that book so much and it stood in for the "treasure" Frank was stealing. At this point, though, I think the Don Quixote parallel is so strong that the joke is a little too heavy-handed. Either Frank should have commented on it himself or maybe we should have settled for something a little less distracting.*

Why do you think we revisit the world of AI, robots, intelligent machinery so frequently in science fiction?

Because we like to play out our current ideas, ethics, values against an "extreme" scenario. It's similar to the interest in zombie movies, I think. We take the things that matter to us in our current world and see how they stack up against something so other, that everything is different. In Robot & Frank, *it was about our values of family, caring for our parents and/or children vs. what if a machine could do it for us? We can justify doing immoral things like stealing if we're doing it with a blank little robot friend; does that make us start to question ourselves? There's endless permutations because the human beings are always different. The robots can stay largely the same in these movies. It's the people and our shared values that we're interested in.*

Automatons (2006)
Writer-Director: James Felix McKenney
Starring Christine Spencer, Angus Scrimm, Brenda Cooney

In the distant future, The Girl lives alone in a bunker. The only connection she has to anyone, aside from the robots who serve her and continue a generation-spanning war, is video footage of the scientist who raised her from an infant. When she discovers that she is a clone designed in hopes of restoring humanity's falling population, she makes a bold decision to join the robot war and aim straight for the heart of the enemy's territory.

Heavy commentary on the real-life war in Iraq and the War on Terror is handled with surprising deftness in *Automatons*, a seemingly fun throwback to the berserk robot films of the 1950s. Though the cast and locations are scant, there are many layers of thoughtful allegory here, from the perception of war through media to the idea of inherited animosity for others. Lest the film become tiresome, there is always a humorously hulking robot in the frame or a cleverly wrought snippet of overly dramatic dialogue to keep the audience entertained as well as enlightened.

∼

James Felix McKenney is a gifted filmmaker whose many talents have been on display in various artistic arenas. Publishing a series of comic books, designing toy lines and working as an associate producer for Larry Fessenden's Glass Eye Pix all readied him for a career as an independent filmmaker and all that includes. Before *Automatons*, he directed the features *CanniBallistic!* (2002) and *The Off Season* (2004). He has also made

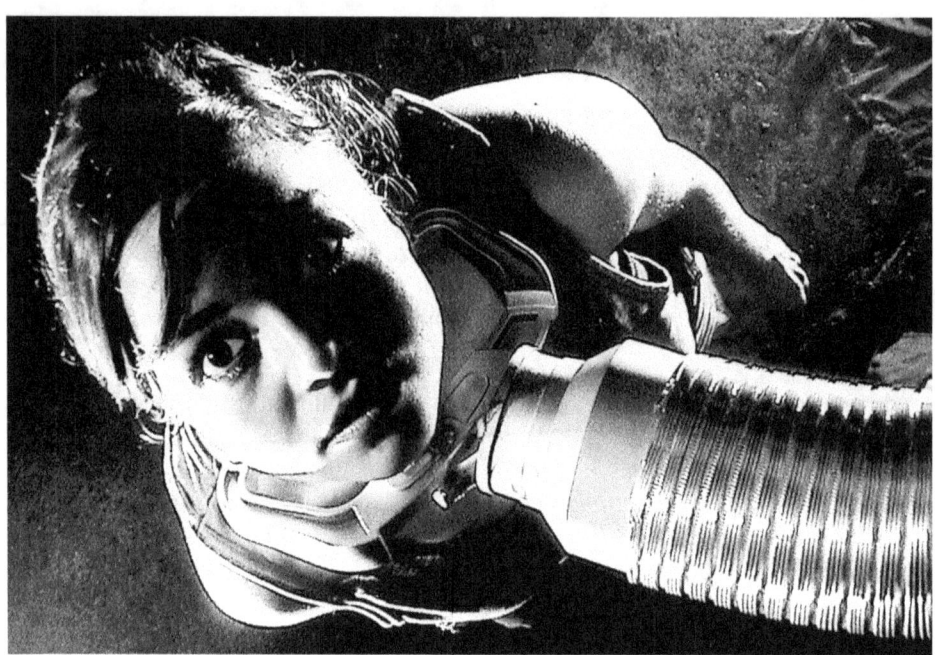

The Enemy Leader (Brenda Cooney) is at the mercy of the robots in *Automatons* (2006).

a love letter to the Christian apocalypse films of the 1970s with *Satan Hates You* (2010) and a throwback monster movie in *Hypothermia* (2010). Many of his films feel like loving remembrances of films seen in childhood.

James Felix McKenney: *Inspiration for* Automatons *came from a couple of places in my childhood. The first was when I was visiting my grandparents around 1976 or so when I was maybe four or five years old. One of my uncles was in the basement watching something on TV. I don't remember what it was, but it had at least one robot in it and that got me really excited. I remember him telling me that there were more things like this out there in the world. I don't know if he was talking about science fiction,* Godzilla *movies,* Lost in Space *episodes or what, but I came away thinking that the Robot Movie was some kind of massive cinema genre. I spent the next ten years trying to find these movies until home video came along and I got access to film books, only to discover that these films featuring epic robot wars only existed in my imagination.*

Though *Automatons* was made in the new millennium, there is a strong sense of analog nostalgia about it. Was that something you did technologically (using real film, practical robot effects and sets, etc.) to be in keeping with the spirit of the idea, which seems to come from classic robot films like *Robot Monster* and *The Day the Earth Stood Still*?

The second thing from my childhood that inspired this film was growing up in a house with no cable television or VCR and being obsessed with science fiction, fantasy and monsters. I would constantly flip through the channels on my little black-and-white TV set with a modified antenna made up of wire hangers and tin foil trying to get in old creature features or cult TV shows.

I was able to get three different PBS stations (New Hampshire, Central Maine, and Southern Maine, which is where we lived) that had late night showings of films like Dawn of the Dead, The Wolf Man, The Fly *and more. Stumbling across shows like* The Prisoner *and* Doctor Who *were like striking gold for me.*

I wanted to capture that almost romantic feeling of watching a horribly degraded black-and-white image of some odd low-budget fantasy production in the middle of the night. Shooting on black-and-white Super-8mm film, which I find to be incredibly beautiful, seemed to be the perfect choice to convey that feeling. If I could get away with it, I would shoot every movie on black-and-white Super-8! I felt that using digital technology and effects would seem really fake and betray the look and spirit of the film. Plus, building all of that stuff was a ton of fun!

The element of Angus Scrimm's performance being entirely confined to monitors watched by the main character: Was that in some way referencing the recent shift in American news consumption, where we only know what we hear from people on screens, radios, computers? It seems like you're trying to show the inherent loneliness of that as the primary form of communication.

Absolutely. This film was made in 2005 during America's invasion of Iraq and the rise of right wing tabloid media into the mainstream. I never understood why anybody would want their information regarding important world events to come from only one source or one point of view, be it from Fox News, talk radio or whatever. It's extremely isolating, yet it seems like the lonelier a person is, the more they are drawn to this stuff.

So here in the film, we have a young woman whose only friends are machines and the only information she has about her world comes in the form of propaganda on a video screen. At least in our world, social media is a two-way street. This lonely woman is not conversing, just absorbing. There's no growth. So she just continues to fight the same war that's been going on for who-knows-how-long. A war that nobody can win, which has already wiped out her people and rendered the planet uninhabitable. If ignorance is all you know, it's hard to recognize how dangerous it is.

The reliance on technology breeds ignorance, and it also breeds a lack of empathy and compassion. One of the things you touch on in *Automatons* is the idea of technology replacing the human element of war. This is a big element of war in the 21st century, isn't it? The impersonality of fighting? In some ways, this film presages drone warfare in frightening ways.

Yeah, who knew? I sure didn't know anything about drones back when I wrote the script in 2005, but I guess that's the whole cliché about science fiction becoming fact.

In the movie, the young woman treats the robots as friends and companions, but at the end of the day, they are just cannon fodder. At the time, I was thinking about the sort of person who has never been through military combat who sits in their safe home in the U.S. or wherever and cries for war without having a personal stake in it or any consideration for the lives lost in the fight.

It's as if to them, these soldiers and civilians on the other side of the world are just automatons or whatever, not human beings. They get angry if the media show images of wounded children or soldiers' coffins. They want conflict, they want to feel like people are being punished or whatever, but they don't want to see or even think about the cost in lives.

So I was thinking less about the technology (again, no idea about drones) and more about the dehumanization of those folks on both sides of the front line.

What is it that you think appeals to viewers about the idea of robots and artificial intelligence? Why are we drawn to have that as an element in so many films, from *Star Wars* to *Her*?

It's a few things. For one, I think we're fascinated by intellectually superior beings. Look at how a character like Sherlock Holmes has endured. The idea of always knowing the answer and being one step ahead of everybody else in the room is really appealing.

There's also the idea of interaction without consequence. In theory, the AI isn't judging you, so there's no danger of embarrassment or awkwardness. With AI, you get a friend without the baggage of having a relationship to an actual human being.

My love of robots is much more superficial than that, though. It's mostly an aesthetic thing for me. There's nothing more beautiful to me than the humanoid (or in the case of Mechagodzilla, the reptoid) form molded in metal or plastic. Call me shallow, I just love robots for their looks!

AI and robot movies used to be cautionary tales about the dangers of a technology that didn't really exist yet. Have you noticed a different attitude about AI and robots in films of the new millennium, now that we're much more exposed to machines in real life that are modern extrapolations of that technology?

I think we're a lot more comfortable with technology than we ever were. I mean, there are the old fears of SkyNet or HAL coming to get us, but not so much that anyone in the 21st century is going to consider for a second giving up the convenience technology has added to our lives.

You mentioned Her earlier, which I don't think is a movie that would have been made more than 20 years ago, but then a film like Ex Machina *really hearkens back to classics like* Frankenstein *and* Metropolis. *So while the way we interact with technology is changing constantly, the old human themes are always there.*

I guess the way modern technology has influenced my stuff is that I'm sort of working against it. I use the tools that are on hand to make my job easier because with the budgets I'm working with, I'm often in the position of functioning as a one-man band. But I love the old film special effects techniques and want to keep those traditions alive.

I'm currently working on a series of science fiction shorts that use everything from rod puppets to stop-motion to traditional 2D animation, just because I love that stuff. If we fans of those techniques don't keep using them, who will?

Other Films of Interest

Robot Overlords (2014)

11

The Fall, and What Comes After

Though there were occasional titles early in film history in which the world faced vast global devastation and a need to rebuild, such as William Cameron Menzies' *Things to Come* (1936), the subgenre of the post-apocalypse film didn't become a fully formed concept until the fear of actually destroying the world became a genuine concern. That concern became frighteningly real in 1945, when scientists in the Manhattan Project invented the atomic bomb and it was dropped on Hiroshima and Nagasaki.

It took Hollywood a few years to digest the immensity of such an event, and independent cinema got there first with titles like 1951's *Five*, the Arch Oboler–directed film about a small handful of people who survive a nuclear holocaust. The studios caught up a few years later; in 1959, Stanley Kramer assembled an impressive roster of stars like Gregory Peck, Ava Gardner and Fred Astaire in the surprisingly dark *On the Beach*.

It would be many years before film flirted with the idea of the post-apocalypse, wanting to tap into the power of the fear but concerned with treating it dismissively. Even in the *Planet of the Apes* series, a science fiction-action film franchise with talking gorillas, the eventual revelation of devastating nuclear warfare bringing about the new world is presented with deadly seriousness.

However, satirical presentations of the nuclear warfare eventually allowed audiences to go to very dark places in the guise of absurdity. Films like *The Bed-Sitting Room* and *Dr. Strangelove* pushed the envelope, and other films were able to explore more serious perspectives in their wake.

In the 1970s, the post-apocalypse subgenre was truly born. *A Boy and His Dog* and *Damnation Alley* primed audiences for one of the most well-known films in the subgenre: *Mad Max* (1979). Combining nuclear fears with new environmental concerns, George Miller created an indelible image of a frightening future and made a blueprint that led to *Le Dernier Combat*, *Cherry 2000*, *Waterworld* and *Six-String Samurai*.

After the Millennium

As technology made the world louder, faster and more complicated, post-apocalypse films ironically became more character-based, singular in their focus, and grittily real. Films like *The Road* and *Book of Eli* were violent, dark road movies whose central themes were touching ruminations on the bonds of father and son and the power of religious faith. *Take Shelter* looked at the coming apocalypse not as a world-changing tragedy, but as an intimate look at the dissolution of a man's sanity and family life.

Religion had its day in the post-apocalypse as well, with 2000 bringing the Christian end times thriller *Left Behind* (which was remade just over a decade later) and 2013 bringing the celebrity-stuffed meta-comedy *This Is the End*, diametrically opposed bookends on the shelf of religious End of Days prophecy.

The Independent Perspective

Much of what independent cinema does best is illuminate the intricacies of human relationships, and the post-apocalypse subgenre allows for a focus on exactly that. From previous co-workers turned reluctant co-survivors in *The Battery* to the breakdown of the family unit in *Time of the Wolf* to the growing passion in 2014's *Chrysalis*, indie cinema turned the attention from the devastation and monsters outside to the heartbreak and isolation within.

The independent world also embraced the aspect of a global apocalypse, bringing forth tales from Brazil (*Beyond the Grave*), Ethiopia (*Crumbs*) and Germany (*Hell*). A new focus on female survival came to the forefront of the subgenre, with strong central women figures in *The Last Survivors*, *Forever's End* and *Bunker 6*.

The Featured Films in this section use the post-apocalypse as an allegory for the events of 9/11, an exploration the idea of reforming humanity through one person's limited perspective, a clear-eyed observation of the dangerous attitudes that lead to global downfall, and a treatise on a girl's journey through adolescence.

Featured Films

5 Shells (2012)
Writer-Director: Paul S. Myers
Starring Chad Brummett, Jordan Grady, Kelsey Hutton

In a post-apocalyptic future, sisters Matti and Joslyn are orphaned when their mom and dad hide them in the basement just before an intruder enters the home and kills them (the parents). Taking the few supplies they have left in the home and a shotgun with just five shells, they leave the house to try and find a safe place to exist. Along the way, they meet several men who appear helpful. But the sisters realize that when they are not together, they're constantly in danger.

Viewing the apocalypse from the perspective of two teenaged sisters, *5 Shells* is a somber, thoughtful film that strips the post-apocalypse world down to its most essential elements: the danger or safety of each human interaction. With a title that telegraphs its existential crisis, the film plays like a melancholy Grimm's fairy tale, even referencing *The Wizard of Oz* as symbolic of their journey *à la* Dorothy Gale.

~

The two films Paul S. Myers directed before *5 Shells* were formative in the creation of its concept. His first film, the short *Putnam*, revolves around a sheriff on a journey to find

Sisters Matti (Kelsey Hutton) and Joslyn (Eve Kozikowski) are on their own in the wild in *5 Shells* (2012).

a man's killer and the futility he feels about his life. His follow-up, the feature film *Southern Belles*, followed two teenage girls looking to break out of their boring lives in a small town. Combining the journey element of his short film with the teenage leads from the second, Myers had the operating premise of *5 Shells*.

Paul S. Myers: *The idea for* 5 Shells *first came about when watching a trailer for another movie. I get a lot of ideas watching trailers. I'll see the first ten seconds, think I know what the movie is, and then by the end of the trailer the film has gone off in another direction. But I'll think, "Man, that would have been great if it was this other thing that I thought it was." It was a movie about two kids who get left in the Old West by their parents in a haunted house, but at the beginning I thought it was just about two abandoned kids in the desert. Then I started thinking about how twins might react to the same situation, and then I started thinking about what kind of world we would leave our kids if society collapsed, and what type of people would thrive, and who these kids would have to deal with. From there, I started writing.*

Yours is the rare apocalyptic film in which the female characters are the leads and are utilized as more than simply sex objects or the possible vessel for a new generation of children. Was part of your motivation for doing this to reflect the large and growing female audience and fandom in the science fiction community?

I actually wasn't thinking about gender roles specifically other than the way that men usually find women to be easy prey, especially in sci-fi or horror movies. One girl definitely falls into the victim category, but the other rejects that label, and is ultimately destroyed because of it. The movie gets pretty rapey as well, and I wanted the villain(s) to victimize with the same toolbox, but in different ways.

Is the apocalypse world you created in some ways a stand-in for our own world that allows us to see the daily indignities of life that women deal with: the harassment, the pornography, the competition, the sense of male entitlement, etc.?

I wasn't thinking that deeply about the "apocalypse" aspect—though now that I've been working on Full Frontal with Samantha Bee *for the last year, I look at things through a "feminist" lens more than I did when I wrote the picture, so I might now. When I wrote it, I thought of the apocalypse as a starting point for the tragedy of the two girls who, at the beginning, have been relatively sheltered from the outside world, and have to go out into it. I'm a huge* Dune *nerd, and in there Herbert says, "God made Arakis to test the faithful." While I don't think that the men, or Matti, in the desert in my movie are "the faithful," I do think they have been hardened by the environment, and at the end of the movie it is only those that are willing to embrace the worst of themselves that are fit to live in that world. I wanted the sparseness of the environment and the cruelty of Frank to be the thing that turned Matti into someone who could survive even if she had to lose her innocence to do it.*

There's a lot of *Wizard of Oz* imagery in the film: the book itself, the journey down a symbolic Yellow Brick Road, the hiding in the cellar to begin the journey just like Dorothy. Why did you draw these parallels? Was it intended as a corollary to the strange new world that the girls now inhabit?

I used Wizard of Oz *as a guidebook because I liked the idea of searching for where you belong. Unfortunately, the main character of my story realizes that she doesn't really have a home any more.*

Why do you think the popularity of the post-apocalypse story has grown so much in recent years? The subgenre is inherently dark and hopeless, but continues to draw viewers and filmmakers.

I think the post-apocalypse setting is a good, and maybe easy, way to comment on today. When I wrote this movie, it was right after the financial collapse of 2008. There were real fears of actual food shortages, real bleak predictions. Now [authors' note: this interview was conducted during the 2016 election cycle], with the looming threat of a demagogue taking control of trade agreements and nuclear codes, those fears have re-emerged. I think those feelings are reflected in the attraction of filmmakers and audiences. Plus, if you do it right, like George Miller does, then it can be goddamn awesome!

One Hundred Mornings (2009)
Writer-Director: Conor Horgan
Starring Ciarán McMenamin, Alex Reid, Rory Keenan

Jonathan and his wife Hannah, along with friends Mark and Katie, fled to a cabin in the countryside just outside of Dublin when rumors spread that some kind of apocalyptic event was on its way: permanent power outages, shortages of food and medical supplies, and a steady erosion of the standard niceties and laws of civilized society. Adding to the difficulty is a recent infidelity within the group that makes the dynamic inside the cabin as volatile as the outside world.

A chamber piece film that uses the microcosm of four people in a cabin to represent the struggle of society to communicate meaningfully in the midst of a crisis, *One Hundred Mornings* is starkly effective in its quiet honesty. Unlike many post-apocalypse narratives, this film begins at the very tail end of the collapse, giving viewers a glimpse of the world crumbling in real time. This is in sharp contrast to the devastated futures of most apocalypse narratives, and the minor change pays off in interesting ways.

Much of writer-director Conor Horgan's career is made up of documentary work. From his early short films *Happiness* and *About Beauty* to his recent feature *The Queen of Ireland*, his style lends itself nicely to a film like *One Hundred Mornings* in which realism is needed for viewers to buy into the premise. Horgan discussed how the film was motivated by a real occurrence.

Conor Horgan: *It wasn't so much an idea as a shock that I got when I went to see the Canadian writer Margaret Atwood speaking at the Dublin Writer's Festival in about 2007. She comes from a science background, and she's a wonderful science fiction writer as well. She gave this great analogy in the form of a question and it goes like this: "There's this test tube and it's full of amoeba food. You put one amoeba in at 12 noon. The amoeba divides in two every minute. At 12 midnight, the test tube is full of amoebas, there's no food left. The question is, 'At what moment in time is the tube half full?'" Intuitively, instinctively you would think, "Well, obviously, it's halfway through, it's six in the evening if we started at 12 noon." But of course, the answer is one minute to midnight. Which is where we are as a civilization now. That's the moment at which all the amoebas are saying, "We're fine and there's half a tube of food left."*

She inspired me to read a book called A Short History of Progress *by Ronald Wright, a very sobering read. He made the case very clearly and in a very inarguable way that all civilizations fall. When you extrapolate from that, all civilizations have a beginning, a middle and an end. It's one thing when it's the Mesopotamian Empire or the Greco Roman Empire or whatever. Now we have effectively a worldwide society and we're so interlinked*

Jonathan (Ciarán McMenamin) and Hannah (Alex Reid) wait it out in a secluded cabin in *One Hundred Mornings* (2009).

with globalization that it's very hard to imagine that if a large part fell, it wouldn't take the rest of it with it. So I suppose that short answer to the question "How did the idea of this film first come about?" is from my own fear, in a way.

They say when writing, you should write about what you know. I say, when writing, write about what scares you. The things that I discovered on a very cursory look at potential breakdowns of society were scaring the hell out of me, so that's what motivated me to write the film and to make the film.

Another thing that I came across during my research was a writer called Alex Steffen. He wrote a great blog post on theworldchanging.com that really kind of resonated with me. In the middle of the blog post is a great statement: "Of all the lies that we tell ourselves, this is the biggest: that there is any world worth living in that involves the breakdown of society."

I'm not a big connoisseur of post-apocalyptic movies or of zombie movies, but I knew enough to know that there was a school of thought, probably predominantly from maybe younger American males: "if the shit hits the fan." It basically means all bets are off and I'll take to the mansions with my guns and my food, and I'll do whatever the hell I want. All societal restrictions will be lifted from me and it will be like the wild west and it will be great and I'll live young wild and free. But of course, if society does break down, or indeed, when *society breaks down* (because it does appear to be an inevitability), it's going to be boring and cold and hungry and lonely. In a way, that's why I wanted to make this film.

You chose to set *One Hundred Mornings* in the immediate aftermath of an apocalyptic event, rather than during the catastrophe itself or the devastated months and years after. What was it that appealed to you about that particular window of time?

It was very clear to me right from the early part of writing the film, I did not want to point the finger and say it's global warming, it's zombies, it's Donald Trump, it's whatever. I wanted it to be just a societal breakdown for any number of possible reasons or a combination of possible reasons. What was interesting for me is, when you start talking to people about this stuff and start reading about it, there is this kind of teeth-clenched optimism. "It's going to be fine." "Why is it going to be fine?" "Because it has to be fine." "How will it be fine?" "They will discover a way." "How will they discover a way to make if fine?" "I don't know but they have to." It's that kind of magical thinking, that forced optimism, that I thought was an interesting aspect to a breakdown. As the world is falling down around the characters, one of them is maintaining this totally unrealistic optimism in the face of what is actually happening, and I think that that he symbolizes a lot of people's attitude, which is totally understandable. When faced with a perfect storm of resources running out and countries becoming more militarized and heading towards people going to war because there are not enough resources left, for an ordinary Joe like me and you, it is very hard to figure out what the hell we can do about it. That forced optimism is possibly a psychologically valid point of view. It's not necessarily going to help, ultimately.

In some ways, the apocalyptic circumstances serve as an allegory for the struggle of being in a personal relationship. Why did you choose to use an apocalyptic setting to tell a personal relationship story?

We have four main characters in the house. Jonathan is putting his own desires ahead of the wellbeing of the group. He's risking the whole social cohesion of the group because he's choosing to sleep with his friend's wife as she is choosing to sleep with him. So, the two of them are risking their own survival by putting their own desires ahead of the wellbeing of the group. So, I'm not really choosing an apocalyptic setting to tell a personal relationship story. I'm choosing to tell a breakdown-of-society story using the metaphor of a personal relationship or a number of personal relationships.

Does the effect and aftermath of the apocalyptic event that precedes the action of the film have any basis in real-world events like market crashes, natural disasters, etc.?

I've been asked this a lot at Q&As for the movie. And my response has always been, "If I wanted to say what it is, it would be in the movie." I don't want to say what it is, and that's not because I have a great secret that other people don't know. It's that I don't know what it is. All I know is that it is more likely than not that society will take a serious hit over the coming years. It may not be in my lifetime, I don't know. It is heading that way inarguably for all kinds of manmade reasons, and the efforts that are being put in to stop it are minimal because it's in everybody's short-term interest to keep going with business as usual. Probably the one thing that would save civilization is that if we are miraculously given the ability to live for 350 years, at which point things would change rapidly.

Most apocalypse stories seem to be from the perspective of first-world, largely English-speaking countries (U.S., Australia and, in this film, Ireland). Do you think that says something about those societies particularly? Is it because of the greater conveniences we have that we're afraid of the day that we're going to lose them all, and that is less of a concern to poorer or less technologically advanced nations?

Is it because we have more conveniences that we're afraid of the day we're going to lose it all? It's not conveniences, it's survival. I've shot documentaries in Papua New Guinea, where people have nothing, no books, no electricity, but they can fish and they can survive and they will survive. These small pockets of people, if the entire global civilization crumbled around them, it's not going to make a lot of difference to them. I mean, global warming would make a lot of difference. I'd have to move up to the mountains instead of the beaches where I'm at, but they'll survive.

I wanted to write about what I knew, and what I know is Ireland. But also, I was very conscious of the fabric of society. People think it's this rock-solid thing, and it's just not. It's a stool, and if you kick one of the legs away, it's going to be very hard to get the stool back up and running again. They say that most modern civilizations or most western civilizations are nine meals away from anarchy. Which is two days.

If you read about what happened in New Orleans during Hurricane Katrina, the rule of law was abandoned very quickly and the cops understandably became the best organized and best armed gang in town. They were looking after themselves because that's all that they could do. Yes, we have a lot to lose, and other people, people who live and work the land, are more likely to get through and are more likely to be less affected by a large-scale breakdown of society.

There's one line in the film where Jonathan is asked what he does. I can't remember what it is now. It's basically computer graphics or something like that. I think that's what was in my mind when I was writing that scene. Something that is absolutely, 100 percent useless in a world where society would break down. People would ask me, "If society broke down tomorrow, how do I think I would fare? I'm a filmmaker, I'm a photographer, I'm a writer." Basically, you're somebody else's breakfast, because these are not transferable skills into a world where growing and catching your own food is going to be the only thing that matters in the end.

The number and variety of apocalypse and post-apocalypse stories has risen sharply in the last 15 years.

End of Days stories always have currency, and some of that comes from simple human egotism. In some sense, it's perversely comforting to think, "Everything is going to fall down. If I'm going to die, then everybody's going to die with me." There is that very human idea of wanting to go right to the edge of a cliff, and part of your body wants to jump. It's similar when you consider apocalyptic or breakdown stories. Having said that, when we were heading towards the year 1000, there were a lot of religious apocalyptic cults, it was almost like Y2K in advance. Once we hit this magical number, everything will fall down or the dead will rise or God will come back or whatever, and there was a lot of fear about that. So, these kinds of End of Days stories have been around for a very long time, but there has never been a time in which the probability of End of Days has been demonstrated so clearly, so logically and so scientifically as it has now. So, of course there are going to be more stories and of course The Walking Dead *is going to be a hit on television, because people know in their bones that it is only a matter of time before the shit hits the fan in a very serious way.*

The Last Man (2000)
Writer-Director: Harry Ralston
Starring David Arnott, Jeri Ryan, Dan Montgomery, Jr.

Alan, the last human being on Earth, devotes some of his time to starting a series of video journals chronicling his circumstances and positing the "way forward" if anyone ever finds his recordings. Then he meets Sarah, a beautiful woman, and while she isn't very interested in him, he is happy; being the last two people on Earth should be enough to give him a chance. But when Alan and Sarah are joined by Raphael, a much more handsome and capable man, Alan hatches a plan to whittle the world back down to just two.

The Last Man is a fun hybrid of the empty city films of the past (*The World, the Flesh, and the Devil* and *The Quiet Earth*) with the neurotic relationship comedies of Woody Allen and Albert Brooks. A quiet but clever commentary about the difference between ideals and executable realities is played out in the juxtaposition between Alan's recordings and his behavior. The movie uses the microcosm of a volatile relationship to show the difficulty of human interpersonal dynamics.

∼

Harry Ralston began his career with the short film *Chicken Delight* (1991); it would be nearly a decade before he made *The Last Man*. In the interim, he built up experience and relationships that would help bring the film to reality. As an actor-producer on the comedy *Men Cry Bullets*, he met Jeri Ryan, who would later star in *The Last Man*. A connection to Roger Avary (who produced *The Last Man*) also led Ralston to work on Avary's *The Rules of Attraction*. Ralston described how the film was born from a single thought that germinated over the years.

Harry Ralston: *In college, I jotted down a line in a notebook: "Dave's Guide to the Universe." I pictured some meek guy as the last person on Earth, who now had the opportunity to teach future people how to live by his own rules and philosophy. Years later, when I was looking for an independent feature to make, it occurred to me that idea might be*

Sarah (Jeri Ryan) and Alan (David Arnott) enjoy each other's company as the last people on Earth in *The Last Man* (2000).

cheap to shoot. I didn't realize getting rid of people was more expensive than keeping them around.

Though the film involves the near-end of the human race, in some ways it's a sci-fi extrapolation of a classic romantic framework: the man, his love interest and the interloper. What interested you about the idea of using a world-altering scenario to reframe a romantic-comedy concept?

Once I had a story of someone thinking they could teach the world how to behave, I knew I needed problems for him to show how that was doomed. Adding a woman he falls for that's out of his league, and then one more man who is slightly better than him in every way, seemed like a good set of problems to show him immediately contradicting everything he taught us. I figured it would be a good microcosm of what led to the end of the world in the first place.

The element of the documentary within the film came about at a time just before the fake documentary movement exploded post–*The Blair Witch Project*. Though this film is narrative, what was your goal in introducing the "documentary" aspect of the story? In some ways, it acts as the expositional best friend character.

I needed a way for him to share his thoughts, so a video guide he's making to teach future generations how to live correctly seemed like a funny way. Then I started to think about how the video he shares with us could expose his hypocritical behavior when contrasted to the film of what's actually happening.

This film taps into some of the empty city films of the past, from *Five* to *The World, the Flesh, and the Devil* and *The Last Man on Earth*. Did these films influence you?

Truthfully, I drew more from Elaine May comedies. She captures desperation better than anybody. But I did want to solve some of the things that bugged me about end-of-the-world films. I figured people wouldn't manage to be as high-minded or productive as some of those films showed them.

Alan's character is remarkably unshaken at the seeming end of humanity, taking it in stride and dealing mostly with his own personal problems. Is it possible that Alan represents the very early origins of the self-obsessed post-millennial generation? I'm mostly kidding. In seriousness, though, does this film in some way reflect a societal shift from investment and compassion to a new ethos of cynicism and self-interest in the (then *brand*-new) new millennium?

I don't think there's anything new in Alan's point of view. He's assured about the lessons he offers us simply because he is completely untested. Once someone he desires enters the scene, and then another person who can take her away, Alan is thrust into a big problem and his philosophy is out the window. His selfishness is just a reflection of the greed, jealousy and desperation that causes most problems. You would hope if you had to rebuild humanity, you'd live up to it, but there's a good chance you'd get consumed in petty fights and waste a lot of time. He does learn from the whole thing, so maybe it's not quite as cynical as it sounds here.

The Mysterious Event (in this film, the vanishing of the human race) is a popular concept in the sci-fi film world. Why do you feel that viewers and filmmakers are drawn to the idea of mysterious events for which we have no explanation, but which we must ultimately accept and deal with?

I always thought that if the world did end, we wouldn't necessarily know how, and it bothered me that movies always neatly explained that. I thought it'd be funny and more realistic if everyone who was left had their own theory about what happened and why.

Stake Land (2010)

Director: Jim Mickle
Writers: Nick Damici, Jim Mickle
Starring Connor Paolo, Nick Damici, Kelly McGillis

The world of the future has been ravaged by a vampire outbreak. People survive on their own or in isolated pockets across America. Young Martin's family was killed by vampires, but he was saved by the mysterious Mister, who has devoted himself to the eradication of vampires. But the vampires aren't the only danger: The Brotherhood, a group of religious fanatics, stalks the streets, trying to spread vampirism among what they consider sinners by dropping vampires in populated areas. Martin and Mister gather a small makeshift family and intend to head to a safe haven called New Eden, but the journey isn't as easy as they hope.

Stake Land is a classic post-apocalyptic zombie story without the zombies. Replacing shambling undead with bloodsucking monsters does nothing to diminish the allegorical power of the story, painting a picture of America as a gaping wound in the aftermath of a great tragedy. The film's frank discussion and confrontation of dogmatic religion and the War on Terror is balanced with the hope of watching disparate pockets of humanity seeking each other out to rebuild.

~

Jim Mickle's route to directing *Stake Land* was circuitous. He worked in the art department and as a grip for much of the early 2000s before teaming with co-writer Nick Damici to make the short film *The Underdogs*. They followed it up in 2006 with *Mulberry Street*. *Stake Land* was the last original premise the two worked on together, adapting the Mexican horror film *We Are What We Are* for American audiences, and bringing two Joe R. Lansdale stories to the big screen (*Cold in July*) and [the small screen] (*Hap and Leonard*). While the themes of *Stake Land* are thoughtful and deliberate, Mickle mentioned how desire and determination were primarily responsible for its inception.

Jim Mickle: *Nick Damici and I were both desperate to get back to making films after* Mulberry Street *a few years before. I was watching some homemade web series at the time, so I brought up the idea of trying to do short serialized things for the Internet. Homegrown genre stories that we could produce in quick bursts while we waited for a feature to get financed.*

The next morning, Nick sent me an eight-page script about a kid taken under the wing of a nomad vampire hunter. It ended with the guy teaching the kid to kill a vamp he had locked in the trunk of his car. It felt very much like Matheson's I Am Legend, *which Nick and I were both huge fans of.*

Over the next few weeks, he'd send two or three of these little scripts a day and all of them were beautiful, self-contained vignettes about these two characters. He just tapped into a zone and couldn't stop writing.

After we had about 25 of them, Larry Fessenden read them, loved them as much as I did, and had the idea to fold them into a feature. The first script kind of glued them back to back, but it didn't really stand without a backbone holding it together. This was all leading up to Obama's election and the end of Bush's run, and the country was growing more and more divided. So Nick took the stories, locked himself in his apartment for a week and wove them all into one script, using the fall of America as the big backdrop that framed all these stories. Then it was just about combing through draft after draft to sculpt it into a single film. But that original eight-page short is the opening of the final film and I don't think we changed a word.

This film, unlike many apocalypse stories, is about people seeking community and togetherness rather than thriving on division and tribalism. Was that an intentional element you and Damici brought to the story?

I think that was Nick's sensibility too. We're both pretty cynical people and we gravitate towards the darkest stories, but even when we get real nihilistic, there's always a dash of hope, family and love mixed in to keep it balanced. It may have something to do with 9/11, which we were both very close to. My biggest memories of that were the initial shock and confusion of being in a city under attack, but then how quickly that brought the city together. I remember that day, walking over the Brooklyn Bridge to get home, looking back at a plume of smoke from the bottom of Manhattan and by the time I reached the other side there were regular neighborhood people accepting strangers, cheering for them, giving us food and water. Random people hugging and crying together. The generosity and bonding was breathtaking. It went right back to being New York City after about a week but that was the experience of shock and then unconditional love and moving forward together as a massive community. Looking back, I think you see a little of that in all our work, so maybe it stems from that.

The portrayal of vampires in this film is different from a lot of modern vampires; they are not suave, tortured and communicative, but rather violent, empty and reactive. Was there some observation either about vampires or about society itself that this portrayal is commenting on?

At the time, Twilight *and that kind of YA (young adult fiction), sexy adolescent vampire was everywhere and I think as horror fans we were offended by it. We wanted to get back to something brutal and scary. Ragged, bestial, soulless things that existed only to tear our characters to shreds.*

I love zombies, and we kind of did them with Mulberry Street, *but it was on such a bare bones budget, I'm sure some of the vampires in Stakeland were about getting that feral undead thing out of our systems. It also gave us some range to create different types of vamps and let the humans in the story use the vamps as a weapon the way the Brotherhood does throughout. They're not meant to be characters or have feelings, they're just nature gone terribly wrong.*

You said many of the themes are related to the events of 9/11 and its aftermath, including the War on Terror. How aware of that were you when writing and filming it? Was it something more organic that became apparent with distance and context?

It was definitely something we were aware of, and I think the earlier drafts of the script felt a little empty before we found some of those themes. Fessenden and I are both political guys, and at that time in the country, we both felt like there was an opportunity to let some of the fear and extremes of the world spill into our story where it could. Damici is always leery of pushing but he was able to weave a lot of that into the script organically.

But I've also done this enough to know that the world around you gets reflected in whatever you do, whether you're reaching for it or not. There's a harmony between real-life turmoil and fiction that can transcend your own point of view if you stay open to it. But the conflicts that inspired Stakeland *seem tame nowadays. One upside to the craziness of the world today is I think it's going to inspire some amazing films and some angry storytelling.*

Was the Brotherhood meant to represent the dangerous effect of religious extremism and zealotry in general, or was there a more specific purpose for their presence?

I think it was about fanaticism, no matter what the fervor is based in. Religion can be a beautiful thing, but when it's pushed to extremes it can be dangerous, ugly, destructive, cruel. Especially when it's used to control. That means Islam, and it also means Christianity.

What is it about the post-apocalypse film that keeps filmmakers and audiences coming back to that same base concept so consistently?

I have no idea, actually. I ask myself that a lot because I'm still reading and thinking about my own apocalyptic stories. Some of it is reflecting the world around us as we're headed down our own self-destructive roads as a civilization. But there's also some wish fulfillment in there. The whole "reset to zero" idea. I was just about to say, we've reached the saturation point and there's no room for apocalyptic stories any more, but now with Trump in office, we may need that genre more than ever. The world is crying out for another They Live.

Other Films of Interest

OzLand (2014), *Ever Since the World Ended* (2001), *Young Ones* (2014), *The Divide* (2011), *Empty* (2011), *Air* (2015), *The Colony* (2013), *Rotor DR1* (2015)

12

There Can Be Only One

Science fiction seems like the most obvious birthplace for the Ultimate Dangerous Competitions subgenre, but it was actually born as a dramatic thriller. One year before he helped bring an iconic horror creature to the screen in *King Kong*, director Ernest B. Shoedsack co-directed 1932's *The Most Dangerous Game*. Based on the story by Richard Connell, the film follows Bob Rainsford, a shipwreck survivor who becomes the prey in an eccentric nobleman's hunting game.

Non-science fiction versions of this story cropped up steadily through the years, including remakes in 1945 and 1956, and even venturing into action star territory with Jean-Claude Van Damme's *Hard Target* (1993). However, science fiction has always offered the convenient veneer of fiction that has allowed filmmakers to discuss issues of the age, and the Ultimate Dangerous Competitions subgenre has more than its share. From 1965's *The 10th Victim* to 2012's *The Hunger Games* to the *Purge* franchise, the competitions in question are often violent games created by totalitarian regimes to keep dangerous populations from acting on their unrest.

Its portrayal in film often stands in for governmental overreach. In 1971, while Richard Nixon was president, Peter Watkins made *Punishment Park*, in which antiwar activists are either imprisoned or given three days to walk over 50 miles through the California desert while stalked by National Guard soldiers and police. *Rollerball* (1975), and to a lesser extent its equivalent *Death Race 2000*, envisioned a world run by corporations, presaging the genuine corporate takeover of most industries in the 1980s.

In the corporate 1980s, deadly competitions became high entertainment, spectacles for viewers to enjoy in the same way that the elites in the films themselves enjoyed the blood sports. *Gymkata* (1985) and *The Highlander* (1986) were high-stakes competitions in which you could lose your life and, in the case of the immortal swordsmen of *The Highlander*, your head. The bloody competition was such a staple of the 1980s that the patron saint of action movies, Arnold Schwarzenegger, starred in a near-parody of the subgenre, *The Running Man*. Ostensibly based on a Stephen King novel, *The Running Man* was a bright, garish satire of America's infatuation with life-threatening entertainment; *Family Feud* host Richard Dawson adds to the meta-commentary as the host of the violent and popular TV show in which a convicted prisoner must fight gladiator-style killers for a shot at freedom.

After the Millennium

Though the remake-rehash boom is generally credited as coming in the new millennium, it got its start just slightly earlier with *Futuresport* (1998), a clear reworking of the *Rollerball* premise. However, the new millennium had more than its share, including new versions of both *Rollerball* and *Death Race* and *Zathura*, a science fiction spinoff of the fantasy board game adventure film *Jumanji*.

There were original ideas in the subgenre, though, beginning in 2000 with the memorable cult hit *Battle Royale*, about school-aged children forced to kill each other until only one remains, in order to combat overpopulation. Interactive technologies of the new millennium led to deadly competitions like *Avalon* (2001) and *Gamer* (2009), which incorporated the innovations of video gaming with the classic life-or-death scenarios.

The Independent Perspective

One big change in the makeup of movie-watching in the new millennium has been the increased availability of films from other territories. Through aftermarket avenues like DVD, video on demand and streaming sites constantly seeking new content, films from all over the world are getting exposure.

Before he made the British sequel *28 Weeks Later*, Spanish filmmaker Juan Carlos Fresnadillo directed the complicated, twisty thriller *Intacto*. His film used the deadly contest as a symbol for the convergence of people from various financial and cultural circumstances who are united by tragedy. Two thousand seven brought a dark exploration of academic ethics in *Fermat's Room*, a Spanish film about mathematicians solving intricate problems to keep from being crushed in a slowly shrinking, locked room.

Some of the mainstream themes continued in the independent arena, with *Stay Alive* revisiting the interactive games theme and *The Tournament* tapping into the everyman struggle that began in *The Most Dangerous Game*. Others reached into new areas. The proliferation of reality television was presaged by Daniel Minahan's *Series 7: The Contenders*, the fake documentary near-future thriller about a TV show where regular people compete to kill each other for money. In the Featured Films section, filmmakers discuss themes as varied as corporate control of medicine, the cutthroat nature of children's education and the American voting system.

Featured Films

The Human Race (2013)
Writer-Director: Paul Hough
Starring Paul McCarthy-Boyington, Eddie McGee, Trista Robinson

During an afternoon, 80 people vanish from their various locations and appear in and around a strange institutional building. Some are deaf, some speak various languages, but somehow all of them hear and understand the same announcement: There is a running route marked out with arrows through the neighborhood around the institution, and all 80 are required to run it. If they don't participate, they die; if they go off the path, they die; if they are passed by everyone twice, they die. As the race begins and people begin dying, the participants become more desperate and more willing to do anything to be the final surviving contestant.

A no-frills exercise that explores the darkest corners of the human psyche in desperation, *The Human Race* hits the ground running as fast as its characters. With an enormous cast constantly whittled down by circumstance, the script keeps the viewer guessing about heroes, villains and likely survivors. The film doesn't provide a simple allegorical premise, varying in possibility from cutthroat modern American society to reality competition TV shows to the impersonality of war.

~

The Human Race was not director Paul Hough's first time observing violent competitions. His first film, the documentary *The Backyard*, chronicled the violent world of backyard wrestling. That experience, combined with his working relationship with actor Eddie McGee, established with the short film *The Angel*, led him to begin his first narrative feature.

Paul Hough: *I actually wrote a big-budget version of* The Human Race, *which one day I still want to make. It's quite different from* The Human Race *I ended up with. After several years of coming close to getting a big movie made, I decided it was just time for me to make a film. So I set out to make a movie called* Remember My Name. *We did some fundraisers for it, and I cast Eddie McGee and Paul McCarthy-Boyington in it.* Remember My Name *relied upon one particular private ranch location, which I had been assured by a producer that I could get. At some point, things from a producing standpoint seemed sketchy, and the location didn't feel secure. But I had raised about 25k. I could either give it back, or make another film. I decided I'd still use Paul and Eddie, and come up with another movie.*

Around the same time, I learned there was a place that had a school, prison and church in it, that was on the California State Film Commission list of places you could film for cheap. It was in Whittier, California, an abandoned youth correctional facility. I was trying to find a place I could shoot a relatively contained (due to costs) movie, and this location seemed perfect. As I was walking around it, I decided I'd adapt my big-budget Human Race *script and try to make a low-budget version. Logistically, my reasoning was that if everyone started the race at the beginning, as they spread out, I wouldn't need to show the large group again. I felt it was a relatively controllable project to shoot. So we started shooting, and we were set for six days in the Whittier facility and four more in a mansion (which was going to be the "asylum"). Originally the script has rules that "the prison, the school and the asylum are safe." This ultimately turned out to be "the prison, the school and the house are safe." Shooting in the Whittier facility wouldn't complete the movie, but I figured I'd work it out after. Again, it was either shoot something or talk about being a filmmaker without actually making a movie. So, on day five of the shoot, I learned that the mansion was not secure. I had to shut down, and re-evaluate. Ultimately, I decided to shoot the rest in my small house, since I knew that at least it wouldn't fall through.*

A few months later, we shot for a few more days, then shut down production again. Then a few more months later, shot again for another two days. During the shutdowns, I would save more money to be able to shoot more scenes. It was a horrible, long process, and the worst way to make a movie. But I was determined to make one. We started shooting in

2009, and the film eventually came out in 2013, so you can see what a long process it was. During that process, the movie The Hunger Games was announced, shot and released. So when my movie came out, it was compared to that, although I had no notion of what The Hunger Games was when I started filming.

Was it intimidating to try and make an independent sci-fi project with such a large scope and an enormous cast?

It wasn't intimidating, just difficult. And not a good way to make a movie. I had to shoot a lot around the actors' schedules. Paul McCarthy-Boyington was always auditioning (he was very in-demand) and that made it very difficult. If I was set for a shoot, and he got a callback, I'd have to shift the entire shoot. One of the hardest things to deal with were the actors' haircuts. There is one scene in particular, with Eddie McGee, where I just had to shoot him from the forehead down, and from a super-low angle.

We shot so much of the movie in my house. At some point, we bought bags of sand from Home Depot and shot the nighttime Afghanistan scenes in my garage.

One of the other things I had to do was rewrite the film as I went along. There was an actor who had a very, very big role, who was so late to a shoot, I just told him to stay home and wrote his character out. As such, I had to be extremely flexible and put everything together like a puzzle. Then there were characters who started out as extras, who became bigger. The three construction workers, for example.

The Human Race *was the type of shoot where everyone did everything. Actors would carry lights. Everyone had to scrub in, literally. After the first day of shooting, I was the one who had to clean the portable toilets. We couldn't afford much, but just had to make do with what we had.*

I believe in equality. It's a running theme in my films. But I don't like to preach to the choir. So, for me, in the film, equality is that everyone has the chance to die, at any time. That's why I kill off anyone at any time. Death is an equalizer, but even more, I wanted to challenge expectations. Stereotypes and social conditioning dictate that you don't expect disabled people to be bad or sympathetic characters to die. But if you believe in equality, you should. That's why in The Human Race, *anyone can die at any time. That is also why I work with Eddie McGee a lot. While he is missing a leg, he is the most able person I've ever met.*

Sol (2012)
Writer-Director: Ben Carland
Starring Jake White, Jake Brown, Colin Conners

In the distant future, young adults compete in a complicated tournament known as the Sol Invictus, in which teams of participants are sent to far-flung planets and challenged to figure out their location and locate Earth's sun in the night sky. As soon as they arrive, they find that they have no communication with home, no way of returning on their own, and they are surrounded by hostile creatures and a dangerous environment. Originally competing against each other, the participants must now work together to survive.

With outer trappings that might remind a viewer of the recent glut of YA sci-fi stories like *The Maze Runner*, *The Hunger Games* and *Divergent*, *Sol* is a smart and sophisticated updating of the classic desert island scenario. Utilizing beautiful and empty practical locations, the film juxtaposes the futuristic drive of competition with the placid

A team of elite academy members faces hostile terrain in *Sol* **(2012).**

exteriors to powerful effect. The simple narrative builds tension slowly and uses the concept of young people in danger to comment on the unreasonable expectations of youth in society.

∼

Ben Carland began his filmmaking career with the short film *The Forgotten Future*, his first foray into science fiction. After working in various capacities on a documentary (*M.I.A. M.D.*) and a drama (*Camión de Carga*), he combined his experience to write, direct, produce and edit *Sol*, his feature debut. Three years later, he followed up with the sci-fi thriller *Shadows on the Wall*.

Ben Carland: Sol *was my very first film out of film school, but I still remember how the story came about like it was yesterday. I was hiking with some friends across a small island in the Atlantic, and it seemed so alien to me there. It was so bleak and primordial— a tiny dot of sand in the middle of the ocean with just a few trees hanging on. No signs of humanity anywhere. It really felt like we had landed on an alien planet. I wondered what it would be like if this really was an alien planet. I'm always trying to imagine what the future may be like, so I thought it would be an interesting story to see how this untouched world might fit into humanity's future and what would happen there. Exploration is one of my favorite themes in writing, doubly so when it's about people who aren't prepared for it, so I began to ask myself how we could get a group of people marooned on an alien world in a stark and harsh way. Luckily, I had something to write with in my pack, so I sat down then and there and started writing it on the beach. About a year and a half later, we were back near that very same beach filming* Sol.

While many of the elements of the film are science fiction in nature, this story hearkens back to tales like *Lord of the Flies*, which focus on the de-evolution of groups of people in desperate circumstances. Was that story an inspiration?

While I don't think Lord of the Flies *really influenced* Sol *directly, it was a large influence for me growing up. I love the idea of exploring what people do when isolated as small groups struggling for survival and putting children in that situation just makes it that much more dramatic. Kids and young adults already face enough uncertainty in their lives by not really knowing who they are or what they can handle. By putting them into a situation that even competent adults wouldn't handle, it just makes the drama of it that much more intense.*

I think I would have written Sol *with a young adult cast either way, simply because I was a young adult myself when I wrote it, but I think* Lord of the Flies *did a fantastic job of showing how far things can fall apart on psychological levels. It also struck me because even though the story and setting in* Lord of the Flies *are so exciting, the real meat of it is about what's going on internally and between the characters as the plot moves.*

Unlike some of the other films in the Ultimate Competitions section, this film doesn't begin as a life-threatening circumstance, but it ends as one. Was this difficult contest between academy members (the Sol Invictus) designed to comment in some ways on the increasingly competitive world of higher education, and the elaborate lengths young people now have to go to?

Absolutely. We're already seeing how much more competitive life can be even before you get out of middle school. In a way, that seems kind of tragic to me: children simply being a product of their time and circumstance rather than just being children. So I thought it would be compelling to see how far that competitiveness may grow in the future and what it might lead to. We're often drilled with these ideas of "Win, win, win!" "Succeed!" at increasingly younger ages, and I thought there was a compelling tragedy to the idea that in the future, kids get thrown into dog-eat-dog competitions over nothing more than prestige and bragging rights.

Though the film is sci-fi, much of the action is planet-bound. While the decision was likely in part based on budget, was this decision also meant to reflect the isolation of the characters in the contest, to show the remoteness and difficulty of their task?

Definitely. Even if we had a better budget, there would have been no space or spaceships, etc., in the film. I wanted it to be all about them being stranded and isolated in every possible way. Anything else would have broken the remoteness of the planet.

Because of the uniform colors and the age of the academy students, I got a bit of a Starfleet Academy vibe. Was that an intentional reference?

I absolutely loved Star Trek *growing up, but the uniforms and academies we hear about in the film are not meant as any kind of reference to it. On some level, it may have inspired me as a visual way to separate and identify people, but really it all boiled down to being a nice way to give some detail about who these people are and where they come from. When world-building on a budget, I think anything you can do to hint at broader elements and leave people wondering is a fun way to get their imaginations going.*

In a good film, there is one challenge; in a great film, there are two challenges. In your film, you have the contest (challenge one), the stranding on the hostile planet without a way home (challenge two) and the hostile wildlife (challenge three). Were these challenges for the characters meant to be allegorical representations of any specific real-life challenges?

No, I don't think I intended there to be any allegorical references to Sol. *I wanted there to be both internal and external struggles, and I wanted there to be so many of them that these poor characters never got a break. As much as I personally might love a movie of just watching people trudge across an alien world and experiencing it, it would have probably bored everyone else to tears. I think the more you can do to ratchet up everything that's working against these people, the more entertaining the story becomes. We actually had several more challenges and threats at work in earlier versions of the film but decided that it was simply too much and was distracting from the meat of the story, so it was trimmed down to just those three.*

The occurrence of the "ultimate competition" story, from *Battle Royale* to *The Hunger Games* to *The Human Race*, has grown steadily in recent years. What do you think it is about the idea of epic, complex, often dangerous contests that interests filmmakers and viewers?

I think they're a lot of fun for films because they let you make worlds within worlds. World-building in films can give writers great blank canvases to work with and these "ultimate competitions" we're talking about essentially doubles the canvas room that writers have to work with. On top of that, it allows filmmakers to run with unbelievable circumstances without threatening the audience's suspension of disbelief. It lets people do a lot of fun, new stuff in films because you can "sell" so many more stories when it's within the framework of "the whole world doesn't necessarily work that way, it's just the rules of this game."

Exam (2009)
Writer-Director: Stuart Hazeldine
Starring Gemma Chan, Pollyanna McIntosh, John Lloyd Fillingham

In a conference room at the headquarters of a huge corporation, eight eager candidates for a position at the company gather. A man comes into the room, giving the candidates a questionnaire page. They are then given three rules: don't speak to him or the guard in the room, don't spoil their papers, and don't leave the room. When the candidates turn over their questionnaire page, all of them are blank.

A fiendishly clever film, *Exam* slowly turns the screws in classic Hitchcock-Agatha Christie fashion. Its framework, about getting a job at an important corporation, seems like a MacGuffin at first, but slowly reveals itself to be one of the film's most important themes: corporate mindset and its effect on human interaction. The movie touches on the wealth gap, the commodification of the medical industry and the cutthroat nature of the business world, all while creating believable tension inside a single nondescript office space.

∼

Stuart Hazeldine was no stranger to complex and controversial narratives when he wrote and directed *Exam*. He started his film career as a producer on the Nazi trial "what if?" film *After the Truth* and then a short film called *Christian*, about Christ visiting a modern-day British high school. His most recent film, the star-studded *The Shack* (2017), revisits similar themes from *Christian* in discussing the place of faith and belief in the midst of violence and tragedy.

Stuart Hazeldine: *I grew up reading about the maverick directors of the '70s, guys like Lucas and Coppola who not only wanted to make great movies, but they also wanted* *creative control and ownership of their work. Then I was blown away by the insane profitability of* The Blair Witch Project, *a cheap little horror movie, and I thought, "If you could come up with a commercial concept that was cheap to shoot and you executed it well creatively, it would be a major result if you could be even a tenth, a fiftieth as successful." I also saw friends who had been first-time director go through purgatory with films that didn't work because of choices that were made for them, things that were out of their control, yet they were blamed for the failure because it's their name listed under "Directed by." I didn't want my directing career to be over as soon as it began because of someone else's bad choices, so for all these reasons I liked the idea of fully financing a low-budget containable debut movie. It didn't need to be shot in one location, but it sure helps.*

I was looking for the right idea for years and had one I was gestating, but it needed to be set in the U.S., while I lived in the U.K. I had shot one short film but was open to making a second before jumping up to features, and a short film funder in London liked my first one. He asked me to write a second which they would hope to finance, so I was on the phone with my best pal Simon Garrity, who had some short ideas he wanted to bounce off me. One was about a bunch of school kids taking an exam who were surprised to find their question papers blank, so in response the kids responded in various ways: expressing themselves through origami, guessing the answer, etc. We moved on to other ideas, but at the end of the call, I went back to that idea and asked, "What if the stakes were higher? What if it was a job interview instead, and it was the ultimate job that you would do anything

Three candidates (Jimi Mistry, Chukwudi Iwuju, Nathalie Cox) subdue a rowdy fourth (Luke Mably) in *Exam* (2009).

to get? What if the people taking the exam were type-A personalities who are prepared for anything except nothing? No guidance." I liked that.

As we developed the idea, I realized I also liked the deeper metaphorical layer inherent in the idea: that life is a blank page and we all have to decide what it means, and often our choice is shaped by our upbringing, our prejudices and biases. So that really made me want to make it. The funder didn't go for it and we'd cut so much to squeeze it into a short film length script that I felt we could expand it to feature-length easily, and I realized this was the debut feature I wanted to finance and control myself.

The film is set in the very near future, but some elements (disease, a shrinking job market) are very real fears in the current world. Did you design the film as something of a commentary on current social concerns and behavior?

I was writing the film as two things were going on. The first was that the bird flu was floating around, and I'd done some background reading and knew that if H5N1 mutated in the wrong way, it was going to trigger a pandemic that would make the Spanish flu of 1919 look like a sniffle. I hate the paranoia of survivalism, but even I had a flu survival kit in my basement just in case. Probably wouldn't have made a difference, but I felt the odds were bad enough that it was worth a little flutter to be prepared, because the world is way overdue for a pandemic. As it applied to Exam, *the carrot of getting a great job is easy: Think of all the power and money you'd want and there you go. But if everyone was motivated by financial greed alone, that's pretty boring dramatically and I needed differentiation. I needed a stick to add to the carrot. And I thought a virus was a great one. What if the world had AIDS, a Big Pharma giant had just found the cure but only had small amounts available, and employees were first in the line for it? Boom.*

The second thing was, the markets were just rising and rising, the property bubble was getting out of control and you could smell the unfettered greed coming from government, business and everyone who owned property. If you've lived through even a couple of crashes, you have to know that a statement like "No more boom and bust!" from the U.K. chancellor is human hubris of the highest order. You know it's going to be a hard landing if the governments of the world don't engineer a soft landing, and so it proved. I wrote it as a prophetic warning. Then Lehmann Brothers collapsed literally as were shooting, I believe. So by the time Exam *was released, it came over like a post-mortem instead. Like anyone would have listened even if it came out before, right? No one was listening even to the economic experts who were predicting disaster. So all you could do was short the housing market, as a few guys famously did, or cash out.*

Was the idea of having the whole film take place in a single room in real time a result of budgeting considerations, or as a way of confining your audience in the same psychological framework as the characters?

Initially it was simply that the original idea took place in an exam hall within the timescale of an exam. I liked the simplicity of that, dramatically and financially. It felt like a challenge to work within those limitations, and make your limitations a strength, a selling point that's part of the concept and the pitch. Look what we did with one room in 80 minutes! And the big strength, as you rightly observe, is it forces the audience to identify with the candidates and feel the anxiety and claustrophobia that they feel. The challenge then was to not let it get so claustrophobic that people wouldn't enjoy watching it.

The film continues an honored tradition of the single-room thriller, from *Rope* to *Lifeboat* to *Cube* to *12 Angry Men*. Were any of these films influential on your scripting and direction?

Honestly, I was really only influenced by 12 Angry Men *and the concept itself. People assume I must have been influenced by* Cube *and yes, I knew the concept of* Cube, *but I only watched it deep into prep when the script was largely set in stone, and I did it because I felt I should, and because I wanted to ensure there were no accidental plot duplications that critics and audiences would assume were copies that actually weren't. When you work in this business, you realize how true it is that there is nothing new under the sun in terms of basic ideas, and differentiation only comes through your unique expression of those same basic story ideas. Things people assume are deliberate copies are often honestly accidental duplications. So I did some basic due diligence to try and avoid that. There was a Spanish movie with similarities that many said* Exam *copied (or maybe they copied us?), and I'd never even heard of it until we released. I still haven't seen it and forget what it was called.* [Authors' note: Hazeldine may be referring to the math-centric single-room thriller Fermat's Room.]

The people in the exam room battle each other, and in so doing, turn themselves into representations of ideas and races rather than individuals. Was the journey from well-groomed applicants to *Lord of the Flies*–esque savages an intentional commentary on the effect of the corporate mindset on regular people?

It was an observation that unregulated capitalism has no place for compassion in the way that armies don't either. They're both aggressive hyper-masculine environments, so any restriction to killing or making money seems like a drag in the short term. But in the long term, acting like humans with empathy is usually the wiser path. We evolved from a base "reptilian brain" mindset for a reason, so any structural, political or economic system that encourages us to regress and abandon our fully evolved adult brains has to be a recipe for mutually assured destruction.

Why does the deadly competition subgenre connect so strongly with filmmakers and audiences?

In a capitalist society, we all have to deal with competition and choice, usually for rewards. So it's not surprising that the flip side of that is the nightmare that we might be forced to compete to avoid pain and death. The perversion of an everyday systemic dynamic into a horrific alternate reality.

Circle (2015)
Director: Aaron Hann, Mario Miscione
Writers: Aaron Hann, Mario Miscione
Starring Michael Nardelli, Julie Benz, Allegra Masters

Fifty people find themselves waking up standing in a circle inside a featureless black room. The people are from all walks of life: a married couple, a pregnant woman, a child, a man who only speaks Spanish, a racist, a devoutly religious person. A countdown starts, and every two minutes, someone dies. They are prisoners in the room; leaving will get them killed. They discover that they have the ability to vote on who will be next, and one after another, people start creating alliances to choose who is worthy of being the final survivor.

A huge cast in a confined space in real time could spell logistical nightmares and a boring result, but *Circle* is a smart thriller that squeezes every drop of possibility out of its simple concept. Allegorically exploring themes of the voting system, scapegoating

Fifty people find themselves in an isolated room, competing for their lives, in *Circle* **(2015).**

and the individual value we put on people based on our limited understanding of them, the film delves into the complexities of human interaction and social structure. Made just before the 2016 election but all the more prescient when viewed after, the film fashions a perfect window into a divided and polarized populace.

Venturing to Los Angeles from the East Coast for a film-related internship, Mario Miscione met up with writer-director Aaron Hann. After working together on a successful online series, they crafted the concept for *Circle*. Its successful execution and effectiveness gave rise to the anthology series *Dark/Web*. Though the ideas behind *Circle* seem ripe for social commentary and character exploration, Miscione discussed the more pragmatic motivations that brought it about.

Mario Miscione: *A few years before* Circle, *Aaron Hann and I created a web series called* The Vault. *The show had been an experiment for us in low-budget storytelling and production strategies, where we tried to tell a cinematic story with a large cast of characters using a single set and a really simple design. The response was better than we could have hoped, and as we wrapped up the storyline, we discussed what our next step would be. We had both wanted to make the jump to feature films, but were well aware of the hurdles we faced, namely the high costs of typical feature filmmaking. We decided to take the ideas that had fueled* The Vault—*large cast of characters in a single, controllable location—and try to apply it to a bigger story. Aaron floated the initial idea to me one day: Fifty people in a room, one person dies every two minutes and the group gets to decide who dies next. From there, we started discussing how such a story would play out, what the scenario was, what we would be trying to say with the film, etc.*

The central plot of this film seems to be an allegory for the voting process, and what it has become in the reality television era: a popularity contest and hard-edged survival mechanism, rather than a tool of opinion and an attempt at change or betterment.

Circle *has always been a story about how people determine value in one another. We do it every day; we size people up, we express opinions about each other's behavior, we decide in small ways what we think each other is worth. We wanted to take this idea and the (often arbitrary) nature of our value systems and apply it to a larger-than-life scenario. What if you took these micro-judgments and made them into a situation where the outcome was life or death? Would we still focus on the little things? Would we go "bigger picture"? Would our system of morality still hold up? Would we have the courage of our convictions to see things through?*

The voting mechanism was the best way, we thought, of articulating these judgments. Votes, by their very nature, are expressions of value. When you vote in the real world, you're choosing the better of the candidates. In Circle, *you're choosing the worse. I don't think we explicitly set out to comment on the political process with the game, but the nature of the situation—the votes, the "campaigning" the characters do, and the inherent biases—emerged as a definite parallel as we went on. Certain moments and conversations are very much rooted in the rhetoric of campaigns. These ways of speaking and appeals to basic values occur in politics because* they work. *It made sense to us that we'd see them in* Circle.

Was the increasingly elaborate structure of voting, and how it can be manipulated to gain a specific outcome, also a commentary on the ease with which the electoral process in real life can be manipulated?

Our concern with Circle *was more commenting on the easily manipulated idea of right and wrong in people. That certainly applies to the electoral process, but we were thinking more broadly. The things that we as human beings believe to be right and wrong can be uniquely personal to each individual. Sometimes, they're part of a larger societal morality, such as "Killing is wrong," and sometimes they're totally arbitrary: "I don't like X type of person because of Y." We wanted to be sure we weren't condoning* any *of the characters' points of view or moral codes. Our goal was simply to show how some pretty commonly held beliefs might spiral out of control in a situation where judgments* had *to be made. Another aspect we wanted to explore was how easy it is to manipulate these supposedly hardwired ethics with rhetorical tricks like appealing to fear or sense of other. We wanted people to question why they believe X or Y and if it's something they'd be willing to die for. If not, why not?*

One theme in the film shows how tragedy or the prospect of it (in this case, certain death) can turn humanity against each other, creating divisions and arbitrary hatred. Is this in some ways an allegory for society in a post–9/11, War on Terror world?

In order to really dig into this idea of "What is the value of human life?," we had to have the prospect of tragedy. In everyday life, people are constantly self-censoring. We are careful what we say and do in polite society; we keep distasteful opinions and comments to ourselves depending on who is around. We hide our biases around some but not others. We're censored by our families, our friends, and what our culture as a whole says is acceptable. Sometimes, this censorship is appropriate, such as when racists don't feel comfortable using slurs in public, and sometimes it's an unfortunate side effect of societal oppression. The sort that doesn't allow people to express their true selves due to stigma or widely held beliefs, like we might see with sexual or gender identities that differ from what's considered "the norm."

For Circle, *we had to strip away that self-censorship a little, and the best way to do that is with the threat of death. When it's life or death, people are a lot more willing to throw each other under the bus, to show their true colors. That being said, there's no way to remove that self-censorship completely. It's so deeply ingrained in us, for one, but also in* Circle, *you need the group to like you and want to keep you alive. You're not going to offer up your racial biases unprovoked because you don't want the negative attention, for example.*

So, as the story goes on, we see characters constantly weighing the risks and rewards of censorship. Some characters make direct appeals to large groups in the circle, attempting to turn them against one minority or another. Others lie about themselves to make their stories more sympathetic or palatable. Emotional appeals, all of them, and though their methods vary, the goal is the same: to keep themselves safe. I suspect that, in the real world, the motivations are similar. Divisive rhetoric is almost always rooted in deeply held fear and ignorance.

Was the story's use of characters, like the child and the pregnant woman, a clever way of giving a concrete representation to the abstract idea of wedge issues, i.e., single issues that divide the voters (like abortion, religion, race, etc.) in the film as well as in real life?

As we developed the story, we knew we couldn't play it safe. That meant including characters that movies traditionally shy away from putting in real danger, namely a small child and a pregnant woman. From a cinematic standpoint, we wanted the viewers to constantly question if we had the guts to do it, to kill off a character that everyone expects to live. From a narrative standpoint, they were chosen as yet another way of commenting on these widely held societal beliefs and how, in some ways, people are slaves to them.

In our society, children (and pregnant women) are valued as the most precious and worthy of protection. It's fairly easy to see why that is: They're not just our most vulnerable, but they're also out future. If we don't care for our children, what happens to us as a species? At the same time, if you're looking at the world from a more natural, wild perspective, children are a burden. If, as the characters suspect, one person can survive the circle and will be left to restart mankind, why should it be a child or a pregnant woman? How capable are they of preserving the species? How valuable are they if they can't survive on their own?

And perhaps more importantly, does the fact that one is a child or happens to be pregnant absolve them of "sin"? Does the pregnant woman deserve to live more, *solely by virtue of being pregnant, than a woman who cannot have children? Does a terrible brat of a child deserve to live more than a kind teenager or adult? How much do these attributes make up for on our value scale?*

Life is full of "wedge issues" that all of us feel strongly about, and undoubtedly, these ideas would come up in a real-life Circle. *Our goal with the film was to address them but not to impart any of our own biases in their depiction. Particularly in the case of the pregnant woman, as we wrote the script, we began to sense that some people might take away from* Circle *that we're commenting on the idea of abortion in one way or another. We actually weren't. In fact, we tried our best to remain neutral in all the issues of our characters and let the story be dictated by a snapshot of society at the time we were writing this. Racial issues, class issues, religious issues, and so on, were and are very present in the national consciousness, and we wanted to address them in ways that felt reflective of how they'd be addressed in the real world. When a group of characters makes a decision in* Circle, *it's not a decision we're saying they* should *have made. It's a decision we believe society at large* would *make, based on things that happen in this country every day.*

In the last 16 years, there's been a sharp rise of stories about people pitted against each other in various contests, usually to the death. What does this say about what filmmakers are seeing in society and reflecting in their films?

I think there is a lot of truth to the idea "Death is the great equalizer." It's something no human is immune to, and as such carries massive emotional and psychological weight for a vast majority of people. Most humans will do anything they can to stay alive, including turn on each other and show their "true" selves. For us, death had to be the consequence. There was simply no better motivator.

I think death is used similarly in other narratives for the same reason. If you truly want to see how a person will behave, put them in harm's way. Will they be noble or self-serving? Additionally, is one reaction better than the other? Why? For Circle, we wanted to use death as a way of pulling back the curtain and revealing the true natures behind these characters. Plus, the fear of death is something all audiences can identify with, so we felt it would immediately help put the audience in the characters' shoes. This was especially important because we wanted viewers to consider the decisions that were being made on-screen. Is killing old people okay because they've lived full lives? Is it okay, when my life is in danger, to turn on someone who is different than me? What would I do in this situation? Is my gut instinct wrong or immoral?

Other Films of Interest

Battle Royale II: Requiem (2003), *Breathing Room* (2008)

13

Dystopian Futures

While many people group the post-apocalyptic subgenre and the dystopian future subgenre together, they are in actuality exact opposites. While one of the defining traits of the post-apocalypse story is the lack of infrastructure, government and oversight of any kind, the dystopia is its dark mirror reflection. Choking its citizens and residents with domineering law and order, the dystopia rules with a totalitarian sense of control.

While the dissolution of society was the great fear and exploration of 1936's *Things to Come*, that post-apocalyptic result seemed a luxury of freedom when compared to the tyrannical rule of the serving class in 1927's *Metropolis*, in which city planners keep workers under their control through manipulative means.

Perhaps the greatest example of the dystopian story is George Orwell's *1984*, made into film versions in both 1956 and 1984. The story follows a government worker who is part of the problem and his journey to enlightenment through love, only to succumb to the machinations of the state. This parable of fascism and the totalitarian state became an allegorical flashpoint, and students of history would reference it in events past and present to show how regimes gain and retain power.

And this is the strongest element of the dystopia: the creation of a false totalitarian government to disguise the discussion of a possible real one. From commentary on the corrupt judicial system in 1962's *The Trial* to the burning of books as a way of keeping education away from the people who need it most in *Fahrenheit 451*, the dystopia allows an imagined narrative to fill in the space for the fear we face in the here and now.

The subgenre was in its heyday in the 1970s, when distrust of the government was at an all-time high. *A Clockwork Orange* questioned the efficacy of the prison system in genuine reform, *THX 1138* was a rallying cry from the independent film world about the chokehold that the dying studio system had on filmmaking, and *Soylent Green* and *Logan's Run* imagined worlds in which the environment was so ravaged that humanity had resorted to cannibalism and forced suicide as solutions. Each of these perspectives came from fears and curiosities of the times.

As was often the case with the 1980s, bigger and more outrageous was better, and the nihilistic perspectives on the future became darkly comical. *Escape from New York* introduced a world of religious leaders who turned New York City into a walled-off prison; *Brazil* showed viewers a world so buried in bureaucracy and paperwork that the vigilante hero at the center of the film was a plumber who simply wanted to fix broken pipes; and in *Dead End Drive-In*, social outcasts were imprisoned inside drive-in theaters and placated with junk food, bad movies and rock music.

The 1990s allowed for more narrative sophistication and artistic merit. Margaret Atwood's novel *The Handmaid's Tale* became a film which confronted religious tyranny, while French directors Marc Caro and Jean-Pierre Jeunet brought the visually inventive, darkly humorous and surprisingly touching *Delicatessen* to the screen. Cinema branched out to unlikely places for dystopian inspiration: Based on a comic book, *Judge Dredd* envisioned a future in which police officers have the full spectrum of the law at their disposal, from arrest to trial, judgment and execution.

After the Millennium

One of the main influences on dystopian storytelling in the new millennium was the release of the 1999 hit phenomenon *The Matrix*. While the story was as much other science fiction subgenres such as Artificial Intelligence and Hidden Societies as it was Dystopia, it was influential on all avenues of sci-fi film. The Wachowskis reinvented the action sequence with the *Matrix* franchise, and films like *Equilibrium* and *Dredd* (the 2012 remake of the 1995 film) took the suggestion and ran with it. *The Island* and *Elysium* used similar action narratives to propel social messages about subjugated people rising up against their oppressors.

Dredd was a comic book adaptation, a new vein of creativity for the new millennium; *V for Vendetta* brought the classic 1980s dystopia comic to the screen as a veiled criticism of George W. Bush's America. The commentary about America moved from foreign affairs to class and race with *The Purge*, about an annual night in which all crime is legal, and the rich sequester themselves as the poor fight among themselves and die. Each dystopia reflects the concerns of each generation.

The Independent Perspective

The cinematic size of a dystopian future is not always easy to capture on the budget and timetable of an independent film. Sometimes, shrinking the world down to a microcosm is the best way to handle the logistics.

Joon-ho Bong's spectacular *Snowpiercer* imagined a world so ravaged by environmental damage that it is plunged into a new Ice Age, and the number of survivors is so small that they can all fit on a single, ever-moving train. The rich occupy the spacious front of the train, while most of the poor live in squalor in the back. A powerful allegory for income disparity and hierarchy, the film connects thematically to the original *Metropolis*.

The new millennium also allowed for an expansion of technologies to tell stories. *Zenith* (2010) embraced alternate reality gaming and transmedia storytelling to augment and add to its initial narrative about a man trying to uncover a conspiracy to keep people docile, distracted and under control.

The satire of the 1980s never went away, it just became more subtle and sophisticated, and it moved into the independent arena. Indie godfather Hal Hartley has worked in fantasy and science fiction several times to great allegorical effect with *No Such Thing* and *The Book of Life*. In 2005, he satirized the commodification of human beings by a totalitarian society in *The Girl from Monday*.

Satire is alive and well in the Featured Films in one of the selections. Other films include discussions on corporate control of everything up to and including the legalization of all drugs and a perspective on global commerce and poverty from the point of view of those most negatively affected.

Featured Films

Visioneers (2008)
Director: Jared Drake
Writer: Brandon Drake
Starring Zach Galifianakis, Judy Greer, Missi Pyle

In a domineering corporate future, George Washington Winsterhammerman is a third-level functionary at the Jeffers Corporation, a company that is helping the move to eradicate individualism and personal connection. His wife is distant, obsessed with a happiness her television tells her is attainable but which she never quite finds. His brother lives in the backyard and keeps practicing to pursue his dream of being a pole vaulter, George's one confidant at the Jeffers Corporation is suddenly gone one day. As George attempts to keep his life from falling apart, he is also in danger of becoming a victim of a rash of spontaneous human explosions spreading through society.

Julieen (James LeGros, left) dreams of pole vaulting, while his brother George (Zach Galifianakis) hopes to keep from exploding, in *Visioneers* (2008).

The laughs are dark, but they hit close to home in *Visioneers*, a pitch-black satire of the corporate takeover of everyday human interaction. The film's main character, a descendant of George Washington, stands in as the bewildered and beleaguered common man, struggling in silence to find the American Dream that was promised to him even though he's not entirely sure what it is. Satirical targets range from company speak to self-help television hosts. The movie's humor allows the commentary to be sharper and stronger than a dramatic perspective could.

~

For his first film, director Jared Drake called on his brother Brandon Drake to create the caustic but somehow hopeful script. Brandon attended the UCLA screenwriting program, winning the Screenplay Competition; he also had experience working in a corporate office, and his experiences there were formative in his concept of the film. Brandon Drake described it as a truly independent project.

Brandon Drake: *My brother and I told ourselves we were going to make a movie. We didn't have any money or connections, so we used our family's house as the main location and I got to work writing up a story to include the elements found there—such as a pole vault pit. Because we were trying to make a movie and follow our dreams, it felt natural to write about a man who was struggling with his own dreams. Yes, I said, let's open up to that place, since that is what we're doing, might as well go all the way, and so we did. From that place, the life of George was born. George is a man in danger of exploding, a man who at some point turned away from his own voice and heart and found himself before long living as a "tunt" [a term used in the world of the film]. George is me, in other words, if I quit writing and did what everyone else told me to do.*

When I wrote this script, my brother and I knew this movie was our one shot. We were scared to death to make it, to go all in and go for it. But, I asked myself, what does the world look like for the man who doesn't go for it? It's a world set somewhere in the future, it's a horrible world, and it is ridiculous. I had had, at that point, my own experiences with an institution that was very much in keeping with the Jeffers Corporation and, well, once you let yourself admit what's really going on here and say "F that!" to the things that bother you most, fun and unique things occur. When you say yes, it all says yes back to you, and before long it oozes out of you and just keeps coming and all you can do is say yes, sure, right, of course he has a kid but we don't have a budget so great he never leaves his room, and so on and so forth ... until you're quoting Robinson Jeffers like you just knew you always wanted to and Judy Greer is crocheting with your mom between takes. That's where Visioneers *came from. The same place that keeps you from exploding, the same place, to put it in a positive sense, that compels you to chase a girl from level four you've never met but sounds like maybe she just might, if you really let yourself believe in wonders and miracles, indeed look like Mia Maestro.*

So much of this film is about the sublimation of humanity into a controllable workforce, from the endlessly bureaucratic jobs to the mind-numbing television to the neutering of rebellious acts like giving someone the middle finger. Was it one of your main intentions to create an allegory for the suffocating plainness of modern society?

Yes. I wanted to make fun of all the stuff we take for granted as being normal but are completely soul-sucking and destructive. And I wanted to put a good man in the midst of all of this garbage and see what he would do with it. I love George. I love where he's at and what he's trying to do, and the beauty and pain of his struggle is that much more poignant when you see how ugly the world he's living in has become.

But, yes, I just wanted to make fun of stupid stuff people do that pissed me off, especially as I often felt pushed to accept those things too, but sure didn't want to. I sat down and said, "Man, George's life sucks, but he's a good tunt. So, what's a sucky life that we can have fun making fun of? Hey, what about your friend's brother's wife who was talking about fd at the barbecue and you wanted to throw stuff at her? Great, so his wife has to watch Oprah all the time and believe every word, because that is what people do, and she should wear the same clothes, and Oprah sucks, but who would be even worse than Oprah?, how about Sahra?, and hey, she should mention Sahra's name when George tries to do her. Yes."

That book 14,000 Things to Be Happy About actually exists.

A strong central theme is the rash of people "exploding." Did you have a specific metaphorical meaning for this (like heart attacks and strokes brought on by work-related stress, etc.)? Or is it more representative of the idea of the myriad health and psychological wellness threats of modern society?

I purposely didn't explain exploding in the film and I didn't allow an explanation for myself. I would say that everyone exploded for different reasons that are known only to them in the moment before they explode. Bern, who knows what he sees as he's drinking during the telethon; same for Todd when he mysteriously loses it after the cuddle crew line. I love that part. I love it so much. In my opinion, there is so much humanity in that moment. So much faith in the goodness of people. Here is this utterly screwed-up world that is telling you to just go along to get along, and here is this guy who can barely drag himself in every day, but he's being asked to hold a teddy bear like it's the answer, and he just can't bring himself to do it, but he's going to try, and then it utters this horrible line and who knows, maybe it brings Todd back to the day he knew he should quit, or a memory from childhood long buried that causes him to snap.... I don't know, but it says to me that for all that they will try to do to contain us, they will fail. Good on you Todd, you should lose your shit there.

On a side note: I've often thought it would be fun to write a sequel to Visioneers *that takes place in the world the people who exploded arrived at after exploding.*

Exploding is a mystery, and in accepting that mystery, it feels true. We all know people who have lost their crap at various moments. They know why. It is usually some tiny detail that rises to the surface again. We know that feeling. It's best not to name it. To leave it vague, but specific to each person. What is uniform is the way we try to escape these feelings.

While this film tackles some serious issues, it does so by being both a science fiction film *and* a satirical comedy.

Comedy is at its core the most sympathetic and honest story form. It tells the greatest truth there is to tell: We are all flawed, we are all failures, we will all fail, and all we can do is keep trying and learn as we go and hold tight to the successes, however they come to us. Sympathy reigns in comedy. Understanding. Awareness of our flaws and of the individual's usually dreary lot in life. So my concern was with George. With one good man doing what he can. Again, when I looked at his life, it was ridiculous. Absurd. Funny.

I think this attitude on my part, along with my belief that man is greater than the stupid world he has built, allows for a positive arc for George and at least some form of hope in the end. He will be all right, even if all else is not. I believe this. So, perhaps that is why I wrote this is a comedy. When we're cannibals, I believe we will still be cannibals capable of falling in love.

This film has a distinctly American sensibility to it, from the commentary on TV to the controlling power of big business to the main character being a descendant of George Washington. Do you feel this film speaks to a specifically American problem, or do you feel it's more universal than that?

I'm American. The movie speaks to what I know and where I come from. Yes. I would say it is definitely rooted there. I do think there are universal themes here, though, that would connect with people anywhere.

We all feel like we are going to explode at times, and I'd bet you'd find that "I'm going to explode" is a phrase that has been used throughout history and in numerous cultures. George is an everyman dealing with a common problem. I'd hope that a Pushti sheep herder who can't figure out why the rope keeps getting untied and why his wife insists on following the example of Gutma the wise, who has a new star chart she's following, knows the feeling. We've all been there.

In fact, as I write this, right now, in a crowded Starbucks, I am feeling a little bit, just a tinge, of some cuddle crew coming on, as my computer refuses to copy and paste this text and behind me, two rowing coaches are talking about rowing as if it is God's gift to universal suffering (rowing will cure it all) and a guy next to me is eating a donut loudly ... and I am not sure why this is bringing on explosive feelings ... perhaps because I know I have other things to do and time is slipping away.... If that goes on long enough, and is ignored enough, eventually you throw that donut across the room and shove the two rowing coaches into a boat made out of the Starbucks sugar and milk stand and dump them into the lake and run off with your computer over your head because that is all it is good for, to block the rain as you run to the mountains and the promise of freedom or at least a quiet death. Or, if you're in Visioneers, *you explode. Or, if you're a mature and peaceful soul, at least in this moment, you take a deep breath and type the text in yourself. Sigh ... yeah, like that. Great. What was I saying?*

Wagers on if I make it to another question? Anyone? Anyone?

By the way, numerous people exploded during the making of Visioneers. *Including, yes, I will admit it, yours truly.*

We're all glad that you've recovered. Why do you think we revisit the world of near-future dystopias so frequently in sci-fi?

For the same reasons we like horror movies. We get to go where we don't really want to go and embrace fears and ideas too terrible in waking life. It's cathartic and therapeutic. It is also a fun logic game to play. What will the world look like? What are the trends and how will they continue? How will mankind adapt? That last part speaks to curiosity about ourselves and our nature. I think we are endlessly fascinated with our own make-up and our own story as a race. We should be. We are a conundrum. Stories in the future, dealing with the problems we are making now, ultimately let us talk about and confront the concerns and questions we have about ourselves as a race. We are part animal, part god, more and more part machine ... capable of great feats of heroism, mundane acts of routine living, and evil—often in the same person, in the same day.

Senn (2013)

Director: Josh Feldman
Writers: Josh Feldman, Britton Watkins
Starring Zach Eulberg, Lauren Taylor, Taylor Lambert

Senn is an assembly line worker on a nearly forgotten, industry-ravaged planet that makes supplies for rich societies off-world. has started having strange dreams and visions which he shares with his girlfriend Kana. Shortly thereafter, a mysterious alien intelligence offers to take Senn and Kana across the universe on a journey to find the Polychronom, an ancient object floating in the emptiness of space; the alien intelligence cannot activate or communicate with it, but for some unexplained reason, Senn seems to be the key to establish contact.

Senn is a film in the tradition of thoughtful science fiction stories that explore global social issues like *Soylent Green*, *Logan's Run*, and *Silent Running*. It smartly plays its limited futuristic elements in contrast with the mostly run-down, derelict locations and costuming to create a lived-in world that is reminiscent equally of *Blade Runner* and *2001: A Space Odyssey*. A cerebral exercise designed to challenge viewers, it is part of a new breed of sci-fi that includes *Arrival* and *Upstream Color*.

～

The film was director Josh Feldman's first feature, but his experience in the arts is extensive; *Senn* was scored by Cubosity, which is actually a musical side project of Feldman's. He is also an author, having written the YA novella *ableYoung*. His most recent film work is the documentary *Conlanging: The Art of Crafting Tongues*, in which he and director Britton Watkins explore the challenging task of creating new languages for cinematic societies (something that was also utilized to great effect in *Senn*).

Josh Feldman: *One day I turned to my husband [Britton Watkins, co-writer and co-producer of* Senn*] and said, "I want to make a movie!" Well, it was more complicated than that of course, but I was feeling like I wanted to do something new creatively, and film was a way of combining all the things that I love doing—music, storytelling, video, fine art, design, photography.... I had done some short films, corporate video work, and animations in the past, but never a feature-length film.*

The film opens with a voice-over monologue that describes about a planet in a way that makes it sound like a real estate listing. That, combined with the mentioned history of the planet itself (the devastating economic downturn and the environmental ravaging

Senn (Zack Eulberg) and girlfriend Kana (Lauren Taylor) dream of a better life in *Senn* (2013).

due to bad business decisions), make this feel like some of the elements may have been taken from real events, such as the 2008 housing crash and the pollution epidemic in South America. Were these influential on the creation of this world?

There were lots of influences—out of control corporations, North Korea, human-caused environmental destruction, Chinese factory workers, deplorable regimes, decaying American cities.... Much of the world in the film is essentially ours extrapolated far into the future.

The film opens with Senn working as essentially a sweatshop employee, assembling cheap trinkets he could never buy for wealthy people living elsewhere. Was this parallel to actual reality intentional, and what was your goal in putting it in the film?

My husband and I have always been fascinated by the idea that Asian factory workers have no idea what they're making. I recently ran across an article about a factory in China that manufactures Christmas decorations—the employees there assumed that the red and green glitter covered stuff they make is for some type of western New Year's celebration, but they aren't really sure.

Is this film in some ways analogous to the immigrant plight? Working a menial job creating cheap goods in the hopes of someday working yourself and your family up to a better status?

Yes, but with the added twist that the company that "owns" you has forgotten that you even exist. The workers in Senn *don't really even have the opportunity to advance, so it's more bleak in some respects.*

Can you talk about the complexity of creating an entirely new written language for this film, and what it was like working with language expert Britton Watkins in the writing stage?

I've seen up close how much work it is to create a new language—I can tell you that those who do it are really dedicated to the craft! Britton and I agreed that having an "alien" language visually appear throughout the film would be a really good way of reminding viewers the story doesn't take place on Earth. It allowed us to achieve extra layers of depth in the world building for relatively little money.

As far as the grammar and writing system, I let Britton create pretty much whatever he felt was appropriate. We then worked together on what phrases would go where, what extra "fonts" needed to be created for different purposes, how aged the letters should look, etc. Occasionally, when I would get an idea for a prop or poster, it took a bit longer to deal with, since Britton then had to go translate the English I came up with into Siinyamda (the invented language in Senn*), or create new words that he hadn't come up with yet.*

Was the element of the Polychronom [a massive, powerful alien "object" in the film] influenced by the monolith in *2001: A Space Odyssey* or the machine in *Contact*?

I don't honestly know where the idea for the Polychronom came from. Probably subconsciously I was influenced by 2001 *and* Contact. *I liked the idea of a machine built by an alien race, who died off long ago, but the machine lives on, its function becoming unpredictable as it encounters new things its builders couldn't have predicted. So I guess I was influenced by the first* Star Trek *movie, too!*

Some of the ravaged locations were actual practical locations. Is that fact a commentary in itself, that you could find real places that could pass as these destitute, devastated locations?

> *Of course we couldn't afford to build sets on our "nano-budget," so we had to find existing locations for everything. Ironically, we live in San Francisco, and with the economy booming here and everything being rebuilt, it was hard to find dilapidated buildings and landscapes! If we were based out of Detroit, it would have been easy.*
>
> *We were lucky to find an old warehouse on an ex-Navy base that we could use. I still had to digitally tweak the background in wide shots to hide signs of renewal and "gentrification," though!*
>
> *Of course, there are real cities and places on Earth that are even more rundown than anything we showed in the film—it's hard for any of us in the first world to imagine what day-to-day life for billions of people living with nothing on our own planet is really like...*

Was the idea of juxtaposition an intentional theme in the film, i.e., love among the ruins of the planet, low-tech vs. high-tech? Even the image of the bed in the forest shows artificial vs. natural.

> *I wanted to have a 180-degree contrast between the first part of the film and the second—gray desolate ruins vs. lush green forest, to highlight the plight of the characters and emphasize the change in their fortunes (for better or worse). There were many intentional contrasts: human warmth vs. cold corporate decay, the familiar vs. the alien, organic vs. artificial, real vs. simulation, etc.*
>
> *One happy "accident" is that when I realized that nothing in the script called for visually showing any technology (computer screens, device interfaces, etc.), I was super-adamant that we not introduce any. I really liked the idea of a sci-fi film that doesn't have any computers or technology visible in it, as that stuff usually dates really badly, so all the more reason to leave it out.*

What do you think it is that appeals to sci-fi film viewers about the dystopian future? It is bleak and somewhat depressing, but viewers continue to watch movies set there.

> *Dystopian themes can get overused obviously (I'm guilty of that overuse, I realize), but I feel it's an expression of where many of us feel our planet is going and of our helplessness at changing its course. Global warming (or global burning, as I like to call it) is clearly accelerating, and with it comes the real threat that the dystopian future that many have predicted will be realized. My husband and I don't have kids, but we have many relatives and friends who do. What will the future be like for them? Right now, it doesn't look good, and there appears to be little anyone can do to stop the long, scary progression.*

Narcopolis (2015)
Writer-Director: Justin Trefgarne
Starring James Callis, Kerry Shale, Elodie Yung

In the near-future, every class of drugs has been legalized. The catch is that they are all now licensed and produced by a corporation called Ambro. Frank Grieves is a detective whose job it is to find the black market dealers selling unlicensed drugs. An unidentified body is found with traces of an unknown substance in its system. His investigations lead him to the conclusion that Ambro has been secretly testing an experimental drug on people. The more he looks into it, the more danger he finds himself in.

There is nothing more sinister than imprisonment disguised as freedom, and *Narcopolis* touches on that concept in interesting and complicated ways. It seems to begin as a commentary on decriminalization and drug use, but then cleverly uses that as a set-up for a more intricate study of the power of corporations. The near-future crime investigation has superficial resemblances to the works of Philip K. Dick, from *Blade Runner* to *Total Recall* to *Paycheck*. Surface elements aside, *Narcopolis* also explores one of Dick's most revisited themes: the shift in human nature as a result of technological advancement.

~

When Justin Trefgarne decided to make *Narcopolis* his debut feature film as writer-director, he was an Emmy-nominated writer for the *Peter Rabbit* TV series and a successful development executive who helped bring *Pride and Prejudice*, *Atonement* and *Hot Fuzz* to the screen. While Dick's work was an influence, Trefgarne had many more basic and relatable inspirations.

Justin Trefgarne: *The film came from two ideas. The first was an image that came to me one day in a storage facility. I rented a locker for a while and I was down in this subterranean vacuum when I wondered if anyone had ever stashed a body in one of these things. That quickly led to the idea of a police investigation surrounding a body being discovered in a locker, and no one knowing where it had come from. The other idea was the drugs. I was playing with the notion of a whole city having narcotics legalized and what that would feel like as a background to a story. Then I put the two together and that was Narcopolis.*

Because of recent societal changes, like marijuana being legalized in many places as well as a backlash about the epidemic of prescription painkiller abuse, this film seems like a strong allegory for actual modern-day events. Did any of these elements inspire the world or the plot of your story?

None specifically, but I did a lot of reading up on the subject—the pros and cons of decriminalization. People on both sides have very strong arguments, and I wondered if that was a better way to proceed. Rather than say "It's good" or "It's bad," I wanted to create an environment where it felt ambiguous. One of the things that was very important to me was to start the story five years into legalization, rather than feature the legalization process itself as the plot. I wanted to drop the audience right into this situation and imagine what society would look like when legal drugs were the norm. But importantly, almost no one talks about drugs in the film. I felt strongly that it would be really cheesy for characters to comment on each other's consumption. I wanted it to be a hard fact so it didn't overwhelm the narrative, which in the end is only partially connected to drugs.

One of the aspects of the drug legalization in this film is that it was achieved with backing from a corporation. Is part of this a commentary on the idea of corporations regulating and charging for medications and drugs in real life, and the monopoly they hold on global health care?

I think whatever your perspective, you have to admit that the minute something becomes legalized and then franchised (which is what would happen), bottom-line economics would play a part. If the subprime crash of 2008 has taught us anything, it's that corporations and governments will do everything in their power to protect the profit margin. People shouldn't be surprised. Capitalism is money first, people second.

The argument, of course, is that money is meant to be a great facilitator—the flow of capital improves the lives of everyone top to bottom. But recent years have shown us that in fact the flow of money goes upwards mostly. If drugs were legalized, that is a fact we would have to face, namely that the companies responsible, like the food industry, the tech industry, etc., would be looking for ever more inventive ways to ensure our addiction to their products. And that will, of course, mean compromises in our health and safety. The drug situation on Narcopolis *is meant to be a microcosm of that reality.*

In an interesting variation on the theme of a dystopian future, the ruling society of *Narcopolis* maintains power by allowing the freedom to do all drugs, rather than the typical dystopia which rules through a strict and rigid set of unreasonable laws. What made you decide to explore that perspective of a dystopian future?

One of the aspects of today that interests me is the notion that we are more "connected: than ever via the Internet, whilst in turn we are more watched than ever. Data are everything. In enjoying the connectivity, we have allowed large, billion dollar corporations to snoop our digital lives to saturation point. But the whole thing is apparently benign—these companies are our friends, or so they would have us believe. When I turned my attentions to drugs and legalization, I wanted the Ambro Corp. to be a friendly face, just like the Internet giants of today. I wanted legalization to look and feel like a libertarian move, a favor to society. Legalizing drugs, in Narcopolis, *is all about freedom, releasing the people from the tyranny of the black market, etc. But what's really happening is that addiction—and these substances are addictive, whichever way you look at it—has been commodified and exploited for profit. It has become a product. And as we know, people who sell potentially harmful products have the most sophisticated ways of packaging them to make them look essential to our happiness.*

The mention of the word Morlock is an obvious reference to The Time Machine, a story which plays into the film in an important way and clearly seems to be an influence. Were there other influences for this film?

Yes, but the danger with science fiction is it quickly becomes all about the influences. I made the mistake of mentioning Blade Runner *a few times and now people compare this film—which was made for under a million dollars–to a movie that cost $60 million 30 years ago and starred Harrison Ford!* Blade Runner *is of course one of the most beautiful films ever made, and I love it deeply, but I didn't ever set out to emulate or borrow from it. My influences were a little more nebulous. I was very interested in looking at the Philip K. Dick universe—the paranoia and delusion, the hallucinatory reality. I wanted some of that fever dream feel to infuse this movie. Part of this film is a fantasy—the time travel and the circular narrative—and I wanted the plot to feel like it could have been hallucinated. Almost as if it was all cooked up by the main character to atone for the huge guilt he feels towards his family, which I guess aligns it with the kind of stuff Philip K. Dick was interested in.*

Cinematically, I am a huge admirer of the early Iñarritu movies and I wanted to retain some of their immediacy and grit. Biutiful *is, in my view, the best film he's ever made. Where it influenced me is, I wanted to bring some of that immediacy and vibrancy to the visuals in* Narcopolis, *the urban decay, the violence and the beauty in that decay. Equally, I wanted the camera to feel light and responsive, to avoid the curse of the low-budget movie feeling locked down and static. We worked incredibly hard to keep the camera fluid and at times improvised; to eschew fancy setups for something that favored performance, allowing the actors to work in a freer way and for the camera to respond accordingly. In this way, I was also heavily indebted to John Cassavetes. I have always been inspired by the "family" approach to film making that he, Coppola and even Kubrick took, whereby the film unit functioned like a mobile family. We would ensure that shooting was as fun as possible, and we'd often use my house as a unit base and bring the crew back for a meal after we wrapped. It was a way of making sure that despite the pressure and the crappy money, that people felt valued and part of something. So those were my influences, and then once the film starts to take shape, other movies recede into the background and it becomes its own influence, shaping your decisions as it starts to take form.*

Dystopias are inherently depressing ideas, and yet viewers and filmmakers alike consistently return to the genre.

Well, the problem with utopia is there's very little scope for conflict, unless that utopia is a lie (in which case it's really a dystopia—as in, say, The Matrix*). Dystopia is more interesting because you have recognizable obstacles to overcome, you have state control (more often than not), and I guess this speaks to the heart of what worries us all the most—that slowly we are handing over power to the state, through the Internet, through our bank accounts, our cell phones.... I guess that's why we want to watch this stuff as it fuels the inherent paranoia that lurks inside us. It's cathartic.*

Other Films of Interest

The Age of Stupid (2009), *Antiviral* (2012), *The Bothersome Man* (2006), *Equals* (2015), *The Giver* (2014)

14

Alongside the Secret Society

The trick to knowing the history of the Secret Society subgenre is to understand the meaning of the subgenre. The title might lead you to believe it is about clandestine groups that meet for rituals and rites, groups like the Bilderberg Group, the Illuminati, the Skull and Bones Society and the Freemasons. While there is some element of the secret duality of man in those stories, the movies in the Secret Society subgenre are about *whole* societies hidden from the view of the rest of the world.

The Secret Society subgenre posits the idea that the world we see and live in is just part of the overall world happening around us. This secret society is only visible and accessible to a chosen few and the occasional accidental interloper.

The subgenre extends as far back as *The Wizard of Oz*, in which a tornado takes Dorothy Gale and her Kansas home to a strange place not normally reachable by human travel. Though she wakes at the end of the film to find it was all a dream, the audience knows better; characters from one world also existed in the other world as doppelgangers, and there is some secret connection between them that is greater than Dorothy's unconscious imagination.

A more physical representation of the secret society is the world that Pat Boone and James Mason discover in 1959's *Journey to the Center of the Earth*. In this story, scientists travel down through an extinct volcano to discover an ancient subterranean city previously hidden from the rest of the world. A similar tale came from the Walt Disney Company with 1974's *The Island at the Top of the World*, in which a previously undiscovered Viking society still exists as it did in the past. Director John Carpenter borrowed from Chinese history in his martial arts adventure-comedy *Big Trouble in Little China*.

The theme of the Secret Society is most often and most effectively used in service of an allegory. In Carpenter's *They Live*, special sunglasses reveal an alien race living amongst us, disguised as human beings with hidden messages everywhere encouraging ambivalence, greed and consumption.

David Cronenberg brought the seemingly unfilmable William S. Burroughs novel *Naked Lunch* to the screen in 1991: The strange city of Interzone in the film is a barely concealed stand-in for the shattered mental state of the drug-addled lead character. *Sandman* creator Neil Gaiman crafted the British TV series *Neverwhere*, which followed the descent of typical man Richard into the hidden shadow world of London Below.

After the Millennium

Many of the previously mentioned titles were revisited post-millennium. In a rush to connect classic properties to new audiences via elaborate special effects with an eye towards starting big franchises, both *The Wizard of Oz* and *Journey to the Center of the Earth* were remade either for TV or the big screen and remakes of *They Live* and *Big Trouble in Little China* have been announced. Gaiman's *Neverwhere* hasn't been remade, but his *American Gods*, about new and ancient gods living among us in disguise and battling for superiority, is strikingly reminiscent. The same can be said for his collaboration with artist Dave McKean, the otherworldly fantasy *Mirrormask*.

By far, the best-known Secret Society in film history was born out of a book series and came to screens in 2001. Beginning with *Harry Potter and the Sorcerer's Stone*, the fantasy series focused on magical school Hogwarts is decidedly not science fiction, but a prime example of how popular the subgenre of the Secret Society can be when a powerful enough allegory is applied. In the case of Hogwarts, the violent extremism and racism of the world is channeled into hatred of non-magic people and children of magic/non-magic couplings, derisively known as Muggles and Mudbloods.

The Independent Perspective

Less money spent on a film means more creative freedom for the filmmakers, and the examples of the Secret Society subgenre in the indies use that freedom to discuss some controversial social issues.

In *Branded*, a young advertising executive discovers that he can see the manifestation of advertising as blob-like creatures subsisting by dangling off the bodies of humans who are susceptible to them. In *Heartless* and *Citadel*, the everpresent danger of wayward youth gone terribly wrong is given a dark, otherworldly spin as violent hooligans in hooded sweatshirts are revealed to be demonic creatures feeding on innocents and spreading chaos.

In *Hard to Be a God*, the humans themselves get to be the Secret Society as a group of human scientists go incognito to live amongst other humanoid aliens just developing into their own medieval era of society. They are there to help the society progress positively, and the movie touches on difficult questions of what is simply being helpful and what is improperly influencing a group without their knowledge or permission.

The Featured Films in this section run the gamut of Secret Societies with a different allegory for each one, from depression to social hierarchies to a religious End Times scenario disguised as a last day at an office building.

Featured Films

Ink (2009)
Writer-Director: Jamin Winans
Starring Christopher Soren Kelly, Quinn Hunchar, Jessica Duffy

The world of dreams is secretly a war zone where the good Storytellers and the evil Incubi battle for the safety and welfare of humanity. An unaffiliated drifter named Ink kidnaps the soul of a sleeping little girl, and the Storytellers are in pursuit. In the real world, the girl's father, John, won't visit the little girl in the hospital; he is bitter and damaged after a car accident claimed his wife. He is unable to face his daughter, burying his sorrow in drugs and alcohol. As the world of dreams and the real world draw closer to each other, John discovers that his actions have far-reaching repercussions that could change the fate of the world.

Ink is a complex, ambitious and passionate film which thinks bigger than should be possible for its budget. Not satisfied to simply stretch the boundaries of science fiction storytelling on an independent level, the film also creates impressive action and martial arts sequences and fantastic makeup and costuming.

∼

Cinematographer-associate producer Jeff Pointer had previously worked in narrative and documentary films like *Earthlings: Ugly Bags of Mostly Water* and *The Shadow Walkers*. He met writer-director Jamin Winans when they worked on a series of short films. Because of the relationship and shorthand they'd developed, Pointer was the perfect person to help Winans bring his ambitious and technically complicated film to reality.

Jeff Pointer: *I first met Jamin Winans around 1999 when I was wrapping up film school. I showed him my reel, which was on VHS. He was impressed and he hired me to shoot a short film called* Blanston. *During* Blanston, *our video assist monitor failed, so Jamin spent the whole day hoping I was shooting good stuff. Can you imagine the anxiety he was under? Not knowing what we were capturing? Anyhow, he loved what I did, and for the next nine years or so, Jamin and I worked together on client projects and his other three films preceding* Ink: The Maze, Spin *and* 11:59.

While the film's budget is low, the concept is high. Were there times when you were worried about being able to create such a complicated and intricate world on such limited means?

Certainly there were moments of fear trying to pull off such a high concept with such a small crew and limited budget. There were three main things we did to overcome this:

1. *What we didn't have in money, we spent in time. I think we shot about 70 days on* Ink. *In other words, we really thought out each scene and how to shoot and light it. I think we should talk about "the production trilemma" at this point: "Good, fast, inexpensive." Choose two because you can't have all three. We chose "good" and "inexpensive," which meant we couldn't move "fast," thus we spent those 70 days moving as efficiently as possible at a slow pace.*

2. *We shot* Ink *on a prosumer Sony V1U camera. Jamin and I are pretty good at knowing how to use a small camera like this and making it look big and expensive. For instance, shooting low F-stops at a big, long focal length. This technique allows one to have a shallow depth of field—in other words, give it a cinematic look. Nowadays, most professional HD cameras have the ability to accept 35mm lenses. That fact alone helps one get that limited depth of field that cinema-style shots are known for. We had to go through a lot of trouble to make that small camera act like a big camera.*

3. Good lighting. Good lighting in the case of Ink meant lots of contrast and pools of light rather than lighting an entire space.

Did you and the creative team discuss any of the film's allegorical elements before filming, i.e., what the alternate world represented and if the Storytellers, Incubi and Drifters were stand-ins for real-life groups or circumstances?

We didn't really discuss this much. Clearly there were alternate realities, but what they mean is up to the viewer. Jamin holds these internal questions quite close and would rather the audience make a determination. He won't even discuss, for instance, what the title Ink means or where it came from.

Fire City: End of Days (2015)
Director: Tom Woodruff, Jr.
Writers: Michael Hayes, Brian Lubocki
Starring Tobias Jelinek, Danielle Chuchran, Keely Aloña

Vine is a demon who is restless and uncomfortable in his job. He lives in an apartment building in a human city, disguised as a human being and in charge of keeping them in various states of misery. One day, he finds himself in a situation in which he has to choose between saving some of his fellow kind or a human woman innocently caught in the middle. This seemingly small and simple decision has enormous ramifications for the delicate balance between humankind and "demonkind" and has the potential to throw the world into war.

In *Fire City: End of Days*, a lot of the classic mythology of the demon world is filtered through a classic film noir, taking the dual nature of flawed heroes in old Hollywood films and making that literal in the shape of conflicted demons. A stark lighting scheme, fantastic makeups and a somber narrative full of complex characters gives this film a leg up on the many post-millennial narratives that build complicated mythologies around classic characters *à la Gods of Egypt* and *The Immortals*.

∽

While many elements make the film a worthwhile view, its success is in no small part due to the expert makeup and practical effects. Director Tom Woodruff, Jr., had decades to hone his craft before embarking on this challenging project. Co-founder of the effects company Amalgamated Dynamics with his partner Alec Gillis (who is featured elsewhere in this book), Woodruff is known for his work in *Alien vs. Predator, Starship Troopers, Mortal Kombat, X-Men: First Class* and the *Santa Clause* series. To create the huge canvas of *Fire City: End of Days*, Woodruff began with a small but important test.

Tom Woodruff, Jr.: Fire City: End of Days *is actually a prequel to a huge project simply titled* Fire City. *It was a move designed by the writer-producers Michael Hayes and Brian Lubocki as a way to introduce audiences to a very rich world of demons among us.* Fire City, *proper, is huge. When the creators were shopping the project around town, it was a serious investment of funds. With no track record other than the script, they were not finding the kind of reception that didn't require severe creative compromise. They were faced with the offer of having the project possibly re-imagined and taken away from them creatively.*

Instead, they stuck to their guns and chose to crowdfund a much more streamlined introduction to Vine and his world. And when you see *End of Days*, this "streamlined" introduction, you can imagine how dense that full world would actually be.

While the plan to crowdfund was being set, I wanted to step up and direct what I thought was a fantastic opportunity to bring realistic demons to life in a world in which they had to interact with each other and with real people on different levels. I've always loved simple "monster movies," but this script was so much more; it was smart and it was engaging. And of everything it boasted, the character of Sara, the little girl, and her relationship with the demon Vine was really inventive and, for me, very attractive.

The guys put together a ten-minute short, *King of Miseries*, as a test. It was a fast pace with a two-day shoot that simply offered a look at our world with two demons conducting

Tobias Jelinek as the demon Vine in *Fire City: End of Days* (2015).

business of their own. We shot fast and lean and, even with losing power for three, four hours the first day, we were able to make a story work.

In this story, there are many actors who, while playing only a single role, actually appear on-screen in two very different ways: as a seemingly normal human and as their actual demon appearance. When casting a movie like this, aside from the skill of performing, do you have to look for certain things in actors, certain features which you know can be utilized or accentuated for the makeup process?

The roles were cast for presence and acting skills. It's funny—I've spent decades designing and creating character makeup effects which are all about look, and wondering why production is casting people whose noses are too big or eyes too small to make the designs fit. I had access to some really accomplished actors who were fresh and willing to take a chance on this little film. The only physical attribute they had to possess beyond being able to play the character, was to not have any claustrophobic reluctance to spend some of their days in full prosthetic makeups.

In the film, the main character's job as a demon is to monitor the human-demon relationships in his apartment complex. Is there some commentary here about the evils of middle management, being the face of evil in a mundane position that brings people sadness and difficulty?

Vine's job was to encourage and allow human misery to flourish in his building. That's what allowed his demon brethren to feed and survive. I always saw him as a provider and a smart businessperson in that he was in charge of his world. I don't think it's going to be good for anyone with a career in film to comment on the evils of middle management— that's how films get made.

One plot element of the film revolves around humanity not dwelling in misery, and the demons growing weak because of it. It reminded me a bit of the dominance of the lower and middle classes by the uber-wealthy and the struggle of the wealthy to keep it that way, a struggle that has recently grown in the real world. Was that an intentional parallel you were drawing in the film?

No, the more basic thought behind that is that each person has the ability to bring himself happiness if he is strong enough to realize it. I see it as more of a job, maybe a duty, to work at each person making himself happy. It's hard work. The idea of class dominance is not an element I wanted to explore other than to say that part of the dominance depends on someone willing to be dominated. I don't see extreme wealth as a bad thing that has to be fought and destroyed. How and why?

I don't think it's going to be good for anyone with a career in film to comment on the evils of extreme wealth—that's how films get made. Oh wait, I already used that!

This film interestingly mixes the idea of a secret demon world with the aesthetic of a film noir. Was that by design because so many film noir stories are about characters struggling with dueling impulses to be good and bad?

From the very beginning, Michael, Brian and I saw this as a film noir tale. It's written that way. Vine is from the Humphrey Bogart mold. I wanted to shoot it in black and white.

There is no better or more human conflict than between good and bad within. Those are high stakes. And setting the main character as a strong character within his evil demon world turns good and bad on its side that really works in a unique way. You end up wanting Vine to succeed even though he is a demon at heart.

The central premise is that the demon world lives clandestinely among us, in a secret society most people never learn of. Why did this concept (hidden worlds within our own) appeal to you?

I love monster movies. That was how I grew up. Long before I even knew what a genre was, I was using the term "monster movie" to talk about the films my small group of friends and I loved to catch on TV, even though at the time it was an embarrassing term for a ten-year old to have to admit to. Today, I embrace it. What are the movies that still resonate today? Everybody loves monsters. And I think that presenting them in their own normal nine-to-five working world gives them a footing to become believable and interesting and more than a creature that waits in the dark to rip off your head and feed on the brains.

End of Days, Inc. (2015)
Director: Jennifer Liao
Writer: Christina Ray
Starring Mark O'Brien, Paulino Nunes, Carolyne Maraghi

On the last night that an inventory processing company is open, many of the laid-off workers are convinced by the unusual owners to stick around after their normal shift for a party. During the party, the owners spring a surprise on them: In exchange for helping them finish their cataloguing business before morning, each of them will receive a bonus of one million dollars. While the employees are working on the task, they start to find evidence that the seemingly harmless cataloguing might have much a more sinister purpose.

This Is the End meets *The Office* in the clever hybrid comedy *End of Days, Inc.* By combining the discomfort of office politics with a secret end-of-the-world scenario, the film allows for humorous observations about both. Skewering bureaucracy, corporate mentality and the proliferation of End Times scenarios in popular fiction, the film allows for a discussion of several modern anxieties through a deceptively simple narrative framework.

Mr. Godfrey (Paulino Nunes) and Esther (Anna Ferguson) have an offer that Janet (Carolyne Maraghi) and their other employees may not be able to refuse in *End of Days, Inc.* (2015).

End of Days, Inc. had a first-time feature director, Jennifer Liao. She had a great deal of experience in many different positions before stepping behind the camera. Aside from directing five short films, including *What You Eat* and *A Tiny Prophecy*, she also wrote and edited several projects. She produced the feature film *Sex After Kids*, playing a role on-screen in the film as well as many others.

Jennifer Liao: *We're very used to apocalyptic narratives in popular culture where the protagonists step up and do extraordinary things to save the day. There's definitely some social commentary and hopefully humor in* End of Days, Inc. *around the fact that most people would not suddenly become fearless action heroes in the face of an apocalyptic threat. The characters in the film aren't used to questioning authority or looking any further than the things that affect them directly, and that idea is taken to an extreme in the film. The personal growth they experience and the actions they take throughout the course of the film are really quite significant for them individually, but all of this happens so late and the impact in the grand scheme of things is limited. Our screenwriter Christina Ray relates the film to the famous passage from the T.S. Eliot poem* The Hollow Men: *"This is the way the world ends. Not with a bang but a whimper."*

Is the idea of these office workers literally compiling and filing human beings (in this case, for the end of the world) also reflecting a sense of depersonalization that many industries are experiencing due to the global nature of business and the use of impersonal technology to communicate? Are we all in our daily jobs just in some way compiling and filing human beings who have no identity to us?

The film is meant to present a satirical reflection of the de-personalization of the worker in modern society, though the intention was never to address it head-on. We want the audience to be entertained by the story and find food for thought in what the characters are going through. The familiar adage of big corporations seeing their employees as nothing but numbers is only getting truer every day, especially if those numbers are costs that can be cut. The massive efficiencies that technology brings about enriches our world (and particular people more than others), but they've also rendered many kinds of jobs obsolete, especially manual labor of the kind that the staff of Godfrey Global Inventory are engaged in. However, in their case, successfully completing the job not only means working themselves into obsolescence on a figurative level, but the entire human race on a literal one! There's an added resonance in the fact that punch cards themselves are such a significant example of an innovation that couldn't seem more archaic today.

This film has a female writer and female director. While female and minority representation in front of and behind the camera still isn't where it should be, have you noticed that there is more of a behind-the-camera presence in the genre community (horror and science fiction) in recent years to start to reflect the large percentage of female fandom?

I hope there are more female directors and writers able to stake their claim to make genre films and TV these days. There may be more notable examples than there have been in the past, but I'd be curious to know how much the numbers have actually gone up. The amount of discussion right now is still far outpacing the actual percentage increases of women behind the camera overall, and I hope that changes soon.

It seems clear the film is somewhat a commentary on corporatism, but given its connection to the End Times scenario in this film, is there some commentary on the idea of the corporatism of religion in recent years as well?

I wouldn't want to dissuade anyone from their own reading of the film's events, but I can't say it was something I was consciously addressing, as organized religion has never been a part of my life and I don't have much personal familiarity with it otherwise.

Other Films of Interest

The Imaginarium of Doctor Parnassus (2009), *Coraline* (2009)

15
Unnatural Selection

The sci-fi subgenre of the Deadly Creature is forever changing, as is our definition of what a deadly creature is. There was a time when creature and monster were interchangeable; even natural animals from real-life ecosystems were sometimes deemed monsters, when they attacked humans. It is no real coincidence that one of the earliest and most iconic creatures in cinema is the so-called monster from 1931's *Frankenstein*, created from parts of dead bodies by a crazed scientist whose main goal was to become a god himself. The tragedy of the story is that the Monster had no say into his birth and could only do what was in his nature.

Later films turned even further away from identifiable human characteristics, presenting a dinosaur in *The Beast from 20,000 Fathoms* (1953) and the scaled aquatic menace of *Creature from the Black Lagoon* (1954). Even then, though, the sharp-eyed viewer could see the tragic plight of the creature, stirred from its natural state and persecuted for reacting as it naturally would. The '50s also brought Godzilla, a radioactive monster attacking Japan; in truth, though, Godzilla was awoken and provoked by American nuclear testing, and is as much a victim as the citizens of Tokyo.

As the subgenre continued, the creatures took on more personality as they became even more deadly. The creatures in both *Gremlins* and *Tremors* wreaked havoc, but also had a personality that drew in fans and brought about sequels. There were many sequels and remakes to *Godzilla*, with each becoming slightly campier and adding more monsters and more personality to the titular figure. The original creature from the 1958 *The Blob* became bright pink and uber-vicious (in keeping with the ethos of the 1980s), and even the deadly T-Rex from Steven Spielberg's *Jurassic Park* somehow gets a hero shot when he (unintentionally) saves the children from a velociraptor's attack. In the last years of the old millennium, giant insects and tentacled undersea dwellers filled the screens thanks to advances in CG animation: In 1997 we had *Starship Troopers* and *Mimic*, followed closely by *Deep Rising* (1998).

After the Millennium

It was human monster vs. creature monster in 2000's *Pitch Black*, the science fiction-horror thriller that put action hero Vin Diesel in the spotlight and began a popular franchise. The new millennium would bring two more entries in the *Jurassic Park* franchise, with *Jurassic World* breaking box office records in 2015.

Straddling the line between fantasy and science fiction is the fun and underrated *Reign of Fire*, in which a devastated England attempts to survive when dragons reawaken and populate the Earth. *Godzilla* was revisited again in 2014, this time spawning a giant monster crossover series that welcomed King Kong back to the screen. Occasional releases like *The Host* hearkened back to smaller scale stories of the past, but that was rare. For the most part, creatures had become as large and unwieldy as the tent pole blockbusters that contained them; *Pacific Rim* and *Cloverfield* reminded us that the big screen demanded a big presence.

The Independent Perspective

There was always entertainment to be had from turning a seemingly innocuous thing into a movie monster; Jonathan King's *Black Sheep* took some of the sweetest and most docile farm animals and turned them into a flesh-eating mob of killers. There was humor in the absurd juxtaposition of slackers trying to save the world from decidedly unusual otherworldly beings in *The Last Lovecraft: Relic of Cthulhu*.

The indie arena also created some of the most affecting and thoughtful social commentaries in the Deadly Creatures subgenre. Mickey Keating's *Pod*, a film about a brother and sister confronting an ex-military sibling who believes he has a monster trapped in his basement, touches on the horrors of war and PTSD. Leigh Janiak's *Honeymoon* weaves a thoughtful narrative about the allegorical terrors of pregnancy and new relationships.

The chamber piece is a staple of the independent science fiction film, and two of the finest of the new millennium placed their characters in confined spaces and let the creature loose on them. *Apollo 18* documents the "lost" expedition to the moon, in which some kind of life invades the ship (and the bodies) of the astronauts. In *Splinter*, a young vacationing couple are taken hostage by criminals, only to find themselves holed up in a middle-of-nowhere gas station when a mysterious being attacks them and starts grafting the bodies of its victims onto itself.

Though there are only two films in the Featured Films section, they cover a great deal of territory, from the aftereffects of the Cold War to climate change to claustrophobia to the roles of women in action narratives.

Featured Films

Harbinger Down (2015)
Writer-Director: Alec Gillis
Starring Lance Henriksen, Camille Balsamo, Matt Winston

In the early 1980s, a Soviet Moon Lander dropped into the Bering Sea. Decades later, college students and a professor set out on a ship to search for evidence of global warming's effect on marine life. While fishing for evidence, they pull up the frozen remains of the Lander onto their boat, along with the body of a cosmonaut. The body goes missing as the students discover that some other form of shape-shifting life survived the crash and the ice and is stalking the isolated boat, killing its passengers one at a time.

One of the many shapes of the changing creature in *Harbinger Down* (2015).

Harbinger Down is a love letter to the effects-driven science fiction films of the 1980s, an homage to the thrillers coming out of the Cold War era in which clear enemy lines were drawn and any scientific discovery or breakthrough was as threatening as a possible tactical advantage for the ideological opposition. Juggling espionage, elements of the space race and even the struggle of scientists to do their jobs in an increasingly divided political world, the film is a big story on a small scale.

Though *Harbinger Down* was the first feature film directed by Alec Gillis, it's possible there was no filmmaker ever more prepared to direct. With an effects career that began in the early 1980s, Gillis, along with his effects partner Tom Woodruff, Jr., worked on some of the most iconic sci-fi films and franchises in modern history: *Tremors*, *The X-Files*, *Aliens*, *Jumanji*, *Cast Away* and many others. Their company, Amalgamated Dynamics, has been on the cutting edge of practical effects technology for decades, and they've worked with the best in the business and created some of the most memorable images in sci-fi cinema history. However, it was an unpleasant work experience that led to the creation of *Harbinger Down*.

Alec Gillis: *We created the animatronic and makeup PFX for* The Thing *[2011]. During post-production, most of our work was replaced by CGI. We started getting questions from disappointed fans who assumed we had screwed up somehow. After the film came and went, we put a five-minute video on YouTube just to show folks what our work looked like. The response was overwhelming. Fans were sad, angry and confused at why great stuff gets cut from films.*

Once I realized there was this kind of support for our art, I decided to see if the fans wanted to crowdfund a film that featured all *practical creatures. Part of the pitch was that I'd write a script that was based on Carpenter's* The Thing *and Ridley Scott's* Alien. *It was a love letter of sorts to those great films of the '80s. It was intended to be cinematic comfort food for fans who have been starved for something "old school."*

The effects in this film are largely practical in design, and there has been something of a renaissance in practical effects lately with films and TV series embracing in-camera effects. Do you think this has come about because of CGI fatigue or nostalgia?

We meet with many younger directors who want to make the kind of movies they loved as kids. The big studios aren't so interested in PFX unless the decision to embrace "real" effects is driven by a powerhouse director like a J.J. Abrams. In the lower budgets, they don't have money to throw around, so they can't afford CGI. We've been having a lot of fun on lower budget films lately. Bryan Bertino's The Monster *is an example. We created a good old-fashioned creature suit for that. Audiences tired of the big-studio pixelfests seem to be looking back to the '80s, when genre films were more contained character pieces.* Stranger Things *is a case in point.*

Was crowdfunding a pleasant new experience for you?

Crowdfunding was a blast, and the only way the film could have been funded. In fact, 25 percent of its budget came from Kickstarter pledgers, and the rest from Sultan Al Darmaki's Dark Dunes Productions. I met the wonderful Sultan through Kickstarter, so without it and him, there would have been no film. Crowdfunding is a huge amount of work, though. I've had meetings with lower-end producers who kind of wink and say, "Hey, grab those Kickstarter bucks, huh?" as if it's a scam or something. My attitude was that our pledgers were our clients, and come hell or high water, we were going to deliver. We had close to 10,000 prizes to deliver in addition to making the movie. I'm very proud of my team for pulling it off with a high degree of pledger satisfaction. Some of the prizes presented a challenge in storytelling. I had to write a couple of parts for pledgers who purchased on-screen roles. That's a bit scary because you don't know who they are or if they can act. I wrote both parts as standalone characters who didn't have much interaction with the rest of the crew so that we could be flexible with the schedule. I lucked out that both Kraig Sturtz and Jason Speer were actually pretty good actors!

The film was influenced in many ways by The Thing [1982] and Alien [1979]. Aside from these foundational influences, were other movies influential on *Harbinger Down*?

I've been around a long time and have been influenced by everyone I've worked with, from Robert Zemeckis to James Cameron to Fincher to Verhoeven. Other than The Thing *and* Alien, *I'd say visually* Alien^3 *was a biggie. In terms of the ensemble, I looked at* Tremors *quite a bit. Aside from* Alien *and* The Thing, *it's one of my favorite ensemble scripts and films. But there are also 1940s influences, too.* Key Largo *is a good one for people standing around being tense.*

Coming from a special effects background as you have for over 35 years, does stepping behind the camera as a director change your perspective of what a film needs?

It was very fulfilling because I was really using my complete skill package. Planning, shooting and working with actors and crew was never daunting. Post-production sound, editing and VFX were less familiar territory.

Is there a vast difference between the storytelling of effects and the storytelling of direction?

I love working with actors. I think being used to the organic, serendipitous nature of Practical FX and puppeteering has prepped me for being open to the incredible spontaneity of actors. I've seen FX people direct as if they're making an animated film, rigidly adhering to a concrete plan and thereby beating the life out of the material. I remember films in the '80s being made a bit more on the fly, and that's where magic happens. Where's the joy in most genre films today? I argue it's squeezed out during pre-viz, when all the studio execs get to weigh in on sequence construction. Yes, pre-viz is needed when you have 9000 VFX shots costing 100 million. Give me a small, organic movie any day.

This film falls into the classic subgenre of the creature-monster-animalistic alien on the loose. What is it about the subgenre that you think continues to draw in both filmmakers and viewers?

I think it's the intimate nature of it. I'd separate the Kaiju movies from this subgenre just due to scale. Those feel more like disaster movies. Body horror resonates because it's the first scare we experience as humans. When you're a little kid and your body does something weird (diarrhea, menstruation, projectile vomiting), you question whether your own body is turning against you. Add the fear of infection, invasiveness of sex and paranoia about those around you and you've got some primal stuff going on. Monsters of a relatable scale are creepy and less expensive, too!

Crawl or Die (2014)
Writer-Director: Oklahoma Ward
Starring Nicole Alonso, Torey Byrne, Tommy Ball

In the distant future, humanity is ravaged by disease and dwindling due to mass infertility. A security team is tasked with transporting the last known fertile female to Earth 2, keeping her safe in hopes of rescuing mankind from annihilation. When a rebel faction attacks the group upon landing on the planet, the team flees underground with the woman. Working their way through an intricate series of underground tunnels, they find themselves being picked off by a monster stalking them through the ever-narrowing passages until only female soldier Tank and the woman are left.

Taking cinema claustrophobia to an all-time high, *Crawl or Die* is a film that operates like a *Terminator* cyborg: a simple, relentless pursuit. Though the narrative boils the essence of action down to its most basic parts, the film still allows room for interesting commentary on gender roles and the role of individuality in an increasingly technology-driven world. Made on a shoestring budget, the movie is an inspiring accomplishment of dedication and passion.

∼

The man responsible, Oklahoma Ward was a producer on several films, including the horror feature *Screen*. He directed his first two short films back to back in 2009–10, *The Isolation of Subject #136* and *The Battle of Tinker*. A lead cast member in all three of those films, Nicole Alonso, was a great partner for Ward on-screen and off. A real-life couple, they reunited professionally to co-produce *Crawl or Die*, with Alonso taking the lead role and Ward writing and directing.

Oklahoma Ward: *Originally, I was a painter living in New York City. It's is one of the great unique cities, because you have to live on top of each other, and so I was living around people of all sorts of races and financial incomes. The majority of them, whether they were in the arts or not, supported the arts, and they all knew artists. One thing that was distressing*

Soldier Tank (Nicole Alonso) is forced into smaller and smaller tunnels to escape a monstrous creature in *Crawl or Die* (2014).

to me was what I saw in the personal friendships I had with artists. The struggle to not give up began to wear them down for many reasons: "Am I ever going to make it?" "How can I make a living?" Nobody's willing to pay for art when you can steal a picture of a painting, have it printed on canvas, and hang it on your wall or you can see any movie you want for free in almost 4K quality. It really started to impact a lot of the artists that I was hanging around and they began to fall off left and right, not because they didn't believe in the arts and not because they aren't talented, but because they just gave up the fight. So my original underlying tone of the movie is, I want to focus on never giving up, even if you know the outcome is not good.

In a way, the film is a symbolic representation of the meat grinder that people are put through trying to find their way in an industry where it's becoming increasingly difficult to make a living in, let alone become successful.

When I'm talking to distributors and I'm talking to sales agents, it's a sci-fi-creature-action film with a tough woman in it. But my side of it, what drove me to spend five years making the movie with no money, is that I have a message underneath it that's important to me. I love to entertain people and I love sci-fi movies, but one thing I think that makes sci-fi movies like Star Wars and Star Trek stand out is that they have a mythology behind them and they're always making you think about things beyond the pure special effects entertainment of it.

The best sci-fi is almost always allegorical; it's standing in for something else, wearing the mask of something that either society is not comfortable talking about or is ignoring. There's some interesting gender commentary in this movie, in the respect that the two most pivotal roles are female characters. One is the warrior and one is the mother. We start the story off with them both being treated like a commodity; one is a soldier that's being ordered around, and one is a woman who literally doesn't have a name, she is just called Package. But our shared experience with those characters helps them to rise out of those standard female roles that they seem to be stuck in. We understand them to be human beings as opposed to just functions.

Another thing that was important to me about the movie was empathy. One of the rules in making a movie is, "You have to give a backstory on characters to make you feel for them." I don't necessarily agree with that. I passed a car wreck about seven or eight years ago, and it was very clear that the family inside didn't make it out of the car wreck; I felt horrible for them. I didn't know their backstory, I didn't know their religion, I didn't know what they believed or what they didn't believe, I didn't know their politics. Because of that experience, I thought, "Can you make a movie without giving the typical backstory and we just observe some people and what they're going through and will we still have empathy for them towards the end of the movie?" That was part of the motivation.

Part of it is also that I have been raised around a bunch of women. My mom is one of three sisters who are all very tough-willed women. I have seen throughout my life when a crisis happens or something very horrible like a child's death, the men will leave the room. They just can't stand to be in there, but all the women, the grandmothers, they will stay there. That's not a commentary saying that women are better than men, it's just an observed difference, and I always thought that I would love to be put into a movie and try to show how strong women are internally. How they can just keep going. That's always intrigued me, it's one of the things I think is beautiful about women, that strength. I wanted to put that in this movie.

One of the film's implicit commentaries is that what makes the character of Tank strong is not that she doesn't have emotions, but that she can have them and continue on. We see a spectrum, we see that she feels fear, she feels remorse and sadness, but she never loses the ability to continue. That's a more honest portrayal of what strength is than the clichéd strong characters that you often get with male action heroes.

Definitely one of the things I tried to drill into Nicole, which she got very quickly, was that I didn't want her to be a superhero and I didn't want her to be a man. I don't want this to come off that I'm male-bashing because I grew up with Rambo *and* Blade Runner, *but it seems that sometimes studios, producers and sales agents see women action characters and feel like they need to be played like a man. But that's what's great about women, they have genuine emotions and that doesn't make them weak. Ironically, Nicole being female, she said, "As a female, I can tell you I'm afraid to show emotion because then the audience will think I'm weak." I told her that it was up to us to make sure that when she shows emotion, it in no way construes that she's weak; it means that she's human.*

I've never seen a film about claustrophobia that is more effectively uncomfortable than yours. You talked about using practical sets, meaning the pipes were real, full pipes she was crawling through with no breakaway sections if they got upset or if they needed to get out. It was a real pipe they were working with. Were there other elements that you tried to tap into to create this unending sense of claustrophobia and dread?

I've always been fascinated visually with movies that handle tunnels and confined spaces, from The Great Escape *to a small section in the movie* Aliens. *I think it's because I truly believe that when you're dealing with situations that you feel are not in your control, your world can become singular and small and you can have tunnel vision. When I was losing a business and I couldn't see the light at the end of the tunnel, it felt like that was the whole world and you forget that there is a life and there is life beyond whatever horrible thing you're going through. That's one of the reasons I wanted to make a movie about claustrophobia. One of the critiques of the movie from producers and sales agents was that nobody was going to be able to sit through a movie that is completely claustrophobic from point A to point B. That's always the decision of the artist, whether you are going to listen to them or are you going to stick with it. We decided to stick with it. I think it was easy to go back to it every single day because, especially when you're making movies, that becomes your whole world. One thing that I tell artists is that when they're getting ready to do a project, if they're not getting paid millions of dollars and they're going to put their heart and soul into something, they might as well pre-pay their bills for the next four months. Clear the calendars, because that should be their whole world. We were in it from day one all the way to the end; Nicole slept in the tunnels some nights. It was extremely difficult, but seeing the results of it daily on the footage made us so excited that we were going to put this out in the world and people were going to be able to experience it. I knew I would be speaking to a lot of artists. I knew for an entertainment value, it would be interesting, but I also knew a lot of artists who would say, "I get this. I don't even care about the story, I just get this feeling." That's what pushed me.*

Your filmic experience was actually quite different from a standard production; in fact, it was only possible with the technology that we have in the new millennium. You had not only a very unconventional production, in the respect that you did it all yourself, but your distribution was different. Your English-language American film had an initial release in Japan before most people saw it here, and you became quite a cult hit over there.

Part of it was designed, and the other part is that technology is changing so fast that distributors don't know how to handle it. They're throwing things against the wall trying to figure it out and catch up. Hollywood has a way of making big tent pole films, they know what works. They throw millions of dollars into p.r. and that will get people to watch the movie. You get beyond that and they don't know what to do. Now you can go anywhere: Netflix, Hulu, content can be found anywhere. So how do you stick out? They decided to go to Japan and release it first because they started to get a little bit of an inkling through Nicole's and my work on social media and Twitter. We started putting images up of Tank, and women in Japan started drawing Tank and sending us pictures and we thought that was very interesting; we were touching on something in Japan with the female audience.

We did that, and I was blown away by the support. Both men and women, but the women of Japan have been crazy in love with Tank. I don't know what that says about their society. All I know is, to this day, we get women sending her clothes, sending her articles, sending her things they make saying, "I want to be like Tank. I want to be that strong." When the distributors saw all these e-mails and all this awareness going on without a single dollar of promotion, then they were willing to spend. Then it rolled out to America, then the U.K. The U.K. was crazy; we premiered on television in the U.K. on the same night as Ant-Man, and we outperformed it on Twitter. We were the number one hash tag in all the U.K. We started getting calls from studios, they wanted to know who our p.r. team was, they wanted to know who we were. Everything changed after that night, and that all is due to technology. Say what you want about the good and bad about social media, but the fans around the world have made our career, and I'll forever be thankful for that.

Social media is actually leading trends now, as opposed to companies using social media to push a trend. Like the marketing campaign for this film, the roll-out for it was largely designed by the feedback you received about it on social media.

Hollywood will say we have to use test audiences, and they'll listen to the test audiences. If we need to make changes to the movie, if we need to amp up the music, whatever. They won't do that with social media; they don't trust it yet.

But it was very clear we had an audience in Japan which panned out, and then it was very clear we were getting a ton of people in the U.K. and Scandinavia. They put our movie out in Blu-ray before we even had DVDs out here in the U.S. It was a huge thing in Scandinavia. I got sent a copy from a fan; it's an amazing cover, it's amazing artwork, amazing menu, they put 5.1 Surround on it. It was a dream come true. All of that led to us getting a decent distribution deal for an independent film in the U.S. because of what we were able to show that distributor.

This film is an antidote to the bloated, over-complicated blockbuster franchise stories that need to build more and more elaborate versions of themselves to get attention. Your film operates in the simple, direct, reality-of-the-moment style of filmmaking that has been lost in theaters lately.

I love complicated, mind-bending stories, but sometimes it's just information piled on information and sometimes it gets overwhelming. I'm not going to bring up any specific titles, but this last summer, there were several huge superhero movies that have 5000 plots going on within one movie. While I can find the enjoyment of that, I also hearken back to John Carpenter films like Assault on Precinct 13, *back to* The Shining, *which in one sense is a very simple story. It's one of the reasons I love* Rear Window. *I'm drawn to that as an artist.*

Other Films of Interest

Area 407 (2012), *The Frankenstein Theory* (2013), *Outlander* (2008)

16

Confronting Global Disasters

Rather than "From the Beginning," perhaps the title of this section should be "In the Beginning," as many of the most famous stories of global disaster have their origins in Biblical storytelling. From the flood that sent Noah and family floating in an ark full of animals to the plagues that tore apart ancient Egypt, Bible stories were the first global disasters. In the modern era, as people were less frightened of (or faithful in their belief of) Bible stories, filmmakers decided to seek fear elsewhere: science.

In 1933's *Deluge*, a massive earthquake destroys the West Coast of the United States, and an enormous wave bears down on the East Coast. No intervention from God caused this; it was simple science, nature doing its job too well.

As science became more complicated and frightening, so too did the uses of it in stories of global disaster. Nuclear disaster reared its head in the 1950s and 1960s, from the "empty Earth" tale *Five* to the family-in-danger aftermath terror of *Panic in Year Zero!* to the quiet dissolution of society in *This Is Not a Test*.

As effects got better and the audience's taste for wanton destruction grew greater, the global cataclysms strayed further from possible reality. *Crack in the World* is a title that described the film's exact concern: a crack caused by drilling into the magma center of the planet. Only slightly less ridiculous was the idea of an asteroid threatening to smash into Earth in *Meteor* (though perhaps the dinosaurs would disagree with the outlandish nature of this film).

The Cold War with the Soviet Union in the 1980s brought back fears that were dormant during the 1970s, reappearing in *The China Syndrome*, *The Day After*, *Testament* and *Miracle Mile*. The fear of asteroids from the 1970s was cyclical, returning in the late 1990s as *Asteroid*, *Armageddon* and *Deep Impact*. Audiences sought tales of global disaster, but filmmakers were running out of unique ways to do it. Canadian filmmaker Don McKellar decided in 1998 to do away with the explanation of the end at all, instead using the destruction of the planet in *Last Night* as a chance to watch humanity cope with their inevitable end.

After the Millennium

The new millennium wasn't just eager to continue the destruction of Earth on the big screen; it was more well-equipped to do so, with the amazing advances in special effects technology. What looked hokey and unrealistic in *Crack in the World* took on a sheen of CGI realism in 2003's *The Core*. The storm in 1939's *The Wizard of Oz* is dwarfed by *Anna's Storm* (2007) and the chaos of *The Day After Tomorrow* (2004).

Asteroids made their illustrious return in the (now comedic) meteoric destruction story *Seeking a Friend for the End of the World*, and trees rose up to destroy their oppressors, mankind, in the (unintentionally comedic) *The Happening*.

This was the era of special effects-driven carnage. Director Roland Emmerich, the king of destruction with titles like *Godzilla, Independence Day, White House Down* and the aforementioned *The Day After Tomorrow*, put an exclamation point on the subgenre with *2012*, in which he utterly destroys the planet and sends humanity floating through space in an ark not too different from Noah's. In Emmerich's tale, it was not God who cleansed the Earth of people, but the Earth itself.

The Independent Perspective

It should come as no surprise that the subgenre of the global disaster film has fewer independent entries than others, given the massive undertaking of destroying the world in a manner that audiences find satisfactory for entertainment value.

Some visionary filmmakers, however, did find the budget and inspiration to do so. Idiosyncratic Lars von Trier put his penchant for histrionic relationships and operatic tragedy to good use in *Melancholia*, a story about a woman so wracked with depression that the coming destruction of the planet by a meteor isn't enough to shake her out of it.

Grim realism and personal narratives populated the global disasters of the independent film world, with nuclear scares focused down to a single man in a house in *Right at Your Door* and a manmade biological disaster seen through the eyes of three couples in *Parts Per Billion*. Controversial filmmaker Abel Ferrara used the lives of a painter and actor as a stand-in for humanity's desperate grab at intimacy in its final hours in the drama *4:44 Last Day on Earth*, and director Jennifer Phang found beauty in the connections of family in her first feature *Half-Life*.

The Featured Films in this section discuss the same type of tragedy, but act as polar opposites. One is a comedic character piece about human interpersonal dynamics, the other an evocative fever dream of a single woman's odyssey as the only hope of stopping the impending destruction.

Featured Films

It's a Disaster (2012)
Writer-Director: Todd Berger
Starring David Cross, America Ferrera, Julia Stiles

At a brunch group's regular meeting, the five couples are all dealing with various issues. One couple is late, one of the guests is bringing her new boyfriend for their third date, and there are buried disagreements among several others. Their minor quibbles take a backseat when a neighbor in a hazmat suit tells them a series of nuclear weapons have gone off across the U.S. The couples first seek survival supplies through the house, but when the late couple finally shows up, the bonds of friendship and trust are tested.

Using a similar premise to the TV series *Jericho*, but replacing the earnest Midwesterners with self-absorbed jerks, *It's a Disaster* is a pitch-black comedy that touches humorously but honestly on the minor human foibles that often take over in the midst of an emergency. A clever combination of a Neil Simon–esque living room comedy and a modern-day *Fail-Safe*, the movie balances observational humor with an unfortunately realistic threat. A cast of recognizable faces stands in as the microcosm of America, unable to put their ridiculous problems aside even in the face of possible extinction.

∽

Todd Berger's work is widespread and well-known, though he is not a household name. With acting performances in films and TV shows like *Southland Tales* and *Parks and Recreation*, he is also known for his writing work in the animated shorts *The Smurfs: A Christmas Carol* and *Kung Fu Panda: Secrets of the Masters*. He did triple duty as writer, director and actor in his first feature *The Scenesters* (2009), a comedy-horror.

Todd Berger: *I set out to write something that I could do incredibly cheap. I wanted to set it in one location and shoot it with friends on the weekends. I had recently read an article about how* Night of the Living Dead, *the classic horror movie from 1968, is now in the public domain because the producers forgot to renew the copyright. So I thought it would be funny to take all of the zombie footage and then shoot a bunch of new footage and intercut it all, kind of like* Dead Men Don't Wear Plaid. *Make a whole new movie about couples getting together for game night in 1968 when there's a zombie attack. The plan was to make it look old and black and white, but then I learned how hard it would be to fake old 16mm film footage. And expensive. So I abandoned that idea but I still liked the concept of having a bunch of couples get together and then something horrible happens outside so they are forced to stay inside and deal with it in a comedic fashion. That's when it hit me: What about some sort of terrorist attack?*

A group of brunch friends (Erinn Hayes, Blaise Miller, Rachel Boston, Kevin M. Brennan, Julia Stiles, David Cross, America Ferrera, Jeff Grace) get uncomfortably close in the midst of an emergency in *It's a Disaster* (2012).

The characters in this film have a hard time focusing on the real disaster happening around them because of the petty bickering and relationship issues amongst themselves. Is this in some way a comment on society's exhaustion with the fear scenarios that have been heaped upon us in a post–9/11 world?

Yeah, I think any genre of film eventually becomes so familiar and oversaturated with audiences that the satirists can then sweep in and exploit the genre's tropes. Take something that's supposed to be dramatic and turn around to make it funny. Post–9/11, there were so many terrorism and disaster and end-of-the-world movies that I think people started getting burned out them, not even being fazed by the destruction on screen any more, which then made the genre ripe for comedies. I mean, It's a Disaster *is basically just a funny version of a film called* Right at Your Door *[2006], a very heavy drama about a man trapped inside his house during a dirty bomb attack.*

Is it a fair reading to say that your film uses the fantastical concept of the disaster as a stand-in for the constant minor indignities of standard social interaction in modern society? With elements like the uncomfortable sexual propositions, the struggle between panicked and knowledgeable people in an emergency, the rejection of the sick couple primarily because of their lateness rather than their illness, and the awkward confrontation of differing religious beliefs in a public setting?

I read once that disaster situations take who you really are in the real world and bring it right up to the surface. So if you're really deep-down a calm, collected leader, then that's who you'll become when the bombs fall. But if you're actually a petty narcissist, a terrorist attack isn't necessarily going to make you a better person—it'll just make you a petty narcissist dealing with a terrorist attack. On top of that, I wanted each one of the characters to represent the stages of grief, which we all supposedly go through when dealing with a traumatic crisis. So there's a character that represents shock, panic, denial, bargaining, guilt, anger, acceptance and hope. I'll let you figure out which one is which.

The disaster film is inherently a dark and somewhat morbid concept. Why do viewers and filmmakers continue to be drawn to stories about unpreventable disasters?

I think since the dawn of storytelling, people like stories they can see themselves in so they can wonder, "How would I have handled that? What would I have done?" Disaster scenarios are the perfect arena for that, because audiences like to imagine themselves as the hero who is going to step in and save the day. I remember reading a Stephen King quote about The Stand, *where he thought it was funny because readers always contemplate which side they would have joined, the good survivors or the bad survivors. But he knew there's actually a 99 percent chance you just would have been dead along with everyone else.*

Also, I think deep down, people just like to see shit blow up.

Magnetic (2015)
Writer-Director: Sophia Cacciola, Michael J. Epstein
Starring Allix Mortis, Chris Bernardi, Rachel Leah Blumenthal

Twentysomething Alice has quit the vibrant but empty life of the big city and returned to the small, rural hometown she left. A strange new employment opportunity presents itself in the form of a boring and endlessly repetitive desk job in an office concealed underneath a farm. Strange visions, messages from mysterious figures and her own broken memories seem to be pointing towards her value in possibly preventing the destruction of Earth by an approaching cosmic object.

Using a single lead character to stand in as every individual human being in the world, *Magnetic* is an audacious and surreal journey. Extrapolating long-held fears of societal breakdown and imminent destruction that surface in times of rapid human advancement or global tragedy, the film's visual flair and stream-of-consciousness narrative turn these fears into intensely personal elements. Commenting obliquely on feminism, free will and the resistance of analog technology to obsolescence, *Magnetic* is undoubtedly one of the more unique and singular films covered in this book.

∽

The two fantastic artistic minds behind the film are Sophia Cacciola and Michael J. Epstein. Before moving into filmmaking, they were already successful musicians; they brought their musical skills to the score and soundtracks for their films. Aside from many short films, documentary subjects and anthology entries, Cacciola and Epstein worked together on two other features, *Ten* and *Blood of the Tribades*. While their first film, *Ten*, was a female-centric horror extrapolation of *Ten Little Indians*, Cacciola wanted to lean heavily into science fiction for their second film.

Sophia Cacciola: *The idea for* Magnetic *started with a short concept I had about a lone female astronaut on a mission in a capsule above Earth when she witnesses Earth being destroyed by a natural event. I wanted to explore what it meant to be the last human and what your responsibility was to humanity at that point. Do you try to leave a record of some kind? Do you bother to try and survive alone? Do you place value on your life itself? What fundamentally is your purpose?*

In some versions, I was playing around with her being pregnant and struggling with those same themes of what one life meant. So, all very heady, unanswerable questions! At the same time, my partner was becoming obsessed with Alice in Wonderland *and, more*

Alice (Allix Mortis) makes her way underground to her mysterious new job in *Magnetic* (2015).

specifically, some of the lesser explored themes of the book. There are numerous ideas, puns and sort of existentialist moments in Alice in Wonderland *that focus on the equal balance of absence and presence rather than absence serving as a lesser, unequal state. The most obvious example is celebrating unbirthdays, but that's just the most heavy-handed use. Our favorite is the dialogue at the tea party:*

"Take some more tea," the March Hare said to Alice, very earnestly.
"I've had nothing yet," Alice replied in an offended tone, "so I can't take more."
"You mean you can't take *less*," said the Hatter: "it's very easy to take *more* than nothing."

Usually when something is Alice*-inspired, it's all very visual, or drug-related, but he was interested in the recurrent theme of nothing being something. This, of course, has a nice tie-in with the blackness of space and empty, drifting meaninglessness.*

When we actually started to combine some of these ideas, we were forced to bring the movie back down to earth as we took stock of the locations and resources available to us on a low budget! Sci-fi is very often about making sense of the individual experience in the context of a giant, uncaring universe. So, we really wanted to tackle that idea of scale with the sun generating a massive event ending life on Earth, which from an outside, universal perspective—such as to an alien creature in another galaxy—it barely registers. Yet, it's the only thing that matters to this individual caught in a pointless, empty life devoid of all positive experience. To that individual, there is the micro experience, and to the viewer seeing the film, they also look at the macro experience. We wanted to understand why existence matters to us, why we fight to go on, why we want to preserve not just ourselves as individuals, but humanity as a collective.

The story was written based on a set of repetitive cycles that parallel most of our lives. We often only exist to wake, work, eat, sleep, repeat. We wanted to tell a story about that on a larger scale. We also wanted the whole movie to focus on how an individual navigates that. That motivated us to not have any other characters in the movie and so we just explored variations of Alice. We really wanted to capture the lonely experience and isolation of this individual. Some people have asked us if we were trying to say the whole world was made up of only Alices, but that wasn't really the idea. It was rather that the world that matters to us consists only of Alice.

We also wanted to explore individual paths in parallel worlds and the tensions between art, science and religion. The same strands of DNA can produce a scientist, an artist, a person of faith. It's choice and circumstance. It's essentially all performance. We wanted to really explore the story of that one person, and we wanted her to make the large-scale choice. The film plays with how one individual, making small changes, can possibly affect all of humanity. We come to the present and close the movie with the butterfly flapping its wings. With each cycle, things are a little different based on those choices.

Was one of the decisions for you to work in the sci-fi film genre (and to cast a strong central female lead) so that the large and growing female sci-fi fan base could be better represented?

Typically, a movie like Magnetic *would probably have starred a man. Whenever I write characters like this, I hope that I can minimize the amount that gender stereotypes impact or appear to impact their behavior. Often, the best female characters in sci-fi films, like Ripley from* Alien, *were originally written as male characters. With* Magnetic, *the goal was to write it without gender and then cast a woman in the role to reinforce the idea that women do not have to play characters who behave as women first. In fact, I think that is the most important female role to present more prominently—a female in a role that has nothing to do with being a woman. The "default" gender is still male and that has to change. This is true across the genre board, but there is definitely still a prominent deficit in sci-fi. I do think visibility and representation of women is hugely important for young people, and at this point, I essentially never plan to make a movie that doesn't star a woman!*

I come from a rock'n'roll music background, where an independent DIY ethic is very ingrained, so I've always just charged in where I don't "belong" and done what I wanted (play drums! scream! make a movie!). I think the film and music industries will open up more and more as women push their way in and overcome the implicit biases against them. I think it's very important for women to be making films, starring in films, having stories told that include "real," fleshed-out female characters with actual plot-advancing motivations. I want young girls to grow up without feeling like outsiders when they get interested in sci-fi, or really any traditionally male-dominated genre.

And this all seems like so little to ask for, but it's still very much missing from mainstream film. One of my favorite aspects of science fiction as a genre is that because it isn't limited to "current day" or "real life" milieus, there is an opportunity to cast women in essentially any role. And what better way to show an egalitarian, utopian future than to show that women are equal to men?

Sci-fi also has a long tradition of telling stories that reflect on socio-political themes at sufficient arm's length safety to get away with being more aggressive. Hey, it's the future or an alternate planet, so it's okay to comment on that "different" society. As a result, sci-fi has really led by example with opportunities for tremendously strong ethical and moralistic subtexts. My favorite movies always leave me with a bigger, subtextual concept to ponder. That's a lot of power for film to wield!

This movie seems to fall into the camp of the hybrid sci-fi-psychedelic arena, entries like *The Prisoner* and *Dune*, stories that have science fiction but a heavy dose of surrealism as well. Were these films influential on *Magnetic*?

I actually devoted my whole band (Do Not Forsake Me Oh My Darling) to exploring the themes of The Prisoner, *and that love of* The Prisoner *definitely extends into some of the themes of* Magnetic, *especially the examination of the role of the individual in society, and ultimately taking responsibility for one's own situation. The most direct reference to* The Prisoner *in the film is one of the characters calling Alice "Number 2" in a science lab scene, but other thematic and visual parallels can be found.*

I also love Dune, *both the series of novels and the David Lynch film. I am a huge fan of Lynch in general. I love his ability to make an entire work that forgoes literal narrative to explore a thematic idea. He is really a master of weaving surrealism into his narrative works. I always prefer interesting images, visual metaphor and the exploration of ideas to a basic, linear plot!*

If I were to make a partial list, Magnetic *was probably influenced by the tonal and visual aspects of films like* Phantasm *(dream-reality blending, and one of the morgues is actually named after the mausoleum in* Phantasm*),* Primer *(looping timelines),* Upstream Color *(cycles and animals connected with the consciousness of people),* 2001: A Space Odyssey *(which is referenced directly via Daisy),* Pi *(getting too close to God),* The Andromeda Strain *(especially the art design),* Blade Runner *(themes of consciousness),* Gattaca *(value of the individual),* City of Lost Children *(cloning, purpose of dreams),* Silent Running *(individual protecting life against all odds), etc.*

The movie Drive *also really opened our minds to a sort of minimalist, music-driven, retro-but-timeless approach. We had been developing the film and looking at going that route, but we didn't feel confident that it could work until we saw* Drive.

One of the aesthetic decisions in this film was to create a mixed-era world, one which contained a lot of classic retro technology. This modern Steampunk aesthetic (I call it the Analog Renaissance) has become more popular in the last few years. What was your inspiration for embracing that?

I watch a lot of older films, and I rarely feel like I want to see a movie set in "present day" with normal clothes and cell phones and things like that. So, we decided to set the movie in the "future-past parallel-universe 1980s," where we had a specific feel we were going for but allowed ourselves to be anachronistic with it.

I wanted Alice's world to be very tactile, so there are many shots of her fussing with cassettes or slowly dialing the phone, for example. I think it's interesting having VHS and cassette tapes and rotary phones and old computers be such a huge part of the film and the grounding of the film, while all that media is quickly slipping away from our world. It becomes almost alien to young people who have never encountered it. We had actually written an explanation for why all of that specific technology was necessary into the plot (there were rules about what could be magnetically transported in the pods), but ultimately, it felt okay to leave it as just a given texture of the world.

And from a production design standpoint, part of it is definitely nostalgia, as I was born in the '80s and still have a lot of positive associations with the technology! I had many mixtapes from when I taped songs off the radio, hurtling across the room and hitting record when I heard the first few notes of the song I wanted. Listening to those tapes was a huge part of my life at the time. Now, finding the song you want to hear is so easy on the Internet! I used to have to work for it! We wanted Alice's emotions to present via the music and lyrics she was listening to at any given moment in the movie. We wanted the viewer to experience the music with Alice. It would have been much less impactful if she loaded a song on Spotify or YouTube or something.

There is an animal motif in the film, from the sheep farm to the spider woman to the animal-headed people she dines with in one scene. Was there a specific intent to the recurring theme of animals, given that it exists alongside the film's intense focus on the machinery and technology she experiences and interacts with?

It's rumored that in Western New York, where we shot the barn scenes, there are many Cold War-era underground missile silos beneath unassuming farms. So we thought that would be a perfect setting for the kind of contrast between the surface's pastoral setting, and the nefarious affairs underground. Sheep serve as a common and clear symbol of our loss of individuality and identity, and thus worked well for us to show in their literal manifestation on the surface of the farm, and then in dreams as anthropomorphized Alice in Wonderland*-esque characters, along with their influencers, the sheepdog and the wolf. The dreams are intended to be sort of disorienting and surrealistically terrifying and weird. They are also the only place where we allow Alice to show her frustration and emotion a bit.*

The characters in the dreams were really important for us because we wanted to show in a sort of physical, visual way how the brain organizes information. One theory, at least, is that dreams are the result of the "resting" brain taking the time to file and contextualize information from the day so that it can be recalled when necessary. Dreams work so that we can understand our sensory experience in the context of all of our prior sensory experiences. Each of the characters in the dream parallels the perspectives, experiences and actions of real versions of Alice. Our protagonist Alice is trying to come to terms with, and reconcile her own varied identity as she experiences her own physical life, but also absorbs the memories of other versions of Alice when they are proximal. We wanted to have those three aspects of mind and memory—Alice's physical experience, Alice's absorbed memories and Alice's dreams. The sheep played a role in each, and represented Alice a different way in each. Each of the worlds has its own set of rules and method of presentation.

As for machinery and its intersection with biology, we were really interested in trying to get at the perceptual experience of life, and how that manifests in the brain, and whether that physical manifestation is really the root of consciousness. It feels like we're pretty close to facing a transhumanist reality where we can preserve our lives, or at least our neural patterns in some form. We might face the very real question of what it means to live and to die. Are those memories that Alice absorbs a separate consciousness?

Other Films of Interest

The Color Out of Space (2010)

17

The Rise of Superpowers

Though heroes from the pages of pulp novels and comic books did grace screens in the early days of film, it wasn't until 1951's *Superman and the Mole Men* premiered, starring live action's first Superman, George Reeves, that superpowers made great heroes into superheroes on a grand scale. DC Comics made it big on the small screen first, and Marvel Comics tried their hand at live-action shows with *Spider-Man*, *Doctor Strange* and *Captain America* in the late 1970s.

But it was a return to the original superhero in 1978's *Superman*, this time starring Christopher Reeve, that made the superhero a viable screen presence who could carry a film and make an impressive profit. However, it would still be years before the formula was perfected; sequels in the *Superman* franchise and a *Supergirl* spinoff were met with shrinking profits, and other DC properties like *Swamp Thing* were interesting but failed attempts. The exploitation company Troma even took inspiration from the comics and turned them graphically violent and sexually explicit with *The Toxic Avenger* (1984). Subversive, disgusting and surprisingly socially conscious, the film somehow spawned a series of sequels and even an animated children's series. Troma would revisit the superhero parody arena years later with 1990's *Sgt. Kabukiman N.Y.P.D.*

Much of the 1980s was spent in an attempt to start new franchises or force new life into dying old ones. *Return of the Swamp Thing* eschewed the dark tone of Wes Craven's original and steered into camp comedy, and comedy seeped into *Superman III* with the appearance of comic Richard Pryor in a supporting role. In 1989 alone, the TV show *The Incredible Hulk* spawned a series of TV movies, *The Toxic Avenger* released the third film in its original trilogy, and audiences were introduced to *The Punisher* and *Batman*.

While much of the 1990s is remembered for its very successful *Batman* and *Teenage Mutant Ninja Turtles* franchises, it also stretched the boundaries of superhero storytelling. *The Shadow* and *The Phantom* looked back into the nostalgic pulp past, *The Crow* showed us a gritty and more realistic present, and *Judge Dredd* warned us of a terrifying future.

As the 1990s began to wind down, studios were recycling and diluting their established characters; *Batman & Robin* put a temporary end to the Dark Knight's big-screen adventures, and *Superman* comic spinoff *Steel* landed with a metallic thud. Unconventional heroes like *Blade* (a half-vampire anti-hero) and *Mystery Men* (a team of reject superheroes who join forces when no one else wants them) brought the only memorable superpowered adventures to screen as the millennium came to a close.

After the Millennium

The Toxic Avenger and *The Crow* both had new entries in their long-established franchises, but the real story of the year 2000 was the emergence of superheroes as adult storytelling material. Bryan Singer, respected indie director of the Oscar-winning *The Usual Suspects*, used his film *X-Men* as an allegory for marginalized people (particularly the gay community), embracing Stan Lee's original narrative of peace vs. militarism in his approach to the heroes and villains dynamic. The film was an enormous hit. M. Night Shyamalan, a young phenomenon hot off the blockbuster horror film *The Sixth Sense*, made a mature, real-world extrapolation of the superhero story in *Unbreakable*, another sign that audiences of the new millennium were supportive of the change of direction for their heroes.

Blade (2002) doubled down—a superior sequel under the skilled eye of Guillermo del Toro; Marvel brought *Spider-Man* back as well, this time to the big screen from horror auteur Sam Raimi, and audiences rewarded the decision to the tune of over $800,000,000. From that point on, any superhero property was a possible hit: *Daredevil*, *The League of Extraordinary Gentlemen*, *Hellboy*, *Constantine*. There were as many failures as hits.

Then, two filmmakers changed the arena forever. Christopher Nolan and John Favreau, popular independent filmmakers venturing into Hollywood territory, made *Batman Begins* and *Iron Man*, flipsides of the same coin: stories about rich men (plagued by past demons) who dress in elaborate costumes and use gadgets to try and make the world a better place. Both films turned into franchises, and both franchises planted the seeds for what would become epic cinematic universes with filmic entries on a yearly basis.

The Independent Perspective

The exorbitant effects and costumes of studio superhero films aren't as easily acquired for indie films, so while there are occasional titles like *Push* and *Kick-Ass* that operate on a similar level stylistically, many of the most interesting indie superhero films tone the action down and the characterization up.

Before he helmed the superhero team film *The Avengers*, director Joss Whedon made a loving homage to the forgotten and misunderstood super-villains in his musical comedy *Dr. Horrible's Sing-Along Blog*. The mundane realities of unrequited love give a frighteningly realistic edge to the classic villain origin story.

Sparks and *Super Capers* were youth-oriented indie releases that tried to move against the flow of the modern superhero wave, bringing back brightly dressed, stalwart heroes with little to no moral gray. Those films had loyal opposition in *All Superheroes Must Die* and *The Scribbler*, dark stories of heroes under threat of murder, with innocent lives at risk and just a hint of psychological breakdown.

The superhero film even explored arenas that had nothing to do with heroes directly. *Shaolin Soccer* showed what a super-powered soccer team might look like, and *The Subjects* employed the gritty violence of a chamber thriller as normal humans are turned into powerful beings through a clinical trial.

The Featured Films in this section explore mind control and governmental conspiracy theories, religious zealotry, the division between public and private lives, and the allegory of superhero origins to the high school experience.

Featured Films

One & Two (2015)
Director: Andrew Droz Palermo
Writers: Andrew Droz Palermo, Neima Shahdadi
Starring Kiernan Shipka, Timothée Chalamet, Elizabeth Reaser

Daniel is the concerned father of adolescent children Zac and Eva. They are growing up, and with that growth comes curiosity and change. But Daniel has greater concerns than most parents of teenagers: Zac and Eva have strange supernatural abilities which allow them to teleport from one place to another. He has moved himself, his wife and his children to an isolated farmhouse surrounded by a fence and a forest, and his sense of desperation has seeped into his style of discipline. Eventually, the children decide to use the powers Daniel fears so much to take them outside the cloistered world he has created for them.

A beautifully photographed coming-of-age drama with elements of Southern Gothic, superhero and family melodrama, *One & Two* is a stunning reinvention of the story of a dysfunctional family. Daniel's fear of his children venturing into the real world can be viewed as an allegory for parental social media anxieties. The added element of the children's unique abilities allows for a reading that includes parents trying to protect their children from the fallout of coming out, being bullied for ethnicity and religion, and even changing gender identity.

∼

Before his narrative feature film debut with *One & Two*, Andrew Droz Palermo had already worked successfully in documentaries with the coming-of-age film *Rich Hill*. He was also a cinematographer, working with director Adam Wingard on *VHS* and *You're Next*.

Andrew Droz Palermo*: The initial ideas came from a number of places. I was reading a lot about Amish and Mennonite communities which surrounded me in Missouri, where*

Eva (Kiernan Shipka) and Zac (Timothée Chalamet) dream of another life outside their confining home in *One & Two* (2015).

I was living at the time, and I started thinking about pushing their beliefs to an extreme. On top of that, I had a scene in mind in which two children laid in a field singing a song together, without vocalizing. Through cutting, we'd understand they were psychically linked.

One of the main themes of this film is isolation: isolation from society, isolation from family, isolation from God or belief. The ability to teleport is a power that should allow for easy interaction with others; did you choose it because of the ironic element it brings to a story about isolation?

After making Rich Hill, *my documentary about three boys in rural Missouri, I thought a lot about what "home" meant. Many people in Q&As would ask, "Why don't the boys just leave?" The answer was simple, because Rich Hill, Missouri, is where their family is. Despite the challenges, harsh realities and traumatic experiences, they ultimately wanted to be home above all else. So, in this sense, the wall in* One & Two *more than anything is a physical manifestation of the bonds that tie you to your family for better or worse.*

The pace and location of this film is entirely unconventional in the traditional superpowers storyline. Is it that juxtaposition of immense power and possibility of these children against the deprivation and stifling of their parent what interested you in telling this story? Does that juxtaposition represent something larger thematically, perhaps something with a greater social context?

It's hard to pinpoint what exactly compelled me to tell this specific story. I often lead with images and feelings, and I had some very vivid ones in the early conception of the film. I always knew that I didn't want the film to feel like traditional comic book films, I wanted it to feel rich and textural yet plain and chaste. A lot of this was drawing on the Amish, Shaker and Mennonite influences of their lifestyle.

With the sick mother, the domineering father, the isolated estate and the outcast children the father believes God has punished him with, this film has as much in common with classic Southern Gothic storytelling as it does with superpower narratives. Did you combine these genres for a specific reason? What do you feel the story gains with the hybrid of the two?

More than anything, I think the regional aspects of the film are drawn from both my real life, and the things in films and novels which speak to me as a Southerner. It also had the simple benefit of being something I hadn't seen, it felt unique, and from my true self. It's a real soup of influences, but I tried to make them congeal in a way that felt as though they were all cut from the same cloth.

Films about superpowers often stand in as stories about adolescence and the struggle to grow up and find yourself. Were you aware of this thematic trend when you started working on your story?

Neima Shahdadi, my co-writer and I, were very aware of this. We talked a lot about what changes, if any, did they go through. We tried a lot of versions of the script where Eva and Zac grew apart from one another as they were pressed by their father Daniel. While Eva turns against Daniel more directly, Zac turned inward and more towards God. Personally, I find that films often have a too-tidy crucial moment where children see their parents in a new light, so I tried to make the turn more subtle.

Films about people with superpowers have become an enormous phenomenon in the new millennium.

I was raised on whatever films I could catch at our local four-screen movie theater. For the most part, that meant big-budget fare, which I loved. Although I have now been exposed to my fair share of art house cinema and my tastes have certainly expanded, my love of populist movies has not changed. With One & Two, *I wanted to make a film that straddled the line between art and popular culture. A movie with genre thrills, lyricism and deep emotion. I can't say why exactly comic movies have exploded, but there is an escapism, I suppose.*

The Posthuman Project (2014)

Director: Kyle William Roberts
Writers: Matthew Price, Sterling Gates
Starring Kyle Whalen, Collin Place, Lindsay Sawyer

Denny and four friends are celebrating the end of their high school career on a rock-climbing trip. The trip ends with the five friends powerful beyond their wildest imaginings due to a genetic alteration. The friends, now nearly adults and preparing to head off into the world, have to deal with life struggles both standard and super-powered.

The post-millennial answer to *The Breakfast Club* combined with a superhero team origin story, *The Posthuman Project* uses superhuman abilities to discuss genuine adolescent concerns. From domestic abuse to the daunting decisions of college and career, the film finds clever parallels with the abilities involved and allows for a complication of the standard clichés of each subgenre.

~

For director Kyle Roberts, a filmmaker just embarking on a feature film career, *The Posthuman Project* was an ambitious first outing, but he was inspired by the challenge.

High school friends Denny (Kyle Whalen), Archie (Collin Place), Lisa (Alexandra Harris), Adam (Josh Bonzie) and Gwen (Lindsay Sawyer) find themselves facing more than just high school problems in *The Posthuman Project* (2014) (copyright Reckless Abandonment Pictures, LLC).

A series of successful viral videos linked him with the writers of the film, Sterling Gates and Matthew Price (with whom he worked on two short features, *Heroes of the Realm* and *The Bulleteers*). When Price first pitched the idea for the film, Roberts knew it was a big project.

Kyle Roberts: I was working at The Oklahoman *at the time, and went into the office of one of my best friends, Matthew Price, the Features editor of the paper, and told him about this crazy idea about a film combining a "John Hughes–like vibe and X-Men, and oh yeah, we're going to do it on a micro budget." He was already working on a story about teenagers that develop superpowers on a camping trip, and I had several viral videos under my belt just coming off of airing on Syfy's* Viral Video Showdown, *so it just kind of escalated from there.*

This film seems very obviously inspired by the John Hughes films of the 1980s, films that attempted to explore adolescent life in a more substantial way than had been done previously. What appealed to you about those films, and what do you feel that style of film could bring to a story about superpowers?

What John Hughes and I have in common is we both feel that teenagers have a real voice. Oftentimes, people overlook teens as just more reckless, ignorant young adults. And although teens do stupid stuff sometimes, they are going through changes very quickly and making decisions that many times affect the rest of their lives and that is what we wanted to capture in our film.

Part of the classic superhero structure is that of the origin story. In some ways, the origin in comics mirrors the struggle of adolescents to find their role in life as they grow into society. It feels like your intention in this film was to merge those two sensibilities together to deepen the impact of both.

Essentially, we used superpowers as a metaphor for adolescence, which is something we really hadn't seen explored before. As you are growing up and everything is changing, you have new responsibilities that you really don't have any training for. In our story, our teens (most seniors in high school) are all freaking out, in their own way, about what they are going to do with the rest of their lives after high school. After being subjected to "zero energy," their powers reflect what they want and need most in life.

This film also seems to focus on some darker real-world problems that the kids deal with. Is this in some way a commentary on the separation recent superhero stories have had from the compellingly relatable characters that first attracted readers to flawed heroes to begin with?

We wanted to show real teenagers going through real problems, while still telling it under a family-friendly bubble. It was important to me to not make this film specifically targeting an anti-bullying or abusive parent campaign, but again to show some real-world issues happening that can make them much more relatable to audiences. This also helps give their characters specific motivations which are reflected in their superpowers. For example, Gwen has a physically abusive stepfather, so she uses that metaphorical fire in here and obtains the ability to create and manipulate physical fire, i.e., pyrokinesis. Archie is the brainiac and gets bullied, so he is the one who ends up getting super strength.

Was it fun to take the clichés inherent in the superhero story and the clichés inherent in the coming-of-age high school story and flip both on their heads by mixing them together? What discoveries did you make about how one genre made the other work better?

It was a blast working on this film! Some trolls, if they just watch the trailer, say, "Oh, that looks so clichéd!" Ding, ding, ding! That's the point. We wanted a teenager who almost everyone can relate to in some way, so by doing that, we heavily used stereotypes to convey our message. Also, it's very hard to make a truly original story today, so I think by mixing and mashing up genres, you can obtain a fresh story. We very intentionally stuck with what we were best at and made this an organically hand-crafted micro-budget independent film, vs. trying to make it feel like a multimillion dollar blockbuster, which of course it is not.

How did you go about rethinking the idea of a villain in a superhero story that was so driven by the realistic, everyday issues that these teen characters were facing?

Matthew Price and Sterling Gates were our writers and came up with the concept, like any good film, to really keep this whole story as centrally focused as possible. So organically making Denny and Archie's uncle the villain made a lot of sense to us. This gave the audience an opportunity to continue to ask questions throughout, like "What happened with Denny and Archie's dad? Why did he walk out?"

In the new millennium, superhero stories have become prolific.

So many people love superhero films! The bottom line is, they keep getting made by Hollywood because the big ones make them a ton of money. There are still few truly independent films like ours because of how much money they cost to make, or how many man hours a smaller crew are willing to do for free. For us, we had 530 visual effects shots and I myself worked them up for over ten months, working three nights a week from about eight p.m. to four a.m. Then I'd take a nap and got to my day job, come home, be a dad-husband for a couple hours, and repeat! Also, we had our daughter, so doing all of this with a newborn was extremely taxing on myself and my wife.

Alter Egos (2012)
Writer-Director: Jordan Galland
Starring Kris Lemche, Danny Masterson, Sean Lennon

In a world where superheroes are nearly as commonplace as lawyers, a hero named Fridge finds himself struggling with a series of life problems. Public support is at an all-time low, the government has pulled much-needed funding, and Fridge is still learning to deal with the fact that his girlfriend seems to be more enamored of his masked persona than she is of his real one. Oh, and he may have to face the man responsible for his parents' deaths—but he's in no hurry.

Alter Egos is an apt title for a film that uses superhero identity as a window into human relationships and questions about public and private personalities. It teases a world where the intricate relationships of an indie drama and the epic good vs. evil battles of a costumed hero adventure not only coexist, but occur to the same people. The modern superhero genre bloomed in the new millennium, and films like *The Avengers* and *The Dark Knights Rises* signaled a giant subgenre ready to be broken down to its component pieces and rethought. *Alter Egos* was up to the task.

After several years as a successful musician, Jordan Galland made a few short films and his first feature, the horror-comedy *Rosencrantz and Guildenstern Are Undead*, which satirized the world of the theater. After *Alter Egos*, he revisited themes of identity and

Fridge (Kris Lemche) and C-Thru (Joey Kern) defeat hunger at a local diner in *Alter Egos* (2012).

lack of control over public identity with the exorcism comedy *Ava's Possessions*. While all the films seem like organic explorations of various kinds of celebrity, Galland's motivation for the film was more pragmatic.

Jordan Galland: *I needed to figure out how to get a second film made for cheap. I had written a bunch of big-budget scripts that were just floating around Hollywood, stalling, going from one producer to the next. And I just wanted to make another film. So I designed backwards, starting with the location. I found a retro, hillside off-season resort and I wrote the script around it. When I brought the team out to do a tech scout, they were amazed at how well it fit the script, because usually you look for a location based on the description in the screenplay. But the pathways, and stairs and cabins, front gift shop check-in area were all exactly as I had described in the script.*

Then I came up with characters with specific actors in mind, people I had worked with on my first film. I first met Kris Lemche and Joey Kern on Rosencrantz and Guildenstern Are Undead *and fell in love with them as actors. They didn't have any scenes together in* Rosencrantz; *Lemche's character died too soon, and Kern only came in at the end. So I wrote* Alter Egos *for them, inspired by them. They're both good-looking, handsome fellows in the classic comic book superhero sense. And I felt that they were different as actors, though equally brilliant. Their differences as actors I think was expressed for me in the differences of the characters I wrote for them, the fundamental philosophy of the industry they work in and their abilities and craft, and how they come to accept each other at the end.*

Then came the VFX (Gary Breslin told me they would be doable for a small budget). Then I decided, "This would be cool if it were superheroes." I set about creating a scenario that I thought felt like "Reservoir Dogs with superheroes." It ended up being less violent and more like "Clerks with superheroes."

This is a world where superheroes exist in large numbers, and are almost an afterthought (if not a disliked commodity in many cases). Is this a commentary on the subgenre itself at this time in history? It went from laughable and rare in the 1970s and 1980s to more commonplace in the 1990s and a virtual cottage industry that has started to exhaust some moviegoers in the new millennium.

I definitely feel overwhelmed by the blockbuster movies that come out, and worry sometimes these lessons are watered down and buried beneath the glossy surface. On the one hand, I think, "My God, when I was a kid I would have loved all these special effects." And on the other hand, I think, "Thank God I got to grow up before all these special effects," because I might not have enjoyed the texts and comic books as much. I spent so much time dreaming about the possibilities of books I read, what they would feel like in real life. And when I see a film now that shows us everything, and puts the audience on a 3D rollercoaster ride of CGI monsters, sure it's fun, but it kind of feels like, "Well, that's it. That's what it feels like in real life. Now I don't have to imagine it any more." And I worry our imaginations will shrink. But I worry a lot.

I do love a film that can use graphics tastefully, sparingly, and so they don't get in the way of the storytelling. I feel the same way about humor. I don't want jokes or CGI to get in the way of storytelling, and I will be angry if I get taken on a tangential detour for the sake of laughs or visual candy.

I see a trend in superhero films to show a real person who becomes a superhero. Like with Kick Ass, Defendor, Super. *And when the superheroes are mutants, like in X-Men, they don't really get to show their human side too much. They do, but it's still in the context of a big action movie. So I wanted to explore the more intimate, internal side of these larger-than-life, colorful celebrities. It's closer to what* Robot Chicken *does when they show the Justice League throwing a birthday party or arguing over a pizza delivery than it is to* Kick Ass, *I think.*

This film is also about people with special abilities who have a hard time getting positive attention or funding for their unique talents. Is the film possibly also an allegory for the life and struggles of the arts and artists in modern America?

When I set down to write the script, there was definitely a lot of that—applying my experiences as a musician and filmmaker, the disappointment, competition and betrayal, to these characters. Money is the cause of stress in everyone's life. Needing to move out of your parents' house or getting fired from your job or losing your funding-financing—these are very relatable circumstances. I found a kind of truth and irony to the idea that superheroes need government subsidies because their services don't generate any revenue otherwise. Fridge/Brendan was also really a metaphor for me shedding off a very indie "rock star" identity which I had cultivated when I had a rock band, and felt like something I could no longer relate to or live up to, but that people expected from me. In the context of superheroes, I found a lot of humor, but also a kind of unexpected sadness to it.

The title *Alter Egos* and the relationship storyline of Fridge/Brendan speak to the idea of the face we share vs. the face we hide. Is there some element to the idea of the superhero life as a representation of public vs. private personas in the real world? Something that has become increasingly tangled in our social media-driven world?

I had just spent a few solid years promoting my music and first film, on Facebook, and I felt uneasy with how this was taking up my time and changing my thought process. So I wanted my superheroes to confront what it means to have two separate identities: one public and one private. I was sort of obsessed with this Internet-induced, multiple personality disorder. There was also the glaring realization of global injustice, that there would be no punishment for anyone on Wall Street who knowingly abused the positions of power and plunged the global community into a financial crisis. There would be no help for their victims. The world seemed to all at once express frustration and outrage at the small group of bankers and traders who had gotten us into this mess, and yet were still inexplicably making tons of money.

Is part of the reason why this film is a comedy-satire because we've reached a point in the life of the superhero film subgenre where the template has solidified sufficiently that we can now evaluate and deconstruct it? That is often the point at which a subgenre needs to change in order to be invigorated, or to wane in popularity after becoming exhausted.

I definitely think there is over-saturation in all genres—horror, sci-fi, rom-com. And in such times, the challenge is to find a fresh new take on that. I just think, we're used to superheroes battling villains; and even when they're battling each other, like in the most recent Captain America *movie, it's all about right and wrong. But I wanted to see them struggle with some more neurotic, Woody Allen–type problems. I thought that would cast the genre in a new light, and show that they can be so much more than just iconic two-dimensional characters, even with a lot less money.*

What do you think the fascination is with superheroes in general??

Superheroes have an undeniable value to society, as much so as a Greek god, for instance. We process and filter the problems of culture through them, as they restate lessons handed down through old mythology. You can see these parallels. As science and medicine made progress early in the 1900s, Superman came along to preach the value of physical fitness in fighting natural and manmade disasters. When the Great Depression brought a cloud of despair over America, Batman showed us that in order to effectively combat darkness, we need to tap into our own dark side. Then later when women and African-Americans were standing up for equality, the superheroes in X-Men comics warned us against the dangers of bigotry and underscored the great strength that comes from underdogs and outcasts.

Today, I think a lot of the draw is just spectacle, and built-in audiences from years of comic books. The outsider kids grew up to be parents who will bring the whole family to the theater, and the studios do a good job of making it feel like an event. Social media also does a good job of turning it into a debate about feminism and sexism and so all these important issues get explored and discussed around the release of these movies, even if sometimes that's not the intention of the storytellers.

Were there specific films (superhero or otherwise) that were influential to you in making this film?

There was no specific superhero film that inspired me, except perhaps The Incredibles *or old* Batman *TV episodes from the '60s. I didn't know at the time I was filming that* Super *was in production, and I had completely forgotten about* Mystery Men, *although that may have been in my subconscious.*

The flashbacks in Alter Egos *were inspired by* Reservoir Dogs *and Woody Allen's* Crimes and Misdemeanors. *I just like the hard, unannounced cut to a memory, sometimes with the ambient sound of the present scene where someone is describing—not narrating—the memory we are watching.*

But what I really wanted was for Alter Egos *to have the feeling like you had stepped into a comic book, but that the comic book was now real, and all around, and felt very natural. So the costumes were bright, skin-tight, and not modern and compiled of military-grade technology the way Christopher Nolan's* Batman *and the Marvel movies have done it.*

Crawlspace (2012)

Director: Justin Dix
Writers: Eddie Baroo, Justin Dix, Adam Patrick Foster
Starring Amber Clayton, Eddie Baroo, Ditch Davey

A distress signal bursts forth from a secret military base in the mysterious Pine Gap area of Australia. A well-trained crew of commandos is sent in to find and rescue the scientists stationed within. They are attacked by mutated animals, and then the strangest thing of all: The team leader finds his wife, previously thought dead, being held as prisoner inside the facility. They try to find other survivors and make their way safely out of the base. As their numbers dwindle, they discover that they might not be the rescue team; they might just be more victims of the experiments.

Combining elements of superpowers, military thrillers and science experiments gone terribly wrong, *Crawlspace* is a hybrid that borrows recognizable tropes from various subgenres and remixes them to fun and dizzying effect. Fans of Australian genre cinema will recognize some of the faces here such as actor-cowriter Eddie Baroo and John Brumpton, a genre staple from horror (*The Loved Ones*) and westerns (*Red Hill*). The film takes place in Pine Gap, a locale steeped in the kind of conspiracy theories which have become secular mythologies in the new millennium.

∼

Before he moved into film directing, Justin Dix worked on several big hit films in other technical capacities; he created props for *Charlotte's Web* and worked on the special effects for *Star Wars: Episode II—Attack of the Clones* and its sequel in his home country of Australia. His experience in effects, coupled with some ideas about the Pine Gap mystery, led to the creation of *Crawlspace*.

Justin Dix: *I'd been writing scripts and heading back and forth to L.A. for a while in between production designing, art directing and having my company, Wicked of Oz, do special effects for other films. It was becoming clear that I was writing what they call "tent pole" movies; another term thrown around L.A. is "high concept"—Batman, Armageddon, that sort of thing. Films that required big-name casts and big-name directors.*

I was meeting lots of great people and having lots of great meetings (by the way, they say you never have a bad meeting in L.A.), but I was not making forward progress. Anyone who knows me knows that I do not like to sit on my hands, doing nothing. So I decided to make an independent film, one that I had complete control over, and that I could put just about everything or anything I wanted to into it.

Also, my father used to be in the Australian intelligence community and used to disappear from time to time and return with beer coasters from the officer's club at Pine Gap. I'd always had a fascination with Area 51, who doesn't?, but something my father said one day got my mind racing. This is not word for word, but it was something like, "Everyone knows about the NSA, CIA or FBI, but no one really knows what the Australian Intelligence community does."

That made me think about Pine Gap, which is virtually right in the middle of Australia, one of the largest deserts in the world, a place hardly anyone goes, due to its isolation. I've driven up to the border of Area 51 from Las Vegas, it's not a hard drive, and for a top-secret base, everybody seems to know exactly where it is.

The other thing was, there had been numerous films and TV shows about Area 51 but virtually nothing about Pine Gap because nobody really paid any attention to it. It was the perfect cover.

From there, the script, using inspiration from one of my favorite films, Scanners. *Yes, I'm a product of the '80s, and I decided that psychic abilities would allow me to not only put anything in the movie I wanted (as it could all be in your mind), but I also loved the idea of messing with memories—what is real, what is not. I tried to be very aware of this while making the film. Careful what I showed and what I didn't.*

Myself, I love a film that could have multiple explanations. [Spoiler alert:] Was she really the wife or not, was the other girl, the blocker, projecting into our hero's head what Caesar wanted Romeo to see? The same is true with the opening of Crawlspace: *I wanted to mess with the audience's minds, showing the finale at the opening of the film, but still telling the story I needed to. Start the journey with a girl with no memory, scared, experimented on and surrounded by carnage, which just happened to make her choose which way she would exit the scene.*

This opening scene, which is actually the end, was the first thing I thought of, and the rest was just me being a kid in a candy store.

One of the elements explored in this film, and many others in the science fiction genre, is the eternal struggle between scientists on the edge of discovery, and the military that is either cleaning up their mess or trying to take their discoveries and utilize them for war-related purposes. This film ultimately doesn't come down clearly on either side. What is your opinion on that struggle between science for discovery and science for tactical advantage (both in the film and in real life)?

You touched on a very specific point that I am very passionate about in storytelling. It is reflected in other scripts I've written, one of which is looking like it may be going ahead about our race to achieve AI. We've all seen The Terminator *or* The Matrix, *even the scientist trying to be the first to create true artificial sentience. But, if you don't try, the other guy will.*

I did a lot of research on DARPA (Defense Advanced Research Projects Agency) and what their mandate is. They will pretty much fund research no matter how ridiculous, just to prove it is impossible, because if they, or someone else, proves otherwise, you're then ahead of the other guy. The unfortunate thing is that most of these advances will always be utilized for military applications first.

The robotics department at DARPA ... these things are scary, and they are getting faster, stronger and more silent. Just wait until they arm them.

I came across some article referring to psychic research and what might come across as fantasy does not get ruled out until it is ruled out as an impossibility. But if successful, you'll never know about it. It would become covert, go underground, and possibly be put in one of the most remote places on Earth.

You used Pine Gap, the Australian site long rumored to be an alien hotbed much like America's Area 51, as a setting for your story. What do you think the draw is to these "black sites," places where supposed secret alien activities have taken place? Do you think they're true, or just a fun element to add into a sci-fi story?

I chose Pine Gap because I wanted to create an Australian urban legend. Rumors of Area 51 are numerous, so I wanted an Aussie conspiracy story of our own. Black Sites are fascinating; I'm not a conspiracy nut, but I love not knowing, it makes me want to know more and that's what draws us to these stories.

I love misinformation, I love the fact that anyone thinking that there are aliens under the Australian desert would be considered a nut job, as all of this works to the advantage of those wanting to keep secrets in plain sight.

I've found that, since making Crawlspace, *I've found my niche: covert military cover-ups. I've written three scripts now, all very different, but all that circles around cover-ups, military advances, the mix of genres, it's a playground that I'm very excited to play in.*

As to whether it's true or not, I don't dwell on that; I love the idea that it could be, but also the idea it may not be. I'm more of a direct proof guy. If I was grabbed by aliens one day, I'd be shouting it from the rooftops, but I would also be seen as one of the nut jobs that claim they were as well. I keep an open mind. I don't discount anything, but I also don't believe in everything you see on the Internet.

In using psychic abilities in this film, you found an interesting way to re-visualize how a battle of psychics could happen.

I storyboarded every scene—in fact, every shot of the film prior to filming the movie, every turnaround for dialogue, and every bit of action. I actually built a 1:6 scale set and used 12-inch action figures to photograph the whole film, even lighting it with pen lights and doing miniature explosions with aerosol cans and a lighter. (Don't try that at home, kids.) The psychic battles were storyboarded the same way, but I knew they would be sound-reliant and need an amazing amount of trust on behalf of the actors for me to accomplish.

The happy accident on set was when my director of photography Simon Ozolins and I started to use torchlight shined into the anamorphic lens to create a bright light source that would intensify as their power did. It ended up being one of my favorite parts of the film. There are lots of favorite parts, but I really loved working with my actors to create believability to those scenes. The whole movie relied on it and I'm extremely proud of Amber Clayton's bravery in trusting that I would not make her look silly. I love that girl, she is so talented, she basically played three characters in that movie. She took it seriously and I'm enormously proud of the character E.V.E. It's not mentioned in the film, but the acronym for E.V.E. is Extraterrestrial Vivisection Experiment.

Other Films of Interest

Zoom (2006), *Gagamboy* (2004), *Astro Boy* (2009), *The Specials* (2000)

18

Science Fiction and Fake Documentaries

The fake documentary is the youngest of the movie genres, and the reason for that is because it was a long time before the technology that allowed for a narrative film to look like a documentary was inexpensive enough to warrant being created. Peter Watkins invented it with his historical battle reenactment film *The Battle of Culloden*, but immediately started utilizing the style for more fantastical stories.

Watkins imagined a nuclear scenario in England with the Oscar-winning *The War Game* (1965), then followed with two critiques of television's unblinking eye on violence with *The Gladiators* (1969) and *Punishment Park* (1971). This was the wave that broke open the dam, and filmmakers with interests different than Watkins' focus on politics and war used the format to great effect.

In one of David Cronenberg's earliest forays into body horror, 1969's *Stereo*, he chronicles the imaginary Canadian Academy of Erotic Enquiry and explores various grotesqueries which were precursors to his later *Videodrome* and *The Brood*. Environmental causes were just becoming realities in the early 1970s; 1971 brought us *The Hellstrom Chronicle*, an apocalyptic insect End Times parable that was fictitious like *The War Game* and likewise Oscar-nominated as Best Documentary.

Another 1971 hit, *The Legend of Boggy Creek*, was a precursor to pseudo-documentary television series like *In Search of ...* and much of the modern Syfy Channel's reality programming. Arthouse directors got into the game as well, with iconoclast Peter Greenaway creating a medical study of a Violent Unknown Event that grants immortality and strange abilities in *The Falls* (1980). Comedian Woody Allen created an entry with 1983's *Zelig*, about a man with such an extreme personality deficit that he began to adopt the appearance and mannerisms of people with whom he spends any time.

After the Millennium

The years following the huge success of 1999's fake documentary *The Blair Witch Project* were surprisingly sparse in terms of other releases, in part because even the Blair Witch franchise didn't follow up with a documentary-style sequel in *Book of Shadows: Blair Witch 2*. It was 2002 before science fiction saw another notable entry; *Dark Side of the Moon* was a straight-faced documentary that tapped into *X-Files*–style paranoia in theorizing that NASA and Stanley Kubrick faked the moon landing.

The satires of documentary cinema continued, with Werner Herzog lampooning his own reputation as a too-involved documentary director in 2004's *Incident at Loch Ness*. The same year brought the humorous but challenging "what if?" doc *A Day without a Mexican*; the film told the story of how California deals with the aftermath of every Mexican resident vanishing overnight.

Two years after *Dark Side of the Moon*, fake documentaries returned to space with *First on the Moon*, telling the story of Russian cosmonauts secretly reaching space a quarter century early, and *Interkosmos*, a tale of a failed German space colonization mission.

The late 2000s saw a boom in the zombie business, and the fake documentary world had its share. While *REC* (and its English-language remake *Quarantine*) was the most famous example of camera crews facing the undead, modern zombie progenitor George A. Romero made the similarly themed *Diary of the Dead*, commenting on the American desire to consume media at an alarming rate. Director Grace Lee even found an interesting take on marginalized communities and self-help support groups with the fake doc-comedy *American Zombie*.

By the end of the first decade of the new millennium, the format was so widely accepted that even high-concept franchise starters were using it style to great effect. The kaiju-style monster movie that *Godzilla* birthed in the 1950s was given the modern treatment in *Cloverfield*, and the superhero story was tweaked in *Chronicle*.

The Independent Perspective

Independent filmmakers not only embraced the newfound freedom of making films with lower budgets and less expensive equipment, they also incorporated the new "film it all" ethos of the post-millennial generation. The ease of recording became an element of the storytelling as well as a filmic device; aliens were still mysterious creatures, but their activities are now being captured frequently in films like *Lunopolis* (about documentarians uncovering a conspiracy of people living secretly on the moon) and *Invasion* (in which static dash-cam footage from a police car captures an alien invasion in real time).

The innocent idea of capturing the miracle of life through videos of pregnant mothers is visited in multiple scenarios as well, both frightening (in *Absence*, a pregnant mother's child vanishes from her womb without a trace) and hopeful (*The Baby Formula* follows a lesbian couple carrying each other's child from an experimental stem cell procedure).

Like pregnancy, romantic relationships are another subject in the purview of independent cinema, and *11 Minutes Ago* explores the struggle of modern relationships by replacing the typical anxieties and life problems with an elaborate non-linear "meet cute" that takes two years for the man and a single afternoon for the woman. Other intimate relationships, like the one humanity has developed with artificial intelligence, are reflected as well. In the aftermath of revelations about NSA spying and behavior recognition software, *Nightmare Code* was a prescient and terrifying view into our tenuous relationship with machines, seen through the eye of the computer itself.

Featured Films

Mr. Jones (2013)
Writer-Director: Karl Mueller
Starring Jon Foster, Sarah Jones, Mark Steger

Scott and Penny are a young couple who have decided to give up city life, move out to the woods for a year and focus their time and efforts on Scott's idea of making a nature documentary. Their relationship suffers from the isolation and Scott's general aimlessness and lack of concrete ideas for a film. That all changes when Scott chases a thief who stole his backpack and ends up at a cabin filled with creepy statues and figures made of sticks, string and other detritus. Scott recognizes the statues as the work of a reclusive artist known only as Mr. Jones, and decides that he will be the new focus of his documentary. But the more he explores the artwork and world of the mysterious man, the stranger the truth seems to be, until Scott and Penny can't tell the difference between reality and the fantasy Mr. Jones creates for his work.

The rare "found footage" film that uses its technical conceit as a way to save money *and* to create an innovative way to shift storytelling expectations, *Mr. Jones* is a remarkably complicated science fiction thriller that comes disguised in the sheep's clothing of a simple cabin in the woods horror film. The film is at times a commentary on media's obsession with chronicling the private lives of celebrities and at other times a genre-busting exploration of the unseen world between dreams and waking. The film is all the better for both elements.

∼

Before *Mr. Jones*, Karl Mueller wrote the screenplay for the claustrophobic apocalypse thriller *The Divide*. He followed up *Mr. Jones* with the script for the more horror-centric

One of the unnerving art installations from a reclusive outsider artist in *Mr. Jones* (2013).

The Devil's Hand, and recently directed his second feature, the psychological thriller *Rebirth*.

Mr. Jones is an interesting hybrid of a film, one which begins in a certain format and style, and changes drastically in its narrative and stylistic form throughout. How did the idea for the film initially come about?

Karl Mueller: Because I've been making my living as a filmmaker for about a decade, and I've had my eyes open during this time; I've become a big believer in the "context creates content" school of thought. Basically, whatever mixture of financier needs and audience taste and genre conventional wisdom and technological capabilities happen to be around at the time of the genesis of whatever book or symphony or movie you're trying to create will have a huge influence on the book or symphony or movie you make.

This is a long-winded way of explaining why I made a cabin-in-the-woods horror movie. They are cheap to make, and there's a proven audience out there who will pay to see them. Or at least, this was the case when I made Mr. Jones. Even before we finished post on the film, this was changing due to the drying up of the DVD market and Internet piracy.

So in total honesty, the following opportunity was offered to me: If you can write a script that is a horror movie in a contained space with a few characters that can be done cheaply, then you can direct this film. So those were the initial conditions I started with. Everything followed from that, and became much more personal: the outsider artist as central figure, the style of the film, the sci-fi elements (such as they are), etc. Making movies in a capitalist society is an eternal dance between convincing an investor that your movie can make them a profit, and expressing your voice within this context. The artistic possibilities change as your opportunities change (for better or worse), but everyone is beholden to that dynamic.

Though the fake documentary has existed since the 1960s, it was 1999's *The Blair Witch Project* that popularized it, and the new millennium has seen a massive growth in the subgenre. Was *Mr. Jones* in part a response to the glut of largely unoriginal or poorly executed films that came in the wake of *The Blair Witch Project*, films that were utilizing the format of the fake documentary without bringing anything unique or original to it?

I guess I see "found footage" as just another of the many tools you can use to create the sense of reality you need in order for a story to affect a viewer. Different genres have different requirements in degrees of verisimilitude. Horror's need is quite high: Basically, the more "real" it feels, the scarier it gets. The more you're aware that the characters you're watching are actually actors on a set, the less effective the movie will be. There's sort of an arms race always going on in horror to get ever more "real" as audiences get numb to the previous generation's techniques. So found footage is a very cozy, natural fit.

Unfortunately, found footage also comes with a lot of baggage. Because you need to justify why anyone would keep filming when shit gets real, you tend to see the same creaky plot machinery over and over, which creates its own set of clichés. Using those tools means you're running the risk of people immediately dismissing the film sight unseen, just because they're sick of the format. However, when it works, it can be really effective. So I said "Fuck it" and just did it.

I suppose I did consciously make Mr. Jones as a "response" to other found footage movies in the sense that I was aware of these other movies (in a general sense) and I wanted to kind of take the found footage movie into its "modernist" phase. Or maybe, more specifically, *its "Cubist" phase. For me, anyway, the format had been exhausted, so the only interesting move was to make it "aware of itself." So ... the movie we see starts out as the documentary the lead character is making about his life in the woods and the story of finding this infamous, reclusive outsider artist. The deeper he gets into the world of the outsider artist, the more the forces around him start "taking over" the movie. It becomes a found footage movie where eventually, the in-movie "director" is actually a malevolent, irrational, dream-logic Other. In layman's terms, the movie gets really trippy. For people who are looking for the standard reflex responses a horror movie is supposed to deliver,* Mr. Jones *is probably a frustrating experience. But for people who are down with a "Cubist" horror movie—they are few, but they are out there—then hopefully it's an interesting ride.*

From what I can tell, there's this huge divide in the horror world. The majority of horror fans are just looking for something scary. It's not a particularly sophisticated audience, so all you need to do is go through the same tried-and-true storytelling methods and they'll get the high they're after. There's nothing wrong with this. A lot of this crowd is made up of teenagers.

But there's also a very active minority of horror fans who are basically high art connoisseurs with very specific, defined tastes. They are extremely aware of convention and genre and history, and they like the horror genre because it's this well-defined space in which an endless amount of variations can be spun. Mr. Jones *is definitely a movie for that "active minority."*

The mind reels when thinking about the response of two horny teenagers who pop Mr. Jones *in just to have something going while they fumble at bra straps and zippers.*

While your film ultimately goes in many directions, one of its initial themes is the seeking out of a famed "outsider artist." This is a phenomenon of the new millennium: Internet and pop culture's need for constant "discovery" of new art, tech, etc. What inspired you to make the unconventional artist a part of your story?

I first learned the term "outsider artist" when I was living in Chicago and heard about this dead guy named Henry Darger. Darger was a serious outcast, worked his whole life as a janitor and died alone at a ripe old age in a hoarder's apartment. When his landlord went into the apartment Darger had lived in undisturbed and unvisited for years and years, he discovered this completely insane, unbelievably long and detailed "novel" the uneducated Darger had been working on his whole life. It was like 7000 pages, complete with hundreds of full-sized paintings, illustrating the story of an epic war between a race of child-like fairies and these really brutal, militaristic adults. The little girl fairies had penises, for some reason. And were always naked. Nobody had any idea Darger was up to this. It's totally bizarre. Nobody really knew him, so no one had any context to explain what drove him to do this. The "novel" he created was both beautiful and highly disturbing. Darger kind of has this Michael Jackson aura around him: He seems like a total innocent who pined for a lost, never-experienced childhood his whole life, but there was this dark side to that where his adult sexuality infected and perverted his obsession with childhood innocence.

Anyway, it was a fascinating story. I got fascinated in the idea of "outsider artist" for a while, specifically socially marginalized people who might have been marginalized for what we would call mental illness issues. People working so far outside of the culture industry that their art would be totally uninfluenced by the trends and unconscious conditioning the rest of us more conventional (insider?) artists were subject to.

Now, what I discovered is that a lot—if not most—of the "outsider art" that's become recognized and displayed somewhere in our culture industry is pretty flat and uninteresting (in my opinion). There's a lot to be said for spending years learning the tools of craft in order to better express yourself. But there's still something romantic and kind of scary about the idea of what an unhinged mind might create. When I was thinking about what kind of figure I'd want to put at the center of a horror movie, this seemed like a natural fit. You could argue that the character of Mr. Jones *is basically Henry Darger transposed to the context of a cabin-in-the-woods horror movie. I didn't really consciously make this connection when I was making it, but it's pretty obvious to me in retrospect.*

Europa Report (2013)

Director: Sebastián Cordero
Writer: Philip Gelatt
Starring Sharlto Copley, Michael Nyqvist, Christian Camargo

A privately funded organization called Europa Ventures has sent a six-man space mission to one of Jupiter's moons to seek out the possibility of new life. After the devastating loss of a crew member in the wake of a ship malfunction, the remaining crew members struggle through depression and isolation in their 20-month trip. Upon arriving, they begin drilling through the ice and into the ocean underneath. During exploration, another technological mishap causes a ship crash, more deaths and the slow descent of the ship into the water. All the while, crew members have been seeing a mysterious blue light in the water...

An ambitious sci-fi thriller, *Europa Report* pays strict attention to the details of science and technology that are often overlooked in similar stories. The beneficial result is a verisimilitude in both appearance and narrative, combining the documentary style and the focus on the inner workings of space exploration to create a quiet and unnerving thriller. The film touches on multiple post-millennial concerns, including the privatization of space exploration, business' influence on scientific discovery and the modern tendency to record everything for posterity.

∼

After an eerily effective premiere writing and directing *The Bleeding House*, Philip Gelatt worked in graphic novel-writing with the historical thriller *Petrograd*. He followed that up with the space-faring series *Pariah*. Transferring some of the same backdrop and interests from his comic series, Gelatt veered from the youth-driven adventure of *Pariah* into hard science fiction with a faux-documentary conceit.

Philip Gelatt: *That was the original intention, to make it a faux documentary. There was talk a few times of abandoning that as a stylistic conceit but, of course, we did end up keeping it. The other idea that was with the project from the start was that it was would hew as close as it could to scientific accuracy and possibility. So wedding a "realistic documentary" style with that focus on realistic science always felt like a pretty strong combination. The idea was that one would bolster the other, to create a certain kind of feeling of reality or "potential future reality" to the project.*

Many science fiction films of the new millennium have become more realistic, both in effects and in the actual exploration of the scientific process. Do you feel this is a result of fans and audiences (as well as the filmmakers) having more knowledge and access to space exploration information now? And why do you think that these films still insist

Daniel Luxembourg (Christian Camargo) prepares for a long journey in *Europa Report* (2013).

on attempting to get the details of mechanics and science right even in the midst of such fantastical concepts?

I can't really speak to other projects and why science was important to them, but on Europa Report, I knew I wanted to do it precisely because, at the time, I felt we hadn't seen a lot of science in science fiction films in quite some time. There was a lot of talk about Kubrick and Clarke's 2001: A Space Odyssey *and the idea of "hard science fiction" when working on the script.*

Generally though, I think science is great for fiction for a number of reasons. Having story rules tends to really help genre fiction, tends to ground the world being presented and allow an audience to really immerse themselves in it. Using science as your set of rules, so to speak, builds on that one degree further. We're not talking about the rule of magic or superheroes, we're talking about real rules as they exist the physical reality that we know.

If you start from a realistic place and move the viewer to some place fantastic, the fantastic will feel more real because the groundwork of what "reality" is in this world had been laid out.

A lot of this film is about the sacrifice that scientists are willing to make in order to make discoveries, which is commendable. But I think the most powerful commentary is the ultimate revelation of the film, which is how human lives are ultimately worth less to the organization funding the exploration than the discovery is. Is this perhaps a commentary on corporatism generally? The idea of profit and innovation being more desirable than how the acquisition of those things affects people?

One thing we definitely didn't want in the movie was to fully indulge the science fiction cliché of "Evil Corporation." The idea was always to keep it morally ambiguous. The corporation got what it wanted—but what it wanted was also this huge, huge discovery, this moment for mankind.

Personally, I much prefer the idea of government-backed space programs. But more and more it seems that's not what we're going to be dealing with, ultimately. So what you're sensing in Europa *is, yes, the discomfort of big science corporatism but also the hope that while it might not be ideal, and it might not care about its people, it might yet provide us with tools and discoveries that are of massive importance. A moral tension, I guess, is what the movie was after.*

I think you can sense, actually, a similar moral tension in the actual history of the original space race. Where, yes, we were doing it "for all mankind," but we were also doing it to compete with the Soviets. It was that clash of culture and geo-political positioning that got us to the moon. If it's a clash of corporations that takes us the next step, I guess I'd be okay with it. Again, not ideal, but I feel very passionately that something needs to spur us upward to the stars.

When you wrote the script, was it already your plan to have the crew members come from all parts of the world, or did that start to come in as you assembled your fantastic international cast?

It's funny, the multi-ethnic cast feels a bit like a ploy to garner a great cast, but it was actually hardwired into the script from the very start. And in fact, in the original drafts the cast of the company men and scientists was more multi-ethnic than it is in the final film. I really wanted a Turkish scientist (for some reason), but he ended up getting swapped out.

But honestly, the idea with the diverse cast was basically the same as the idea behind the hard science. It felt realistic. The future of space travel doesn't belong just to America and it's important to remember that. Before writing the script, I had a good number of conversations with JPL (NASA Jet Propulsion Laboratory) people and one of my favorite conversations was all about just how many nations have space programs. Now most of them aren't very well-funded, or haven't done much, but they have *them.*

And yeah, that cast was fantastic. I'm still a little startled by it, to be honest.

Why do we continue to be drawn back to the idea of space travel?

I think there is an essential need in mankind to push at its limits. Exploration is kind of hardwired into us. So the idea that there is this vastness out there ... not to anthropomorphize it too much but, waiting for us ... that's a very rich idea. But in terms of actual space exploration and in terms of telling stories about it.

Put another way, I guess, space is kind of blank canvas of the future. And there's a great appeal in painting something on there. Trying your hand at stories that say, "What if in the future, things go this way?"

Other Films of Interest

The Mother of Invention (2009), *Ghosts with Shit Jobs* (2012)

19

The Fantastical Worlds of Musicals

The musical is an interesting film genre; ostensibly, any other kind of genre can become a musical through the mere introduction of musical numbers into the narrative. However, more often than not, the musical genre is limited to singing versions of otherwise standard dramas, comedies and romance films. On occasion, a popular entry will crop up that successfully unites the musical with another genre: action film (*Streets of Fire*), religious epic (*Godspell* and *Jesus Christ Superstar*), drug propaganda film (*Reefer Madness*) and documentary (*This Is Spinal Tap!*). More often than not, though, it is a passing fad that doesn't stand the test of time, and musicals revert back to their natural state.

This is true of the science fiction musical, seen in the early talkie years with 1930's *Just Imagine*. The film leaves no science fiction trope unexplored, with the lead character frozen in the 1930s and thawed out in the 1980s, characters with number-letter combinations as designations, vast social chasms, food in pill form and an expedition to Mars. Three years later, *It's Great to Be Alive* brought song and dance to the depressing concept of a single fertile man left on Earth after a devastating epidemic.

Listed elsewhere in this book as a pseudo-science fiction film, 1939's *The Wizard of Oz* must therefore be mentioned here as well. After that film, however, the science fiction-musical hybrid disappeared from sight, only popping up briefly in 1965 with the weird cult film *Gonks Go Beat*, in which a future society is divided between rebels and suits who each have their distinct musical preferences.

The 1970s were a crossroads of the dying studio system of the past and the daring fledgling artists of the new Hollywood that led to some truly unusual offerings. Olivia Newton-John tried to capture sci-fi fantasy magic twice, first with director Val Guest in *Toomorrow* and then with co-star Gene Kelly in *Xanadu*. While 1971's *Willy Wonka and the Chocolate Factory* might not seem like science fiction at first glance, magical flying elevators and televisions that transmit candy bars across the world are enough to earn it that status. In 1975, the concept of science fiction musicals found its most popular cult icon: *The Rocky Horror Picture Show*. Shocking in its day for the frankness of its dialogue and lyrics and its mainstreaming of the conversation about fluid sexuality, the film attained a midnight movie status that kept it playing for decades, leading to a movie sequel (*Shock Treatment*) and a television remake over 40 years later.

The corporate ownership of the studios in the 1980s didn't seem to stifle the mainstream weirdness of other hybrid films like *Big Trouble in Little China* and *The Adventures of Buckaroo Banzai Across the Eighth Dimension*, and musical hybrids were no exception. *The Apple* (1980) was a tale of drugs and show business in the far-flung future world of 1994, while

1983's *The Return of Captain Invincible* spoofed not only musicals but old-fashioned superheroes as well. The newest trend in the 1980s was to combine aliens, outer space and hard rock, resulting in the decent *Earth Girls Are Easy* (1988), the animated (and unusual) *Rock & Rule* (1983) and the questionable but interestingly cast *Voyage of the Rock Aliens* (1984), starring Pia Zadora, Craig Sheffer and Michael Berryman. The 1980s even saw a genuine critical hit with *Little Shop of Horrors* (1986), based on the Off-Broadway musical which was in turn based on the original Roger Corman film *The Little Shop of Horrors* (1960).

After the Millennium

Though there was a huge resurgence in the occurrence of science fiction musicals in the years after the millennium, nearly none of them were films made by studios. The fantasy-tinged *Moulin Rouge* (2001) was a fantastically rendered film which received Oscar nominations and reignited a mini-musical revival that included *Chicago*, *Hairspray* and *Across the Universe*, but most of the musicals that embraced science fiction elements were little indie films like *Sci-Fi High: The Musical* (2010).

The Independent Perspective

The freedom of new technologies, accompanied by the renewed interest in exploring defunct corners of the cinematic past, led independent filmmakers to create a spate of new films that either looked boldly forward, or nostalgically into a nonexistent past. Director Cory McAbee followed up his cult hit *The American Astronaut* with the science fiction musical hybrid *Stingray Sam* (2009) that added westerns into the mix. *Bang Bang Baby* (2014) went into a candy-coated rock'n'roll past that let science fiction darkness peek around the corners of its seemingly idyllic setting.

The darkness was on full display in director Darren Lynn Bousman's *Repo! The Genetic Opera*. Bousman, who started his career with the *Saw* films and later returned to high-concept musicals with *The Devil's Carnival* and its sequels, told the apocalyptic story of a repo man whose job included collecting organs from delinquent medical clients.

And in true independent fashion, there were films which defied even the already outlandish framework of the sci-fi musical. *The History of Future Folk* (2012) was an inexpensive and endearing film about alien musicians who come to Earth to save it. It was based on the real-life musical act of musicians Nils d'Aulaire and Jay Klaitz, who built their live performances around an elaborate sci-fi backstory.

The Featured Films in this section explore the vast reaches of outer space, explore gender disparity on this planet and others, and travel the entire galaxy just to bring a father and son closer together.

Featured Films

The American Astronaut (2001)
Writer-Director: Cory McAbee
Starring Cory McAbee, Rocco Sisto, James Ransone

Interplanetary trader Samuel Curtis arrives at a galactic saloon to deliver his cargo, a cat. He meets up with old friend Blueberry Pirate, who tells him of a job with a huge reward: deliver the Boy Who Actually Saw a Woman's Breast to the Southern belles of Venus in exchange for a very valuable human body. Embarking on the journey, he comes across a colony of human miners who beg him to return their offspring, a young man named Body Suit, to Earth so he can live out a normal life. Little does Samuel know that his nemesis Professor Hess is on his trail and waiting for the opportunity to kill him…

It is rare to find a film that is almost entirely unfamiliar in plot, characters and execution, and it is one of the chief joys of experiencing *The American Astronaut*. The film is a western set in the far reaches of space and enhanced by an eclectic set of musical numbers, all constructed with an endearingly shopworn DIY sensibility that would fill Wes Anderson with jealousy. The film was born in the valley just between nostalgia for a previous era of filmmaking and the new world of digital video and streaming distribution, and it combines the best of both worlds.

Samuel Curtis (Cory McAbee) wearing full space gear in *The American Astronaut* (2001).

Though *The American Astronaut* was the first feature film Cory McAbee wrote and directed, he had been building towards it for several years with other projects. He formed his style in the short films *The Man on the Moon* and *The Ketchup and Mustard Man*, and the musical sequences and soundtrack for the film came from his band, Billy Nayer Show. Those pieces, combined with some personal events in his life, led to the creation of the film's narrative.

Cory McAbee: *I was working as the head of security at nightclubs in San Francisco for several years. At one point, I quit my job and lost my apartment. I started living out of people's carports. I got by through filling in part-time as a doorman and by doing occasional performances. I was also very much involved with helping to raise my two young nephews. Most of* The American Astronaut *was inspired by all of this. I wrote ideas constantly. After three years, when I was finally able to afford an apartment, I wrote the first draft based on my notes.*

The aesthetic of the film is a retro-future. Were there considerations beyond the final budget of the film that factored into your decision to use that look for the film?

The film was inspired by my family. My father was an auto mechanic. He worked in garages. The science and mechanics resembled his surroundings. My mother's father was also a mechanic. He lived in a mobile home in the middle of the Nevada desert. I spent my summers with him. My character's appearance, my tools and the technology of the world within The American Astronaut *was based on their surroundings. The choice to use paintings instead of computer animation or models to show space travel was a practical choice. I was able to do the paintings myself. I did over half of them.*

This film falls into two distinct subgenres: the sci-fi musical and the sci-fi western. Beyond the challenge of doing it, and the fun of hybridizing those elements, did you feel there were advantages to embracing so many disparate genres within a single film?

Dennis Potter was a huge influence on me. He was the reason I wanted to make musicals. When I first discovered the Singing Detective *[series] and* Pennies from Heaven *[feature], I realized that musicals could be more, or at least different, than what I had grown up seeing. The sci-fi element was, at first, just a metaphor. It quickly became a license to experiment. Researching information to support ideas became a way of educating myself.*

Many films of the new millennium have looked to the past for inspiration about the future, digging into the *Buck Rogers* perception of tomorrow. Your film, though taking place in the past, taps into a similar sensibility. Why do you think yesterday's fantasy of tomorrow's technology and discoveries is more interesting to filmmakers than the genuine technologies and discoveries happening around us?

The science fictions of our past were born of optimism and hope. Space travel was new. It became part of our collective conscious after Yuri Gagarin became the first man in space and the space race became high profile. Five years later, Star Trek *premiered. In 1969, the first men walked on the moon, and David Bowie released* Space Oddity. *Pop culture reflected our hopeful achievements. Three years later, Bowie released "Star Man" while Elton John released "Rocket Man." We were inspired and curious. That optimism may seem quaint today, but today's discoveries are the product of those times.*

Films this unique and high-concept would have been relegated to obscurity or marginal cult status in previous generations. Has the advent of the Internet allowed fans and new viewers to connect more with you and the film, and give it a life that might not have been possible 20 years earlier?

Chesterton once wrote, "Where does a wise man hide a leaf? In the forest." The Internet is the forest, the artwork is the leaf, but there are a lot more people in the forest looking for leaves, so ... yes and no.

There has been a surge in the number of sci-fi musicals in recent years, from *The American Astronaut* and your follow-up *Stingray Sam* to films like *Ripped!* and *Bang Bang Baby* and *Repo! The Genetic Opera*. Why do you think fans and filmmakers have suddenly started embracing a genre that was never that popular or prolific to begin with?

I have no idea. When I began writing The American Astronaut *in the mid–90s, I was trying to create something that didn't resemble anything that I had seen before. I wanted it to be likable, but I needed it to be unique. When I wrote* Stingray Sam, *I reworked ideas from* The American Astronaut *to create a sci-fi parody of our political environment. Part of the story structure and filmmaking was in anticipating how films would be seen on emerging technologies. Today, I am more interested in the effect that a film can have on viewers, and on the people who become involved with its creation.*

Are there specific films or TV shows that were influential to you in making this movie?

The Ghost and Mrs. Muir. *The black-and-white photography, the camera movement and the simplest of in-camera effects to tell a story. These had an impact on me from a young age.*

The Ghastly Love of Johnny X (2012)

Director: Paul Bunnell
Writers: Paul Bunnell, Steve Bingen, Mark D. Murphy, George Wagner
Starring Will Keenan, Creed Bratton, Reggie Bannister

Banished alien Johnny X and a few of his loyal friends are living on Earth disguised as a gang of greasers. Johnny X is the inventor of a resurrection suit that a woman named Bliss has stolen. Others desire the suit, including concert promoter King Clayton, who wants to use the suit on Johnny X's long-lost absentee father, recently deceased rock star Mickey O'Flynn. Plans are hatched for an army of zombies, and love blooms in the most unusual of circumstances.

The Ghastly Love of Johnny X is an updated reinterpretation of several classic genres: the science fiction alien film, the youth in trouble story, the 1950s musical and the "starcrossed lovers" romance. The brilliance of the film is not just the way in which it weaves disparate filmic elements together to tell an outlandish but ultimately very sweet story, but also how it uses its far-fetched sci-fi plot to discuss the roots of juvenile delinquency, the dangers of weapons in the wrong hands and the societal taboos of certain kinds of relationships.

∼

The wealth of Hollywood film history hidden throughout the film should be no surprise coming from director Paul Bunnell, whose obsession with filmmaking began at an early age. A long career full of small supporting roles and short films led Bunnell to his first feature film, the surreal *That Little Monster*. Using his experience as a writer, director, producer, cinematographer and editor, he assembled a cast of cult stars like Reggie Bannister and Creed Bratton for *The Ghastly Love of Johnny X*, a film born of a single intriguing central concept.

Johnny X (Will Keenan) and the Grand Inquisitor (Kevin McCarthy) pictured on a lobby card for *The Ghastly Love of Johnny X* (2012) (courtesy Ghastly Johnny X, LLC).

Paul Bunnell: *I've always loved old science fiction movies, and had been kicking around ideas for making one myself for years. When I came up with the basic concept of the resurrection suit, I knew it could work as the linchpin on which I could build an intriguing story. This would be my tribute to those sometimes awful but always fun low-budget films of the past. The initial story regarding the resurrection suit started off very differently from the final product, but I was very happy with the end result.*

This film clearly has an affection for the sincere but cheesy sci-fi films of the 1950s and 1960s. This has become a recent mini-phenomenon, with films like *Plan 10 from Outer Space, The Lost Skeleton of Cadavra* and others which try to recreate the performance style, set design and aesthetic of films which now seem dated or clumsily executed. What is your opinion on why that has become something of interest in the new millennium?

People are always rediscovering outdated stuff and finding out that, regardless of technological advances or current attitudes, there is real value in otherwise forgotten styles and techniques. For example, when compact discs proved so popular, for their immense storage space, high fidelity and ease of care, vinyl record albums became a thing of the past. But they never completely went away, and every so often, a new generation embraces vinyl all over. Fans pick up on some intangible element that makes them seek out either vintage LPs or newly issued collectible vinyl albums and 45s, because there is something warm and fuzzy about that type of product missing from the digital world. The same school of thought can be applied to the cheesy films of the past. In the best of those endeavors, everyone involved was putting on a show the very best that they could. It didn't always turn out the way they wanted, and yes, it was a business and they were hoping to turn a profit, but their heart and soul was up there on the screen.

My heart and soul is in every frame of The Ghastly Love of Johnny X. Of course, I did want to replicate the feel of those wonderful old black-and-white sci-fi "classics" of yesteryear, but I also wanted to put out a professional-looking product. It is not intended to come across as self-consciously bad or cheap-looking. Those filmmakers who deliberately set out to create movies bursting with poor acting, low-rent sets and so forth, are only entertaining themselves. I hope to entertain a larger audience, so we do the very best we can. That said, the ongoing resurgence of the low-budget sci-fi look can only be a good thing, since it perpetuates interest in the 1950s and 1960s originals, which are too good (or so bad they're too good) to be forgotten!

Though they seem ill-suited together, there has been a recent surge in science fiction-based musicals. Why do you think these disparate genres have recently been combined so frequently? Why has it become so popular?

That is a good question! The Ghastly Love of Johnny X was not initially conceived as a musical, actually. As various drafts came and went, it just seemed that certain scenes played out better in song. It was a surprise to me, too! From the beginning, there were always a couple of spots that incorporated music. There would have been at least one concert number, for example, since part of the story revolves around a pop singer. And because I was paying tribute to various other genres anyway, I planned one big musical number for the cast, which is the "Fantasy Diner" sequence. This bit is fairly long in the finished film because it was intended to be my big statement on old movie musicals. As such, it incorporates a few different styles, including the rousing fight chorus, the rock'n'roll solo and the sweet love ballad. I was covering all the bases in one number, and I thought it worked pretty well. However, at different points during completion of the script, I found songs actually worked much better than the written word at conveying some plot points and character development. Before long, I realized the movie was now just as much a musical as it was a science fiction story!

As for why it seems to be a popular trend to incorporate music into sci-fi or horror, I imagine it is because a lot of audiences these days are dismissive of musicals as an art form. The musical will always be around, of course, and every now and then there is a hit amongst the duds. But sophisticated moviegoers don't take people bursting into song seriously, and they haven't for years. If a filmmaker is already telling a story that requires a certain amount of suspension of disbelief anyway, which is most sci-fi and horror, then why not just go whole hog, as it were, and toss in some musical numbers at the same time? It helps to separate your movie from the pack. When it is done well, this can be a lot of fun, although there are some not-so-terrific ones out there, too.

With aliens, resurrection suits, zombies, love stories, music and greasers, it feels like there's some sort of satirical element in this film that comments on sci-fi's love of the endlessly elaborate and complicated narrative. Was the "kitchen sink" approach to the sci-fi elements of this film in some way a comment on that?

Well, the satirical element is deliberate, yes. And it is important to note that The Ghastly Love of Johnny X is not a parody. My movie is having fun with genres of the past, but it is not making fun of them. Combining so many disparate story types was my way of celebrating those classic old flicks, which frequently piled on complicated plot twists and elements out of left field in an effort to surprise their audience, or at least keep them interested. Generally speaking, the "kitchen sink" approach is a sign of desperation, meaning nobody making the movie is exactly sure what works, so they try a little bit of everything. In my case, we put in many of these wildly diverse movie staples because they truly moved an admittedly weird story along.

Incidentally, I personally have no issues with flat-out parodies and spoofs. I love a well-crafted, genuinely funny comedy. One of my all-time favorite theatrical features of the 1960s is actually It's a Mad Mad Mad Mad World! When I draw the line of distinction with The Ghastly Love of Johnny X, it is to reassure my audience that it was never conceived of as being primarily a comedy. There are definitely humorous moments, of course, and the concept is so "out there" that you wouldn't be expected to sit grim-faced and thoughtful throughout the picture. But I wanted the characters to have some kind of real emotional investment, and directed the actors to approach the material with a straight face, not a wink to the camera. Well, not too many winks, anyway! And for me, the best science fiction movies, new or old, are presented respectfully, rather than as a big joke.

Why do you think the genre of the science fiction musical has had a renaissance in recent years?

That is hard to answer. I think there will always be an audience for science fiction films in general, because of the endless possibilities. Sometimes that audience is smaller in number, and not so vocal, and sometimes it is trendy to embrace sci-fi, such as when a big studio, mega-budget blockbuster comes out. But I can't say for sure why the specific sub-subgenre of the science fiction musical is popular at any given time. I just think that some directors, like myself, find themselves working on a fantasy project of some kind, and realize that putting in a couple of musical numbers might breathe a little more life into the story. Sometimes they try to be more realistic, having a dance number set to music actually depicted as playing on screen, for example, and sometimes they just embrace the notion outright, with characters singing and dancing to unseen orchestras like they did in those old-fashioned big screen musicals, which is not at all realistic. But it is always interesting.

Ripped! (2014)
Director: Rod Bingaman
Writers: Andrew Barlow, Rod Bingaman
Starring Hallie York, Quentin McCuiston, Elise Rovinsky

The year is 1967. In the halls of the British Space Agency, four young lads (Norman, Colin, Andy, and Reg, collectively known as the pop group Norman's Normans) work as janitors. After a mishap involving a BSA-trained chimpanzee, the lads are shot into outer space. They arrive on the planet Hormone (which is populated entirely by women), where Norman catches the eye of Princess Noxema. This angers Queen Fallopia, who throws the lads in prison. But trouble is brewing with a nearby planet of men, and Norman's Normans might be the only thing standing in the way of intergalactic war.

The film may have been produced in 2014, but *Ripped!* is a musical whose origins and inspirations are straight out of the era in which it is set. It is a clear love letter to the subgenre of the jukebox musical, which began in the 1940s and reached its peak popularity with the Beatles film *A Hard Day's Night*. The film is charmingly old-fashioned with some clever gender commentary; its smartest move is in combining the infectious characters and musical numbers with a satirical science fiction story no doubt influenced by female-centric but decidedly un-feminist films like *She*, *Aelita Queen of Mars* and *Barbarella*.

~

Director Rod Bingaman and producing partner Maura Shea were no strangers to recreating films of a bygone era; their previous film, *Hooray for Mister Touchdown*, a 1930s period piece about a football player, also had science fiction plot elements. Bingaman had a few other films and genre tropes from the past that inspired his second film.

This is a hilarious, unique concept. I'm curious how the idea came about.

Rod Bingaman: *Wow, thanks! I wish more people felt that way! I think in retrospect, I probably over-indulged myself, but it's great when someone gets what you're trying to do. Andrew Barlow and I cooked this up over a pitcher of beer 20 years ago as an Elvis movie that was never made. We both enjoyed the campiness of those movies.* Ripped! *is full of references.... It got put away for a while as "too ambitious" until we decided to dust it off and then I brought the Norman's Normans characters over from a Matt Helm–type script I had written.*

It's a movie I always wanted to make because I like making music and Help! *is a favorite of mine. The concept is what used to be called jukebox musicals, which were eventually replaced by music videos. So the banter of the group is Beatles-inspired (Norman is the charmer, Reg the cute hair guy, Colin the sensible one, Andy the clown). The space theme was inspired by the Herman's Hermits movie* Hold On. *The "beam trip" in the middle is by way of the Monkees'* Head. *Some* Barbarella *got tossed in, too.*

There seemed to be this quaint idea in the '60s and '70s that cute guys could show up anywhere with guitars and everyone would melt. I guess I probably got that from Bye Bye Birdie. *We patterned the look of the two female leads after Ann-Margret and Shelley Fabares.*

Princess Noxema (Hallie York, center) and her royal assistants (Cait Johnston, Mandy Brown, Lindsay Goranson, Rachel Sweeney) find trouble from Earth in *Ripped!* (2014).

Norman's Normans is clearly a satirical version of the "movie band" à la the Monkees, Herman's Hermits, the Beatles in *A Hard Day's Night*. Why did you decide to make a meta-musical about the band that was playing the music in the movie? Is this film in some ways a commentary on the kind of "do-it-all" music celebrities that the Beatles wrought (now you now have to sing, have a perfume, clothing line, act in an indie film, produce a game show, etc.)?

Meta-musical ... interesting. In some ways, any time you make a period film, you are referencing the form, but I think I just wanted to experience it on some level, which sounds very Method, but I like living in the idiom, so to speak. If I think too much about broader intentions, I tend to get in my own way.

The element of the female ruling class on the alien planet feels like a clever way of talking about the questionable gender politics of the day in a modern satirical light. What were you hoping to illuminate about the time in which the film is set, and what makes it stand out in contrast to the world now?

Yeah, that was certainly part of the thinking; it's a shame there isn't a more stark contrast. In the '70s, I really thought we would have come farther by now, but I underestimated how long change would take. Sexual politics are also part of it, although a jukebox musical would be very coy about that. It's all about selling records. At the time, the idea that women could survive without men was hard for most people to conceive. Surely Rod Taylor needed to show up and save somebody? This is why the entire Hormonal culture is based on the Cult of Isis—philosophically spelled out in the song "Come With Me," where even God is a woman—a woman of color (a rare sight in these movies). It seems like acceptance of our sexuality has outpaced our acceptance of changing gender roles. I wish now (in the current cultural climate) that I had addressed race as well.

Recent years have brought about the phenomenon of reaching back into our past to find the fake futures, the retro futures that never were, and to embrace them and make stories about them. What do you think the draw is there?

It may be a product of the times. I think when we were kids, we imagined a more interesting future than we've gotten. I feel like there was a lot more optimism in the air when I was young. My students take a snarkier view of those times, as if we were incredibly naïve about the future. That's accurate, although when the cultural context is removed, so is the reality of the moment. Those were some heady, interesting days.

Although it might seem counterintuitive, musicals and science fiction have somehow become comfortable bedfellows in the last few years. Do you have any thoughts on why two such disparate genres would suddenly be so frequently combined, especially considering the lack of musicals of any kind in recent history?

I can only guess. There are probably just more musicals in general than 10, 15 years ago. Baz Luhrmann, music videos, singing cops—all have changed the perception of what a musical should be. Second, it's easier to do low-budget special effects than it used to be. Third, there is so much material out there competing for your attention. It kind of invites the exotic and the eccentric (i.e., mixed genres).

Other Films of Interest

Interstella 5555: The 5tory of the 5ecret 5tar 5ystem (2003)

20

The Romance of Science Fiction

In the musical *Aida*, Elton John and Tim Rice wrote a song called "Every Story Is a Love Story." Perhaps an exaggeration, but only slightly. The idea of the romantic plot or subplot in a story predates film, and has been a staple of film since its inception. Because of that, the idea of romance in the midst of any kind of story has long been accepted as foundational and normal.

We don't just overlook the romances in adventure stories like *The Last of the Mohicans* and *Raiders of the Lost Ark*; we often appreciate the stories *because* of them. From the tragic horror romance of *The Phantom of the Opera* to the cultural divide of the Wild West in *Dances with Wolves*, genres often find the most success by placing romance front and center in their narratives.

Science fiction is no exception. Though the numbers of films focusing specifically on romance in a science fiction setting are not as high as other genres such as the historical epic, there are obvious classic examples. *Bride of Frankenstein* is a sequel entirely predicated on the desire of a single, lonely creature to have someone who understands and connects to him; that the love ended up unrequited is in keeping not only with horror, but with many bittersweet romances.

One of the great science fiction romances is 1980's *Somewhere in Time*, a tale of a man so taken by a painting of a woman that he breaks the laws of time and space to travel back in time to be with her. Stories of people from two different worlds are as old as Tristan and Isolde, but a science fiction facelift can refresh the ancient concept; just in the year 1984, science fiction romances brought us a man and a mermaid in *Splash*, a woman and an alien in *Starman* and a girl and a computer in *Electric Dreams*.

After the Millennium

Happy Accidents (2000) revisited the time-tossed romance seen in *Somewhere in Time*, a motif that repeated itself many times throughout the new millennium: time travel building a new relationship in *Somewhere in Time*, time travel putting strain on a relationship in *The Time Traveler's Wife*. Even the big-budget 2002 version of *The Time Machine* had romantic tragedy at the core of its origins: Dr. Hartdegen would never have constructed a way to travel back in time had it not been for the untimely death of his beloved.

But all relationships don't suffer solely from bad timing and missed opportunities. In *The Fountain* and *Cloud Atlas*, souls who were meant to be together didn't allow something as simple as death, rebirth, generations of separation and changing genders to stop their protagonists from finding their true loves. *It's All About Love* stared a terrifying future in the face, one full of genetic manipulation and the slow degradation of gravity, and still found beauty in the embrace of a single other person.

Technology worked its way into the picture as well, with the millennium reminding us that machines now have a prominent role in our relationships. From *Her* to *Timer*, technology aided our conquests and confused our sensibilities. *Scott Pilgrim vs. the World* embraced video game aesthetics to show that an increasingly connected world makes moving past old relationships more difficult than in previous generations. Science fiction even used allegory to great effect in *Warm Bodies*, showing how love can be a literal healing factor. In *The One I Love*, a lake house occupied by doppelgangers reminds a mildly unhappy couple that real relationships deal with actual people rather than idealized perceptions.

The Independent Perspective

After shattering the expectations and limitations of time travel and cloning with *Primer*, director Shane Carruth explored co-dependency on a personal and global level with *Upstream Color*, a story about two people in love and the organism that somehow brings them even closer together. A similarly unexplained phenomenon allowed the characters of *In Your Eyes* to see and hear what the other was doing; the metaphorical act of walking in someone else's shoes bridged the gap of geography, gender, economics and expectation.

The theme continued in compelling ways with *I Remember You*, in which a female scientist saves the life of an actor, and the two discover that something greater than themselves has somehow destined that they be together. Like *The Adjustment Bureau* before it, *I Remember You* would allow nothing to come between people destined for each other. The relationships explored in this Featured Films section run the gamut from ancient beings experiencing young love to a UFO revealing hidden troubles in a marriage to a global disaster somehow making love the most valuable commodity left on a devastated planet.

Featured Films

Spring (2014)
Director: Justin Benson, Aaron Moorhead
Writer: Justin Benson
Starring Lou Taylor Pucci, Nadia Hilker, Jeremy Gardner

Young American Evan has been spending his time taking care of his mother, who is slowly dying of cancer. After her death, he goes on a night of drinking that ends with him assaulting someone. He leaves the country for Italy, finding a job at a local farm and courting a local girl named Louise. She initially rejects his advances, but then sleeps with him. Louise pushes him away in the days after that, and when he pursues her, Evan discovers that her reasons for pushing him away were much darker than he thought.

A classic romance story updated for the millennial age and tinged with the science fiction horror of H.P. Lovecraft, *Spring* is a beautiful and confounding parable about the strange journey to love. It repackages questions of destiny and free will by entangling them with new myths based in the world of genetics and science and a touch of body horror. The result is a rumination on the foundational elements of humanity that isn't easily categorized, and that's a good thing. The two leads have fantastic chemistry, and the cinematography in the scenic Italian locales is an effective juxtaposition to the darkness Louise is hiding.

∼

Directing team Justin Benson and Aaron Moorhead first collaborated on a feature film with 2012's *Resolution*, a clever reinvention of the found footage sci-fi-horror film. After teaming again for an entertaining segment in the trilogy-ending *VHS: Viral*, they started brainstorming on interests they shared, and *Spring* began to take shape.

Justin Benson: *I thought a story about a woman who metabolizes the stem cells that result from pregnancy to live eternally would be fun and connect well to a love story. I called my dad and told him that, and he was like, "That sounds good, you should write it." Wrote a screenplay real quick and tossed it in the back seat of Aaron's car, and we developed it further into the movie you see, basically just the two of us on the story and screenplay and all that. We've actually never shot anything where we collaborate with anyone outside our two-person collective on the screenplay. But of course people like our producer David Lawson, sound mixer Yahel Dooley and our composer Jimmy Lavalle make it all come to life.*

Aaron Moorhead: *I'll be honest, I've never given much care to zombies, werewolves,*

Evan (Lou Taylor Pucci) and Louise (Nadia Hilker) have more to conquer than just cultural differences in *Spring* (2014).

vampires and other traditional monsters. I know it's a bit heretical to say in some places, given my Stephen King–Twilight Zone roots and "horror director" title. But when I dive a bit more into that, I realize that the stories I've always been attracted to had a large element of the unknown, and Spring creates an entirely new myth. Instead of using it to solely scare the hell out of you, we were able to talk about things that interest me like love and immortality, and we have a great relationship, environment and mythos to boot.

This is a movie that toys with traditional story structure. The first half has a very specific feeling, that of an international romantic drama, and it isn't until about the halfway point that the film reveals itself to also be a complex sci-fi–horror hybrid. What did you feel was the goal in structuring the film like that, aside from keeping the audience surprised?

Moorhead: *We had a lot of resistance to the final act of* Spring *in script phase, until it was made and audiences could see the result. It just was never going to be that movie. In our heads when getting it going,* Spring *always was exactly as it is now: He leaves America, meets her, she has a secret, we find out the secret, and they figure out what to do from then out. Changing that structure or significantly truncating a piece of it just wasn't ever really in the cards, because the movie just was always like that. It wasn't a deliberate attempt to vandalize the Rules of Storytelling, it was just that the movie only makes sense to us one way. Still wouldn't change a thing.*

Benson: *There's a lot of structure rules, especially in genre film, that if you throw out the window, you'll be rewarded. Getting to a certain event by 10 or 15 minutes into a movie is sometimes dulled by the expectation of thousands of movies that do this. So allowing more time to get to know the characters before the scary thing happens can have so much more impact. That was the idea, anyway. It could also be that in writing, I usually see the concept as a backbone for the good material that you can attach to it, a lot of times this material being attached is simply interesting conversation.* Spring *is a movie where the real merits of the movie are the things you attach to the plot, not the plot itself. Richard Linklater is the all-time master of this and it's weird when people make the comparisons because no one can come even close to the genius of what he does.*

This film clearly seems to be influenced by the style of H.P. Lovecraft. Were any of the films based on his works influential to you in the making of this film? I'm also reminded of the amazing William Sansom story "A Woman Seldom Found."

Benson: *I actually didn't know who Lovecraft was when writing* Resolution *and* Spring, *but I do now and now he actually is influential. Weird how that works…. Making movies and reading the reviews actually made me more cultured. I had read a lot of Stephen King and* House of Leaves *and stuff like that, though.*

Moorhead: *Seconding that, didn't know Lovecraft until after the comparison was made. Again, heresy. Now I've read Lovecraft and, of course, we all stand on his shoulders. I think the big thing that draws that comparison (besides that one shot in which Louise has a tentacle) is what Lovecraft called "cosmic horror." You get the impression in* Spring *there's something else going on, something deeper than just Louise's affliction, like nature's encroaching on their romance. That's likely why it feels a Lovecraftian film. Nothing else directly inspired it, except in reactionary ways (in which she's* not *a vampire, werewolf, alien, etc.). That said, I don't know how much of the massive amount of Stephen King or* The Outer Limits *or* Unsolved Mysteries *I consumed as a kid influences our work, but that's definitely there in other mysterious ways.*

This film cleverly toys with many genres at once, from romance to science fiction to horror, even veering occasionally into indie comedy. Was your goal in utilizing so many genres to keep the audience from expecting or feeling completely comfortable assuming anything about the characters or the story in the film?

Benson: Very honestly, I'm terrible at genre categorization. I very sincerely just don't care, and Aaron doesn't develop scripts from a genre category perspective. So, in my writing, I just do what seems interesting at the time, and then way later the distributor who acquires the film figures out the genre.

Moorhead: In some ways, yes, that's absolutely what we did and why, but I think it comes from more of a conceit of doing what we think is right in the moment, as long as the general tone of the movie isn't consistently violated. The general theory is that you do whatever it takes to make you care about the characters, be that laughing with them or being terrified for them or being thrilled by their decisiveness, and in doing so, you kind of bounce from what people would call a comedy to a horror to an adventure. As long as that stays interesting, the genre matters less and less. A Coen Brothers movie is often categorized as a Coen Brothers movie before it's given another genre; its Coen-ness is what comes first in their identities.

While there are ancillary characters in both your films, *Spring* (like *Resolution*) primarily focuses on the relationship between two characters, and the complications that arise. In one, a man is addicted to drugs; in the other, a woman is using injectable material to maintain her fragile physical state. Is this an intentional pattern you're creating in your films?

Moorhead: We like the amount of focus you can put on relationships between only two people, but also, frankly, it's much more accomplishable within the scope of an indie film than ensemble pieces. We won't always do that, but right now it makes sense for the stories we wanted to tell.

Benson: There's usually some human conflict examined, that's intentional, but the small number of characters involved is more of a logistical thing. We worked on a movie script with five main characters, and if you don't want to use archetypes that people already know, it's incredibly difficult to keep the thing from becoming so damn long because there's so many people to get to know and relationships to show.

One element of the film that is most interesting is the idea of a quantifiable measure of love between two individuals, something which the world in your film hinges on finding out. Was this element in the story in any way a commentary about the changing attitudes towards love in an increasingly isolated, cynical and scientific world?

Benson: I know it's going to sound corny, but very literally love is treated as real Magick in Spring. That whole third act is about two people via time and communication forming a bond they have no control over. Take all the data you want about these two people and you could have never predicted the bond, like real life.

Moorhead: Many common themes try to put a very definite morality on love (e.g., love requires hard work, love and hate look similar, love can hit you at inopportune times and from unexpected places, etc.). What we wanted to do was to say that love is a whole bunch of things, most of all unknowable and unpredictable. By trying to measure it with our oxytocin device, or by Evan trying to make her say out loud a binary "I do/don't love you" is asking all the wrong questions, so that the answer can and should still surprise.

Spring joins an increasing number of films in the new millennium that combine high-concept sci-fi and romance in a way that is not reductive to either, but rather complements the best elements of both. What drew you to the idea of working on a "science fiction romance"?

Moorhead: *I never thought of the film as part of a movement, and in fact we got a lot of resistance to the idea of combining romance with horror-sci-fi. Outside of* The Fly, *we had nothing to point to in order to say "See, this works"! I think we wanted to talk about the first steps of a romance, but our brains just automatically aim towards sci-fi, because it makes possibilities a lot more limitless. That said, when I think of all my favorite movies, often there's sci-fi and human connection combined in there at least in small ways* (Blade Runner, Her, Children of Men...).

Benson: *Never thought about it in those terms, just thought Evan and especially Louise were really interesting people, and that within the beauty of their courtship we could put some stuff to really get under an audience's skin, that it would be really thrilling.*

Alienated (2015)
Writer-Director: Brian Ackley
Starring George Katt, Jen L. Burry, Taylor Negron

Outside his house, Nate sees a UFO. When he goes back inside, he is hesitant to share the information with his wife Paige. The two are obviously struggling in their relationship, and the revelation of his belief in the UFO triggers buried issues between the two of them. Their neighbor Griffin is blind but seems to be more aware of something brewing than either of them...

Alienated uses the common science fiction device of the UFO sighting to get to the heart of most human struggle: the inability to communicate or see another's viewpoint. From Paige's lack of interest in Nate's video of the UFO incident to their insistence on arguing about the smallest of things (like optimum water temperature for dishwashing), the film explores the very human instinct to adopt adversarial positions, whether in personal relationships or in group dynamics.

∼

After his feature film debut in 2009's *Uptown*, writer-director Brian Ackley brought *Alienated* to the screen. Previous experience producing features, directing and acting prepped him for the challenge of creating a contained feature film with only three major characters whose themes are much larger in scope than the physical production itself.

Brian Ackley: *The concept came from my producing partner, Princeton Holt. Searching for a high-concept low-budget project, he pitched me the idea of a guy who sees a UFO but doesn't know how to tell the people in his household. It took several weeks for the situation to resonate, and when it finally did, it caught fire within me. I pared down the drama so that it would ping-pong between two central characters, each right in their own way, but each equally wrong. In the venomous dynamic between these two people, I drew inspiration from real-life couples I had the misfortune of being too close to, as well as the fictional couples in the highly successful plays (and films)* Who's Afraid of Virginia Woolf? *and* Hurlyburly.

This is a film that uses some of the trappings of a science fiction film to tell a story that is actually a very relatable human drama. What was the thinking behind combining such disparate genres?

Nate (George Katt) and Paige (Jen Burry) can't stop arguing, no matter what's happening around them, in *Alienated* (2015).

The thinking behind structuring a drama or melodrama within the framework of a sci-fi was multi-tiered. From the start, our main goal was to make a marketable film. Science Fiction sells. Our company One Way or Another Productions has made several features, and they'd all been character-driven dramas. None of them had made any money, so it was time to try something that would reflect the data our research were showing, which told us that genre films (horror, sci-fi, action) find audiences much more easily than non-genre films (dramas and comedies).

As I developed the material, I found a great place to play inside the mind and imagination of our main character, Nate, the one who sees the UFO. It became more exciting to me to explore the psyche of the character than to show the spectacle of what he believed. In this way, I invited our audience to experience these circumstances the way the character did, and given such extraordinary scenarios both the audience and the character become susceptible to frustration, doubt and even madness while figuring out if what's being perceived is real, and then considering the implications if it is. What started as a challenge became a fun, innovative game to find ways to bring together elements of sci-fi and drama, to work out the right combination to make these genres compatible.

An argument can be made that these genres are innately compatible (or perhaps all genres are) as they consider, study and/or reflect the human condition. Sci-fi is a genre of ideas; it can be a projection of our thoughts and cognitive desires. The genre becomes fertile ground for philosophical discussion and debate. "Your scientists were so preoccupied with whether or not they could that they didn't stop to think if they should." (Ian Malcolm, speaking of the genetically engineered rebirth of dinosaurs through preserved DNA in Jurassic Park.*) The drama genre provides the perfect forum to explore these ideas and their implications, simply by assigning different backgrounds and perspectives to different characters. In my opinion, the most impactful science fiction material ties into human drama. One* *asks a universally profound question (perhaps, who are we or why are we here?), while the other relates its significance to our everyday lives. It was wonderful to discover a link between Nate's dark, fantastical imagination and obsessive tendencies with the universal truth that we all have the gift of love within us. It was wonderful to make such a connection between love and fear so pronounced, especially within the confines of such a simple story with few characters. For better examples of this kind of union, revisit M. Night Shyamalan's work. Signs and* Unbreakable *were big influences on* Alienated.

In the end, the best result from merging these two seemingly dissimilar genres comes in the form of a metaphor. Breaking up with a loved one feels like the end of the world.

If my job as a filmmaker has you more concerned about the dynamic of this crumbling relationship than an imminent alien invasion, then I've succeeded.

This film taps into a theme of recent millennial films about worldwide disasters, which is that human beings are often so obsessed with the issues in their personal lives that they don't notice external problems or events until long after they should. Is there some commentary in this film about that mentality of self-absorbed modern society?

Nope. At least not intentionally. It's a really cool theme to play with, though, and I see this accidental lesson-commentary in Alienated.

Was the idea of putting a relationship drama at the forefront and an alien story in the background an intentional reversal of the clichéd "hero gets the girl while fighting the monsters" dynamic we've seen so many times?

Not exactly. I do work diligently against clichés and general things I've seen before. My work needs to be original and challenging in order for me to be interested in it. For Alienated, *the process was more organic. I started from Princeton's pitch, where a guy sees a UFO and doesn't know how to share the news to his loved ones. Why would a person not share such a dramatic event? Perhaps because he knows he wouldn't be believed. Why wouldn't he be believed? Perhaps because he's shared similarly outrageous tales and they were not fully believed. This inner dialogue quickly led me to explore the dynamic between a conspiracy-believing, out-of-work artist husband and a passionless but hardworking, breadwinning wife, which in turn created ripples, then waves of emotional interactions, all centering around the characters. The most interesting aspects of the story unraveled themselves until they were essentially a play. Add to this my creative temperament where I knew we'd be working on a tight budget and I tend to be attracted to character-driven stories, and the outcome cannot be surprising.*

Because of the smaller cast, the dialogue-driven story, and the contained locations, this film has the sensibility of a stage play. Was there another form of this story before it became a film, or were those choices more budgetary in origin than stylistic?

In origin, choices were made for budgetary concerns. Once I embraced this, I drew great inspiration from Who's Afraid of Virginia Woolf?, *and subsequent choices were made thematically and stylistically. I sat with the basic concept for a week or two. By the time I was ready to commit to writing, I knew I would essentially be writing a play. I constructed each sequence almost like a musical movement, where stretches of dialogue would slowly reveal more and more background, and the shift in power would forever teeter from husband to wife, back to husband, and so forth, eventually building tension to a point of no escape.*

I loved the process. The characters couldn't wait to climb out from my head to do battle with each other. Writing this film was so much fun that I adapted it into a play. I always knew it would play better as a play. It certainly feels better as a play, but that's also because I finally found my ending. We had the toughest time figuring out our ending for the film, and that probably shows.

Taylor Negron plays the blind neighbor who "sees" more than you might think. Is there an allegorical purpose for his character beyond being a sounding board about the relationship? The wisdom combined with his blindness gives him the feeling of being a sage or a Greek oracle of some kind; was this intentional?

Yes, there's a hidden meaning in the wisdom of this character. I'm afraid we contradict ourselves when we move forward with the idea of the film ending with an alien invasion. In my favorite version of the script, the aliens visit the planet at the end, but it's suggested that they may be good, not evil. It's therefore implied that Taylor Negron's character is an alien, an outside observer, offering advice from a place of compassion. As a human, he is blind because as an alien, his species does not need the sense of sight. His wisdom comes from a universal truth, understood by everything connected in the universe, even by humans, though we more often keep these secrets locked up with fear.

The resolution in this version comes when Nate chooses selflessness over narcissism, as well as a willingness to be open to positive things, first by being positive himself. The final frame would have been from inside a kitchen where bright lights flood through the windows. Nate takes Paige's trembling hand and escorts her out the door, where nothing but bright lights consume them. Are they walking into danger? Are they walking into certain death? They could be, but at least together they walk with open minds and they walk without fear. Robert Zemeckis's Contact was another influence.

Though the relationship in this film isn't what you might call traditionally "loving," the film nonetheless falls into a subgenre of sci-fi film that combines science fiction elements with the more intimate human dynamics of romantic relationships. Why do you think that the incidence of stories with strong romantic or relationship elements have grown recently in the sci-fi film arena?

I think romance is popular. Apparently, it's not too popular as a genre itself (in the indie world), but it's hugely popular as a storyline in so many genres. It makes sense that romance would find its way into sci-fi, particularly the more marketable projects put out by studios and big production companies.

From a producing standpoint, if it sells, it should be more available. People relate to romance stories and relationship dynamics. It's a major component of our lives. So it stands to reason that we buy these stories and we watch them. I guess we can't get enough romance, really, so we're starting to appreciate it when it pops up in new ways.

Beyond (2014)
Writer-Directors: Joseph Baker, Tom Large
Starring Richard J. Danum, Gillian MacGregor, Paul Brannigan

Cole, an aimless and unmotivated young Scottish man, meets Maya at a party, and they begin dating. When a meteor is discovered hurtling towards Earth, Cole becomes serious about their relationship with Maya, and they marry. Devastation from the meteor and a subsequent alien invasion divide Cole and Maya about their collective future. Violence, tragedy and possible new life push the couple from mere survival into an existence with meaning.

A rare instance of a high-concept science fiction premise that is entirely subservient to a fascinating two-person story, *Beyond* issues a separate and equally intriguing challenge to its audience: the non-linear narrative. The film bounces back and forth between the past before the meteor strikes and the devastated present; Cole and Maya's ordeal stands as a literal representation of every young couple's struggle with independence, their future and questions of procreation in an increasingly troubling world.

∼

Writer-director Tom Large and co-creator Joseph Baker were no strangers to writing intimate narratives about big ideas. *Beyond* was their fourth film, following the equally thoughtful *And Darren*, *Fly Trap* and *Wounded*.

Tom Large: *We'd always wanted to do a relationship drama and we were keen to combine this with our love of sci-fi. A potential apocalyptic event felt like a unique backdrop to explore a couple's relationship from its inception right through its eventual breakdown.*

The film shifts back and forth through the relationship of the main characters as well as through the science fiction events happening around them. What was the thinking behind the non-linear format? Is it reflective of the idea of surprise and change inherent in starting a relationship with someone?

Non-linear storytelling is a great way to provide an immediate and stark juxtaposition between where the characters are at the beginning of their journey and where they end up. It gives the audience a great hook in wanting to know how the characters went from one extreme to the other. It was important for us to show both positive and negative elements of Cole and Maya's relationship throughout the film, rather than simply portray the happy times at the beginning and load the second half of the film with all the heavy stuff.

Though the asteroid-aliens play a role in the film, they are often seen primarily in the background or merely referenced. Is this because they are a symbolic stand-in for the standard problems of the world that either keep people apart or force them together?

Absolutely. The extraterrestrial elements of the film provided an original and interesting backdrop for the real focus of the story (namely, Cole and Maya's relationship). The arguments they have about survival in the post-apocalyptic landscape are the same arguments they would be having in the real world about struggling to make ends meet. Everything that happens in the post-apocalyptic world is a representation of the pressures, trials and tribulations that have been building in the pre-decimated world.

Were you interested in juxtaposing the sci-fi elements and the romantic and dramatic elements because you were able to use science fiction to make subtext into text and vice versa? To play around with the meaning of events and themes that would seem clichéd or mundane if placed in a straightforward dramatic narrative?

Exactly. Depending on your perspective, there is a great deal of romance in the idea that the world is going to end and a great deal of tragedy in the idea of surviving it. In many respects, an impending apocalypse means you can forget all your woes and concentrate on enjoying whatever time you have left with the ones you love. Surviving it almost certainly means a whole new struggle.

We loved the idea of exploring a relationship within these parameters. Imagine falling in love just before the planet is (potentially) about to be wiped out. Imagine getting pregnant. These experiences are intense at the best of times, but against the backdrop of such monumentally portentous circumstances, everything is twisted and magnified to such a degree, it is genuinely difficult to imagine how one would actually deal with that situation. This gave us a fascinating lens through which to examine the ideas of marriage and parenthood in ways which a conventional dramatic narrative wouldn't have.

Were there any events or circumstances playing out socially or politically that were influential on the creation of this story?

There weren't any political or world events playing out that influenced the story (certainly not on any conscious level anyway). From a personal perspective, it's probably no coincidence that we were a similar age to the Cole and Maya characters at a time when many of our friends were starting to get married and have children. On some level, the story reflects aspects of our own anxieties about marriage and parenthood at that particular time in our lives. But mostly we were motivated by the idea of conveying a very human relationship as meaningfully as possible. In this respect, Blue Valentine *was a major influence, particularly in terms of structure. For the overall sci-fi tone of the film,* Another Earth *was another movie we were huge fans of.*

The concept of the sci-fi romance story is one that has been around nearly since the beginning of the sci-fi genre. Why do you think we continue to revisit stories about romances in fantastical settings?

Science fiction is only limited by the imagination, which means there will always be new and interesting ideas for sci-fi films of every genre, not just romance. Since love is a limitless emotion that we still have very little scientific understanding of, it makes sense that we will continually be drawn to stories which push the boundaries of imagination to explore it further.

Other Films of Interest

Safety Not Guaranteed (2012), *Mr. Nobody* (2009), *The Lobster* (2015), *Z for Zachariah* (2015)

21

The Future of Our Cinematic Futures

Science fiction is by nature forward-looking, which is why no book exploring the various subgenres can be complete after simply looking at the past and the present. With such an impressive array of science fiction filmmakers willing to speak about their own films, it seemed appropriate to ask them about the future of the genre which they love and for which they created unforgettable images and memories.

At the end of each interview, the filmmakers were asked a series of questions about the future of science fiction film, questions about their personal tastes and the direction of the genre, what would remain popular and what might change completely based on changing opinions and technologies.

All of the many responses can be broken down into four essential categories:

1. As technology changes, society's perceptions often shift, and the way we feel about a technology when it first appears is vastly different from how we feel about it after we have become accustomed to (and even reliant on) its presence. That's why the first of the four categories is the question "What kinds of technologies would you want to see science fiction films cover in the future?" Here are the filmmakers' thoughts:

Daniel Myrick (*The Objective*): AI and robotics is a big subject which I think has incredibly far-reaching ramifications for us as a species. At what point do we reach that singularly with AI where it takes on a life of its own and what are the potential downfalls with that? When AI becomes more empowered, do they develop a consciousness indistinguishable from our own? I've always found that to be a fascinating topic to explore.

BP Cooper (*Time Lapse*): I'm sure there are a handful of great stories that can be told around the Large Hadron Collider at CERN. The implementation of nanotechnology in both society and humans has certainly been used in movies but I feel it has a larger potential for use in the right story.

Geoff Marslett (*Mars*): I have written a couple like that, that I hope to make. As we better understand the mathematics of time and consciousness, I'd like to see some films play that out. I'd like to see my films play that out!

Frankly, I love robots. Robots! Robots! Robots! Did you ever see my short film *Monkey vs. Robot*? [Authors' note: *Monkey vs. Robot*, a hilarious animated film with Andy Samberg voicing the monkey, is well worth seeking out.]

Clive Dawson (*The Last Days on Mars*): Nanotechnology is one area rich in possibilities. I'm surprised that Michael Crichton's *Prey* was never filmed.

2. Beyond simply the discussion of new technologies on screen in films, there are other ways in which technology will change the landscape of filmmaking in the future. In fact, the industry is already in the midst of it, with technologies like high frame rates and Virtual Reality and Augmented Reality and streaming services. That is the basis of the second question: "Are there technologies that you are interested in seeing utilized to tell new stories?" Given the timing of the questions, many of the answers focus on one particular technology, but the various perspectives are telling. Here are the filmmakers' reactions:

Tom Large (*Beyond*): Virtual reality will be incredible for the sci-fi genre. Provided the technological advancements of the next few years don't eclipse the importance of real grounded human drama and characters, we should all be massively excited.

Brian Ackley (*Alienated*): I could write a chapter describing my mixed feelings on the topic.... It seems much of the filmmaking community is preoccupied with new technologies to tell stories that they don't bother to take their time to tell their stories well. Where's the craft? Where's the quality content?

At the other end, if you give this new technology to great storytellers, we can see some amazing things. I certainly wonder where our entertainment industry is going—gaming, virtual reality, interactive play. But I'm not waiting around or dreaming for all this magic to happen. For one, I'm forever entertained by old and new classics like *Ghostbusters* and *Guardians of the Galaxy*. Secondly, I try to contemplate only things that I have control over, such as my own creative output.

What excites me the most about new technology has nothing to do with making films, and everything to do with releasing and sharing them. The greatest challenge for filmmakers of my generation is finding a way to share our work. What technology would allow us to connect with people who would appreciate our voices? What technology would help us develop relationships with our viewers for the benefit of both parties? How do we best use technology we now have to achieve these goals? These are the questions that stir in my mind. These will be the answers that my film career depends upon.

Aaron Moorhead (*Resolution* and *Spring*): Now you're talking about my favorite realm, speculative fiction. I honestly think that most popular emerging technologies should not have a film made about them. They sound like films that won't stand the test of time no matter what, it's a little too current events–ish—and it'll be very hard not to moralize or sound preachy. What excites me about tomorrow's sci-fi is not much to do with current trends or current technology, but more current and future voices. My favorite sci-fi films of recent times could have been made decades ago, besides what's available with CG. So honestly, rather than a specific technology being either the subject or the vehicle for a movie, I just want to see what brilliant filmmakers and writers put together to talk about the future.

Rod Bingaman (*Ripped!*): I think everyone anticipates a more virtual sci-fi experience, which will probably arise out of gaming. Interactive is just more fun. I'm not a gamer, but the creative possibilities are intriguing.

Andrew Droz Palermo (*One & Two*): VR is in such early days and it's going to look as rudimentary as an Atari in a few short years, but I think what it can do is really transportive. I'm not sure it'll replace traditional filmmaking, but I've had some great experiences already. As far as films I'm excited about, generally I'm just thrilled to see something well-told and original.

Alec Gillis (*Harbinger Down*): I'm sure that VR and AR [augmented reality] will be big game changers, and I'll happily partake, but I still love being in the hands of a storyteller and taking that journey. Interactivity seems chaotic and rambling. In a way, it's more like life than movies are. I like to escape from life while reflecting on it. Any movie or art form that helps me do that is where I'll be.

Tom Woodruff, Jr. (*Fire City: End of Days*): There is something really compelling about VR technology and how close it is to being a really engaging technology for storytelling. Technically, it's there. I look forward to advances that allow you to immerse yourself in a world that gives you freedom to interact. This is something new and different, something in which a single person is engaged but so completely that you don't need the advantage of a whole audience sharing emotions. But I do jump ahead to being able to "watch" a VR story unfold and have others "join" you in that world. You can go there 20 different times and see it from 20 different ways. It's going to take some incredible writing to make it work. But if the technology is there, what a fascinating way to tell stories this will be.

Jeff Pointer (*Ink*): I'm not much of a science fiction fan, actually. I'm far more into films about real people, real situations and stories that represent the real human spirit as we (or I) know it on the Earth that's in front of me. As far as technology, I think it's very important to mix any new technology with good writing. No one has invented a gizmo to write a great story. As far as I'm concerned, good stories will always trump the latest camera or technology.

Justin Trefgarne (*Narcopolis*): I am always excited by technology, but the truth is what excites me most are stories that justify the technology. In other words, I want to continue to see stories that are challenging, rich and about something more than the effects, the bangs, etc. You take a film like *The Martian*, an old-fashioned yarn in some ways but utilizing state-of-the-art technology. What makes it remarkable is how completely engrossing that story and that character are. Or *District 9*, which is a masterpiece. The CGI was seamlessly woven into one of the most compelling, thrilling sci-fi narratives and settings I'd seen for years. I am also very excited by the work of people functioning at a smaller level. Shane Carruth is a genius, and his modestly budgeted films belie the epic, mind-blowing narratives he is attempting. It's always got to be story first.

Mario Miscione (*Circle*): I think we need to be more careful. Often, they can be a gimmick that doesn't really expand the experience in a meaningful way. Technology like 3D is neat, but is it ever necessary? Rarely, I think. Still, it's nice to give viewers an option. It might also be interesting to experiment with interactivity in film. Imagine, for example, if *Circle* was an interactive experience. If the audience could vote on who died next, and the film changed in real time! It'd take a lot of planning on the part of the filmmakers, of course, but the narrative possibilities and replayability of that kind of experience would be really compelling. I think we're reaching a point where the line between interactive media and film are blurring, and though some purists might roll their eyes at it, I think it's a really interesting direction. Some of the best, most cinematic sci-fi stories are being told through video games these days.

From the production side of things, it's never been easier for aspiring filmmakers to get access to the equipment needed to make professional-looking pieces. That's maybe the most exciting thing for me, when I think about the future of film and sci-fi. If you have a story to tell, now you have no excuse not to get out there and tell it.

Stuart Hazeldine (*Exam*): I'm torn because on the one hand I am a paid-up member of the Nolan school that believes 35mm is the apex of the curve as a capture medium. I've seen 48 frames per second remove the painterly gauze and show me a hyper-real movie reality, and I'd like the painting back, please. I also like to see the frame towards the periphery of my vision at widest, ideally well within my vision, because it brings pleasing compositional dynamics with it. I like paintings and photos, so I like films within a frame. I see frameless reality all the time, so to put a frame over still or moving images repackages reality in a different, aesthetically pleasing way. I will spend time and money to consume and appreciate that difference. Without that frame, we filmmakers stop being painters and start being ringmasters only.

That said, it isn't a bad thing to be a ringmaster, which has its own rules and attractions. All filmmakers want to push the envelope, innovate and do something new: usually within the boundaries of the storytelling itself, but it's no great leap to want to innovate in terms of the shooting and presentational medium itself. So anything new that comes along—IMAX, 3D, HFR—I want to be first in line to see it and ask, "Does it work for everything? If not, would it be suited to tell particular kinds of stories?" If I'm persuaded, I'm persuaded. It just doesn't happen much.

Cinema has always been about spectacle, and I want to provide that where possible, especially if it makes audiences want to pay to watch a movie in a big dark room rather than at home on TV or (God forbid) on their phone. But primarily movies for me are an artistic and emotional medium, and both those boxes can be ticked by filmmaking in the existing shooting medium of film or HD within a widescreen frame, so that will always be my primary focus.

Ben Carland (*Sol* and *Shadows on the Wall*): I can't wait to see what happens with virtual reality. I think VR will succeed where High Frame Rate and 3D have largely failed. It's just in its infancy and has a long way to go on the capture side and streamlining exhibition, but the few times I've seen it done well, it was absolutely astounding. I imagine it was similar to what people watching the very first motion pictures felt. I can't wait to see what it allows filmmakers to do and how it will unlock story experiences to viewers.

Paul Hough (*The Human Race*): I think as technology advances, the creators' imagination can go to new places. Right now, drones are the big thing. I think it would be awesome to see a movie shot entirely with drones, in the sky. Maybe there will be a movie about people trapped in a hot air balloon, or a UFO movie utilizing drones. Drones are exciting to me, since they enable you also to get shots that you once had to spend a fortune on to get. Anything that enables the actual realization of the imagination is brilliant.

Shane Acker (*9*): I think VR has the possibility to give you an experience like that as well, but the traditional narrative possibilities of VR seem very narrow. It seems to be all about the interactive possibilities. That is what is truly interesting to me.

Geoff Marslett (*Mars*): The most exciting thing is that science is moving faster than ever before, and the faster it moves, the more revolutionary ideas fall into the laps of storytellers. That can pollinate some pretty amazing tales. So I hope people keep running with them. Things like *Black Mirror* happen. Things like *Embers* happen. Things like *Mars* happen. I want that to keep happening!

Timothy Lanzone (*Travelling Salesman*): I certainly think in the next ten years, we're going to have these movies where you're going to have your own headset or you're going to be provided one and you're literally going to be present in this film. Technologically speaking, we're close to that.

There's also the Woody Allen side of me that laments this shrinking reality of standard cinema, of not shooting in 35mm, or shooting with crazy dolly moves and cranes and special effects. One of my favorite filmmakers is Fellini; human stories shot simply and beautifully. We don't have that as much in American cinema as in European cinema. There's a part of me that wants to push for more technology in film, to push for more CG and 3D, but those things do take away from the idea of pure filmmaking and storytelling. Like everything else, film evolves. The medium has evolved in the 120 years or so that it's been around, so I guess that's to be expected.

Anouk Whissell (*Turbo Kid*): There's a whole lot of technologies that would be very interesting to explore, but also technologies that do not exist yet. A lot of past movies were visionary in that way. We're open to what the future brings as to new technologies in cinematography, but we know we're not fond of CG fests, as it often creates a disconnect between the audience and the screen. That's why we're really looking forward to Denis Villeneuve's *Blade Runner*, which is said to be using CGI only when they *had to*, and that's the way to go!

Timo Vuorensola (*Iron Sky*): One of the big topics in the future of film will be the topic of how virtual reality will challenge the reality by being simply a much better alternative. Spike Jonze's *Her* and Alex Garland's *Ex Machina* are excellent examples of today's science fiction films, ones which discuss the threats and possibilities of today's technology. Personally, I'd love to tell a story using augmented reality—a bit like a game of *Pokemon Go*, but in a narrative format, so that the story would be not enjoyed in one place, but actually all around you, through your mobile device.

James Ward Byrkit (*Coherence*): Clearly someone is going to make a *Citizen Kane* equivalent in the VR space someday, and that's going to be amazing. We are only scratching the surface in blending games and storytelling and once that door is unlocked, we will be in another universe of possibility.

B.P. Cooper (*Time Lapse*): The advancement of VFX has done wonders for all genres, sci-fi perhaps being the biggest recipient of such innovation. I'm excited to see the leaps and bounds of realistic world-building and visually seamless integration of practical and digital sets, props and overall creations. Additionally, it's becoming more and more cost-efficient to achieve this on an independent film. Most of all, I'm excited to see new stories and characters from the minds of wonderfully crazy people utilize these tools both within and outside of the Hollywood system.

Michael Kospiah (*The Suicide Theory*): I see that whole virtual reality thing becoming a movement. I have a feeling that'll become more and more a part of films in the future. Kind of like the way 3D has found its way into our cinematic experiences, whether in theaters or at our homes. I feel like VR, more than any other gimmick, will provide us with that extra-sensory experience that we've been searching for. Though I'm curious how they would include that in a movie theater experience. It all sounds very expensive.

I didn't have a cell phone until I was 20 years old. Now, I couldn't imagine *not* having one. And I didn't have computers as a child. I learned to type on a typewriter. Now I'm naked without my laptop. I'm curious as to what the next big thing that we "need" will be.

Daniel Myrick (*The Objective*): Virtual reality is starting to take on a new urgency today with VR glasses. I've got a pair myself that I've been using as R&D on another project that I'm working on. They are brought up in news and commentary regularly, and I find them fascinating to talk about and explore.

3. As interesting as the technologies seen in film are the ways in which those technologies are used in the stories. Many subgenres have been around for decades, but are given new life when a smart and innovative filmmaker finds a new perspective on the seemingly tired idea.

This important element to the survival and fostering of science fiction film led to our third question: "Are there science fiction films or ideas that you still want to make?"

Chance Shirley (*Interplanetary*): I've often said that if someone was foolish enough to give me a couple hundred million dollars to make a movie, I'd like to make a dinosaur adventure in the spirit of *Jurassic Park*. Though that movie is rightfully heralded for its groundbreaking CG effects, and it features some amazing traditional animatronic effects like that incredible full-size animatronic T-Rex. It also features plenty of solid meat-and-potatoes filmmaking: dynamic lighting, solid camerawork, charming actors and a tight screenplay.

Even though it is more than 20 years old at this point, few films have found that sweet spot between traditional and CG effects like *Jurassic Park*. On the indie side, Duncan Jones' *Moon* and Aronofsky's *The Fountain* are both gorgeous movies that smartly combine old and modern effects techniques. I hope more filmmakers consider this best-of-both-worlds method in the future.

Paul S. Myers (*5 Shells*): I think the Singularity is the most interesting subject that I'd love to tackle. In fact, I'm kind of obsessed with AI. It hasn't really been done well since *2001: A Space Odyssey*, which touches on it, but since that concept of a Singularity wasn't really being talked about much in 1969. HAL doesn't really explore the idea thoroughly. I was working on an idea about meshing the Singularity with the Clarke quote "Any sufficiently advanced technology is indistinguishable from magic." The idea being that if a super intelligence explosion happened, then the story could meld from a techno sci-fi movie into a supernatural horror film seamlessly because the AI could achieve things that our puny brains would only understand as sorcery. I did tons of research, and hopefully I will get a chance to follow through, hopefully before the Singularity happens and it brings about the apocalypse, and we have to walk the desert hunting rabbits and fending off pharmaceutical lobbyists with hobby shotguns.

Conor Horgan (*One Hundred Mornings*): The next film I'm writing is a love story that has a small technological advance added. It's a bit like *Eternal Sunshine of the Spotless Mind*; that kind of science fiction is something that I really like. I do hope that I will still be able to make films, that there will still be films in the time I have left to make them.

When I think about what I said about earlier, about having non-transferrable skills, it would depend on if everything falls down tomorrow. I do have ability as a writer, I do have some ability as a dramatist, so if it meant telling stories around the campfire and getting fed as a result, you never know. I might just make it.

Tom Wooruff, Jr. (*Fire City: End of Days*): Conceptually, I want to be able to grow off of *Fire City* and its characters. Whether it's horror or science fiction or a monster movie, I want to tell stories that are real to the characters on screen and embrace the audience with that world.

Alec Gillis (*Harbinger Down*): I only think in terms of films I want to see, and those are the kinds of films I want to direct. I'm no longer of the demographic that big Hollywood pursues (as a viewer or a director), so I really don't care about most summer blockbusters. I hope to direct some smaller scale films with interesting alien characters interrelating to other characters. *Ex Machina* is a good example.

Cory Mcabee (*The American Astronaut*): New technologies have allowed me to connect with people to make a collaborative feature film. That's what I'm involved with now. It's called *Small Star Seminar*. A strong human element is built into the production and carries into the story. *Small Star Seminar* is a science fiction, but a very different kind of science fiction. I hope it can find its audience.

Brian Ackley (*Alienated*): Princeton Holt is producing and directing my latest screenplay, called *Butterfly Chasers*, which is a sexy sci-fi dramedy. Who can keep track of genres? It's vastly different from anything I've written and once again the concept started with Princeton. It's based on a romantic comedy he wrote several years ago. We added sexbots. It's awesome. I'm also slowly writing a sci-fi thriller novel based on a friend's screenplay. I guess I can work kind of randomly; that is, if an idea catches my attention, I may cling to it, explore it. I don't actively seek sci-fi stories that I want to develop. I'm just pulled into certain ones.

4. *Ultimately, every one of the filmmakers who worked so hard to produce a science fiction film did so because they believe in the power of science fiction. The reason for that belief is because, before they were science fiction filmmakers, they were science fiction fans. That passionate belief, not just in your own film, but in its genre and in the loyal fans that support that genre, is integral in finding staying power, creating emotional resonance, and having the impact of your story last beyond the moment the story ends.*

That brings about the fourth and final question: "As fans of science fiction, what do you hope to see in the future? What excites you about science fiction film?"

Jamie Nash (*Altered*): Things like *Ex Machina* would normally be my answer, or *Moon*, the small kind of tales that also need a budget. *Cube* was one that I liked, and those kinds of movies seem to be coming back in a big way. The things I gravitate towards now are sci-fi movies that are barely sci-fi movies, like *The One I Love*. It's a sci-fi movie, or is it? Or the movie *Safety Not Guaranteed*. They don't have all the special effects and things like that. People are generally willing to go with these sci-fi conceits without laser guns and robots and spaceships; the movies are centered on ideas.

Clay Liford (*Earthling*): I get excited about the circularity of art, history repeating itself, and I'm ready for it. I'm excited about sci-fi stories about human beings and genuine character interaction. I get my hopes up when I see a film like *Arrival* doing so well. I want a return to intelligent films, or even just films that are about something. It's criminal that there wasn't better traction here with Joe Cornish's *Attack the Block*, the heir apparent to *Gremlins*. It has smart characters and is really accessible, but it tanked in America because distributors were afraid the London language wouldn't be understood by American audiences. It's heartbreaking.

I get excited about movies with smaller stories. Not every story has to end with the destruction of a major American city. It's the Marvel problem. You don't need to do that. You can have emotional stakes on a personal level that feel bigger than the artificial bigness we have now. If you bring the budgets down, then you don't have to do that.

Michael Kospiah (*The Suicide Theory*): I was never a big fan of huge, epic science fiction stuff. Movies like *Independence Day* don't do it for me. I'm not a huge *Star Wars* kind of guy, either, though I do enjoy them overall (outside of *Attack of the Clones*). I enjoy more personal, smaller scale stuff that still manages to say something, reflecting us as people and our society. I absolutely *love* that *Black Mirror* show on Netflix. It reminds me of *Outer Limits* but strictly focusing on how the media and technology affect us.

Merlin Dervisevic (*Cruel & Unusual*): The thing that excites me about any film is innovations in telling the story. It's not the technologies so much, it's how we tell the story. A good example of that is *Memento* by Christopher Nolan. I really appreciate that kind of thinking as a filmmaker because he told a story in a way we haven't seen before and we rarely come across that any more. It seems like everything that's being made these days is told in a structure that has worked in the past over and over again. I'm always excited when I hear about a film that has been told in a different way, some innovation in the way it's been structured or just something. I'm always looking for fresh ideas. Those are the things that really excite me.

BP Cooper (*Time Lapse*): I'm always hoping to be wowed by concepts I've never heard of or seen before. That's a rarity of course, as most everything tends to be an amalgamation of pre-existing ideas. However, I'm sure every sci-fi fan would like to be constantly entertained by truly inventive concepts and storytelling, so I'd love to see more odd and offbeat sci-fi created in the future.

Kurt Kuenne (*Shuffle*): I want to see stories that surprise us, stories we've never seen before. I am so sick of the flood of remakes and sequels that keeps coming our way every year. It's like we're living in a cultural recycling bin. When I see films like *Inception* and *Looper*, they get me excited about movies all over again; those films dream big, take huge risks and take us to places we've never been before. I'm not really a technology guy, but I am someone who loves big, bold, audacious flights into uncharted territory. I hope to have the opportunity to do some of that work myself, but I wish for all of us to be able to get out from underneath all the branded properties, which tend to be predictable pieces of commerce, and to find ideas that truly excite us, then get them financed and in front of mass audiences. It's a hard road and it keeps getting harder. But it's worth the effort.

Darren Paul Fisher (*Frequencies*): I really like how the independent sci-fi film scene is shaping up in the social media era. Audiences are really connecting and discussing ideas based sci-fi as opposed to action-based sci-fi. Don't get me wrong, I love action-based sci-fi also, but they can very easily become over-simplified chase sequences with little for the audience to engage with. *Frequencies* became part of a new genre that fans are calling mind-fi or sci-phi which I love, but probably highlights a problem with the term sci-fi, that it's a wrapper, not a genre in its own right. A mind-fi what? A mind-fi actioner? A sci-phi drama? The fact that genre film festivals are now getting mainstream recognition can only be beneficial for films that push the audience's imagination.

Personally, I've never really liked heavy dystopian stories, so would love to see a lighter, more playful approach. But there's space—and audiences—for everything. I'm kind of a technological agnostic, so I don't really care what something is shot-edited-projected on just as long as it's the right tonal choice for the material and the story is compelling. That said, stories that are based in science fact and will help inspire the next generation of scientists, inventors and dreamers would be something I'd like to see more of. We need more Elon Musks! I also have a very soft spot for Steampunk, so I'd like to see more films out there in those universes. Alternate reality anachronistic worlds are a fantastic sandbox to play in.

Jeff Waltrowski (*It Came from Yesterday*): I hope the future of sci-fi is bright. I think we are living in a unique time when technology is available to anyone. Let's use that technology to talk about times we are living in. Let's bring sci-fi back to what it should be, which is to discuss our lives as humans. Whether it be our political landscape, our fears, or how we live with one another. The indie filmmakers are the people to do this. Hollywood is about razzle dazzle and crowd-pleasers. As much as I enjoy that form of entertainment, I also want to see personal stories, or stories that have a deeper meaning and some substance. For as silly and lighthearted *It Came from Yesterday* was, I was telling a story about many things; family, living with your past, fear and paranoia, etc., disguised as a goofball parody. I'm excited to see what indie filmmakers can create that comes from the heart.

James Ward Byrkit (*Coherence*): I love that the availability of technology gives so many people license to play with smart ideas that in past years would have never been made. I hope people push the limits of the imagination more and more, to experiment with bending time and narrative in ways that approach our dreams.

I'm very compelled by the science fiction tales that have an aura of reality to them, like *Chronicle* and *District 9*. Filmmakers can shoot something cheaply and then do amazing post work on their own time, like *Monsters*.

Timothy Lanzone (*Travelling Salesman*): One of my favorite science fiction movies of all time is *The Day the Earth Stood Still*, which is now close to 70 years old. I don't necessarily think any innovative technologies or techniques like James Cameron does for the *Avatar* movies will make for better films than *The Day the Earth Stood Still*.

Brett Ryan Bonowicz (*The Perfect 46*): Science fiction and futurism is always reflective of the time in which that prediction or projection of the future was made. *2001: A Space Odyssey* is a reflection of the 1960s, *Gattaca* is almost directly tied to Dolly the sheep in the 1990s, and *The Perfect 46* is absolutely a reflection of direct-to-consumer genetics in the early 2000s. Tomorrow's science fiction will always be a reflection of the time and I really like the time capsule element of it all.

Personally, I'd like to see more films depicting the potentials of a utopia. What our obsession with it is, in history, and in depiction of the future. The one science fiction project I wish I could see is Francis Ford Coppola's *Megalopolis*. It was to be this sprawling epic science fiction film and that's something he's never really done in his career—unless you're counting *Captain EO*.

Geoff Marslett (*Mars*): More stuff like *The Twilight Zone* and less stuff that is really fantasy. A good sci-fi for me is one that is basically realism but with a postulate that changes some fundamental building block, and then the whole sci-fi world is shifted from regular reality by that. We get to see how important each piece of our world really is. I love that kind of sci-fi more than just an adventure with new gadgets and technologies. But don't get me wrong, I love those, too.

I don't need heavy CGI and armies of fantastic machines and creatures. I need a few characters I can't get enough of. I want a couple ideas that lodge in my brain and I think about all night after watching the film. I want the sci-fi to be so thought-out that I really wonder, "What if that was our reality?"

I want sci-fi to be a way of telling stories, and I truly love it when that way is used to combine unexpected genres. I want sci-fi romance and sci-fi comedy and sci-fi action and sci-fi horror and sci-fi drama! I loved *Moon*, I loved *Alien*. I loved those because they were not just space adventures but movies about other stuff that the space setting enhanced. I also loved *Star Wars* (or at least all the *Star Wars* except episodes I–III) because they were a world-building set of films with open doors in every direction outside of the films. And I think the industry has caught on to the world-building aspect—so we will get more of that, but I hope they keep encouraging the small-fi too. So my short answer is *way more* lo-fi sci-fi!

Chance Shirley (*Interplanetary*): It's funny. As everyday life becomes more like the science fiction of my youth, I find myself drawn more to traditional approaches to sci-fi filmmaking. Though I'm not crazy about the movie on the whole, I really love the craft of Christopher Nolan's *Interstellar*. The IMAX camerawork is often stunning, and the filmmakers utilized many old-fashioned practical effects techniques.

The same can be said for the latest *Star Wars* movies. After three prequel movies that relied heavily on greenscreen work, digital effects and digital video, the filmmakers working on *Star Wars: The Force Awakens* moved back in a more analog direction, shooting on film and utilizing more practical sets.

Clive Dawson (*The Last Days on Mars*): This may not be a popular view but, personally, I'd like to see far fewer blockbuster epics of the *Star Wars* and *Independence Day* variety. Science fiction should be intelligent and push the boundaries. When it's used merely as a pedestrian backdrop to an action story, then I don't view that as true science fiction. Obviously, there's a balance to be struck between telling an entertaining story and making people think, but often profound human insight can spring from a populist, commercial movie, if it's intelligently conceived. Some would perhaps argue that *Last Days on Mars* didn't in any way push the boundaries. If that's true, it wasn't for lack of trying. Either way, I'd like to see more sci-fi movies that explore the deeper complexities of the human condition; *Ex Machina* is one that springs to mind.

Shane Acker (*9*): I've been enjoying all of these space exploration movies, *The Martian*, *Interstellar*, etc. I think they make the concept of space travel and exploration more tangible, I can feel it more through the human characters' struggles and by feeling like I'm having the experience. Space is a deadly fucking place, and very isolating.

Harry Ralston (*The Last Man*): I like metaphysical ideas played out in movies, to show the test of people's behavior. There is no shortage of films that do this, but I would enjoy more good comedies on the subject.

Christopher Ford (*Robot & Frank*): What excites me most about the future of sci-fi is that it will be *in* the future. When William Gibson's novels are now basically set in the present, it's fascinating to see how the advancing imagination will push even further than before. The human side of the stories will always be the same, but hopefully more attention will be paid to that side of things. At least in movies and TV, we have entered an era where more nuanced, smaller and sophisticated stories are possible to be told as science fiction. So I'm excited for that as well.

Jim Mickle (*Stake Land*): I've been way into this "personal sci-fi" genre that's been popping up lately. Big science fiction stories about small, intimate human emotions. *Gravity* was one. *Arrival*. Even *Black Mirror*. I'd love to see science fiction be used to tell human stories with a twist. Sci-fi loses me when it gets too gadgety or overly complex, but when it's just off from the world today, it can be really moving. I hope we get more conceptual sci-fi and less stupid shiny things.

Ben Carland (*Sol* and *Shadows on the Wall*): I am so excited for the future of sci-fi as a genre. It's not my favorite genre because I love space and aliens (even though I do); it's my favorite because it gives us a blank canvas to explore our own humanity with. For instance, I think some of the *Star Trek* shows are not only the best science fiction of all time, but some of the best fiction of all time. Not because of the fantastic plots, great characters or inventive filmmaking, but because of the questions they make us ask about ourselves. Who are we and where are we going? Any genre can ask those questions, but I think sci-fi is the most effective and fun way to explore that right now.

Stuart Hazeldine (*Exam*): Philip K. Dick was ahead of the curve when he saw that AI was going to blur the dividing line between the human and the artificial, so what is it uniquely that makes us human? How much of what we consider to be human can you strip away and still be human, not animal or artificial? That is a scientific, spiritual, philosophical and technological question, and it's only going to become a larger and larger preoccupation as human society continues to transfer its evolution from slow-paced biological to fast-paced technological and techno-biological.

Mario Miscione (*Circle*): I want to see more risks taken in film. I want to see more unconventional concepts, executions, and more weirdness in general. I believe that you can make amazing films inexpensively if you're smart about it, and I'd like to see more low-budget, independent sci-fi films done outside the studio system. Studios can be fantastic, but the real risks are taken outside of that arena, I think. I also want to see films embrace diversity more. We're beginning to see that now and it feels as though we're on the cusp of really seeing cinema open up from a diversity perspective. I want underrepresented people to have their day on film. Again, another reason why independent excels.

Brandon Drake (*Visioneers*): I think it's time for a new epic saga. Something huge and sprawling that tries to pull together the threads of technology available today, problems in society, and problems in philosophy and psychology and offer it all up on a massive plate with a cool premise and smart story. I'd read or watch that.

I see sci-fi as an optimistic genre. Because it says, boldly, in its premise, that mankind will survive, has survived, or can survive. I like that. I think the only way we do survive is by continuing to reach for bigger and bigger things as a species. I'd love to see a story that digs into the darkest crevices we have now as a race a decade and a half into the 21st century, takes all the potential we have as individuals, and marries it to the farthest flung technological advances we can imagine—and then sees what happens.

Whatever the case may be, we need stories and we need to keep telling stories. We need characters and heroes. We need beliefs, principles and universal values sought out by and explored by passionate storytellers. We need empathy and, if not truth, then at least the search for it. A good laugh doesn't hurt either.

Josh Feldman (*Senn*): I, like a lot of people, want to see movies with new stories and new ideas, but it's becoming increasingly harder for those types of films to be made, at least at the big-budget level. Too many have flopped, causing studios to stick with existing "safe" franchises—thus the overabundance of superhero films and rehashes of old ideas.

The technology required to create low-budget sci-fi is becoming more and more affordable, which means that the new, innovative stories that I want to see will increasingly come from the indie film world. Which is a great thing!

Tom Woodruff, Jr. (*Fire City: End of Days*): I still think the theater is the place where movies live and breathe. Watching a story unfold as part of an audience allows you to share that world, and in sharing that almost communal feeling with the audience, it takes on more significance than watching it alone. I'll watch a movie a few times at home, classics for dozens of times. But that first time, I like to have it happen in a theater, preferably with a big audience.

Philip Gelatt (*Europa Report*): I'm all for science fiction becoming weirder. I love this trend of scientific science fiction films, but I kind of yearn for the days of *Zardoz*. When science fiction was just utterly bizarre and imaginatively free.

Ever since *Star Wars*, there has been this kind of tyranny of narrative that surrounds not just science fiction films but most films. We've come to expect stories to be told a certain way, with certain beats.

I'd love to see science fiction as a genre break through that. Movies that *feel* like the future as much as they are *about* the future. Sort of, ironically, what George Lucas was trying to do with *THX 1138*, ultimately.

Cory McAbee (*The American Astronaut*): I hope to see something that I have never seen. New ideas have to be expressed in the simplest terms, or no one will understand them. I want to understand it, so it needs to speak in human truths. All of the best science fiction does that.

Justin Benson (*Resolution* & *Spring*): Would love to see intelligent risk-takers like Shane Carruth get the big movie business behind them to make their more ambitious stuff. Especially at the studio level, there's as much stale sci-fi as anything else, but more than ever there are people out there who can give us something new.

Brian Ackley (*Alienated*): This is hard for me to answer. I'm more inclined to fill a void than to complain about one. I'm more interested in creating than criticizing. I don't have a particular hope for sci-fi films. The deep, enriching ones will get my attention, especially if they offer a bit of originality. And if there is a story I want to tell—something I haven't seen yet—I'll write it.

Paul Bunnell (*The Ghastly Love of Johnny X*): I always hope to see good storytelling in movies, science fiction or otherwise. I want to be moved by honest acting and unpredictable plots. Obviously, I am a big fan of science fiction, although I don't just want more of the same. Tell me a story that hasn't been done to death. As technology continues to advance, it is always fun to see bizarre subject matter and futuristic concepts realized on the screen, more realistically than ever before. But put your best foot forward, don't churn out some half-hearted mess in an effort to turn a buck, and then tell the critics and audiences that your poor efforts were intentional, just part of the joke. I'd rather re-watch an old, nearly forgotten feature that someone really believed in than sit through something brand new, but genuinely bad (purposefully or not). I do look forward to many new, wonderful sci-fi movies, and I know there will always be some little gem just around the corner, because, as I said before, the possibilities are truly endless!

Further Reading

Chapman, James, and Nicholas J. Cull. *Projecting Tomorrow: Science Fiction and Popular Cinema*. New York: I.B. Tauris, 2013.

Johnston, Keith M. *Science Fiction Film: A Critical Introduction*. London, New York: Bloomsbury Academic, 2011.

Rickman, Gregg. *The Science Fiction Film Reader*. New York: Limelight Editions, 2004.

Sanders, Steven. *The Philosophy of Science Fiction Film*. University Press of Kentucky, 2009.

Sobchack, Vivian. *Screening Space: The American Science Fiction Film*. New Brunswick, NJ: Rutgers University Press, 1997.

Telotte, J.P. *Science Fiction Film (Genres in American Cinema)*. Cambridge University Press, 2001.

Index

Abbess, Shane 89
ableYoung 152
About Beauty 123
Abraham Lincoln: Vampire Hunter 67
Abrams, J.J. 170
Absence 199
Acker, Shane 110–113, 230, 236
Ackley, Brian 221–224, 228, 233, 238
Across the Universe 207
The Adjustment Bureau 217
Advantageous 76
The Adventures of Buckaroo Banzai Across the Eighth Dimension 55, 58, 206
Aelita, Queen of Mars 5, 214
Afghanistan 10–11, 56
Africa 15
After (2012) 27
After the Truth 138
The Age of Stupid 157
A.I. 109
Aida 216
AIDS 100, 140
Air 131
Akira 113
Alcala, Nicolas 89
Alice in Wonderland 180–181, 183
Alien 89, 94, 169–170, 181, 235
Alien Abduction (2014) 7
Alien: Covenant 89
Alien 3 170
Alien Trespass 15
Alien vs. Predator 161
Alienated 221–224, 228, 233, 238
Aliens 169
All Superheroes Must Die 186
Allen, Woody 126, 194, 198, 231
Almost Human 7
Aloña, Keely 161
Alonso, Nicole 171–172
Alter Egos 191–194
Altered 7–10, 233

The Amazing Race 63
The American Astronaut 207–210, 233, 238
American Gods 159
American Psycho 26
American Zombie 199
And Darren 225
Anderson, Paul W.S. 89
Anderson, Wes 208
Android 109
The Andromeda Strain (1971) 100, 182
The Andromeda Strain (2008) 31, 101
The Angel 134
"The Animators" (short story) 95–99
Ann-Margret 214
Anna's Storm 177
Another Earth 18, 226
Antisocial 101
Antiviral 157
Apollo 18 67, 168
The Apple 206
Arau, Sergio 19
Area 51 196
Area 407 175
Armageddon 176, 195
Armstrong, Neil 88
Arnott, David 126–127
Aronofsky, Darren 232
Arrival 152, 233, 237
Assault on Precinct 13 175
Astaire, Fred 119
Asteroid 176
Astro Boy 197
Atonement 155
Attack the Block 233
Atwood, Margaret 123
Austin Powers: International Man of Mystery 29
Automata 110
Automatons 115–118
Avalon 133
Avary, Roger 126
Ava's Possessions 192

Avatar 7, 235
The Avengers 186, 191
Awake 18

The Baby Formula 199
Babylon 5 70
Back to the Future 29, 37
The Backyard 134
Baez, Joan 15
Baker, Joseph 224
Balance 111
Baldoni, Emily 60
Ball, Jonas 10
Ball, Tommy 171
Balsamo, Camille 168
Bang Bang Baby 207, 210
Bannister, Reggie 210
Barbarella 214
Barclay, Danny 79–80
Barlow, Andrew 213
Baroo, Eddie 195
Bass, Saul 17
Batman (character) 194, 195
Batman (1989) 185
Batman (TV series) 194
Batman & Robin 185
Batman Begins 186
The Battery 120
The Battle of Culloden 198
The Battle of Tinker 171
Battle Royale 133, 138
Battle Royale II: Requiem 145
Battlestar Galactica (2003) 65
The Bay 101
The Beast from 20,000 Fathoms 167
The Beatles 213
The Bed-Sitting Room 119
Begos, Joe 7
Bekmambetov, Timur 111
Believers 11
Benson, Justin 19, 217–221, 238
Benz, Julie 141
Berger, Todd 177–179
Bernardi, Chris 179
Bertino, Bryan 170

Beyond 224–226, 228
Beyond Re-Animator 69
Beyond the Black Rainbow 54
Beyond the Grave 120
Bicentennial Man 109
Big Hero 6 110
Big Trouble in Little China 51, 158, 206
Bigelow, Kathryn 75
The Bilderberg Group 158
The Bill 95
Bill & Ted's Excellent Adventure 28
Billy Nayer Show (band) 209
Bingaman, Rod 213–215, 228
Bingen, Steve 210
The Birds 17
Biutiful 156
Bixby, Jerome 59
Black Book 69
The Black Hole 89
Black Mirror 231, 234, 237
Black Sheep 168
Blade 185–186
Blade Runner 109, 155–156, 182, 221
Blade Runner 2049 231
The Blair Witch Project 11, 61, 128, 139, 198, 201
Blanston 160
The Bleeding House 203
Blindness 101
The Blob 167
Blood of the Tribades 180
Blood Punch 41
Blood Simple 37
Bloom, Eric 79–80
Blue Valentine 226
Blumenthal, Rachel Leah 179
BMX Bandits 72
Bogart, Humphrey 161
Bond, Christopher 50
Bond University 47
Bones 38
Bong, Joon-ho 147
Bonowicz, Brett Ryan 84–87, 235
Bonzie, Josh 189
The Book of Eli 119
The Book of Life 147
Book of Shadows: Blair Witch 2 198
Borders, Cary 92
Boss, Hugo 69
Boston, Rachel 178
The Bothersome Man 157
Bounds, Sydney J. 95–99
Bousman, Darren Lynn 207
Bowie, David 209
The Box 15
A Boy and His Dog 119
Boyle, Danny 89
The Boys from Brazil 66
Brainstorm 75

Branded 159
Brannigan, Paul 224
Bratton, Creed 210
Brazil 113, 146
The Breakfast Club 189
Breathing Room 145
Brendon, Nicholas 60
Brennan, Kevin M. 178
Bride of Frankenstein 216
Bridge of Spies 64
Britt, Alison 92
The Brood 198
Brooks, Albert 126
Brown, David 92
Brown, Dru 22
Brown, Jake 135
Brown, Mandy 214
Brownlow, Kevin 66
Brummett, Chad 120
Brumpton, John 195
Bubblecraft 90
Buck Rogers 58, 209
The Bulleteers 190
Bunker 6 120
Bunnell, Paul 210–213, 238
Burgess, Tony 105
Burman, Barney 40
Burroughs, William S. 106, 158
Burry, Jen L. 221–222
Burton, Tim 50, 51, 111, 113
Bush, Pres. George W. 11, 129, 147
Butterfly Chasers 233
The Butterfly Effect 39, 41
Bye Bye Birdie 214
Byrkit, James Ward 60–62, 231, 235
Byrne, David 91–92
Byrne, Torey 171

Cabin Fever (2002) 101
Cabin Fever (2016) 101
Cacciola, Sophia 179–184
Caesarea 105
Cain, Leon 22–23
Callis, James 154
Camargo, Christian 203–204
Cameron, James 170, 235
Camión de Carga 136
CanniBallistic! 115
Captain America 185, 194
Captain America: The First Avenger 67
Captain EO 235
Carland, Ben 76–79, 135–138, 230, 237
Caro, Marc 89, 147
Carpenter, John 6, 51, 91, 158, 169, 175
Carriers 101
Carruth, Shane 229, 238
Cassavetes, John 156
Cast Away 169
Catholic Church 10

The Cell 44, 87
Cement Suitcase 35
Cemetery of Splendor 18
Chalamet, Timothée 187
Chambers, Munro 72
Chan, Gemma 138
Chappie 110
Chariots of the Gods 12
Charlotte's Web 195
Cherry 2000 119
Chicago 207
Chicken Delight 126
Children of Men 84, 221
China 15
The China Syndrome 176
Christian 138
Christie, Agatha 138
A Christmas Carol (book) 28, 33, 38
A Christmas Carol (2009) 29
Chronicle 199, 235
Chuchran, Danielle 161
Chrysalis (2014) 120
Cilella, Peter 19
Circle 141–145, 229, 237
Citadel 159
Citizen Kane 231
The City of Lost Children 43, 50, 51, 89, 113, 182
Clark, Wesley 10
Clarke, Arthur C. 12, 204, 232
Clayton, Amber 195
Clerks 192
A Clockwork Orange 146
Close Encounters of the Third Kind 6, 10, 64, 91
Closer Than We Think 85
Cloud Atlas 217
Cloverfield 168, 199
Clown 113
Coen Brothers (Joel and Ethan) 220
Cohen, Robyn 84
Coherence 60–62, 231, 235
Cold in July 129
The Cold War 17, 58, 67, 69, 169, 176, 183
Cole, David John 79
Collateral 26
The Colony 131
The Color Out of Space 184
Columbus, Chris 38
The Comedian at The Friday 85
Comet 56
Commander Cody 58
Communion 9
Conan Doyle, Sir Arthur 42
Concrete Island (novel) 103
The Congress 43
Conlanging: The Art of Crafting Tongues 152
Connell, Richard 132
Connelly, Jennifer 110
Conners, Colin 135

Constantine 186
Contact 89, 153, 224
Contagion 101
Containment 101–105
Cooney, Brenda 115–116
Cooper, B.P. 34–37, 227, 231, 234
Cop Car 114
Copley, Sharlto 203
Coppola, Francis Ford 138, 156, 235
Coraline 56, 166
Corder, Shannon 62
Cordero, Sebastián 203
The Core 177
Cornish, Joe 233
The Corridor 27
Coscarelli, Don 56
The Cosmonaut 89
Countdown 88–89
Cox, Nathalie 139
Crabbe, Buster 58
Crack in the World 176–177
Crawl or Die 172–175
Crawlspace 195–197
The Crazies (1973) 100
The Crazies (2010) 101
Creative Control 76
Creature from the Black Lagoon 167
Crichton, Michael 75, 100, 109, 228
Crimes and Misdemeanors 194
Cronenberg, David 75, 100, 158, 198
Cross, David 177–178
Crossworlds 55
The Crow 185–186
Cruel & Unusual 30, 234
Crumbs 120
CSA: The Confederate States of America 67
Cuaron, Alfonso 89
Cube 75, 83, 140–141, 233
Cubosity 152
Curran, Vinny 19
Currie, Andrew 67
Cypher 87

Damici, Nick 128–129
Damnation Alley 119
Dances with Wolves 216
Dante 01 89
Danum, Richard J. 224
Darabont, Frank 56
Daredevil 186
Darger, Henry 202–203
The Dark Knight Rises 191
Dark Portals: The Chronicles of Vidocq 54
Dark Side of the Moon 198
Dark Star 88, 91
Dark/Web 142
DARPA (Defense Advanced Research Projects Agency) 196
d'Aulaire, Nils 207
Davey, Ditch 195
Dawn of the Dead (1978) 117
Dawson, Clive 95–99, 228, 236
Dawson, Richard 132
The Day After 176
The Day After Tomorrow 177
The Day Before the Wedding 90
Day Break 18
The Day the Earth Stood Still 5–6, 116, 235
A Day Without a Mexican 18, 199
DC Comics 1
Dead-End Drive-In 146
The Dead Guy in the Trunk 23
Dead Men Don't Wear Plaid 178
Dear Zachary: A Letter to a Son About His Father 38
Death Race 133
Death Race 2000 42, 132
Deep Impact 176
Deep Rising 167
Defendor 193
Delicatessen 89, 113, 147
del Toro, Guillermo 186
Deluge 176
Demon Divas and the Lanes of Damnation 58
Demonitron: The Sixth Dimension 73
De Niro, Robert 80
Le Dernier Combat 119
Dervisevic, Merlin 30, 234
The Devil's Carnival 207
The Devil's Hand 201
Diary of the Dead 199
Dick, Philip K. 155–156, 237
Dickens, Charles 28
Dickinson, Benjamin 76, 114
Diesel, Vin 167
Dietze, Julia 70
The Dirt Bike Kid 72
Disney World 64
District 9 7, 229, 235
Divergent 135
The Divide 131, 200
Dix, Justin 195–197
Dr. Horrible's Sing-Along Blog 186
Dr. Plonk 30
Doctor Strange 185
Dr. Strangelove 119
Doctor Who 117
The Dog That Stopped the War 73
Don Quixote (novel) 115
Donnie Darko 30
Donovan's Echo 27
Dooley, Yahel 218
Doomsday 101
Douglas, Kirk 66
Dracula 75
Drake, Brandon 148–151
Drake, Jared 148
Dredd (2012) 147
Drive 183
Drive-In Movie Memories 38
Duffy, Jessica 159
Dune (novel) 122
Dune (1984) 43, 182
Dune (2000) 43
Dunst, Kirsten 51
Duplass, Mark 90
Durant, Nicole Lee 76–77
Dyke, Robert 67

Eagle Eye 110
Earth Girls Are Easy 207
Earthling 13–16, 233
Earthlings: Ugly Bags of Mostly Water 160
Edge of Tomorrow 29
Edwards, Gareth 7
84 Charlie MoPic 69
Einstein, Albert 83
Eklund, Michael 30
Electric Dreams 216
11:59 160
11 Minutes Ago 41, 199
Eliot, T.S. 165
Elysium 147
Embers 231
Emmerich, Roland 7, 177
Empty 131
End of Days, Inc. 164–166
The Endless 19
Enter Nowhere 27
Epstein, Michael J. 179
Equals 157
Equilibrium 147
E.R. 61
Escape from New York 146
Esmail, Sam 56
E.T.: The Extra-Terrestrial 6, 9, 10, 63, 64, 91
Eternal Sunshine of the Spotless Mind 76, 232
Eulberg, Zach 151–152
Europa Report 203–205, 238
Event Horizon 89
Ever Since the World Ended 131
"Every Story Is a Love Story" 216
Everything Changes 90
Evil Dead II 8, 10
Ex Machina 110, 118, 231, 233, 236
Exam 138–141, 230, 237
Exists 8
Explorers 74
Extracted 87
Extraterrestre 15
Extraterrestrial 15

Fabares, Shelly 214
Facebook 59

Fahrenheit 451 146
Fail-Safe 178
The Fall 44
The Falls 198
Family Feud 132
Fantastic Voyage 75
Fatherland 66
Faust (play) 106
Faust (2000) 69
Favreau, Jon 186
A Feast of Flesh 58
Feldman, Josh 151–154, 238
Fellini, Federico 231
Ferguson, Anna 164
Fermat's Room 83, 133, 141
Ferrara, Abel 177
Ferrera, America 177–178
Fessenden, Larry 115, 129
Fido 67
Fight Club 8, 26
Fillingham, John Lloyd 138
The Final Countdown 66
Final Destination 56
Fincher, David 170
Finn, George 34
Fire City: End of Days 161–164, 229, 233, 238
Fire in the Sky 9
Firefly 89
First Men in the Moon 87
First on the Moon 199
Fisher, Darren Paul 47–49, 234
Five 119, 128, 176
5 Shells 120–122, 232
Flash Gordon 58
FlashForward 18
FLIR (forward-looking infrared) 12–13
Flourish 35
The Fly (1958) 117
Fly Trap 225
Folman, Ari 43
For a Few Zombies More 93, 95
Forbidden Planet 88
Ford, Christopher 113–115, 236
Ford, Harrison 156
Ford, Henry 83
Forever's End 120
The Forgotten Future 77, 136
Foster, Adam Patrick 195
Foster, Jon 200
Found in Time 41
The Fountain 217, 232
A Four Course Meal 13
4:44 Last Day on Earth 177
14,000 Things to Be Happy About 150
Fox, Tim 76–77
Fox News 117
The Frame 27
Frankenstein 1, 75, 113, 118, 167
The Frankenstein Theory 175
Frankenstein's Army 67–69, 71
Franklyn 44–46

Fraser, Daniel 47
Freejack 29
Freemasons 158
Frequencies 47–49, 234
Fresnadillo, Juan Carlos 133
Fringe 18
Frost, Robert 60
Full Frontal with Samantha Bee 122
Funnybones 95
Futuresport 133
Futureworld 109

Gabe, Jessie 50
Gagamboy 197
Gagarin, Yuri 209
Gaiman, Neil 158
Galaxy Quest 6
Galifianakis, Zach 148
Galland, Jordan 191–194
Gamer 133
Garai, Romola 95–96
Gardner, Ava 119
Gardner, Jeremy 218
Garland, Alex 231
Garrity, Simon 139
Gates, Sterling 189–190
Gattaca 182, 235
Gelatt, Philip 203–205, 238
Gelb, David 76
George Méliès 1
Gervais, Ricky 43
The Ghastly Love of Johnny X 210–213, 238
The Ghost and Mrs. Muir 210
Ghost World 91
Ghostbusters 228
Ghosts of Mars 99
Ghosts with Shit Jobs 205
Gibson, William 236
Gilliam, Terry 51
Gillis, Alec 161, 168–171, 229, 233
The Girl from Monday 147
The Giver 157
The Gladiators 198
Glass Eye Pix 115
Glover, Crispin 110
Goat 8
Gods of Egypt 161
Godspell 206
Godzilla 116, 167, 177, 199
Godzilla (2014) 7, 168
Golden Age 93
The Golden Compass 43
The Golden Girls 15
Gonks Go Beat 206
The Good Dinosaur 67
Goodwill, Craig 50–51
The Goonies 73
Goranson, Lindsay 214
Grace, Jeff 178
Grady, Jordan 120
Gravity 89, 237

The Great Escape 173
Green, Eva 44
Greenaway, Peter 198
Greene, Peter 13
Greer, Judy 148–149
Gremlins 167, 233
Groundhog Day 25, 29, 30, 37
Guardians of the Galaxy 55, 228
Gwilym, Robert 67
Gymkata 132

Hairspray 207
Half-Life 177
The Handmaid's Tale (1990) 147
Hangar 10 15
The Hangnail 111
Hann, Aaron 141
Hap and Leonard 129
The Happening 177
Happiness 123
Happy Accidents 216
Harbinger Down 168–171, 229, 233
A Hard Day's Night 213, 215
Hard Target 132
Hard to Be a God 159
Harmon, Richard 30
Harris, Alexandra 189
Harry Potter and the Prisoner of Azkaban 29
Harry Potter and the Sorcerer's Stone 159
Hartley, Hal 91–92, 147
Hartsell, Chuck 93, 95
Hauer, Rutger 66
Hayes, Erinn 178
Hayes, Michael 161
Hazeldine, Stuart 138–141, 230, 237
HBO 25
He-Man 55
Head 214
Heartless 159
Heat 80
Hell 120
Hellboy 67, 186
The Hellmouths of Bewdley 105
The Hellstrom Chronicle 198
Helm, Matt (character) 214
Help! 214
Hemsworth, Chris 89
Hemsworth, Liam 89
Hemsworth, Luke 89
Henke, Brad William 7–8
Henriksen, Lance 168
Her 110, 113, 118, 217, 221, 231
Herbert, Frank 122
Herman's Hermits 214
Heroes of the Realm 190
Hertford, Whit 84
Herzog, Werner 199
Hide and Creep 93
High Rise 103
The Highlander 132

Hilker, Nadia 217–218
Hiroshima 119
The History of Future Folk 207
Hitchcock, Alfred 17, 26, 138
Hitler, Adolph 66–67
The Hive 108
Hold On 214
The Hole (2009) 56
Hollobaugh, Nathan 56
The Hollow Men 165
Holmes, Sherlock 118
Holt, Princeton 221, 233
Honeymoon 168
Hooper, Tobe 9
Hooray for Mister Touchdown 214
Horgan, Conor 122–126, 232
The Host 168
Hot Fuzz 155
Hot Tub Time Machine 29
The Hot Zone 99
Hough, Paul 133–135, 230
Houle, Lisa 105
House of Leaves 219
Howard the Duck 55
Huertas, Jon 10
Hughes, John 190
Hulu 174
The Human Race 133–135, 138, 230
Humanity's End 99
Hunchar, Quinn 159
Hunger 85
The Hunger Games 89, 132, 135, 138
Hurlyburly 221
Hutton, Kelsey 120–121
Hypothermia 116

I Am Legend 101, 129
I Remember You 217
I, Robot 110
The Ice Pirates 43
I'll Follow You Down 41
Illuminati 158
The Imaginarium of Doctor Parnassus 166
The Immortals 161
In Search Of... 198
In Time 29
In Your Eyes 217
Inbetweeners (2001) 47
Inception 76, 84, 234
Incident at Loch Ness 199
The Incredibles 194
Independence Day 6, 177, 234, 236
Independence Day: Resurgence 7
Indiana Jones 56, 58
Infini 89
The Infinite Man 87
Inglourious Basterds 67
Ink 159–161, 229
Intacto 133

Interkosmos 199
Interplanetary 92–95, 232, 236
Interstella 5555: The 5tory of the 5ecret 5tar 5ystem 215
Interstellar 236
Invasion 199
Invasion of the Body Snatchers 6, 97
The Invention of Lying 43
The Invisible Man 75
Iraq War 45, 115
Iron Man 76, 186
Iron Sky 70–72, 231
Ironside, Michael 72
The Island 147
Island at the Top of the World 158
The Isolation of Subject #136 171
It Came from Yesterday 56–59, 235
It Happened Here 66
It's a Disaster 177–179
It's a Mad Mad Mad Mad World 213
It's All About Love 27, 217
It's Great to Be Alive 206
Iwuju, Chukwudi 139

Jack the Ripper 29
Jack Waltzer: On the Craft of Acting 52
Jackman, Hugh 110
Jackrabbit 76
Janiak, Leigh 168
Jarry, Alfred 106
Jaws 10
Jelinek, Tobias 161–162
Jericho 178
Jesus 12, 67
Jesus Christ Superstar 206
Jeunet, Jean-Pierre 51, 147
John, Elton 216
John Dies at the End 56
Johnston, Cait 214
Johnston, Joe 75
Jones, Duncan 232
Jones, Sarah 200
Jonze, Spike 113, 231
Journey to the Center of the Earth 158, 159
JPL (Jet Propulsion Laboratory) 205
Judge Dredd (1995) 147, 185
Jumanji 133, 169
Jurassic Park 167, 222, 232
Jurassic World 167
Just Imagine 206

Kalesniko, Michael 70
Katt, George 221–222
Katt, William 13
Kauffman, Chris M. 76–77
Kaufman, Adam 7–8
Keating, Mickey 168

Keenan, Rory 122
Keenan, Will 210–211
Kelly, Christopher Soren 159
Kennedy, John F. 67
Kern, Joey 192
The Ketchup and Mustard Man 209
Key Largo 170
Kick-Ass 186, 193
Kier, Udo 70
Kill Bill 65
King, Bradley 34
King, Jonathan 168
King, Stephen 18, 132, 179, 219
King Kong (1933) 132
King Kong 168
Klaitz, Jay 207
Kochalka, James 91
Kospiah, Michael J. 22–27, 231, 234
Kostic, Goran 96
Koteas, Elias 95–96
Kozikowski, Eve 121
Kramer, Stanley 119
Kubrick, Stanley 156, 199, 204
Kuenne, Kurt 37–41, 234
Kuhn, Michael 97
Kuklinsky, Richard 25
Kumiko the Treasure Hunter 15
Kung Fu Panda: Secrets of the Masters 178
Kyson, James 84

Labadie, Elle 40
Lagan, Matt 80
The Lake 55
The Lake House 29
Lanbert, Taylor 151
Lang, Fritz 42
Langella, Frank 114
Lansdale, Joe R. 129
Lanzone, Andy 79
Lanzone, Timothy 79–83, 231, 235
Large, Tom 224–226, 228
The Last Barbarians 73
The Last Days 101
The Last Days on Mars 95–99, 228, 236
The Last Lovecraft: Relic of Cthulhu 168
The Last Man 126, 236
The Last Man on Earth 100, 128
Last Night 176
The Last of the Mohicans 216
The Last Starfighter 89
The Last Survivors 120
The Last Woman on Earth 17
The Lathe of Heaven (1980) 55
The Lathe of Heaven (2002) 55
Launstein Brothers 111
Lavalle, Jimmy 218
Lawrence, Don 69
Lawson, David 218

The Lazarus Effect 76
The League of Extraordinary Gentlemen 67, 186
Leboeuf, Laurence 72
Lee, Grace 199
Lee, Stan 186
Left Behind 120
The Legend of Boggy Creek 198
LeGros, James 148
LeGuin, Ursula K. 55
Lemche, Kris 191–192
Lemon, David 101
Lennon, Sean 191
Levin, Ira 109
LFO 87
Li, Jet 56
Liao, Jennifer 164–166
Life Tracker 76
Lifeboat 141
Liford, Clay 13–16, 233
Linklater, Richard 219
Listen 87
Listening 76, 82
Little Shop of Horrors (1960) 207
Little Shop of Horrors (1986) 207
The Lobster 226
Loch Ness Monster 13
Logan's Run 146, 152
Looker 75
Looper 234
López-Gallego, Gonzalo 67
Lord of the Flies (novel) 136–137, 141
Lord of the Rings 103
The Lord of the Rings: Return of the King 111
Lost 18
Lost in Space 116
The Lost Skeleton of Cadavra 211
The Lost World 42
Love & Teleportation 87
Lovecraft, H.P. 218–219
The Loved Ones 195
Lovely Molly 8
Loves Her Gun 90
Lubocki, Brian 161
Lucas, George 42, 138, 238
Lullaby Procedure 93
Lunopolis 199
Lynch, David 182

Mably, Luke 139
MacGregor, Gillian 224
The Machine 110
Mad Max 72, 101, 119
Maestro, Mia 149
Magnetic 179–184
Major Damage 111
The Man from Earth 67
Man in the High Castle 71
The Man in the White Suit 75

Man of Steel 40
The Man on the Moon 209
The Man Who Fell to Earth 6
The Man Without a Head 52
Mangan, Catherine 7
The Mangler 18
Manhattan Project 82, 119
Maraghi, Carolyne 164
Marlowe, Christopher 106
Marooned 88
Mars 90–92, 227, 230–231, 235
Marslett, Geoff 90–92, 227, 230, 235
The Martian 89, 229, 236
Martin, Trevor 50
Marvel Comics 1
Masters, Allegra 141
Masters of the Universe 55
Masterson, Danny 191
Matheson, Richard 129
The Matrix 109, 147, 157
Maximum Overdrive 18
May, Elaine 128
The Maze 160
The Maze Runner 135
McAbee, Cory 207–210, 233, 238
McCarthy-Boyington, Paul 8, 133–135
McCuiston, Quentin 213
McDonald, Bruce 105–108
Mcenery-West, Neil 101–105
McGee, Eddie 133–134
McGillis, Kelly 128
McHattie, Stephen 105
McIntosh, Pollyanna 138
McKean, Dave 159
McKellar, Don 176
McKenney, James Felix 115–118
McManus, Don 84
McMenamin, Ciarán 122
McMorrow, Gerald 44–46
McQueen, Steve 85
McWilliam, Joss 22
Mechagodzilla 118
Megalopolis 235
Melancholia 177
Memento 234
Memory Lane 87
Men Cry Bullets 126
Men in Black 6
Men in Black III 29
Menzies, William Cameron 119
Meteor 176
Metropolis 42, 109, 113, 118, 140, 147
M.I.A. M.D. 136
Mickey Mouse 28
Mickle, Jim 128–131, 237
Midnight Cowboy 26
Miller, Blaise 178
Miller, George 119, 122
Milton Is a Shitbag 90
Mimic 167

Minahan, Daniel 133
Miracle Mile 176
MirrorMask 159
Miscione, Mario 141–145, 229, 237
The Mist 56
Mr. Jones 19, 200–203
Mr. Nobody 226
Mistry, Jimi 139
Mitchell, Chris W. 67
Moebius 111
Mohammad 12
Mollow, Andrew 66
The Monkees 214
Monkey vs. Robot 227
The Monster 170
Monster House 64
Monsters 7, 235
Montague, Emily 19
Montgomery, Dan, Jr. 126
Monty Python 51
Moon 90, 232–233, 235
Moonlight 8
Moore, Alan 67
Moorhead, Aaron 19, 217–221, 228
Morgan, Glen 56
Morocco 13
Mortal Kombat 161
Mortis, Allix 179–180
The Most Dangerous Game 132–133
The Mother of Invention 205
Moulin Rouge 207
Mousehunt 60
Mouzakis, Steve 22–23
Mueller, Karl 200–203
Mulberry Street 129–130
Mumbai 54
The Mummy 75
The Muppets 28
Murphy, Mark D. 210
Myers, Paul S. 120–122, 232
Myrick, Daniel 10–13, 227, 232
Mystery Men 185, 194
Mystery Science Theater 3000: The Movie 109

Nagasaki 119
Naked Lunch 158
Narcopolis 154–157
Nardelli, Michael 141
Nash, Jamie 7–10, 233
Negron, Taylor 221, 224
Netflix 174
The Neverending Story 73
Neverwhere 158–159
The New Women 18
New York City 54
Newberry, Luke 67
Night of the Comet 17
Night of the Creeps 73
Night of the Living Dead 95, 107, 178

The Nightmare Before Christmas 113
Nightmare Code 199
9 110–113, 230, 236
Nine Minutes 93
The Nines 65
1984 (film) 50, 146
Ninja Eliminator 4: The French Connection 73
Nixon, Richard 132
No Such Thing 147
No Tomorrow: A Turbo Kid Tale 73
Nolan, Christopher 84, 186, 194, 230, 234, 236
Northeast 52
Nothing (2003) 27
Nunes, Paulino 164
Nyqvist, Michael 203

Obama, Barack 129
O'Bannon, Dan 91
The Objective 10–13, 227, 232
Oboler, Arch 119
O'Brien, Mark 164
The Off Season 115
The Office 164
Office Space 94
Oklahoma! 106
The Old Negro Space Program 67
O'Leary, Matt 34–35
Olivier, Laurence 66
The Omega Man 100
On the Beach 119
One & Two 187–189, 228
One Hundred Mornings 122–126, 232
The One I Love 18, 217, 233
Oosterhoorn, Bart 69
Oppenheimer, J. Robert 111
Orlando (book) 14
Osombie 67
Otto, Götz 70
Our Hero 31
Outbreak 99, 100
The Outer Limits 219, 234
Outlander 175
OzLand 131

Pacific Rim 168
Pacino, Al 80
Pal, George 28, 58
Palermo, Andrew Droz 187–189, 228
Panabaker, Danielle 34
Pandemic 108
Pandorum 99
Panic in Year Zero! 176
Paolo, Connor 128
Papua New Guinea 125
Paradox 41
Paramount Pictures 2
Pariah 203
Parks and Recreation 178

Parts Per Billion 177
Pataphysics 106
Patch Town 50–51
Patton, Mark A. 10
Paul, Stephanie 70
Paycheck 155
Pearl Harbor 66
Peck, Gregory 66, 119
Peggy Sue Got Married 29
Pennies from Heaven 209
The Perfect 46 84–87, 235
Peter Rabbit (TV series) 155
Petrograd 203
Pettler, Pamela 110
Phang, Jennifer 76, 177
Phantasm 56, 182
The Phantom 185
The Phantom of the Opera 216
Phase IV 17
Phase 7 108
Phillippe, Ryan 44
The Phoenix Project 76, 78, 82
Pi 75, 83, 182
Pine Gap 195–196
Pirates of the Caribbean (2003) 60
Pit Boss 63
Pitch Black 167
Pittsburgh 58
Place, Collin 189
Plan Nine from Outer Space 92
Plan 10 from Outer Space 211
Planet of the Apes (1968) 42, 119
Planet of the Apes (2001) 29
Plotnick, Jack 89
+1 30
Pod 168
Point Park University 58
Pointer, Jeff 160, 229
Pokemon GO 231
Poltergeist 10, 63, 64
Pontypool 105–108
Pontypool Changes Everything (novel) 106
Popcorn (2007) 47
Popo 69
Possession 77
The Posthuman Project 189–191
Potter, Dennis 209
Pressing the Public Opinion 85
Prewitt, Bobbie 62–63
Prey 228
Price, Matthew 189–190
Pride and Prejudice 155
Primer 30, 36, 78, 82, 182, 217
Prince of Tides 10
The Prisoner 117, 182
Professor X 29
Project: Valkyrie 57–58
Prometheus 89
Psycho 26
Pucci, Lou Taylor 217–218
Pugh, Owen 47
The Punisher 185

Punishment Park 132, 198
The Purge 132, 147
Push 186
Puskala, Jarmo 70
Putnam 120
Pyle, Missi 148

Quarantine 101, 199
Quatermain, Allan 56, 58
Quay Brothers 111
The Queen of Ireland 123
The Quiet Earth 17, 126
The Quiet Hour 15

Raaphorst, Richard 67–69
Rabid 100
Radar Men from the Moon 58
Radio Free Albemuth 74
Raiders of the Lost Ark 55, 216
Raimi, Sam 186
Ralston, Harry 126, 236
Rango 60
Ransone, James 207
Ray, Christina 164–165
Raymond, Marc 80
Real Steel 110
Rear Window 36, 175
Reaser, Elizabeth 187
Rebirth 201
REC 101, 199
Re-Cycle 56
Red Hill 195
Red Planet 99
Reefer Madness 206
Reeve, Christopher 185
Reeves, George 185
Reid, Alex 122
Reign of Fire 168
Reilly, Georgina 105
Repeaters 41
Repo: The Genetic Opera 207, 210
Reservoir Dogs 192, 194
Resident Evil 101
Resolution 19, 218, 228, 238
The Return of Captain Invincible 207
Rhodes, Paula 37
Rice, Tim 216
Rich Hill 187–188
Richardson, Miranda 66
Richings, Julian 50
Richmond-Peck, David 30
Right at Your Door 177, 179
Riley, Sam 44
Ripped! 210, 213–215, 228
Rivera, Alex 76
The Road 119
Road to Pecumsecah 80
Roberts, Kyle William 189–191
Robinson, Ruairi 96
Robinson, Trista 133
RoboCop 10
Robot & Frank 113–115, 236

Robot Chicken 193
Robot Monster 116
Robot Overlords 118
Robot Stories 110
Rock & Rule 207
Rocket Man 209
The Rocketeer 58, 69, 75
The Rocky Horror Picture Show 206
Roden, Karel 67
Rollerball (1975) 132
Rollerball (2002) 133
Romeo and Juliet 52
Romero, George A. 199
Rope 140
Rosencrantz and Guildenstern Are Undead 191–192
Roth, Eli 67, 113
Rotor DR1 131
Rovinski, Elise 213
The Rules of Attraction 126
Run Lola Run 55
Runaway 75
The Running Man 132
Russo, Nayli 56
Ryan, Jeri 126–127

Sabiston, Bob 91
Safety Not Guaranteed 90, 226, 233
Samberg, Andy 227
Sánchez, Eduardo 7–10
Sandman 158
Sansom, William 219
The Santa Clause 161
Sarandon, Susan 113
Sarsgaard, Peter 113
Satan Hates You 116
Saturn Awards 52
Saw 207
Sawyer, Lindsay 189
Scanners 196
Scenesters 178
Schreiber, Live 95–96
Schreier, Jake 113
Schrödinger's Cat 62
Schwarzenegger, Arnold 132
Sci-Fi High: The Musical 207
Scott, Jason Thomas 62–65
Scott, Ridley 89, 169
Scott Pilgrim vs. the World 217
Screamers 109
Screen 171
The Scribbler 186
Scrimm, Angus 115, 117
Scrooge, or Marley's Ghost (1901) 28
Seeking a Friend for the End of the World 177
Seiple, Tyler 80
Senn 151–154, 238
September 11, 2001 (9/11) 1, 6–7, 10–13, 56, 64, 70, 101, 129–130, 143, 179

Serenity 89
Sergeant, Peta 70
Series 7: The Contenders 133
Serling, Rod 62
Seventh Moon 8
Sex After Kids 165
The Shack 138
The Shadow 185
The Shadow Walker 160
Shadows on the Wall 76–79, 136, 230, 237
Shahdadi, Neima 187
Shale, Kerry 154
Shallow Moon 36
Shaolin Soccer 186
She 213
Shea, Maura 214
Sheen, Martin 66
Shelley, Mary 113
Shelton, Michael 93
The Shining 175
Shipka, Kiernan 187
Shirley, Chance 92–95, 232, 236
Shivers 100
Shock Treatment 206
Shoedsack, Ernest P. 132
A Short History of Progress 123
Shuffle 37–41, 234
Shyamalan, M. Night 186, 223
Siemer, Ben 70
The Signal (2007) 101
The Signal (2014) 15
Signs 223
Signs and Voices 85
Silent Running 15, 88, 152, 182
Simard, François 72
Simon, Neil 178
S1m0ne 110
A Simple Plan 37
Singer, Bryan 186
Singh, Tarsem 44
The Singing Detective 209
Sisto, Rocco 207
Six-String Samurai 73, 119
The Sixth Sense 186
Skull and Bones Society 158
Sky Captain and the World of Tomorrow 43, 58
Slash 13, 16
Slaughterhouse-Five 28, 39
Sleep Dealer 76
Sleepers 10
Sliding Doors 55
Small Star Seminar 233
Smith, Will 29
The Smurfs: A Christmas Carol 178
Snowpiercer 147
Snyder, Zack 67
Sol 77, 135–138, 230, 237
Solanas, Juan 51–54
Solaris 15
Solaris (1972) 89
Solaris (2002) 89

Solstice 11
Somewhere in Time 216
Sony 2
Sound of My Voice 41
Source Code 56
Southern Belles 121
Southland Tales 178
Soviet Union 5, 67, 88, 176
Soylent Green 146, 152
Space Oddity 209
Space Station 76 89
Space Truckers 89
Spall, Timothy 51
Sparks 186
Special 35
The Specials 197
Spence, Rebecca 13–14
Spencer, Christine 115
Spicy Sister Slumber Party 58
Spider-Man 185–186
Spider-Man: Homecoming 113
Spielberg, Steven 6, 9–10, 63, 64, 167
Spin 160
Splash 216
Splatter Movie: The Director's Cut 58
Splinter 168
Sprayberry, Dylan 40
Spring 19, 217–221, 228, 238
Stake Land 128–131, 237
Stalker 15
The Stand 100, 179
Star Man 209
Star Trek 40, 46, 55, 58, 65, 70, 94, 137, 153, 172, 209, 237
Star Trek: The Next Generation 15
Star Wars 10, 42, 58, 91, 94, 109, 118, 172, 236, 236, 238
Star Wars: Episode II—Attack of the Clones 195, 234
Star Wars: The Force Awakens 236
Star Wreck: In the Pirkinning 70
Starbucks 151
Starman 216
Starship Troopers 161, 167
Stay Alive 133
Steel 185
Steger, Mark 200
The Stepford Wives (1975) 109
The Stepford Wives (2004) 110
Stereo 198
Sterling, Maury 60
Stiles, Julia 177–178
Stingray Sam 207, 210
Stone, Chris 37
Stranded 99
Strange Days 75
Stranger Things 64, 170
Strangers on a Train 26
Street of Crocodiles 113

Streets of Fire 206
The Stuff 100
Sturgess, Jim 51
The Subjects 186
The Substitute (2007) 15
The Suicide Theory 22–27, 231, 234
Sultan Al-Darmaki 170
Sunshine 89, 95
Super 193, 194
Super Capers 186
Super 8 64
Super Mario Bros. (1993) 55
Supergirl 185
Superman (character) 185, 194
Superman (1978) 185
Superman and the Mole Men 185
Supernatural 31
Swamp Thing 185
Sweeney, Rachel 214
Synchronicity 29

T Is for Turbo 73
Take Shelter 120
Taken (2002) 9
Tarantino, Quentin 65, 67
Tarkovsky, Andrei 13, 15
Taxi Driver 26
Taylor, Lauren 151–152
Taylor, Rod 215
Technicolor 59
Teen Wolf 40
Teenage Mutant Ninja Turtles 185
Tejada-Flores, Miguel 67
Ten 179
Ten Little Indians 180
Tenenbaum, David 62–64
The 10th Victim 132
The Terminal Man 75
The Terminator 114, 171
Terminus 2015
Testament 176
That Little Monster 210
Thespian X 45
They Live 131, 158
The Thing (1982) 6, 169–170
The Thing (2011) 169
The Thing from Another World 5, 95
Things to Come 119, 146
This Is Not a Test 176
This Is Spinal Tap! 206
This Is the End 120, 164
This Island Earth 88
Thor 89
III: The Ritual 65
THX 1138 146, 238
Thyne, T.J. 37
Time After Time 28
Time Bandits 29, 113
Time Lapse 34–37, 227, 231, 234
The Time Machine (novel) 156

The Time Machine (1960) 28
The Time Machine (2002) 29, 216
Time of the Wolf 120
The Time Traveler's Wife 29, 216
Timecrimes 30, 36
Timeline 35
Timequest 67
Timer 54, 217
A Tiny Prophecy 165
Toomorrow 206
Total Recall 37, 155
The Tournament 133
The Toxic Avenger 185–186
Transformers 110
Travelling Salesman 79–84, 231, 235
Treasure Island (novel) 115
Trefgarne, Justin 154–157, 229
Tremors 167, 169–170
The Trial 146
Triangle 30
A Trip to the Moon 1, 88
TRON 109
True Stories 91
Trust 91
Trumbull, Douglas 75
Trump, Donald 125, 131
Turbo Kid 72–74, 231
12 Angry Men 80–81, 140–141
12 Monkeys 29, 100, 113
20th Century Fox 2
28 Days Later 97, 101
28 Weeks Later 133
20,000 Leagues Under the Sea 75
Twilight 130
The Twilight Zone 17, 23, 24, 38, 62, 65, 219, 235
Two Front Teeth 8
2009: Lost Memories 74
2001: A Space Odyssey 15, 88–89, 91, 94, 153, 182, 204, 232, 235
2012 177
Tympanum 62–65

Ultrasonic 19
Unbreakable 26, 186, 223
The Underdogs 129
Undertow 102
Universal Pictures 2
The Unprofessionals 31
Unsolved Mysteries 219
Upside Down 51–54
Upstream Color 152, 182, 217
Uptown 221
The Usual Suspects 186

V for Vendetta 147
Validation 38
Van Damme, Jean-Claude 132
Vanishing on 7th Street 27

The Vault (web-series) 142
Verbinski, Gore 60
Verhoeven, Paul 170
VHS 187
VHS 2 8
VHS: Viral 218
Videodrome 75, 198
Vietnam 43
Villeneuve, Denis 231
Vimana 11–12
Viral Video Showdown 190
Virus (1999) 18, 109
Visioneers 148–151
The Visit: An Alien Encounter 15
Vonnegut, Kurt 39
von Trier, Lars 177
Voyage of the Rock Aliens 207
Vuorensola, Timo 70–72, 231

Wachowskis (directors) 147
Wagner, George 210
Waking Life 90
The Walking Dead 126
The Wall (2012) 27
WALL-E 110
Walt Disney Pictures 2, 51, 158
Waltrowski, Jeff 56–59, 235
Waltz with Bashir 43
The War Game 66, 198
War of the Worlds (book) 113
The War of the Worlds (1953) 6
War of the Worlds (2005) 6
Warcraft 15
Ward, Oklahoma 171–175
Warm Bodies 217
Warner Bros. Pictures 2
Warning Sign 100
Watchmen 67
Watergate 6
Waterhole Cove 85
Waterworld 119
Watkins, Britton 151–153
Watkins, Peter 66, 132, 198
Watros, Cynthia 90
Watts, Jon 114
Wayne, John 10
We Are What We Are 129
Weil, Liza 90
Wells, H.G. 28, 113
West Side Story 52
Westworld 75, 109
Whale, James 75
Whalen, Kyle 189
What You Eat 165
Whedon, Joss 186
Where Have All the People Gone? 17
Whissell, Anouk 72–74, 231
Whissell, Yoann-Karl 72
White, Jake 135
White House Down 177
"Who Goes There?" (short story) 95

Who's Afraid of Virginia Woolf? 221
The Wild Blue Yonder 15
Wilder, Gene 64
Williams, Michael C. 8, 10
Williams, Olivia 96
Willy Wonka and the Chocolate Factory 64, 206
Winans, Jamin 159–161
The Wind in the Willows 95
Winfrey, Oprah 150
Wingard, Adam 187
Winston, Matt 168
The Wizard of Oz 1, 120, 122, 158–159, 177, 206
The Wolf Man 75, 117
Wolverine 29
"A Woman Seldom Found" 219
Wong, James 56
Wood, Elijah 110
Woodruff, Tom, Jr. 161–164, 169, 229, 233, 238
Woodruffe, Antony 101
Woolf, Virginia 13–14
The World, the Flesh, and the Devil 126, 128
World War II 66
Wounded 225
Wright, Robin 43
Wright, Ronald 123
Wuss 13, 16
Wyld, Eleanor 47

The X-Files 15, 169, 199
X-Men 186, 190, 193–194
X-Men: Days of Future Past 29, 67
X-Men: First Class 67, 161
Xanadu 206

Yesterday Was a Lie 54
York, Hallie 213–214
Young Ones 131
You're Next 187
Yung, Elodie 154

Z for Zachariah 226
Zadora, Pia 207
Zanzarella, Nicol 62–63
Zardoz 238
Zathura 133
Zelig 198
Zellner, David 15
Zemeckis, Robert 89, 170, 224
Zenith 147
Zero Theorem 87
Zombi 1 69
Zoom 197

www.ingramcontent.com/pod-product-compliance
Lightning Source LLC
Chambersburg PA
CBHW081548300426
44116CB00015B/2801